Ordnance Survey *Ireland*

KU-354-790

City Atlas Series

6th Edition

Dublin

City and District Street Guide

General Travel Information	Route Planner	I
	M50 Map	II
	Outer Orbital Route	III
	Inner Orbital Route	IV
	Dart, Luas and Suburban Rail Network	V
	Dublin Bus Route Network	VI
Dublin City and District Maps		1
City Centre Maps		69
Tourist Information	Places to Visit	73
	Churches and Cathedrals	77
	Libraries	78
	Art Galleries	79
	Museums	80
	Famous People associated with Dublin	81
	Dublin's Parks and Gardens	83
	Embassies	85
	Dublin Bus Services	86
Index to Hospitals		88
Industrial Estates and Business Parks		89
Index to Street Names		91

Compiled and published by Ordnance Survey Ireland, Phoenix Park, Dublin 8, Ireland.
Arna thiomsú agus arna fhoilsiú ag Suirbhéireacht Ordanáis Éireann, Páirc an Fhionnuisce, Baile Átha Cliath 8, Éire.

Sáraíonn atáirgeadh neamhúdaraithe cóipcheart Suirbhéireacht Ordanáis Éireann agus Rialtas na hÉireann. Gach cead ar cosnamh. Ní ceadmhach aon chuid den fhoilseachán seo a chóipeáil, a atáirgeadh nó a tharchur in aon fhoirm ná ar aon bhealach gan cead i scríbhinn roimh ré ó úinéirí an chóipchirt.

© Suirbhéireacht Ordanáis Éireann 2006

SPECIAL THANKS TO FÁILTE IRELAND, DUBLIN CITY COUNCIL, DÚN - LAOGHAIRE RATHDOWN COUNTY COUNCIL, FINGAL COUNTY COUNCIL AND SOUTH DUBLIN COUNTY COUNCIL.

Map data compiled from the OSi Database and validated to September 2005.

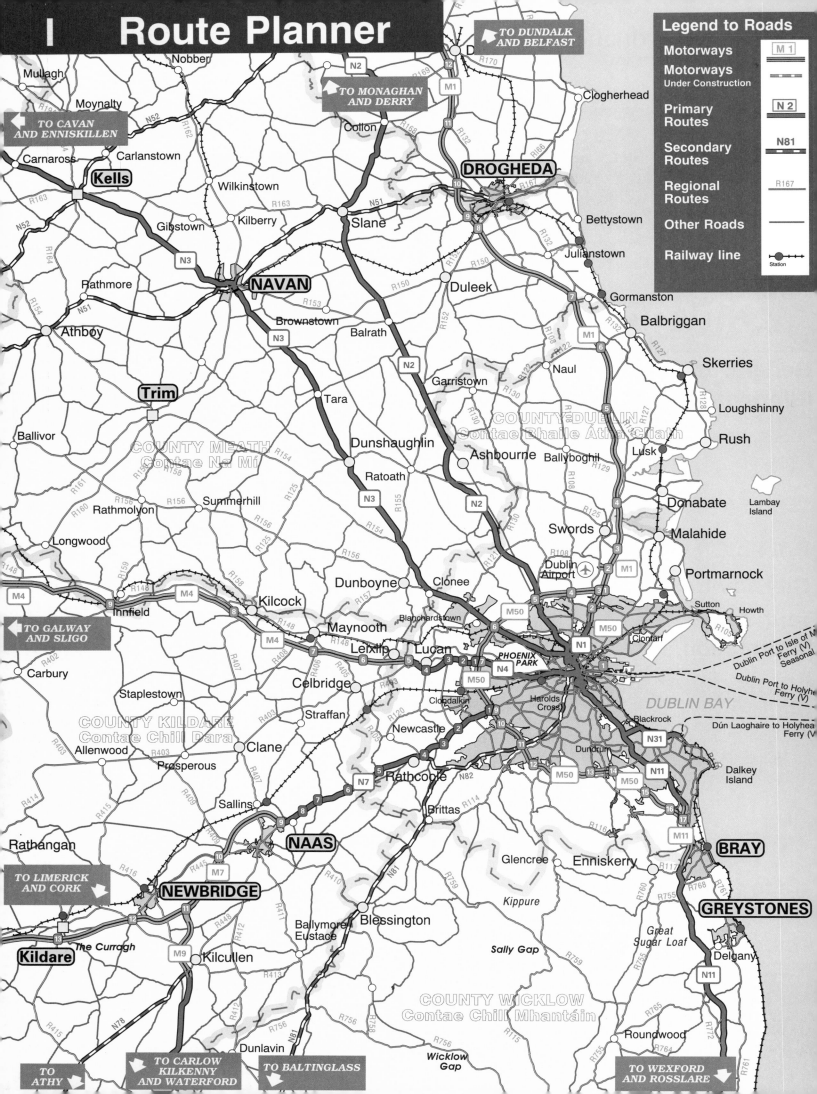

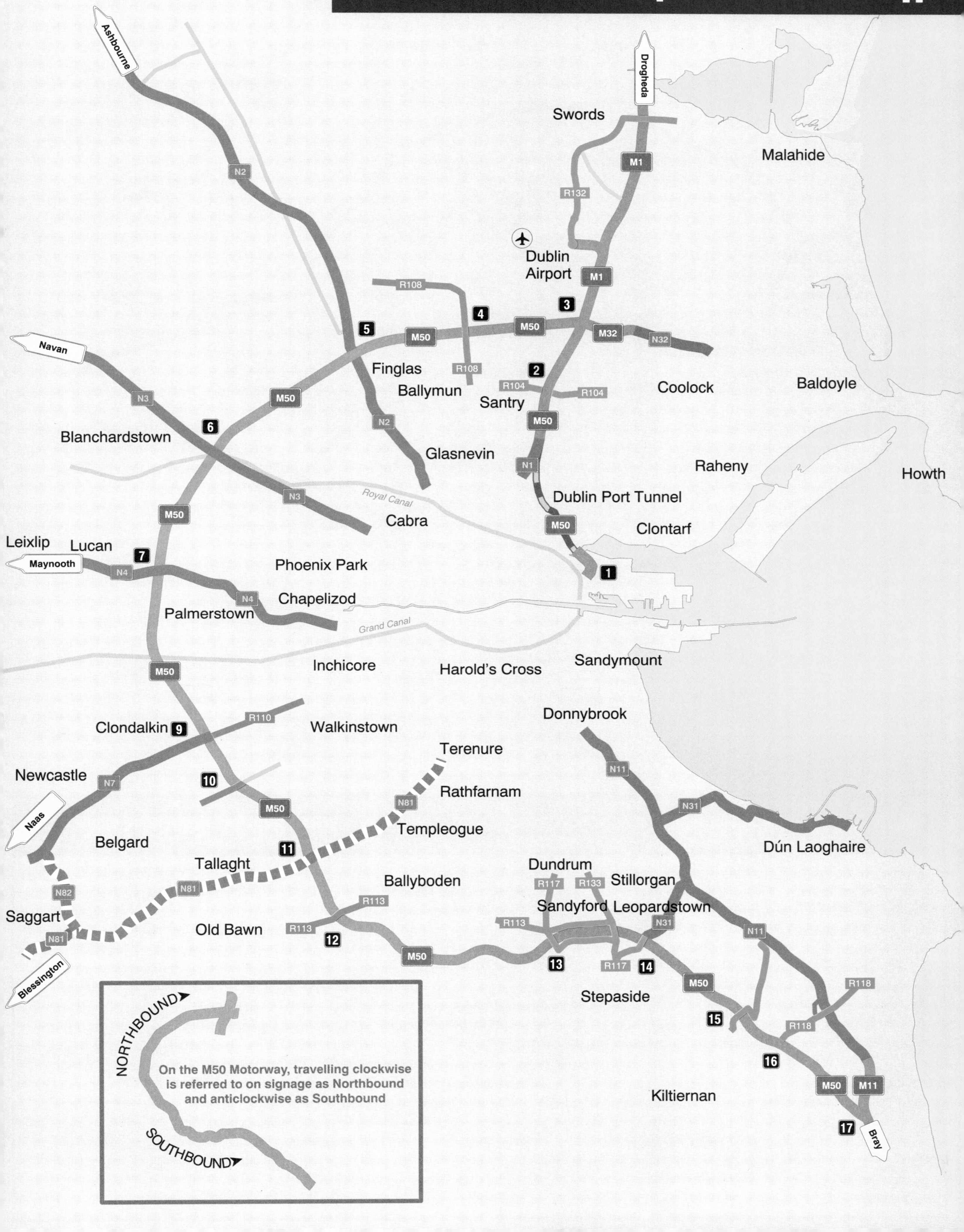

M50 Map

II

Ashbourne

N2

Drogheda

Swords

Malahide

M1

R132

Dublin Airport

M1

R108

5

4

3

M50

M50

M32

N32

Navan

N3

Finglas

R108

2

Ballymun

Santry

R104

Coolock

Baldoyle

M50

R104

6

Blanchardstown

N2

Glasnevin

M50

Raheny

Howth

N3

Royal Canal

Cabra

N1

Dublin Port Tunnel

M50

Clontarf

M50

Leixlip

Lucan

7

Maynooth

N4

Phoenix Park

Chapelizod

M50

N4

Palmerstown

Grand Canal

Dublin Port Tunnel

Inchicore

Harold's Cross

Sandymount

M50

Donnybrook

Clondalkin

9

R110

Walkinstown

N11

Terenure

Newcastle

N7

10

Rathfarnam

N31

Dún Laoghaire

Naas

M50

N81

Templeogue

11

Belgard

Dundrum

Stillorgan

Tallaght

Ballyboden

R117

R133

Sandyford

Leopardstown

N82

N81

R113

R113

N31

N11

Saggart

R113

12

M50

R113

13

R117

14

M50

N11

R118

N81

Old Bawn

Stepaside

15

R118

Blessington

16

Kiltiernan

M50

M11

17

Bray

NORTHBOUND

On the M50 Motorway, travelling clockwise is referred to on signage as Northbound and anticlockwise as Southbound

SOUTHBOUND

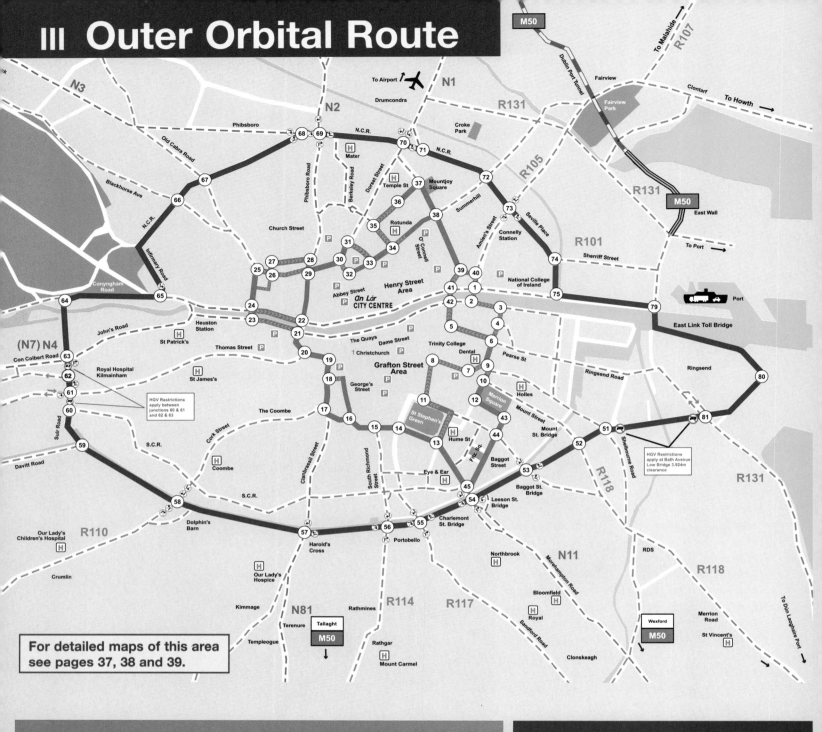

III Outer Orbital Route

For detailed maps of this area see pages 37, 38 and 39.

INNER ORBITAL JUNCTIONS INDEX

J1   Custom House Quay / Talbot Memorial Bridge
J2   Talbot Memorial Bridge / City Quay
J3   City Quay/Lombard St. East
J4   Lombard St. East / Townsend St.
J5   Pearse St. / Tara St.
J6   Pearse St. / Westland Row
J7   Clare St./Lincoln Place
J8   Dawson St. / Nassau St.
J9   Lincoln Place / Westland Row
J10 Clare St. / Merrion Square
J11 St. Stephen's Green / Dawson St.
J12 Merrion St. Upr/Merrion Sq. Sth.
J13 St. Stephen's Green / Leeson St. Lwr.
J14 St. Stephen's Green / Harcourt St.
J15 Wexford St. / Kevin St. Lwr.
J16 Kevin St. / Bride St.
J17 Kevin St. / Patrick St.
J18 Bride Rd. / Patrick St.
J19 Christchurch Place/High St.
J20 High St. / Cornmarket
J21 Bridge St./Merchant's Quay
J22 Inns Quay / Church St.
J23 Ushers Island / Blackhall Place Bridge
J24 Ellis Quay / Blackhall Place Bridge
J25 Blackhall Place / King St.
J26 King St. / George's Lane
J27 George's Lane / Brunswick St. Nth
J28 Brunswick St. Nth. / Church St. Upr
J29 King St. / Church St.
J30 Nth. King St. / Bolton St.
J31 Bolton St. / King's Inns St.
J32 Parnell St. / Ryder's Row
J33 Parnell St. / King's Inns St.
J34 Parnell St. / Parnell Square West
J35 Parnell Square West / Granby Row
J36 Parnell Sq. Nth. / Frederick St. Nth.
J37 Gardiner St. Upr. / Mountjoy Square
J38 Summerhill / Gardiner St.
J39 Gardiner St. Lwr. / Beresford Place
J40 Amiens St./Beresford Place
J41 Eden Quay / Butt Bridge
J42 Tara St./Butt Bridge/Burgh Quay
J43 Merrion Sq. Sth. / Fitzwilliam St. Lwr.
J44 Fitzwilliam St. Lwr / Baggot St. Lwr
J45 Fitzwilliam Place / Leeson St. Lwr

OUTER ORBITAL JUNCTIONS INDEX

J51 Shelbourne Rd / Haddington Rd
J52 Mount St. Lwr. / Haddington Rd
J53 Baggot St. Br. / Mespil Rd
J54 Leeson St. Br. /Grand Parade
J55 Charlemont St. Br. / Ranelagh Rd.
J56 Portobello / Rathmines Rd
J57 Harold's Cross Br. / Clanbrassil St.
J58 Dolphin's Barn / Crumlin Rd.
J59 Davitt Rd. / Suir Rd.
J60 Suir Rd. / SCR
J61 SCR / Old Kilmainham
J62 SCR / Inchicore Rd.
J63 SCR / St. John's Rd. West
J64 SCR / Conyngham Rd.
J65 Parkgate / Infirmary Rd.
J66 NCR / Blackhorse Ave.
J67 NCR / Prussia St.
J68 NCR / Cabra Rd.
J69 NCR / Phibsboro Rd.
J70 NCR / Dorset St. Lower
J71 NCR / Belvidere Road
J72 NCR / Summerhill
J73 Amiens St. / Seville Pl.
J74 Sheriff St. / Guild St.
J75 Guild St. / North Wall Quay
J79 North Wall Quay / East Link Br.
J80 Sean Moore Rd. / South Bank Rd.
J81 Sean Moore Rd. / Beach Rd.

Inner Orbital Route IV

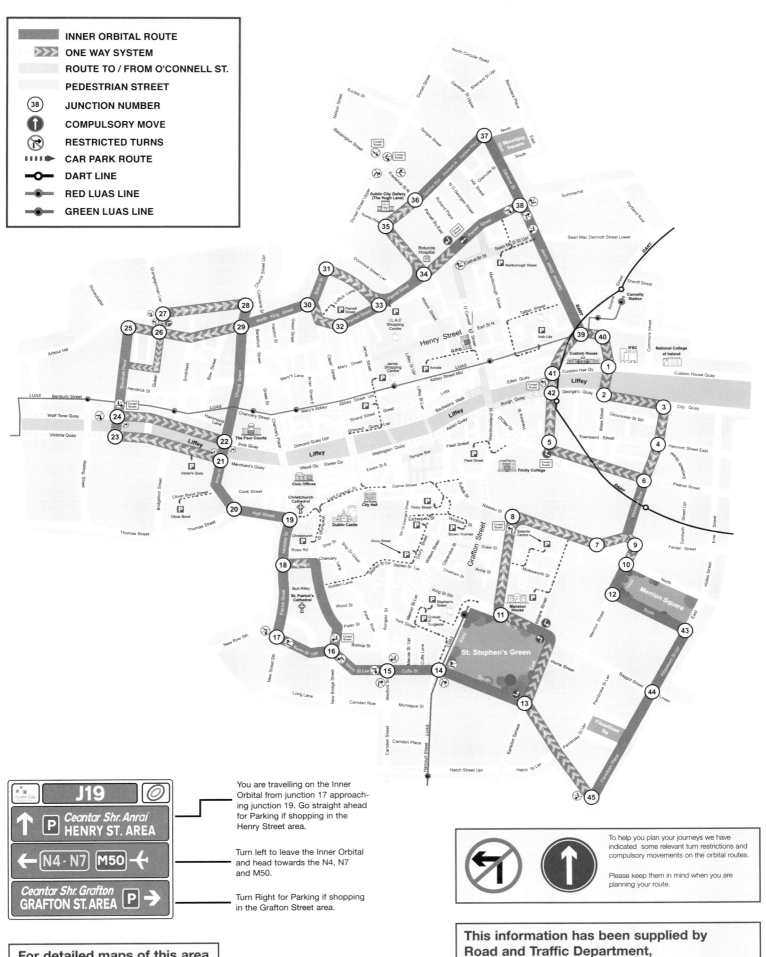

Legend:
- INNER ORBITAL ROUTE
- ONE WAY SYSTEM
- ROUTE TO / FROM O'CONNELL ST.
- PEDESTRIAN STREET
- (38) JUNCTION NUMBER
- COMPULSORY MOVE
- RESTRICTED TURNS
- CAR PARK ROUTE
- DART LINE
- RED LUAS LINE
- GREEN LUAS LINE

J19 Dublin City

↑ P Ceantar Shr. Anraí HENRY ST. AREA

← N4 - N7 M50 ←

Ceantar Shr. Grafton GRAFTON ST. AREA P →

You are travelling on the Inner Orbital from junction 17 approaching junction 19. Go straight ahead for Parking if shopping in the Henry Street area.

Turn left to leave the Inner Orbital and head towards the N4, N7 and M50.

Turn Right for Parking if shopping in the Grafton Street area.

For detailed maps of this area see pages 69, 70 and 71.

To help you plan your journeys we have indicated some relevant turn restrictions and compulsory movements on the orbital routes.

Please keep them in mind when you are planning your route.

This information has been supplied by Road and Traffic Department, Dublin City Council

V Dart, Luas and Suburban Rail Network

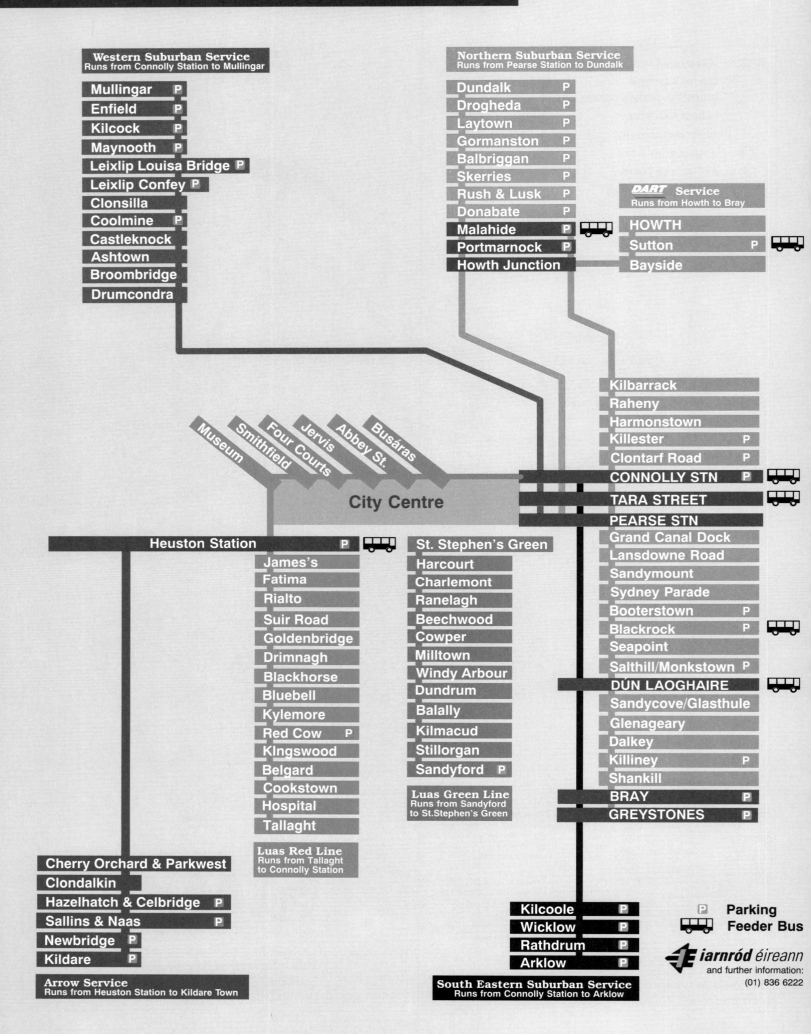

Western Suburban Service
Runs from Connolly Station to Mullingar

Mullingar P
Enfield P
Kilcock P
Maynooth P
Leixlip Louisa Bridge P
Leixlip Confey P
Clonsilla
Coolmine P
Castleknock
Ashtown
Broombridge
Drumcondra

Northern Suburban Service
Runs from Pearse Station to Dundalk

Dundalk P
Drogheda P
Laytown P
Gormanston P
Balbriggan P
Skerries P
Rush & Lusk P
Donabate P
Malahide P
Portmarnock P
Howth Junction

DART Service
Runs from Howth to Bray

HOWTH
Sutton P
Bayside

Kilbarrack
Raheny
Harmonstown
Killester P
Clontarf Road P
CONNOLLY STN P
TARA STREET
PEARSE STN
Grand Canal Dock
Lansdowne Road
Sandymount
Sydney Parade
Booterstown P
Blackrock P
Seapoint
Salthill/Monkstown P
DÚN LAOGHAIRE
Sandycove/Glasthule
Glenageary
Dalkey
Killiney P
Shankill
BRAY P
GREYSTONES P

Museum
Smithfield
Four Courts
Jervis
Abbey St.
Busáras

City Centre

Heuston Station P

James's
Fatima
Rialto
Suir Road
Goldenbridge
Drimnagh
Blackhorse
Bluebell
Kylemore
Red Cow P
Kingswood
Belgard
Cookstown
Hospital
Tallaght

Luas Red Line
Runs from Tallaght to Connolly Station

St. Stephen's Green
Harcourt
Charlemont
Ranelagh
Beechwood
Cowper
Milltown
Windy Arbour
Dundrum
Balally
Kilmacud
Stillorgan
Sandyford P

Luas Green Line
Runs from Sandyford to St.Stephen's Green

Cherry Orchard & Parkwest
Clondalkin
Hazelhatch & Celbridge P
Sallins & Naas P
Newbridge P
Kildare P

Arrow Service
Runs from Heuston Station to Kildare Town

Kilcoole P
Wicklow P
Rathdrum P
Arklow P

South Eastern Suburban Service
Runs from Connolly Station to Arklow

P Parking
Feeder Bus

iarnród éireann
and further information:
(01) 836 6222

Dublin Bus operates the bus network in the greater Dublin area. This network extends from Balbriggan in North County Dublin to Kilcoole in County Wicklow and westwards as far as Kilcock, County Kildare.

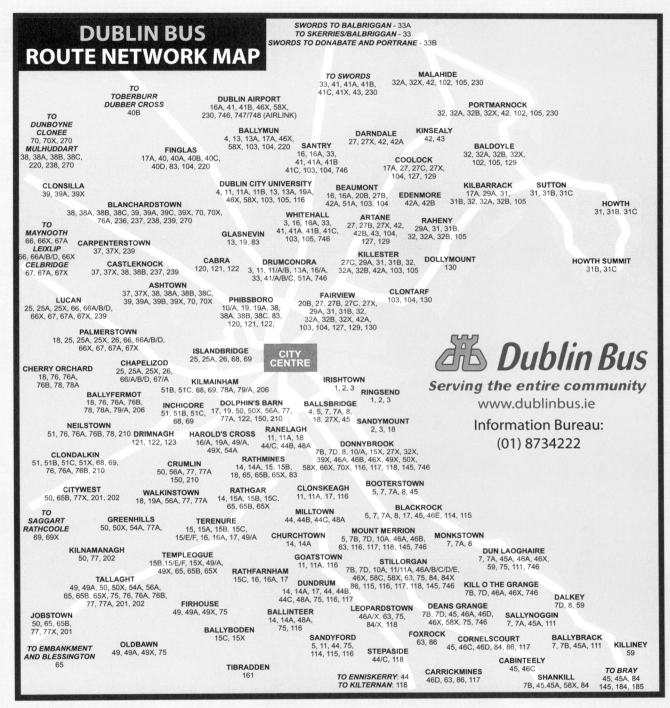

Contact Information

Our Head Office is located at 59 Upper O'Connell Street, Dublin 1 and our opening hours are as follows:

Monday: 0830 – 1730hrs   Tuesday to Friday: 0900 – 1730hrs   Saturday: 0900 – 1300hrs

Please note that the Dublin Bus Head Office is closed Sundays and Bank Holidays.

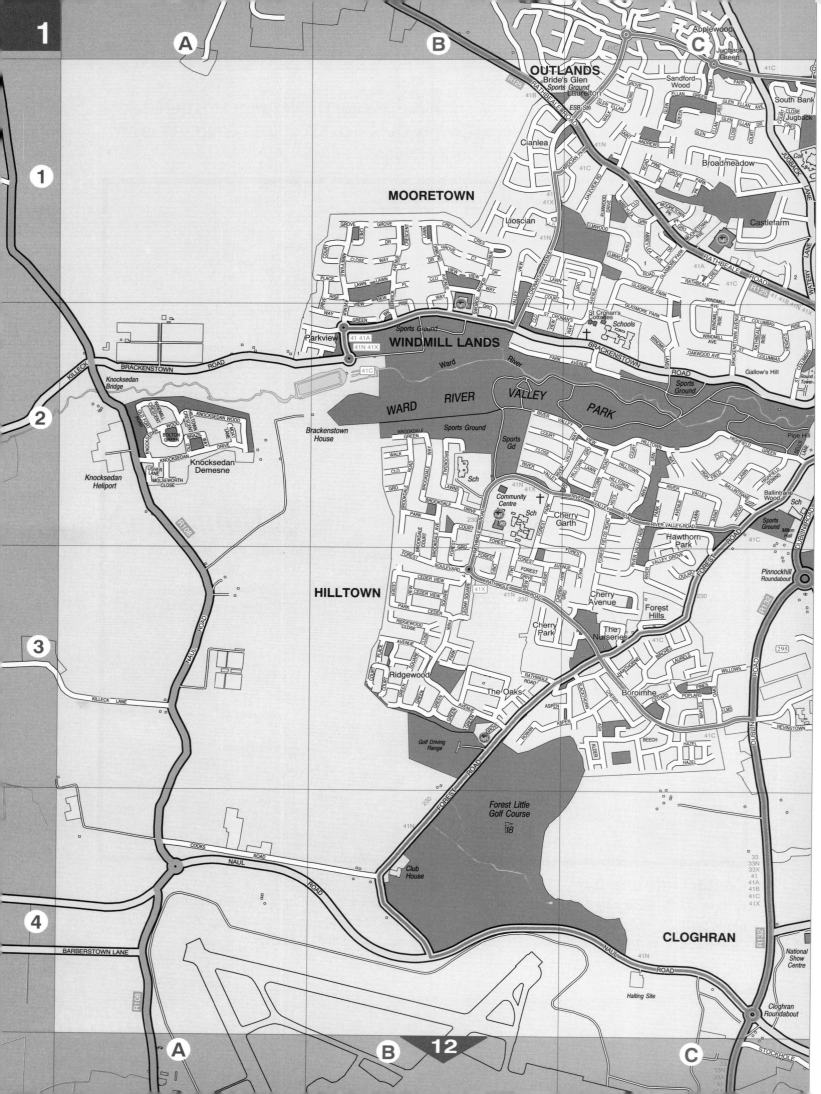

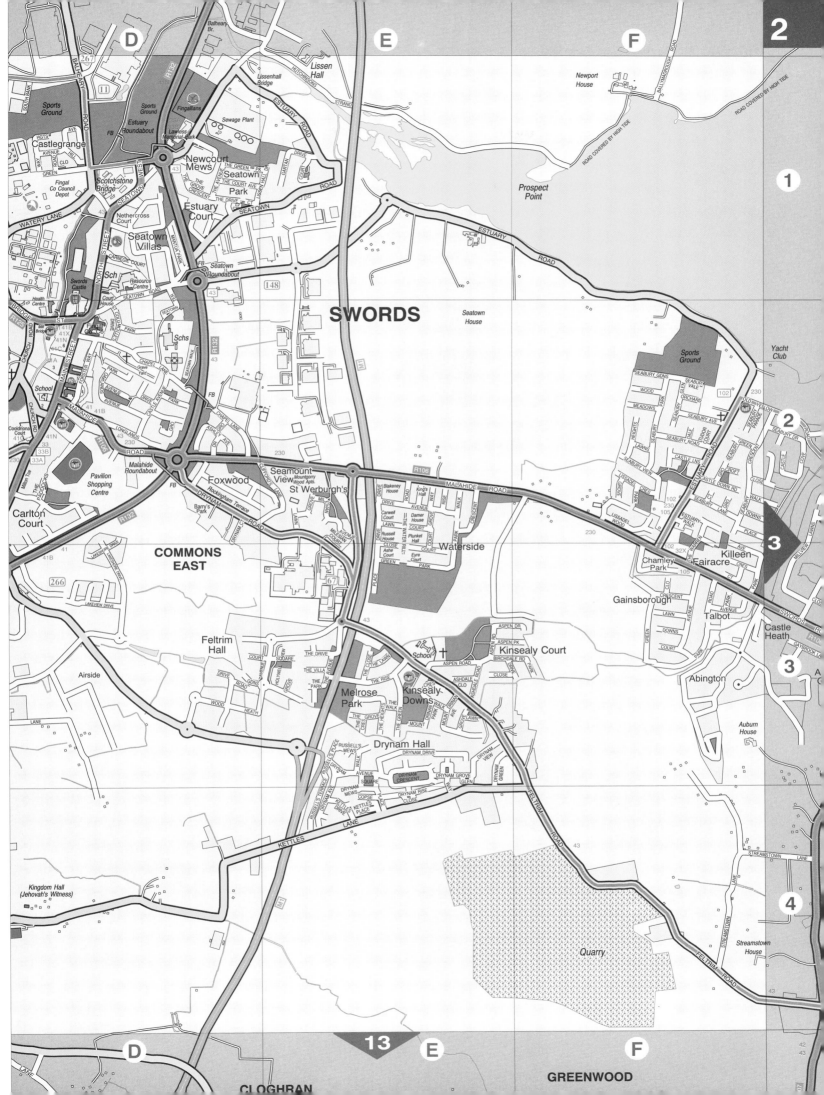

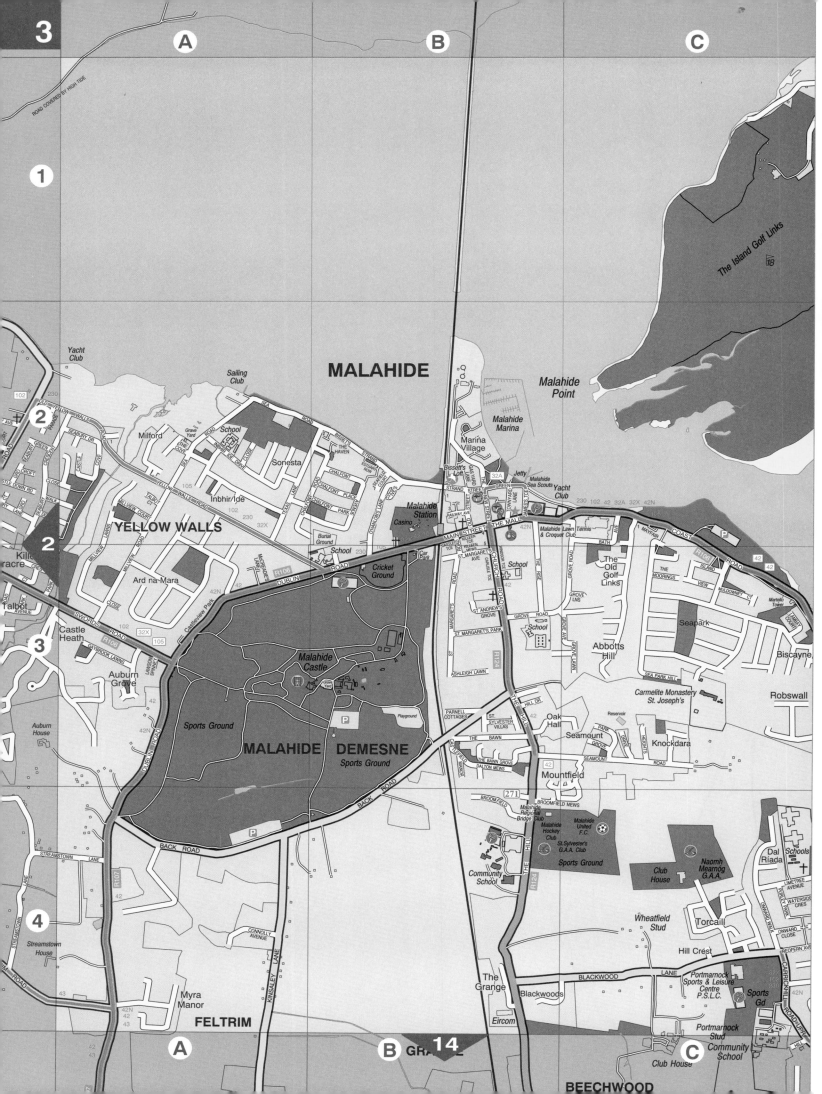

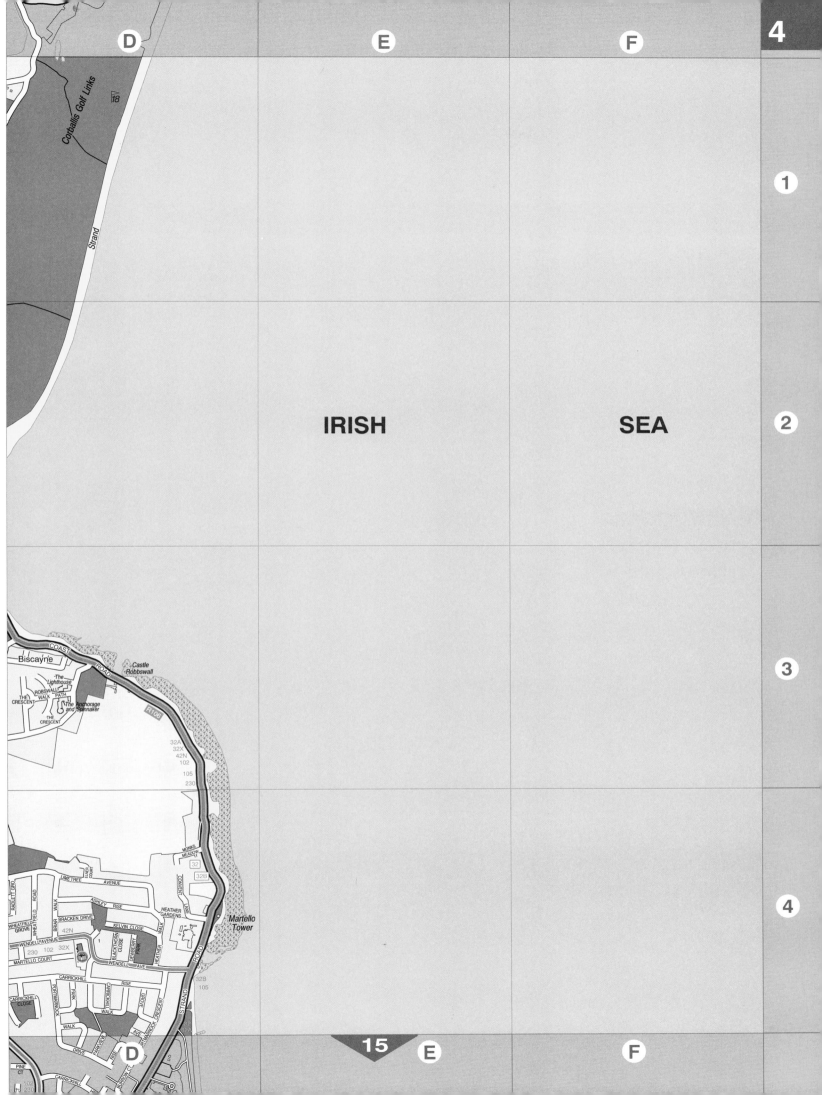

4

D　　**E**　　**F**

Corballis Golf Links

18

Strand

1

IRISH　　**SEA**

2

COAST

Biscayne

Castle
Robbswall

The
Lighthouse

ROBSWALL
WALK
PATH

THE
CRESCENT

The Anchorage
and Spinnaker

R106

THE
CRESCENT

3

32A
32X
42N
102

105
230

MONKS
MEADOW

32

Martello
Tower

LIMETREE
ELMER
COURT

AVENUE

32B

CONNOR
LANE

RADLETT GRO

ASHLEY
RISE

HEATHER
GARDENS

4

WHEATFIELD
GROVE

WHEATFIELD
ROAD

BRIAR
WALK

BRACKEN DRIVE

KELVIN CLOSE

BLACKTHORN
CLOSE

DEWBERRY
PARK

HEATHER
WALK

42N

WENDELL
AVENUE

230
102
32X

1

STRAND
ROAD

MARTELLO COURT

WENDELL
AVE

CARRICKHILL

32B
105

PORTMARNOCK

CARRICKHILL
CLOSE

CARRICKHILL
WALK

PARK

ROHIRD

RISE

PARK
WALK

PORTMARNOCK CRESCENT

PINE
CT

ELDRON CT

CARRICKHILL

DRIVE

PARKVIEW

102
230

D　　**15**　**E**　　**F**

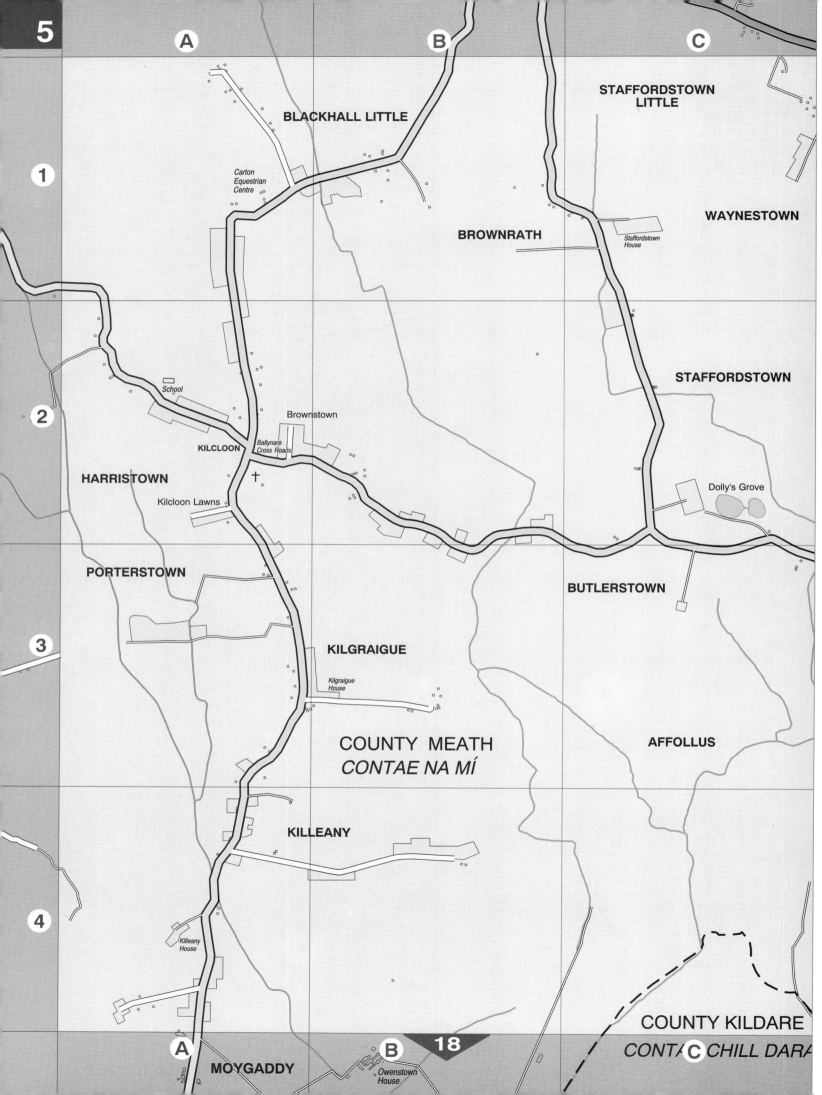

5

A   B   C

1

STAFFORDSTOWN LITTLE

BLACKHALL LITTLE

Carton Equestrian Centre

BROWNRATH

Staffordstown House

WAYNESTOWN

2

School

Brownstown

KILCLOON

Ballynare Cross Roads

STAFFORDSTOWN

HARRISTOWN

Kilcloon Lawns

Dolly's Grove

PORTERSTOWN

BUTLERSTOWN

3

KILGRAIGUE

Kilgraigue House

AFFOLLUS

COUNTY MEATH
CONTAE NA MÍ

4

KILLEANY

Killeany House

COUNTY KILDARE

A   B   **18**   C

MOYGADDY

Owenstown House

CONTAE CHILL DARA

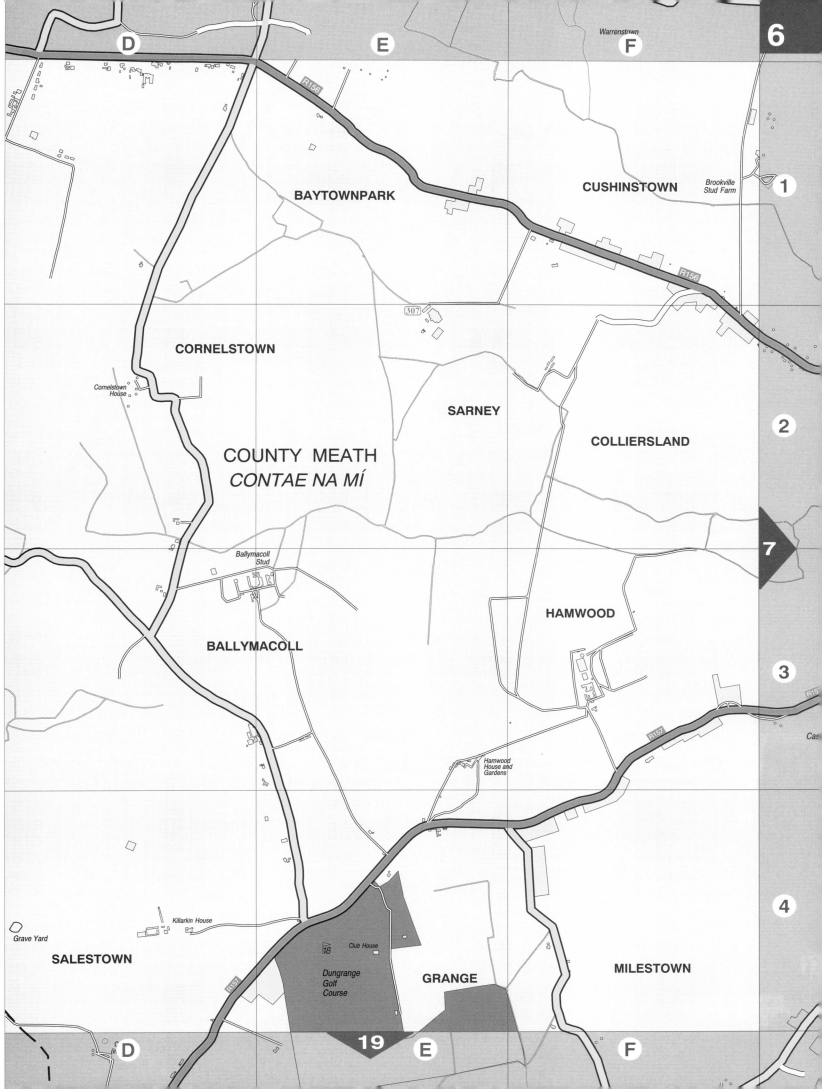

Warrenstown

R156

BAYTOWNPARK

CUSHINSTOWN

Brookville
Stud Farm

R156

307

CORNELSTOWN

Cornelstown
House

SARNEY

COLLIERSLAND

COUNTY MEATH
CONTAE NA MÍ

Ballymacoll
Stud

HAMWOOD

BALLYMACOLL

Killarkin House

Hamwood
House and
Gardens

R157

R157

R15

Cas

Grave Yard

SALESTOWN

18
Club House

Dungrange
Golf
Course

GRANGE

MILESTOWN

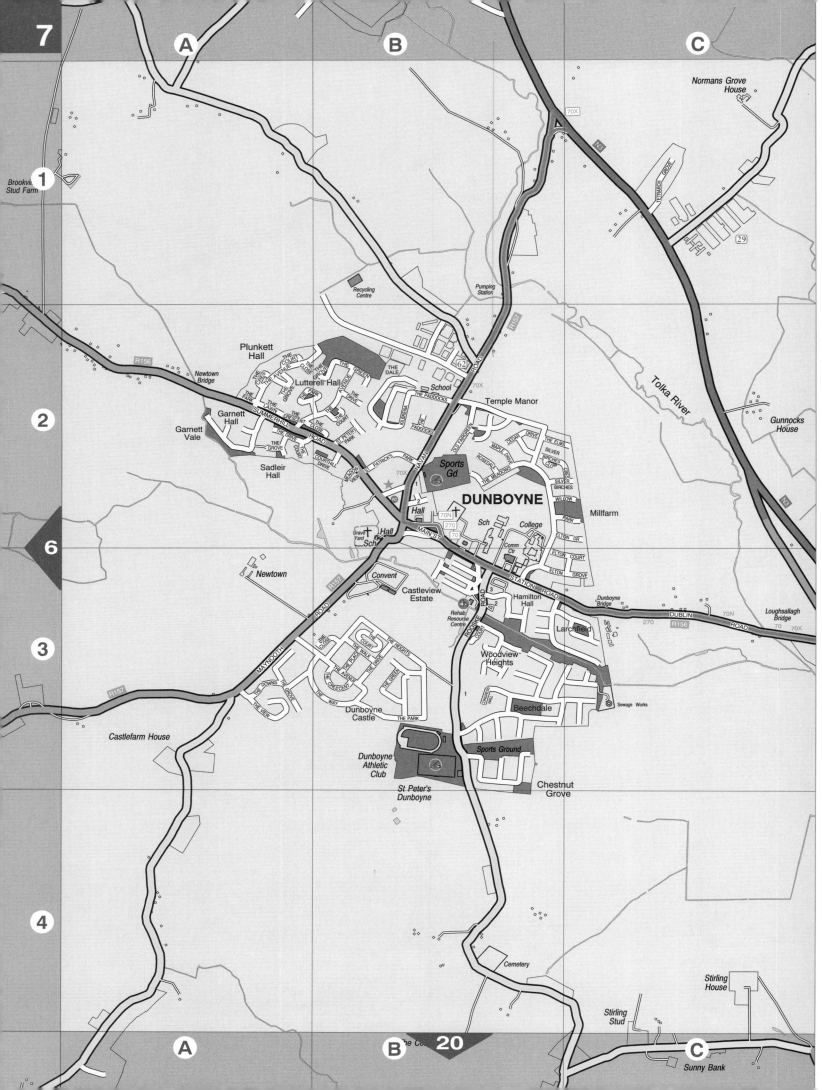

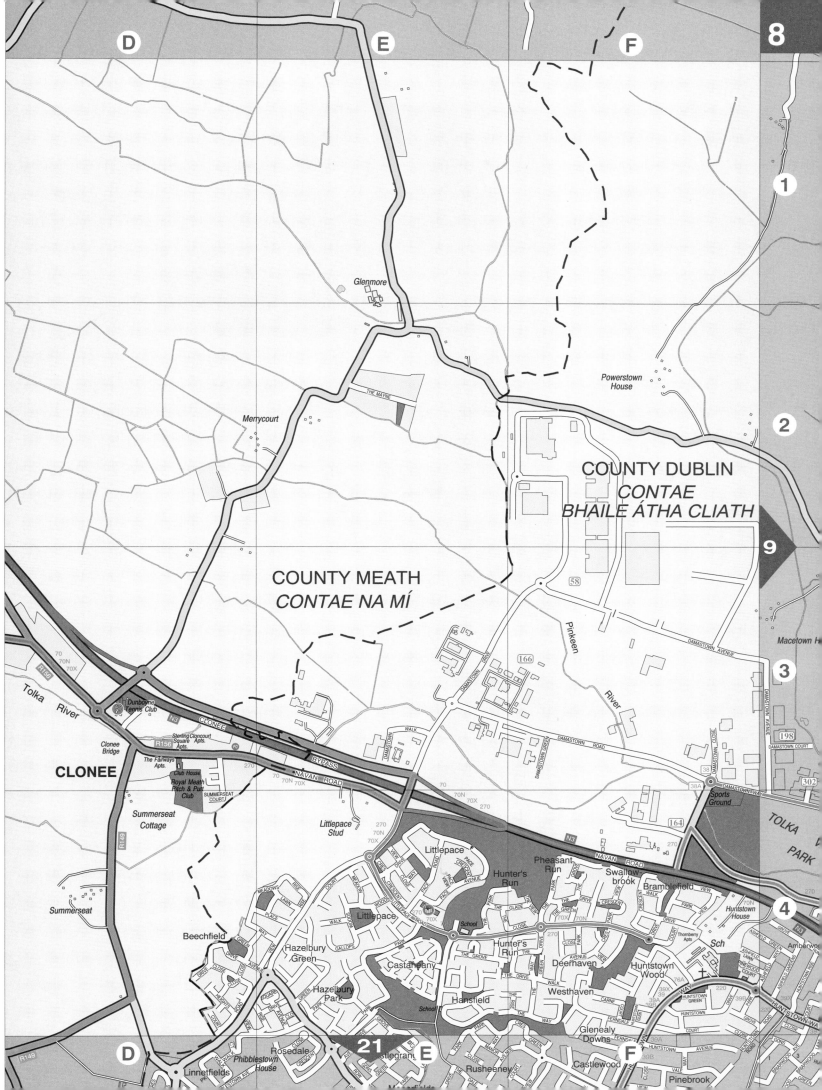

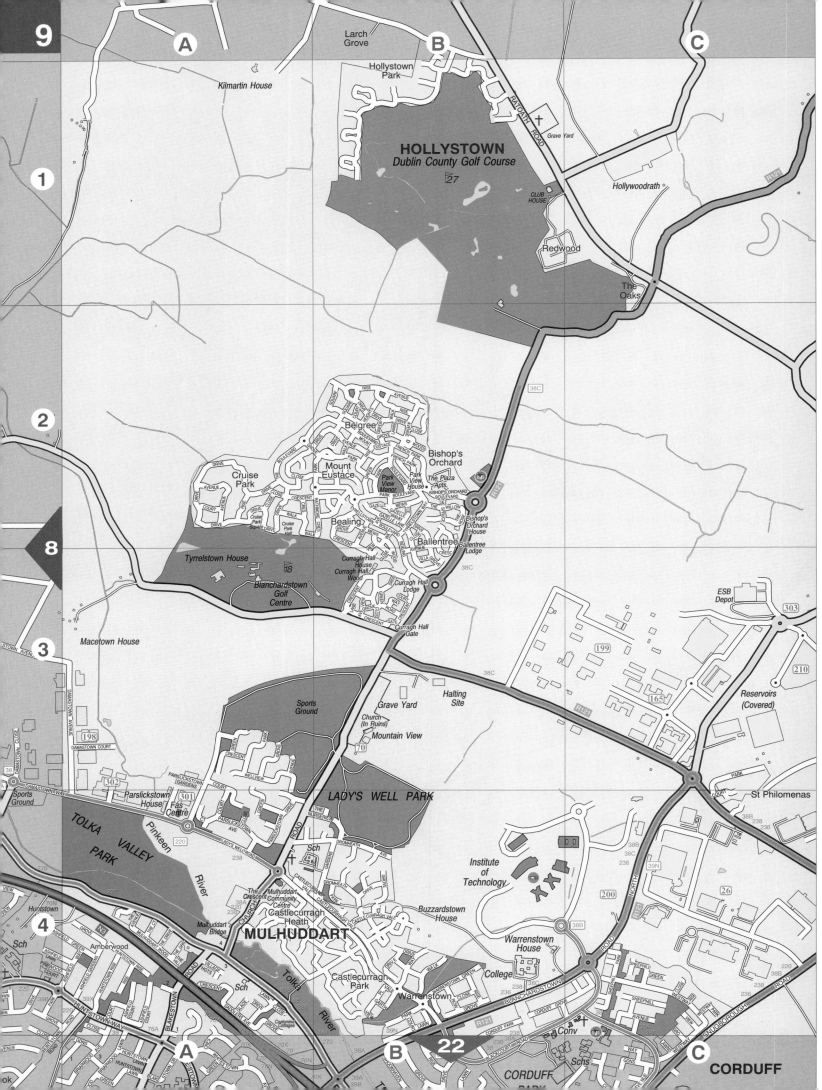

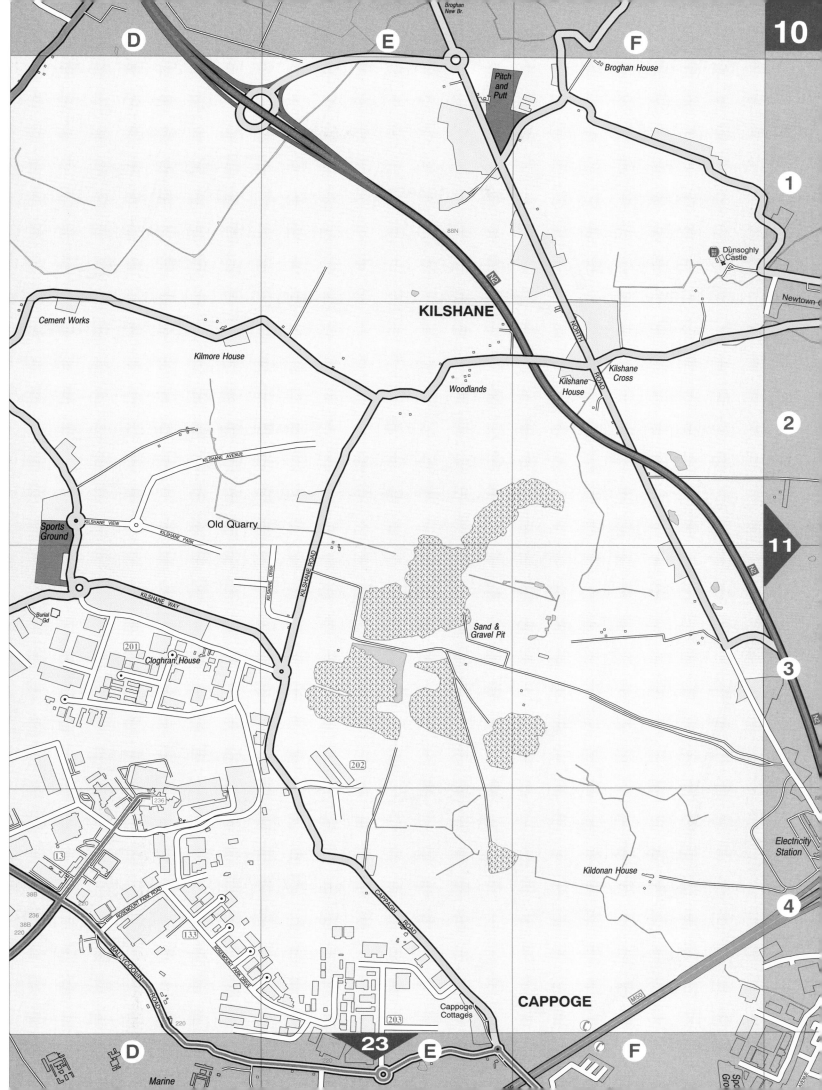

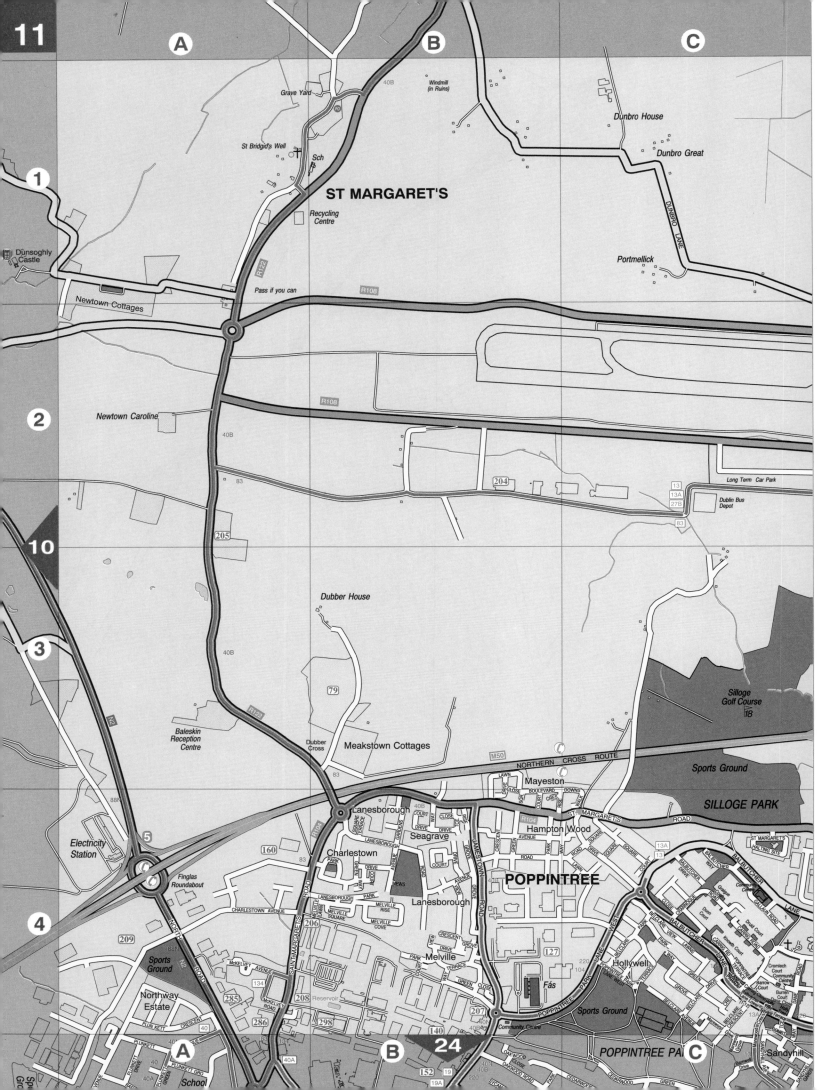

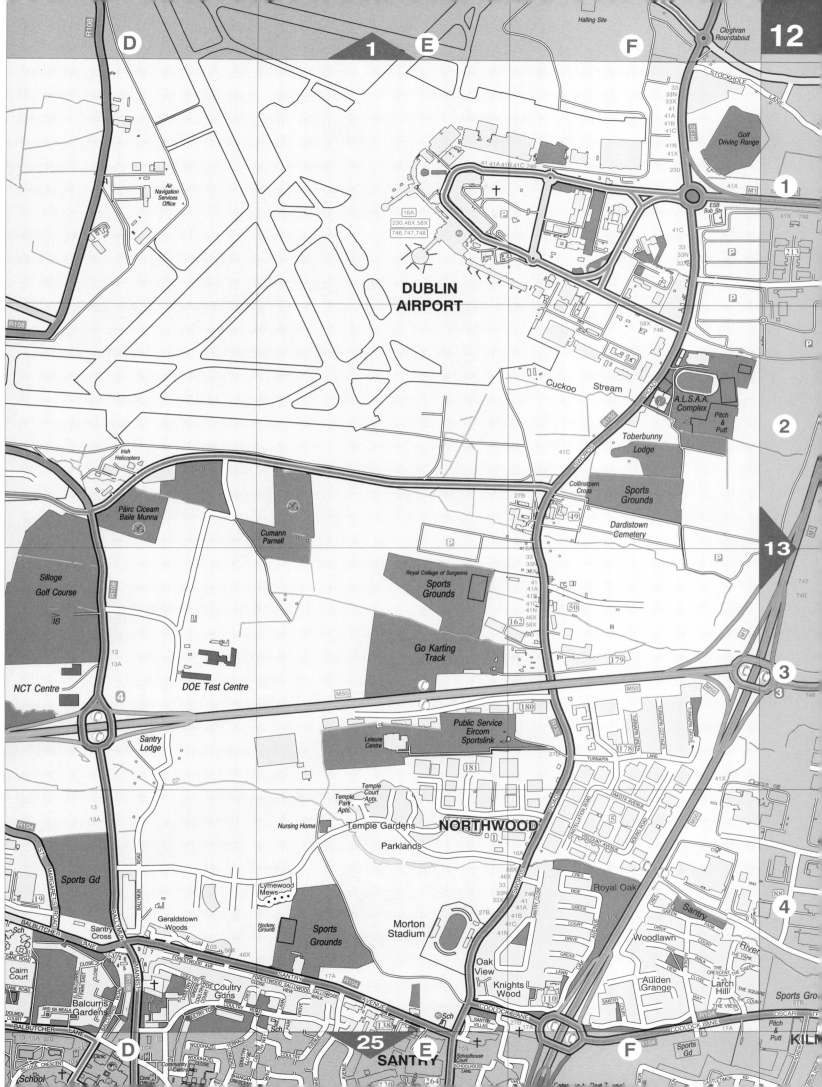

DUBLIN
AIRPORT

Cloghran
Roundabout

Halting Site

STOCKHOLE

Golf
Driving Range

ESB
Sub Stn

33
33N
33X
41
41A
41B
41C
41N
41X

230

41X

M1

1

41X 748

P

P

213

41C

41A 41B 41C 746

Cuckoo   Stream

A.L.S.A.A.
Complex

Pitch
&
Putt

58X 746

R132

Toberbunny
Lodge

SWORDS

2

41C

Collinstown
Cross

Sports
Grounds

49

27B

Dardistown
Cemetery

P

13

747

748

Air
Navigation
Services
Office

R108

R108

Irish
Helicopters

27B

Páirc Ciceam
Baile Munna

Cumann
Parnell

Silloge
Golf Course

R108

18

13

13A

Royal College of Surgeons

Sports
Grounds

16A

33
33N
33X

41
41A
41B
41C
41N
46X
58X

162

50

ROAD

179

NCT Centre

4

DOE Test Centre

Go Karting
Track

M50

M50

180

3

3

M50

M50

748

Santry
Lodge

Leisure
Centre

Public Service
Eircom
Sportslink

R132

178

TURNAPIN GREEN

TURNAPIN COTTAGES

TURNAPIN GROVE

41X

13

13A

R104

Temple
Court
Apts.

Temple
Park
Apts.

181

27B

TURNAPIN
LANE

DAKOTA AVENUE

CONSTELLATION ROAD

5

VISCOUNT AVENUE

88

Nursing Home

Temple Gardens

Parklands

NORTHWOOD

16A

SWORDS   ROAD

BORRIS ROAD

Sports Gd

19

Lymewood
Mews

58X
46X

33
33N
33X

746
41
41A
41B
41C
41N

27B

CRES

RISE

GREEN

COURT

DRIVE

GROVE

Royal Oak

Santry

Woodlawn

Aulden
Grange

Larch
Hill

River

THE CRESCENT
THE GREEN

THE SQUARE

Sports Gro

ST. MARGARET'S ROAD

BALLYMUN

Geraldstown
Woods

Hockey
Ground

Sports
Grounds

Morton
Stadium

Oak
View

Knights
Wood

COOLOCK LANE

DRIVE

RISE

VIEW

WALK

CLOSE

SANTRY

WAY

THE VIEW

THE COURT

4

Santry
Cross

BALBUTCHER LANE

Sch

Cairn
Court

DANE ROAD

DANE ROAD

CLOSE

BALCURRIS
PARK EAST

Balcurris
Gardens

DOLMEN
COURT

ARD NA MEALA

13 13A 220

R108

MAIN ST.

9

7

4

BALCURRIS ROAD

Coultry
Gdns

FORESTWOOD AVE

COUNTRY DRIVE

COULTRY CLOSE

SALLOWOOD
VIEW

COUNTRY TCE

WOODHAZEL TERRACE

COUNTRY

SANTRY

SALLOWOOD
WALK

58X 46X

17A

R104

Sch

AVENUE

138

25

SANTRY

School

Clinic

Community
Centre

Civic
Offices

WOODHAZEL
CLOSE

SHANGAN

SILLOGE CRESCENT

104

COULTRY
PARK

COULTRY
WAY

Sch

Schoolhouse
Court

SCHOOLHOUSE
LANE

103

Santry
Villas

E

F

R104

COOLOCK LANE

17A

CASTLETIMON RD

Pitch
&
Putt

Sports
Gd

KILM

264

110

16A

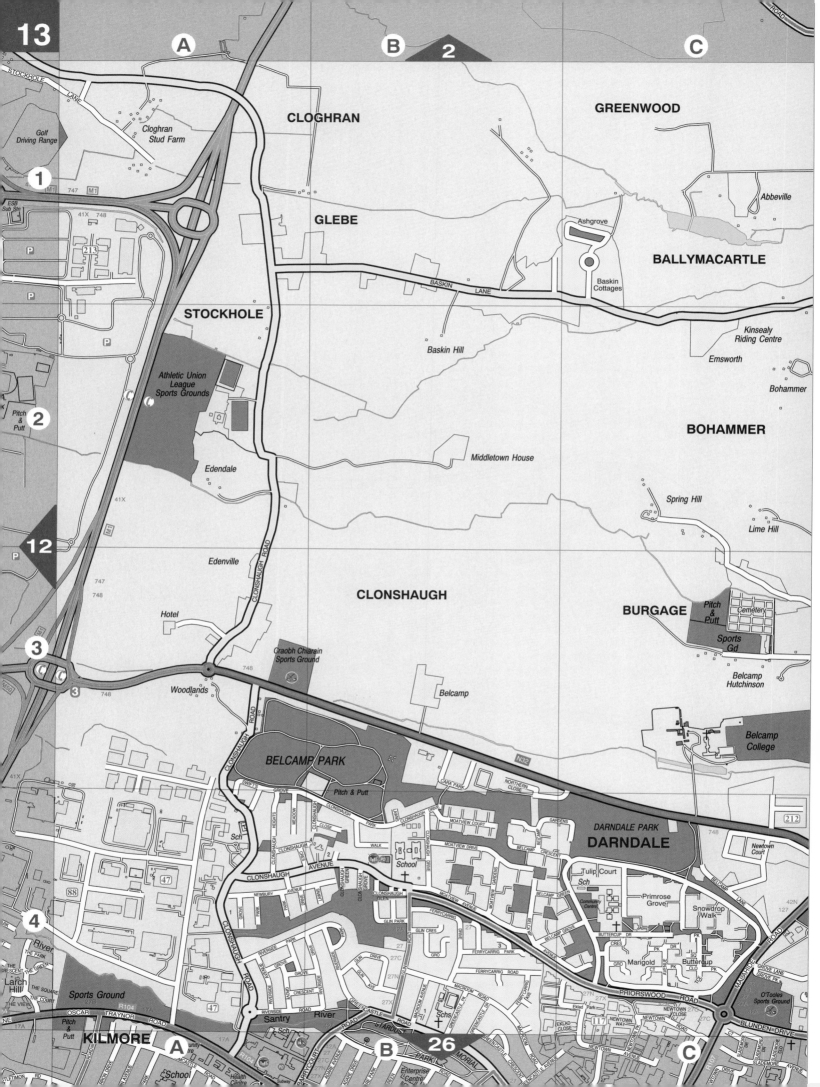

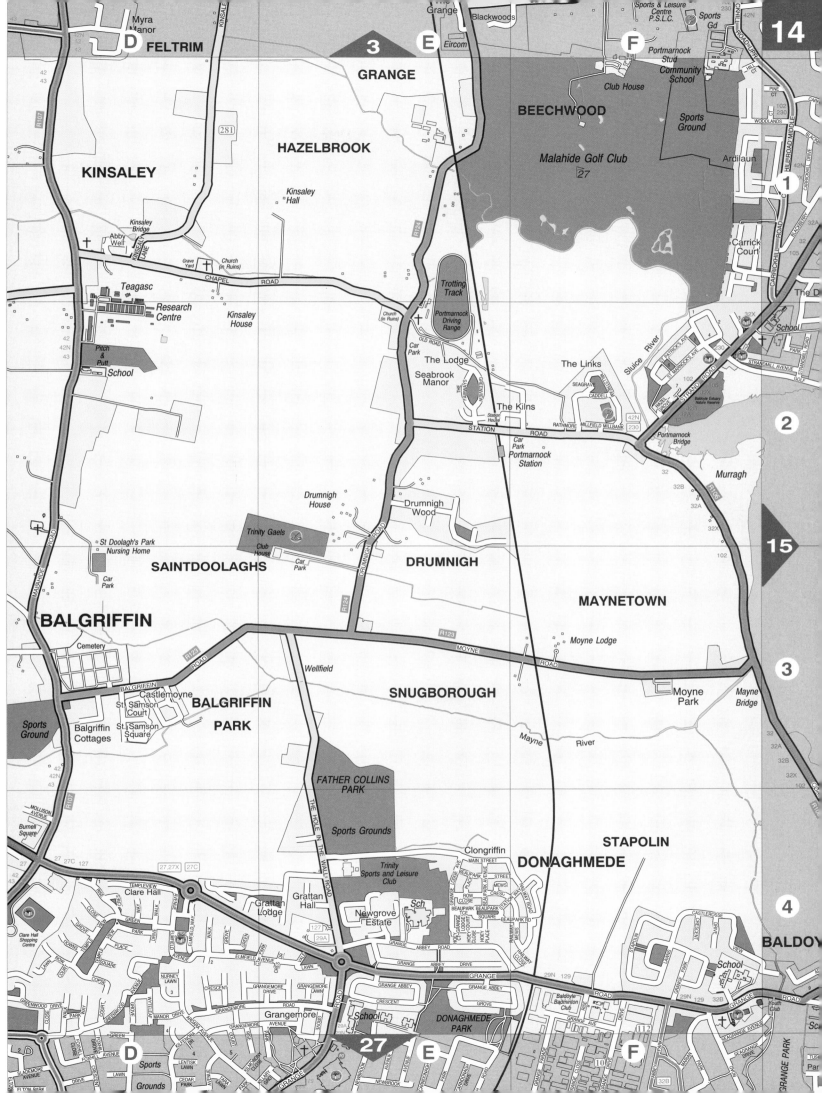

The Steer
Tower

Ireland's Eye

Carrigeen Bay

Rowan Rocks

Thulla Rocks

Thulla

Lighthouse

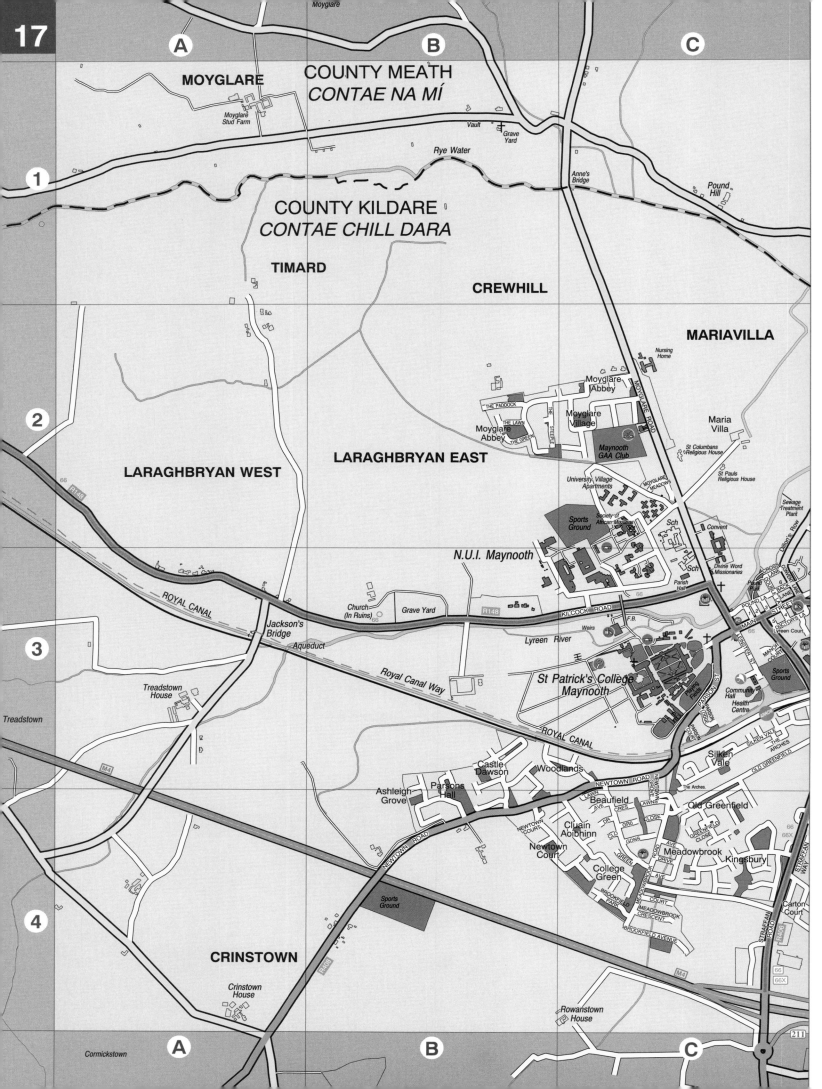

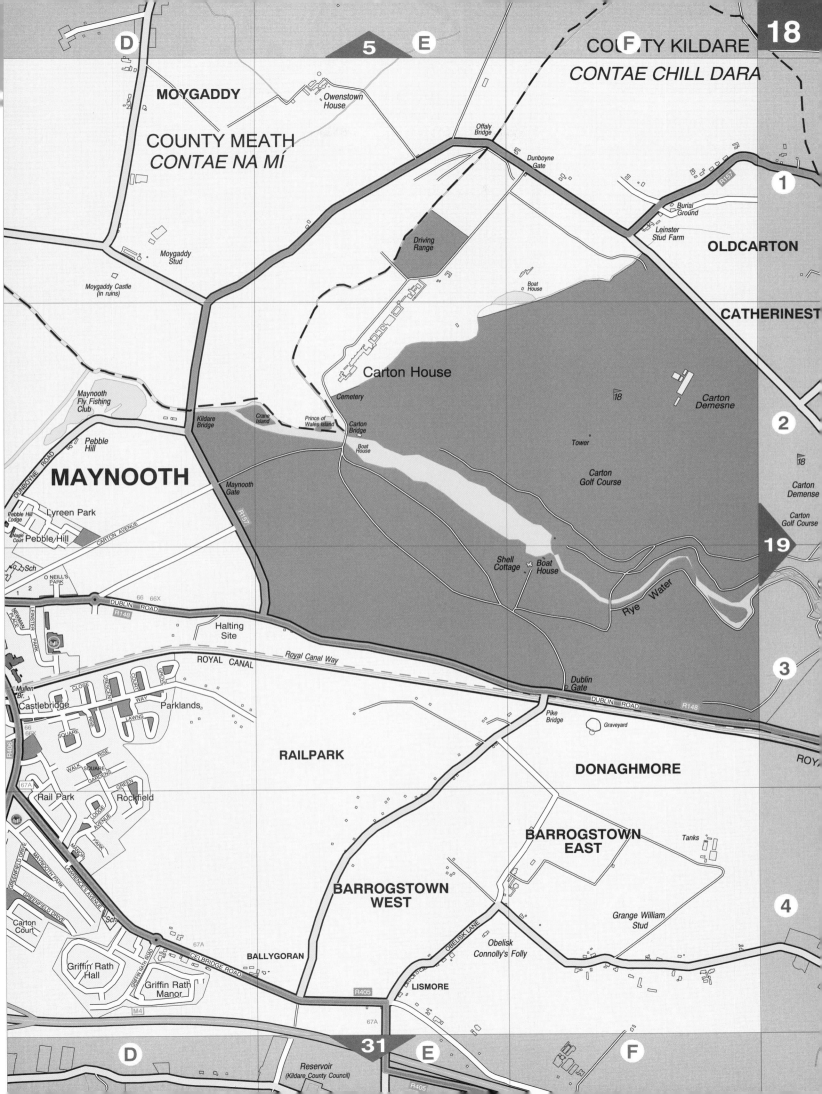

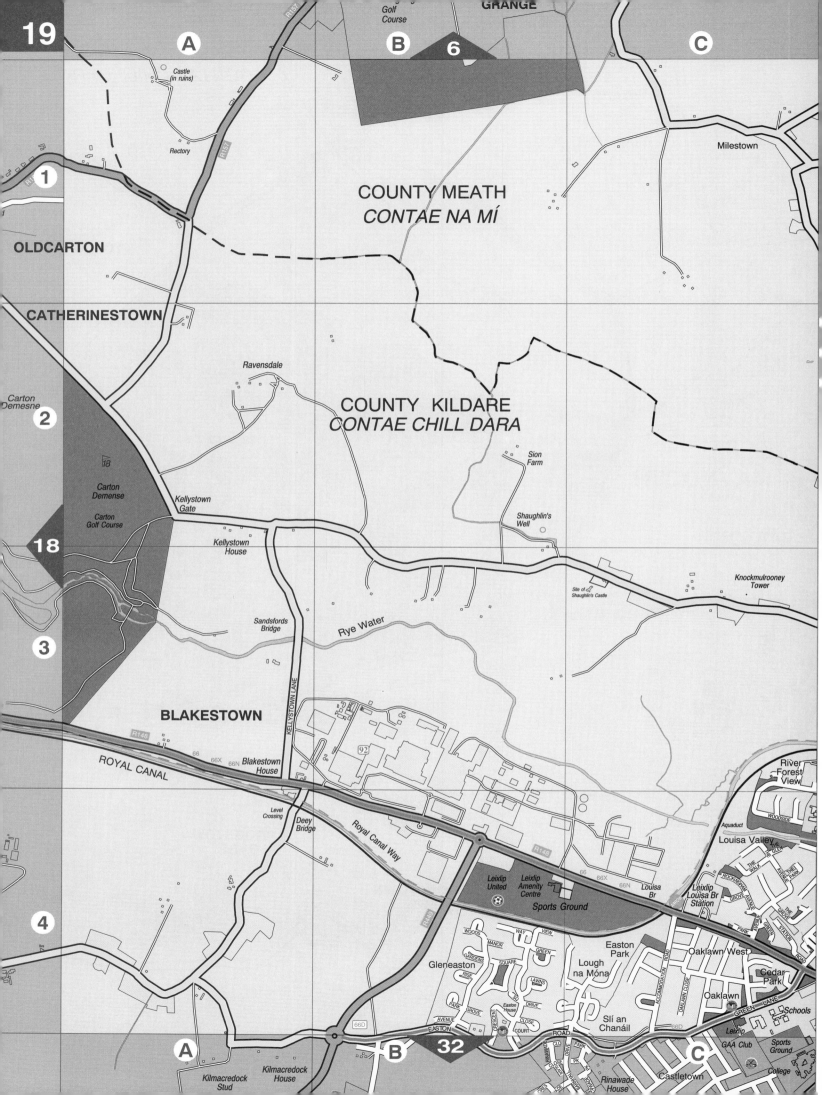

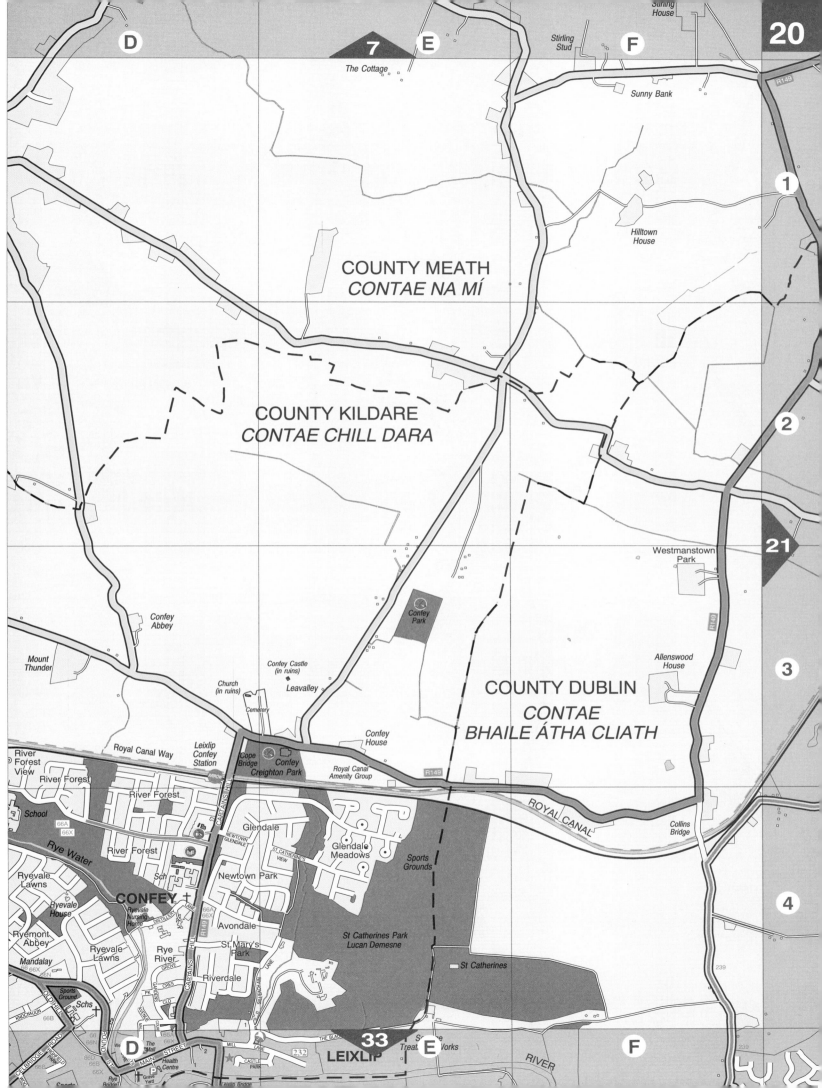

Stirling House

Stirling Stud

Sunny Bank

The Cottage

COUNTY MEATH
CONTAE NA MÍ

Hilltown House

COUNTY KILDARE
CONTAE CHILL DARA

Westmanstown Park

Confey Abbey

Confey Park

Allenswood House

Mount Thunder

COUNTY DUBLIN
CONTAE
BHAILE ÁTHA CLIATH

Confey Castle (in ruins)

Church (in ruins)

Leavalley

Cemetery

Confey House

River Forest View

Royal Canal Way

Leixlip Confey Station

Cope Bridge

Confey Creighton Park

Royal Canal Amenity Group

R149

ROYAL CANAL

Collins Bridge

River Forest

River Forest

River Forest

School

Rye Water

Glendale

Glendale Meadows

Sports Grounds

Newtown Glendale

St Catherines View

Ryevale Lawns

Newtown Park

Ryevale House

Ryevale Nursing Home

Ryevale Lawns

Avondale

St Mary's Park

St Catherines Park Lucan Demesne

Ryemont Abbey

Rye River

Riverdale

St Catherines

Mandalay

Sports Ground

Schs

CONFEY

Rye Bridge

The Mall

Health Centre

Castle Park

Grave Yard

Mill Lane

LEIXLIP

Leixlip Bridge

Treatment Works

RIVER

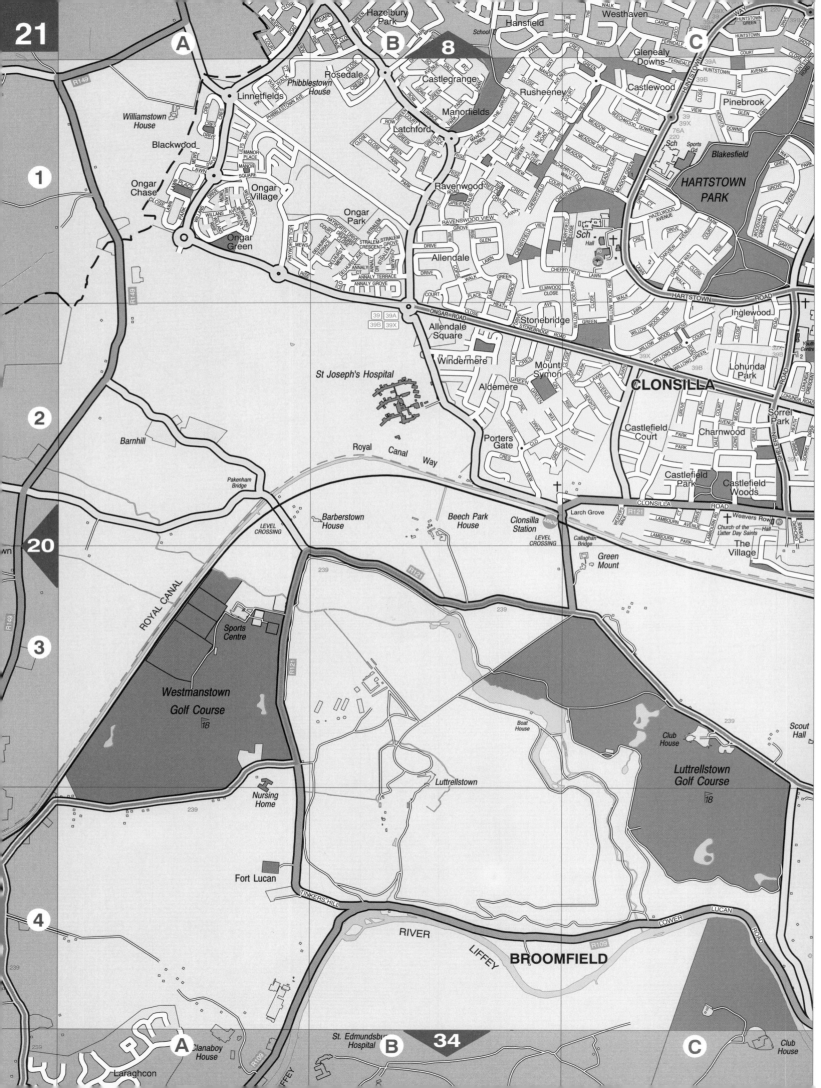

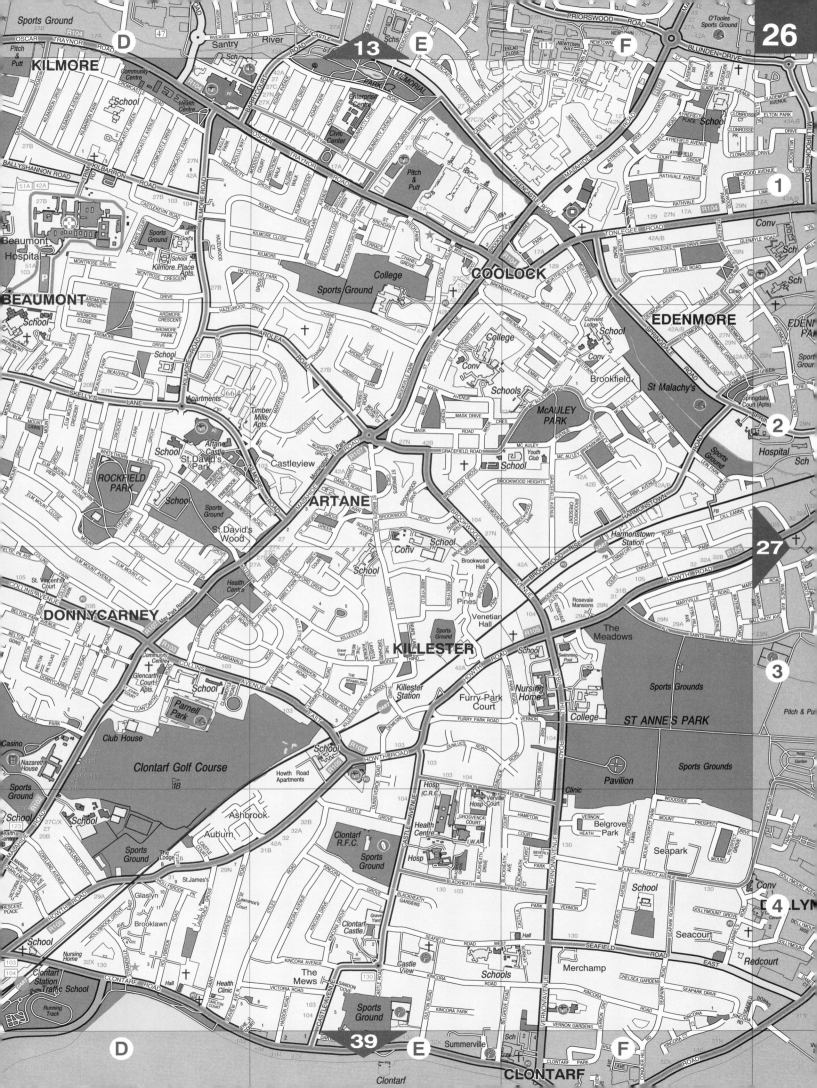

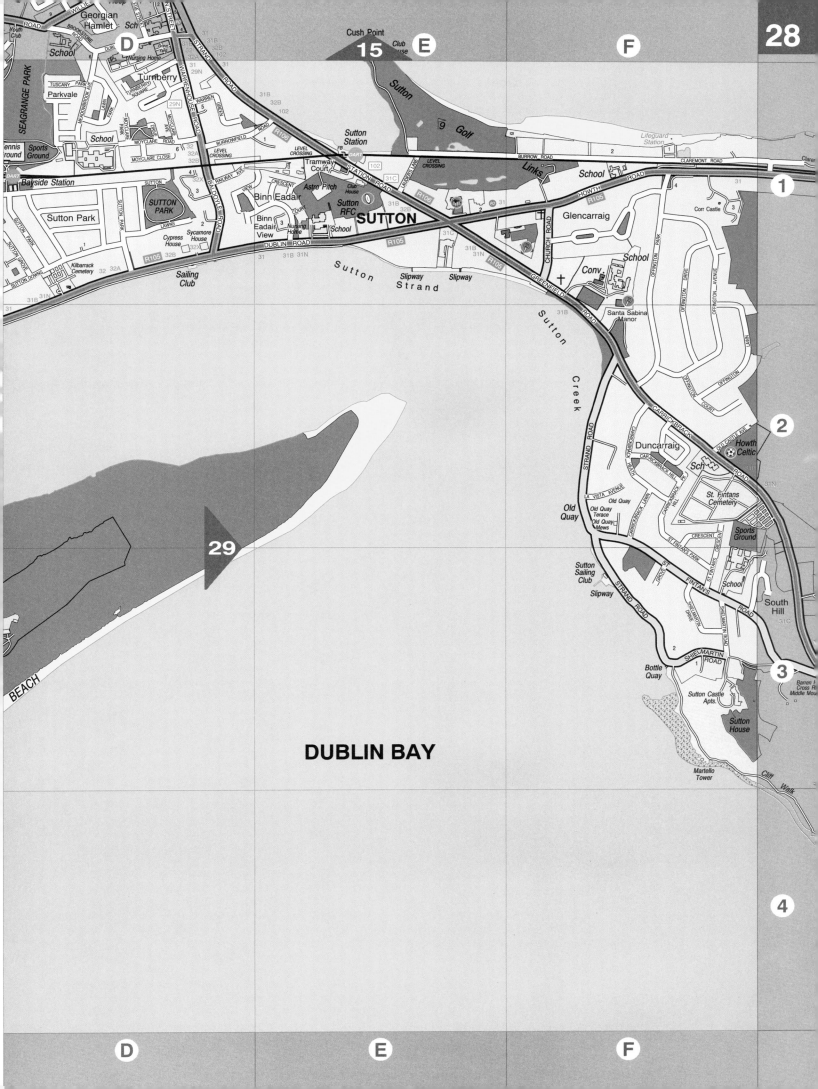

DUBLIN BAY

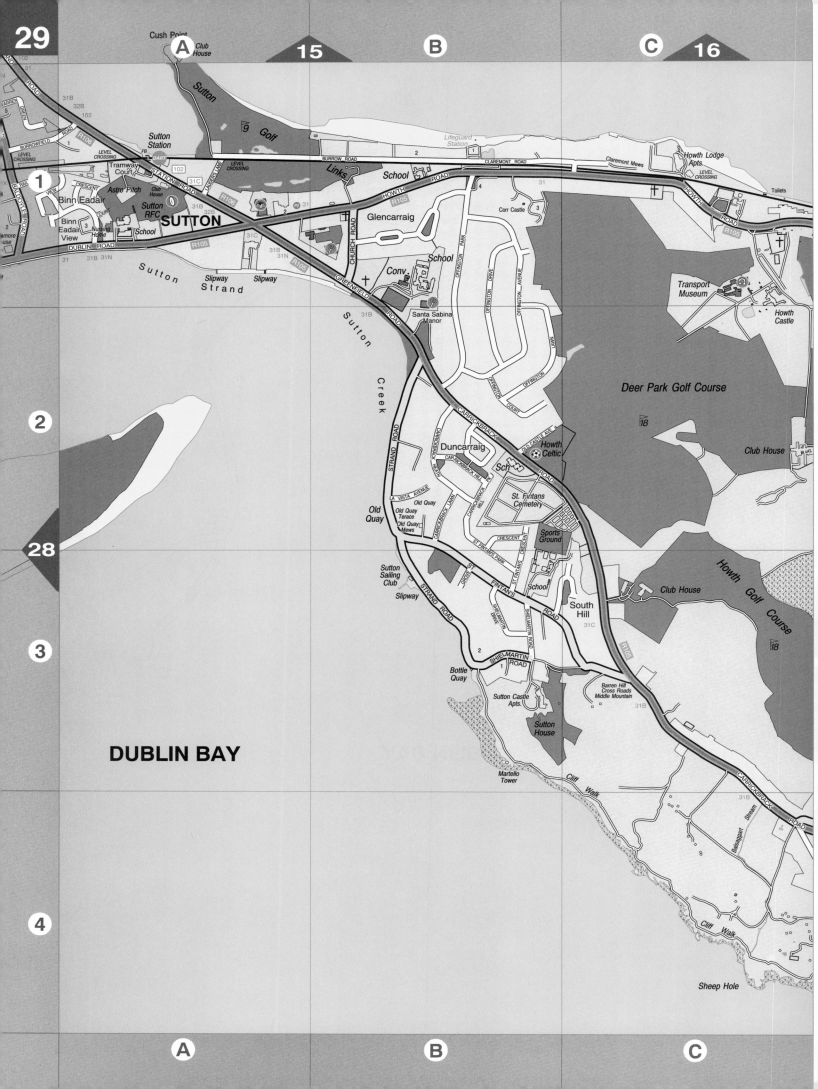

A Cush Point
Club House

Sutton *Golf*

Sutton
Station

1

Links

School

HOWTH ROAD R105

Claremont Mews

Howth Lodge
Apts.

LEVEL
CROSSING

Lifeguard
Station

Toilets

Tramway
Court

BURROW ROAD

CLAREMONT ROAD

LEVEL
CROSSING

Astro Pitch

Club
House

Binn Eadair

Sutton RFC

SUTTON

Glencarraig

Corr Castle

Binn
Eadair
View

Nursing
Home

School

School

DUBLIN ROAD

R105

Conv.

Santa Sabina
Manor

Transport
Museum

Howth
Castle

Sutton *Strand*

Slipway

Slipway

CHURCH ROAD

GREENFIELD ROAD

OFFINGTON PARK

OFFINGTON DRIVE

OFFINGTON AVENUE

OFFINGTON LAWN

OFFINGTON

2

Sutton Creek

Deer Park Golf Course

18

Club House

28

Duncarraig

CARRICKBRACK ROAD

CARRICKBRACK HILL

Howth
Celtic

OLD CASTLE AVE.

STRAND ROAD

La Vista Avenue

Old Quay

Sch

St. Fintans
Cemetery

Old Quay
Terace

Old Quay
Mews

CARRICKBRACK LAWN

ST. FINTAN'S PARK

CRESCENT

Sports
Ground

Old Quay

Howth Golf Course

Club House

Sutton
Sailing Club

Slipway

STRAND ROAD

ST. FINTAN'S ROAD

SHIELMARTIN DRIVE

SHIELMARTIN ROAD

HOWTH ROAD

School

South
Hill

18

3

31C

R105

Bottle
Quay

SHIELMARTIN ROAD

Barren Hill
Cross Roads
Middle Mountain

31B

Sutton Castle
Apts.

Sutton
House

DUBLIN BAY

Martello
Tower

Cliff Walk

CARRICKBRACK ROAD

31B

Balsaggart Stream

4

Cliff Walk

Sheep Hole

A **B** **C**

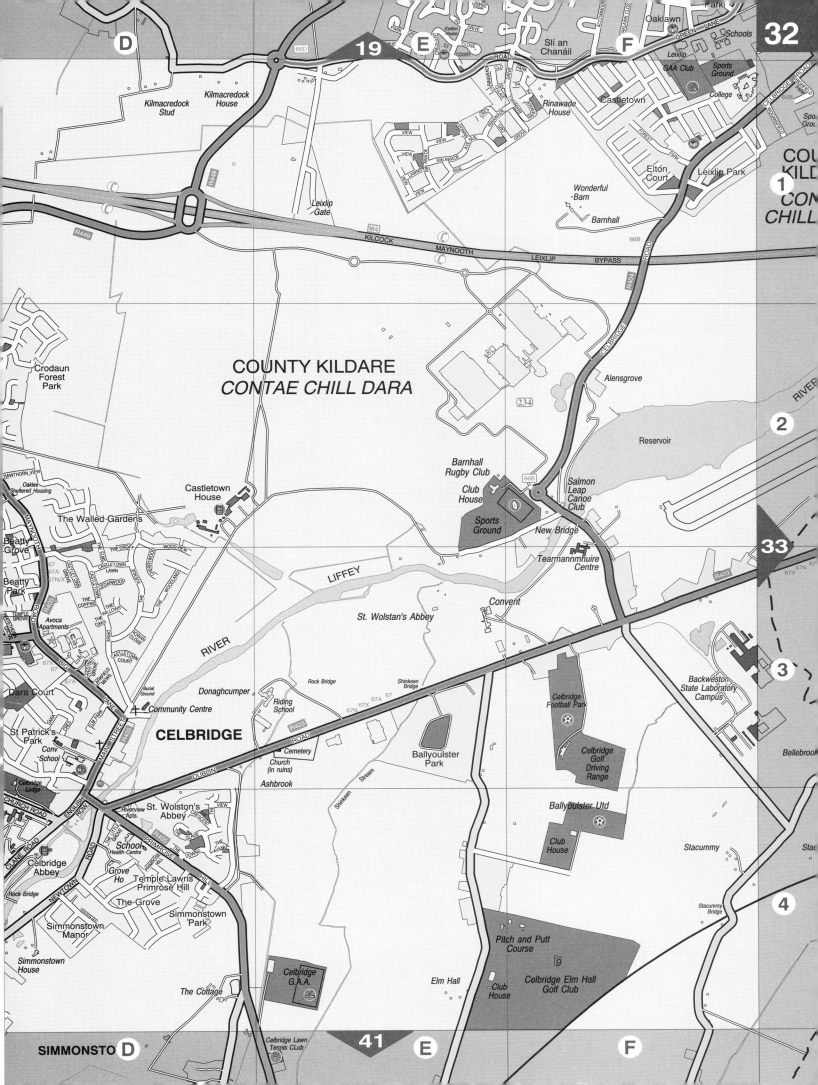

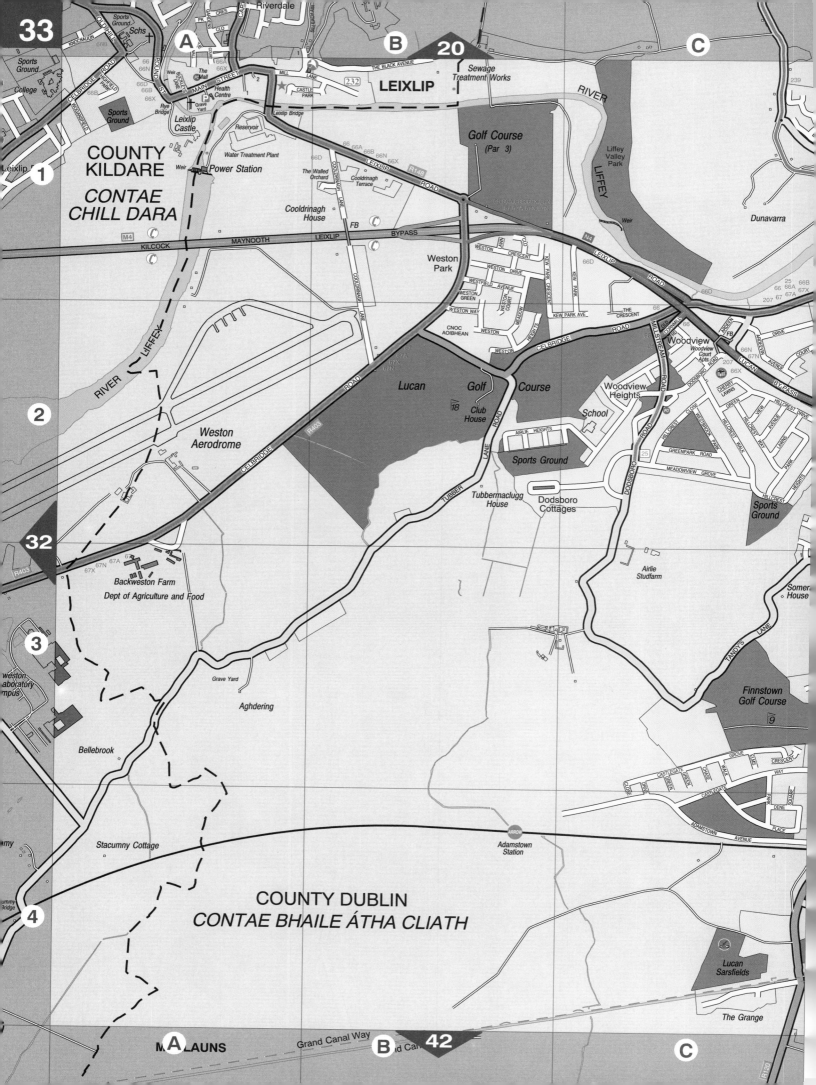

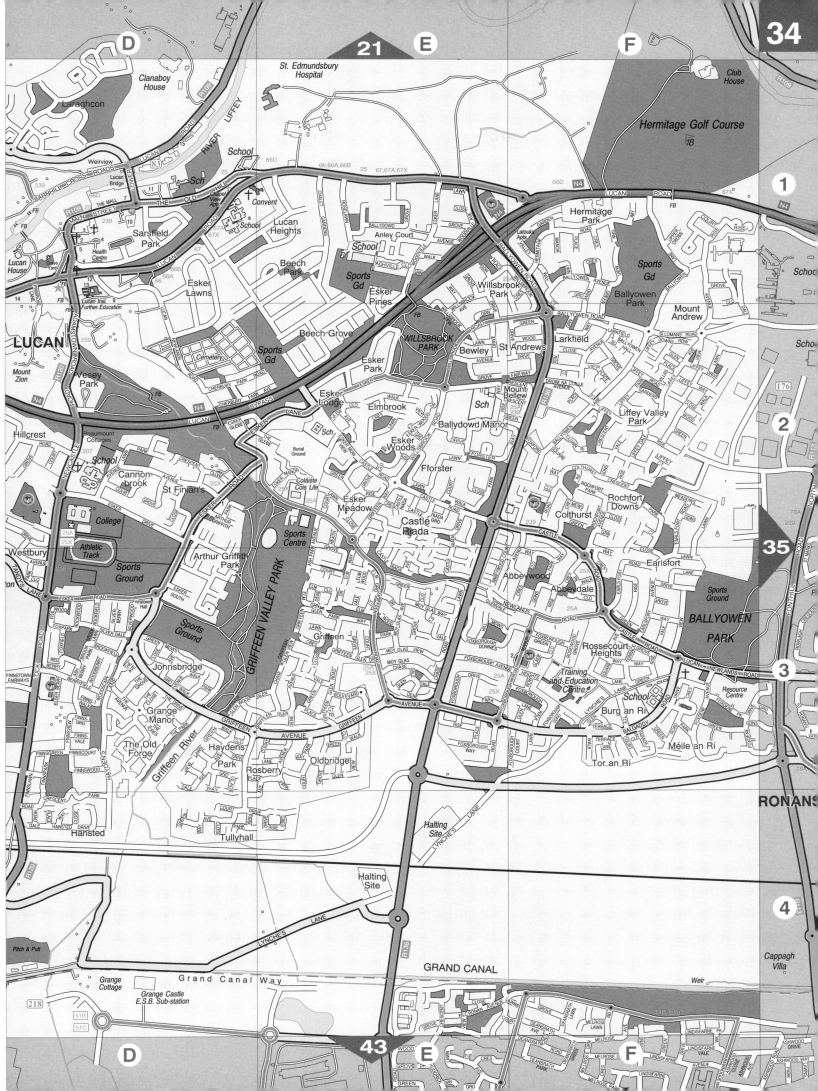

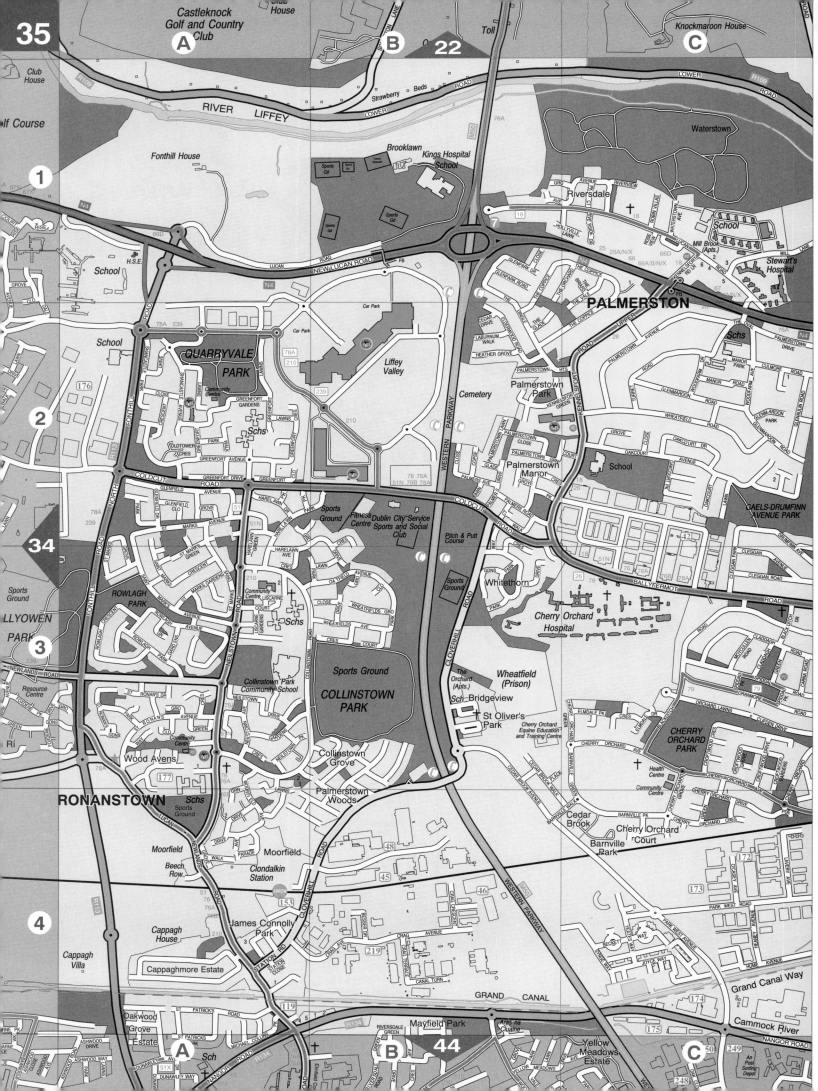

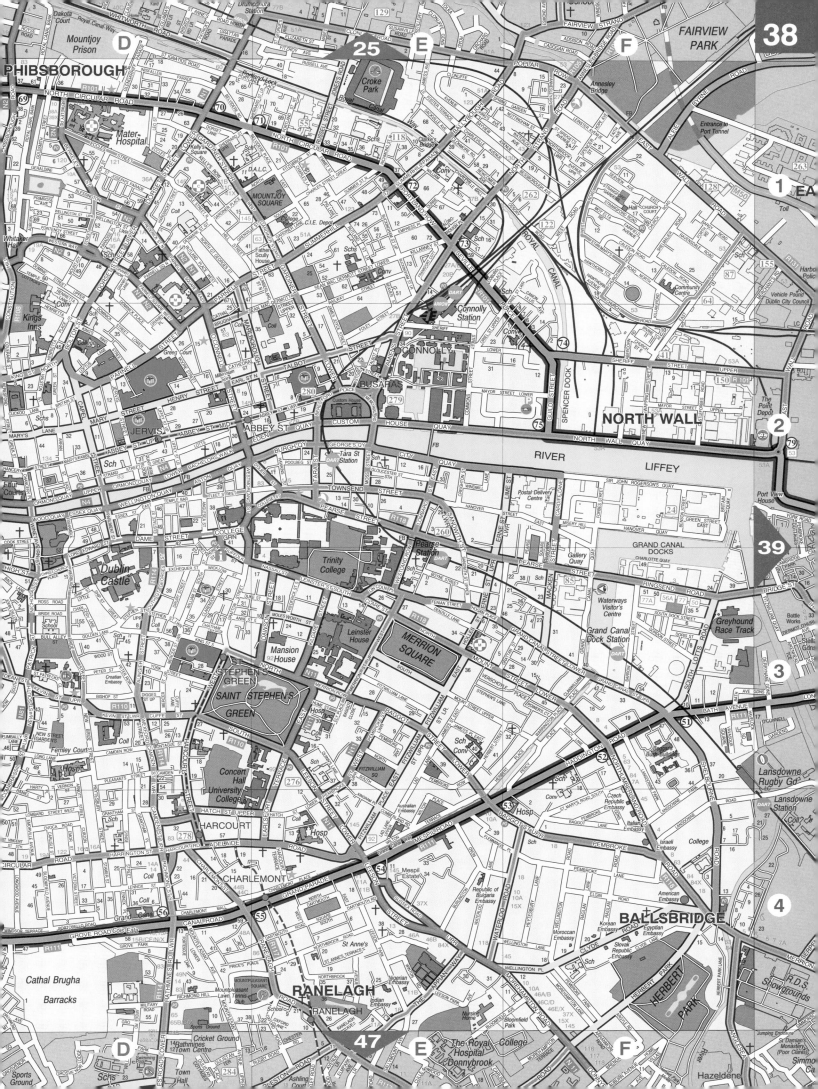

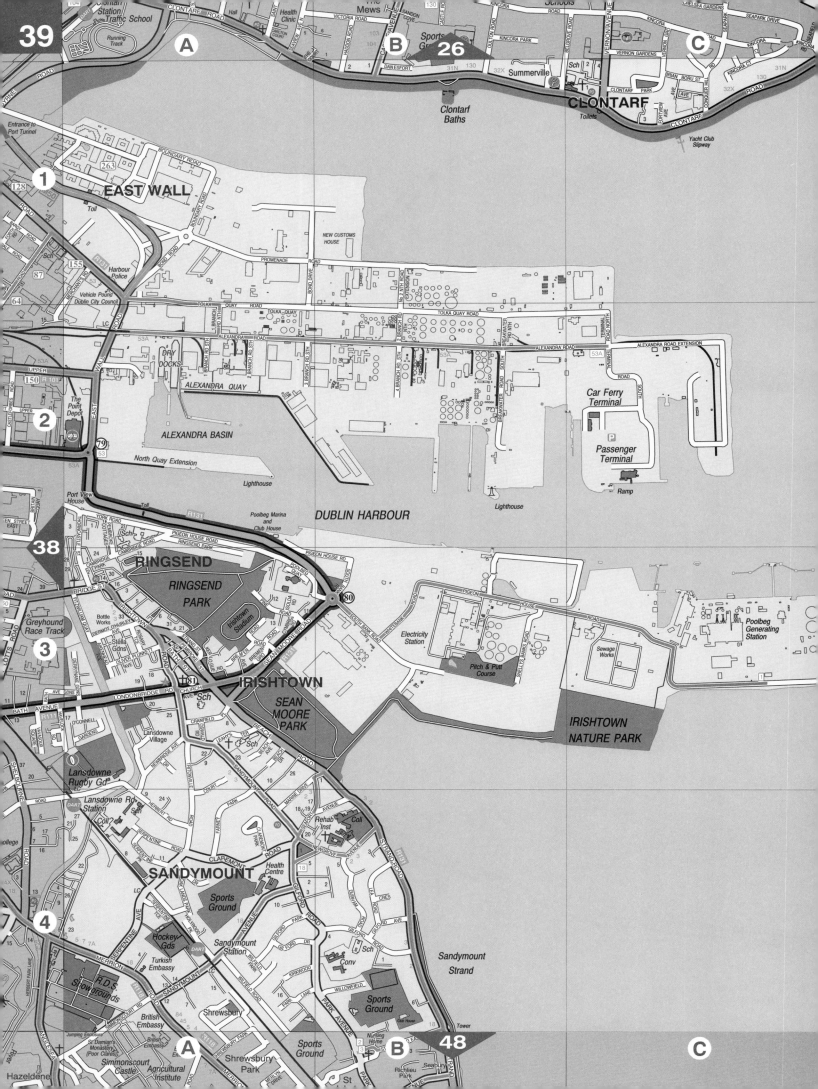

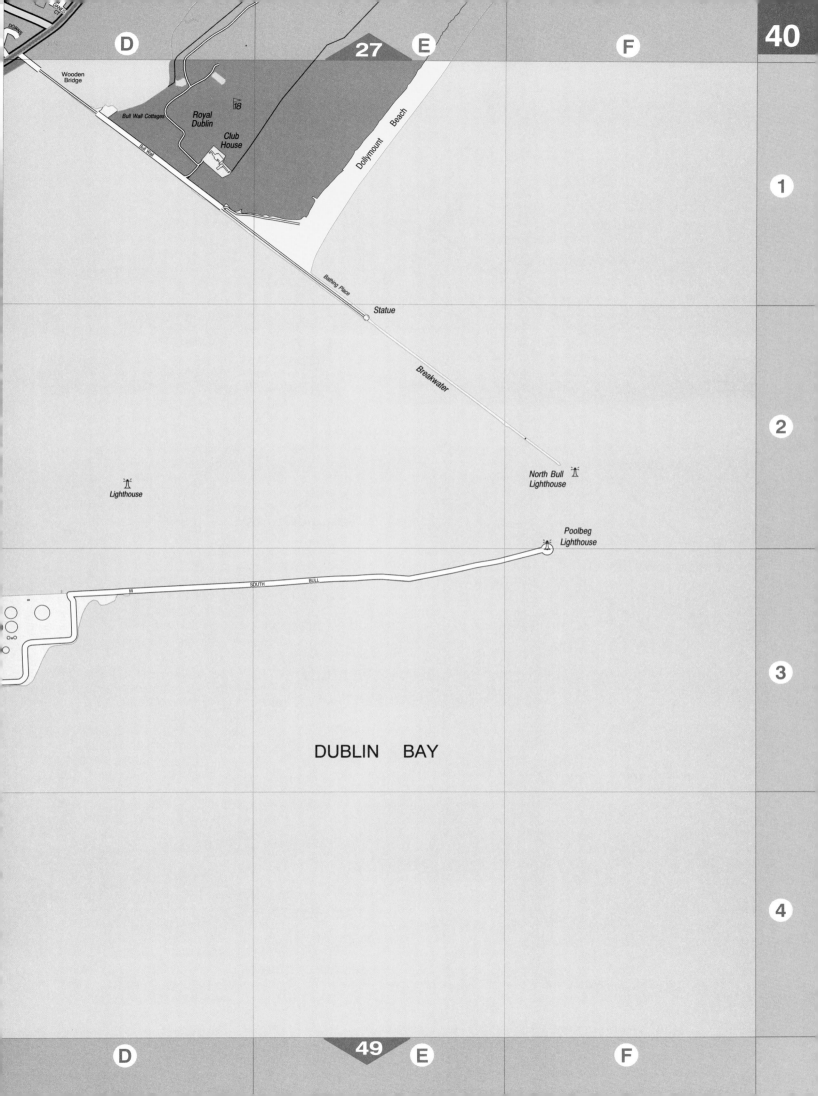

Wooden
Bridge

Bull Wall Cottages

Royal
Dublin

Club
House

↟ 18

Dollymount   Beach

Bull Wall

Bathing Place

Statue

Breakwater

1

North Bull
Lighthouse

2

Lighthouse

Poolbeg
Lighthouse

SOUTH   BULL

3

DUBLIN   BAY

4

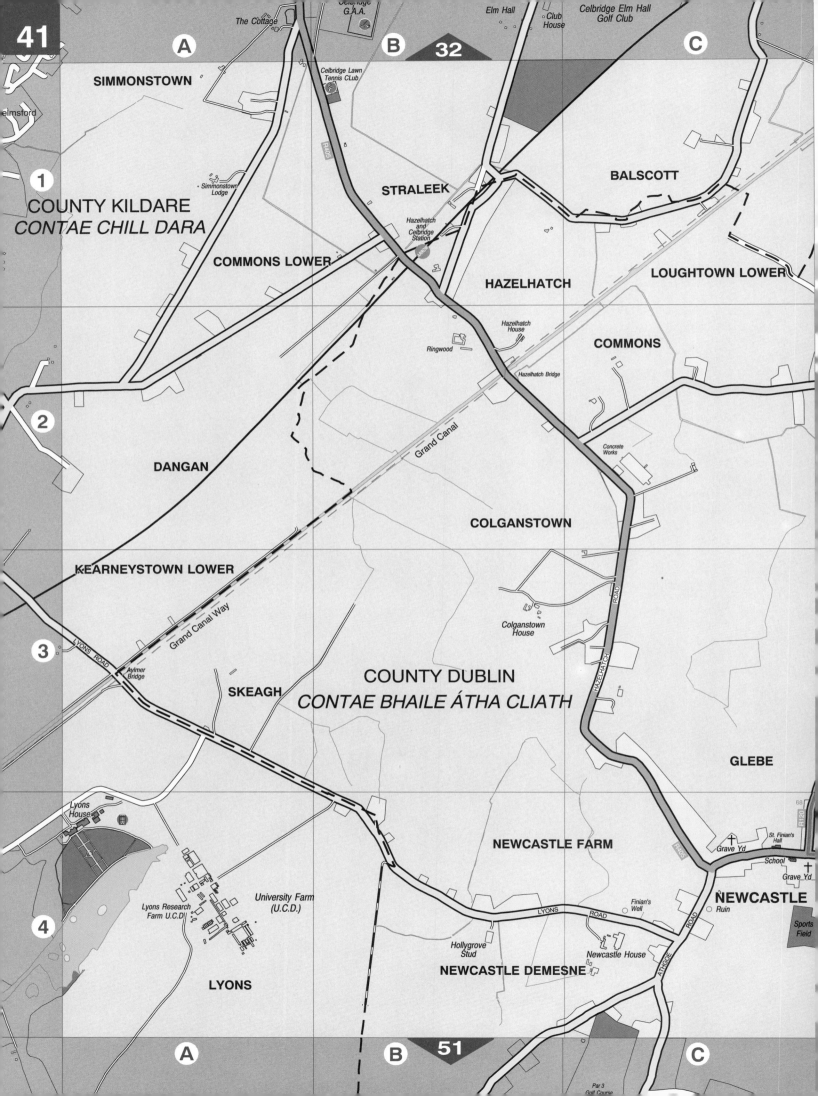

SIMMONSTOWN

elmsford

1

COUNTY KILDARE
CONTAE CHILL DARA

Simmonstown Lodge

COMMONS LOWER

The Cottage

Celbridge G.A.A.

Elm Hall

Club House

Celbridge Elm Hall Golf Club

Celbridge Lawn Tennis Club

STRALEEK

Hazelhatch and Celbridge Station

BALSCOTT

HAZELHATCH

LOUGHTOWN LOWER

Hazelhatch House

Ringwood

Hazelhatch Bridge

COMMONS

2

DANGAN

Grand Canal

Concrete Works

COLGANSTOWN

KEARNEYSTOWN LOWER

Grand Canal Way

3

LYONS ROAD

Aylmer Bridge

SKEAGH

Colganstown House

COUNTY DUBLIN
CONTAE BHAILE ÁTHA CLIATH

HAZELHATCH ROAD

GLEBE

Lyons House

Lyons Research Farm U.C.D.

University Farm (U.C.D.)

4

LYONS

Hollygrove Stud

NEWCASTLE FARM

LYONS ROAD

Finian's Well

Newcastle House

NEWCASTLE DEMESNE

ATHGOE ROAD

R403

Grave Yd

St. Finian's Hall

School

Grave Yd

NEWCASTLE

Ruin

Sports Field

R120

Par 3 Golf Course

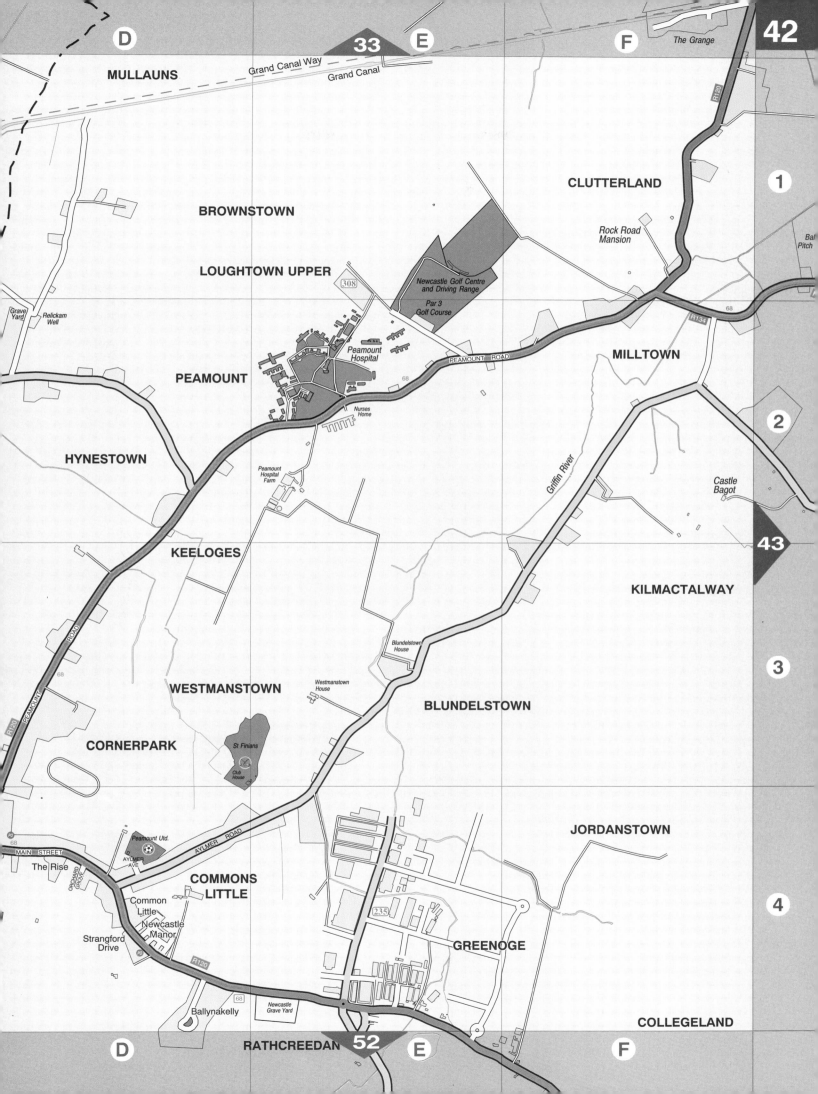

The Grange

MULLAUNS

Grand Canal Way
Grand Canal

CLUTTERLAND

BROWNSTOWN

Rock Road
Mansion

Bal
Pitch

LOUGHTOWN UPPER

Newcastle Golf Centre
and Driving Range

Par 3
Golf Course

R134

308

Grave
Yard

Relickam
Well

PEAMOUNT

Peamount
Hospital

PEAMOUNT   ROAD

MILLTOWN

68

68

Nurses
Home

HYNESTOWN

Peamount
Hospital
Farm

Griffin River

Castle
Bagot

R120

ROAD

KEELOGES

KILMACTALWAY

68

Blundelstown
House

WESTMANSTOWN

Westmanstown
House

BLUNDELSTOWN

CORNERPARK

St Finians

Club
House

JORDANSTOWN

PEAMOUNT ROAD

R120

P

AYLMER ROAD

Peamount Utd.

MAIN STREET

AYLMER
AVE

The Rise

ORCHARD GROVE

COMMONS
LITTLE

Common
Little

Newcastle
Manor

235

Strangford
Drive

R120

GREENOGE

COLLEGELAND

Ballynakelly

Newcastle
Grave Yard

68

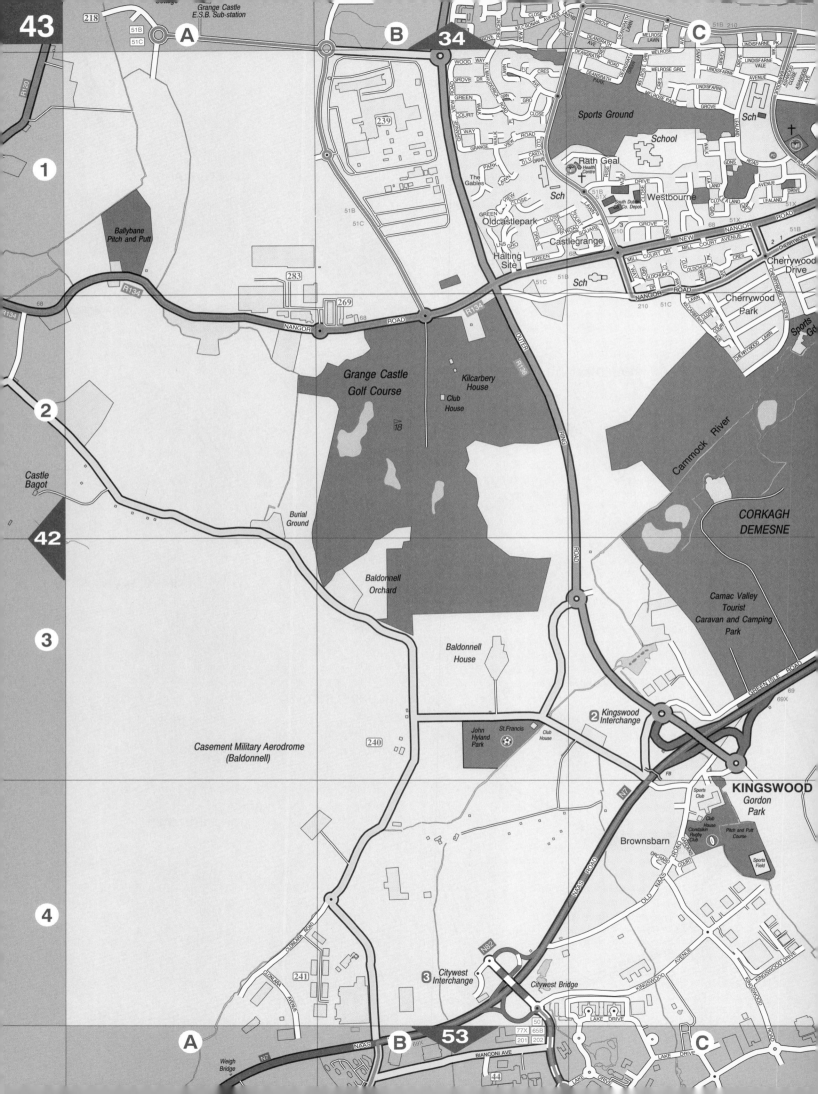

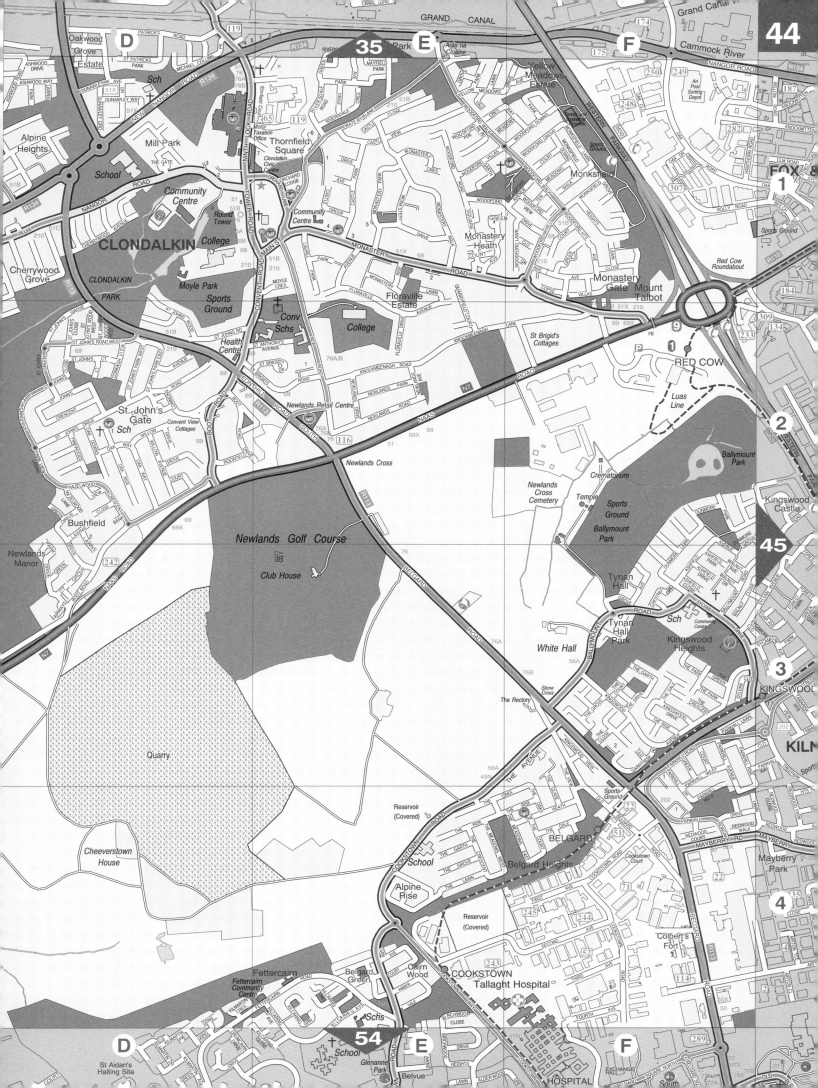

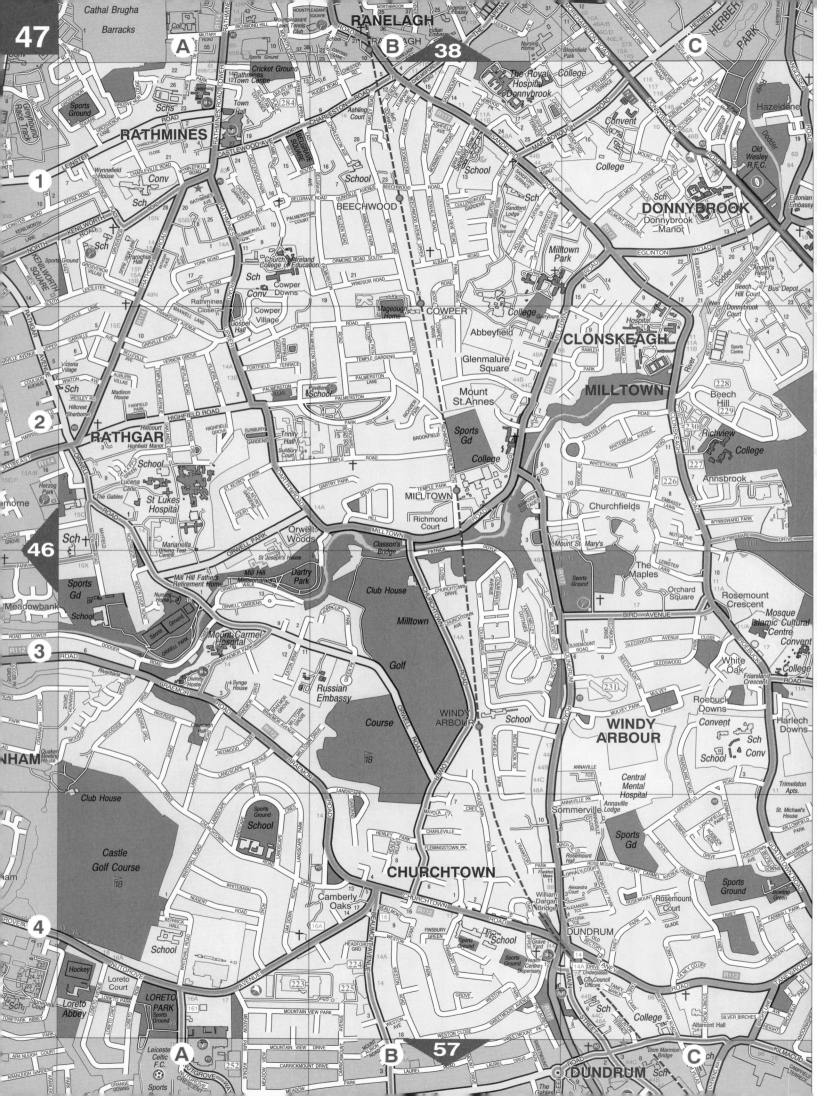

D

E

F

Lighthouse

PIER

Lighthouse

Harbour

EAST PIER

Car Ferry
Terminal

7B	746
45A	46A
46X	59
75	111

Yacht Club

i

Car Ferry
Terminal

Band Stand

HARBOUR ROAD

CROFTON ROAD

NGTCOURT

25

26 27 28

Dún Laoghaire
Station

Yacht Club

Yacht Club

Geographical Pointer
Toilets

GEORGE'S PLACE

18 Harbour
View

Harbour
Square

Dun-Laoghaire/Rathdown
Co. Council

Town
Hall

QUEEN'S ROAD

7A

Hosp

Sch

Maritime
Museum

DÚN LAOGHAIRE

GEORGE'S STREET LOWER

16

MARINE RD

ERANA AVE

111

MORAN
PARK

P

Baths

CONVENT ROAD

Sch

CUMBERLAND STREET

2

DOMINICK
ST

24

19

MELLON AVE

13

Scotsman's Bay

Forty Foot
Bathing Place

TCE N

CROSS
AVENUE

4

Health
Centre

GEORGE'S STREET UPPER

20

CLARINDA PARK NORTH

PARKROAD

PEOPLE'S
PARK

P

Harbour

SANDY COVE AVE WEST

SANDYCOVE POINT

TIVOLI TERRACE EAST

Nursing
Home

45A 111

WINDSOR TCE

P

Baths

Sandycove
Tower

SANDY COVE AVE EAST

PATRICK

MULGRAVE TERRACE

23

CLARINDA PARK EAST

GLENAGEARY RD

SUMMERHILL PARK

Sandycove/
Glastule
Station

NEWTOWNSMITH

14

MARINE
PARADE

10

MULGRAVE
STREET

11

15

CLARINDA PARK WEST

ROSMEEN GDNS

22

SANDYCOVE AVE NTH

Gowran
Hall

20

SANDYCOVE
LANE. E

ROAD

CORRIG

10

ROSSMEEN PARK

EDEN PK

7

8

BALLYGIHEN
AVE

7D

15 16 17 18

7

R119

E.H.B.
Nursing
Home

18

Children's
Home

D

R118

CLARINDA PARK

GLENGEARY RD

LB

GLASTHULE ROAD

LINK RD

BURDETT

21

60

MAR

E

BREFFNI

Bullock
Harbour

F

Clarinda
Manor

EDEN
TCE

EDEN RD UPR

EDEN RD

Coll

Schs

19

10

Gowran
20

SANDY COVE ROAD

13

14

Schn

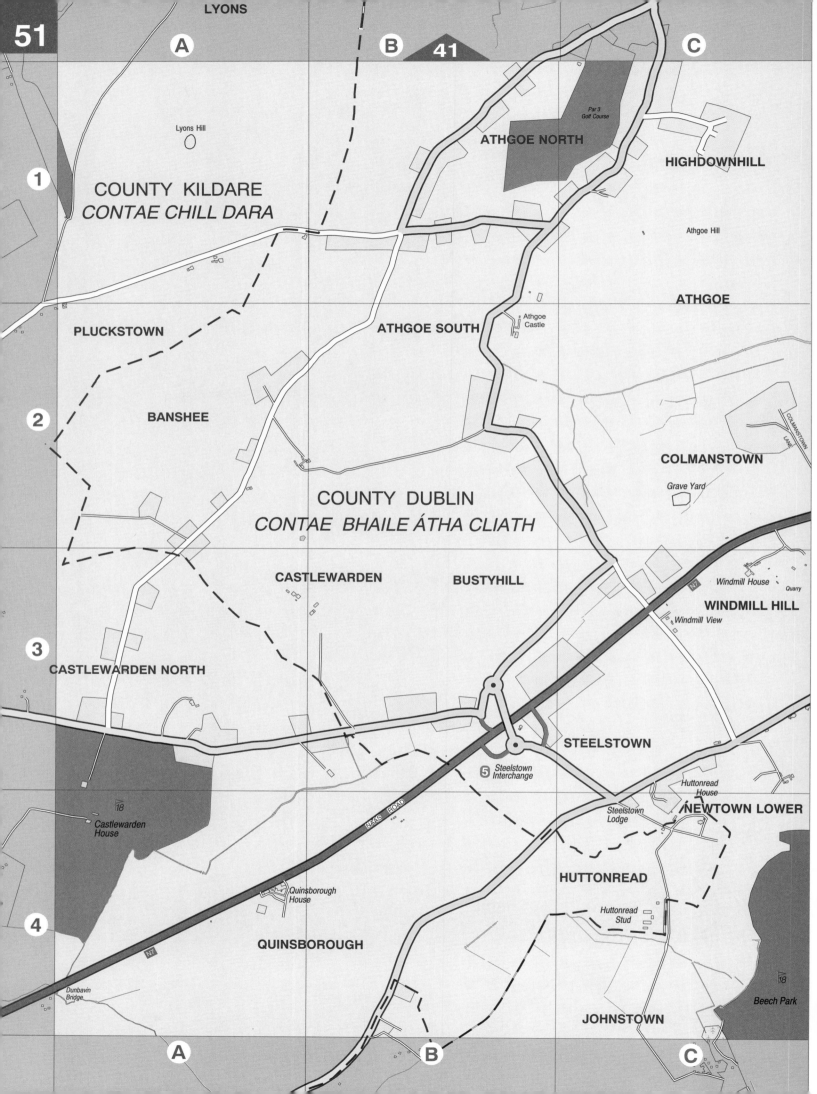

A

B

41

C

LYONS

Lyons Hill

1

COUNTY KILDARE
CONTAE CHILL DARA

ATHGOE NORTH

Par 3
Golf Course

HIGHDOWNHILL

Athgoe Hill

ATHGOE

PLUCKSTOWN

ATHGOE SOUTH

Athgoe
Castle

2

BANSHEE

COLMANSTOWN

Grave Yard

COUNTY DUBLIN
CONTAE BHAILE ÁTHA CLIATH

COLMANSTOWN LANE

CASTLEWARDEN

BUSTYHILL

N7

Windmill House

Quarry

WINDMILL HILL

Windmill View

3

CASTLEWARDEN NORTH

STEELSTOWN

5 Steelstown
Interchange

Huttonread
House

18

Steelstown
Lodge

NEWTOWN LOWER

Castlewarden
House

NAAS ROAD

HUTTONREAD

4

Quinsborough
House

Huttonread
Stud

QUINSBOROUGH

18

Dunbavin
Bridge

N7

Beech Park

JOHNSTOWN

A

B

C

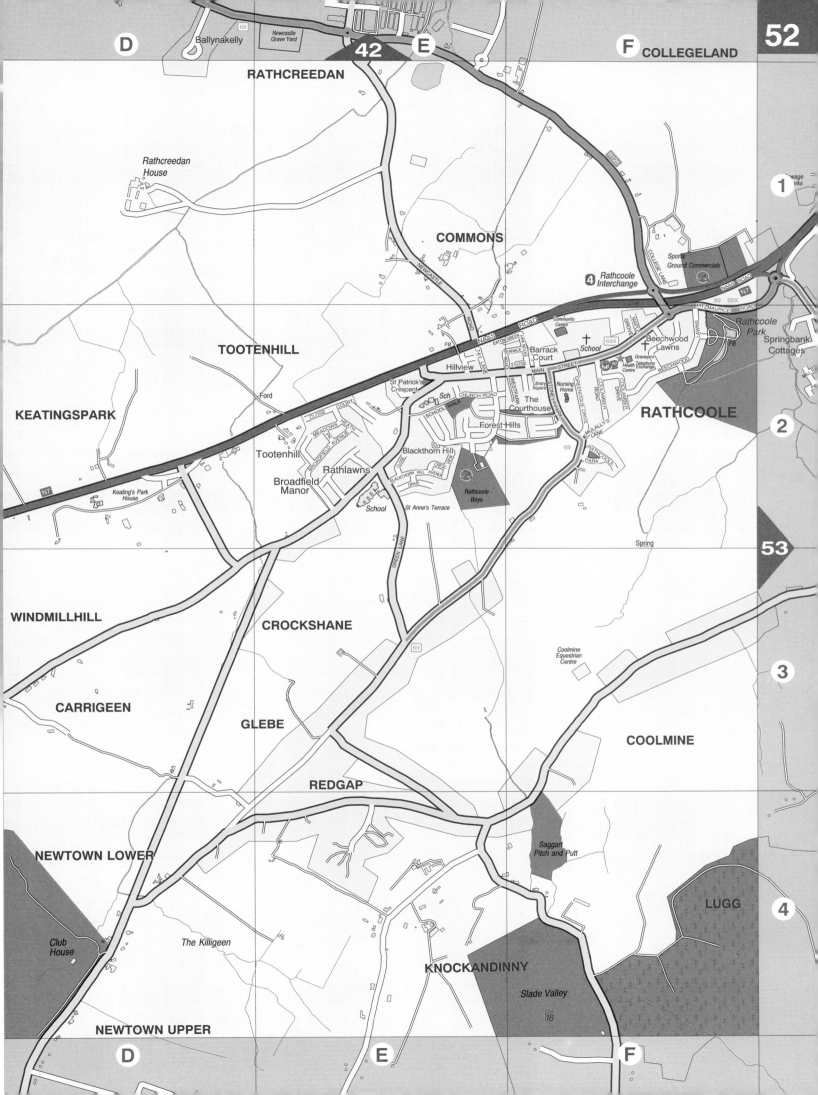

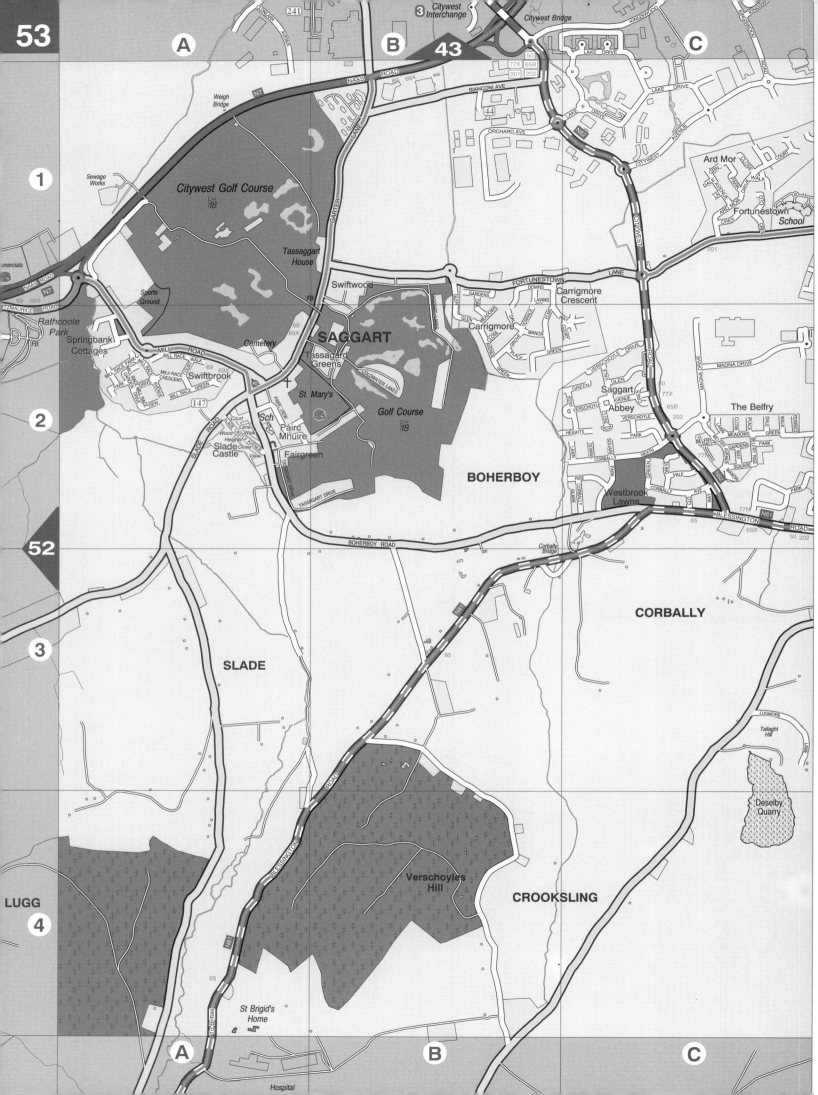

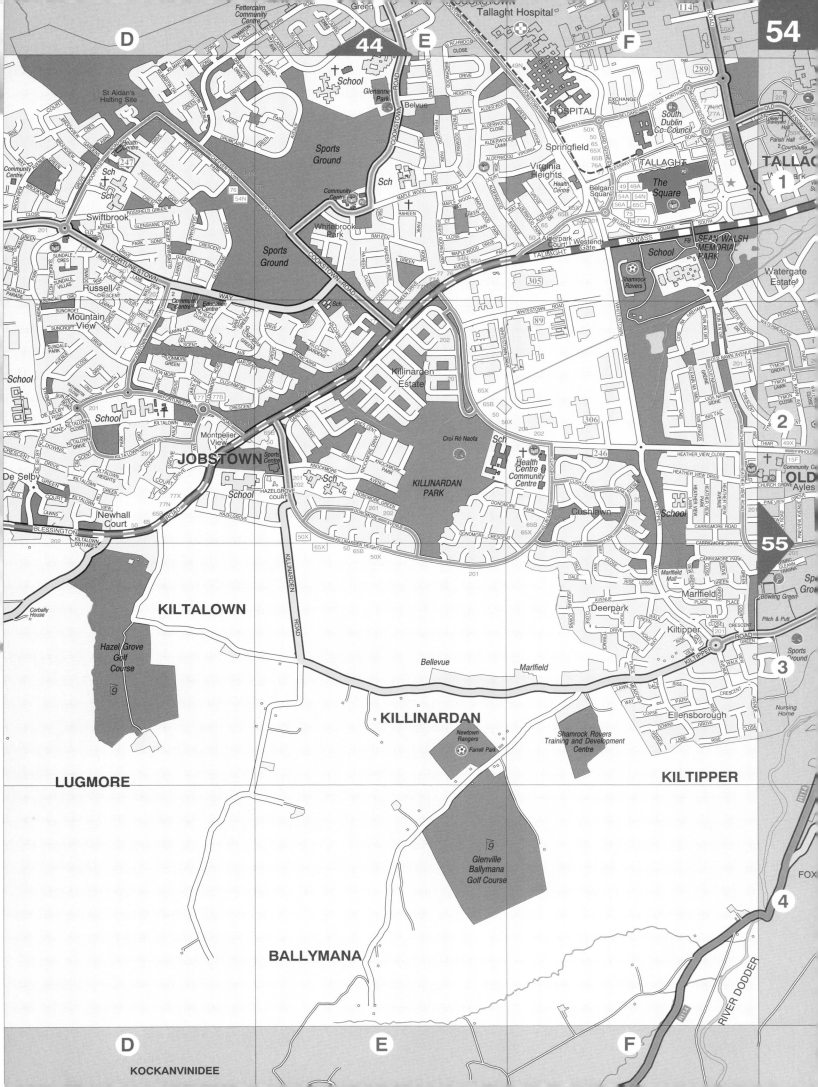

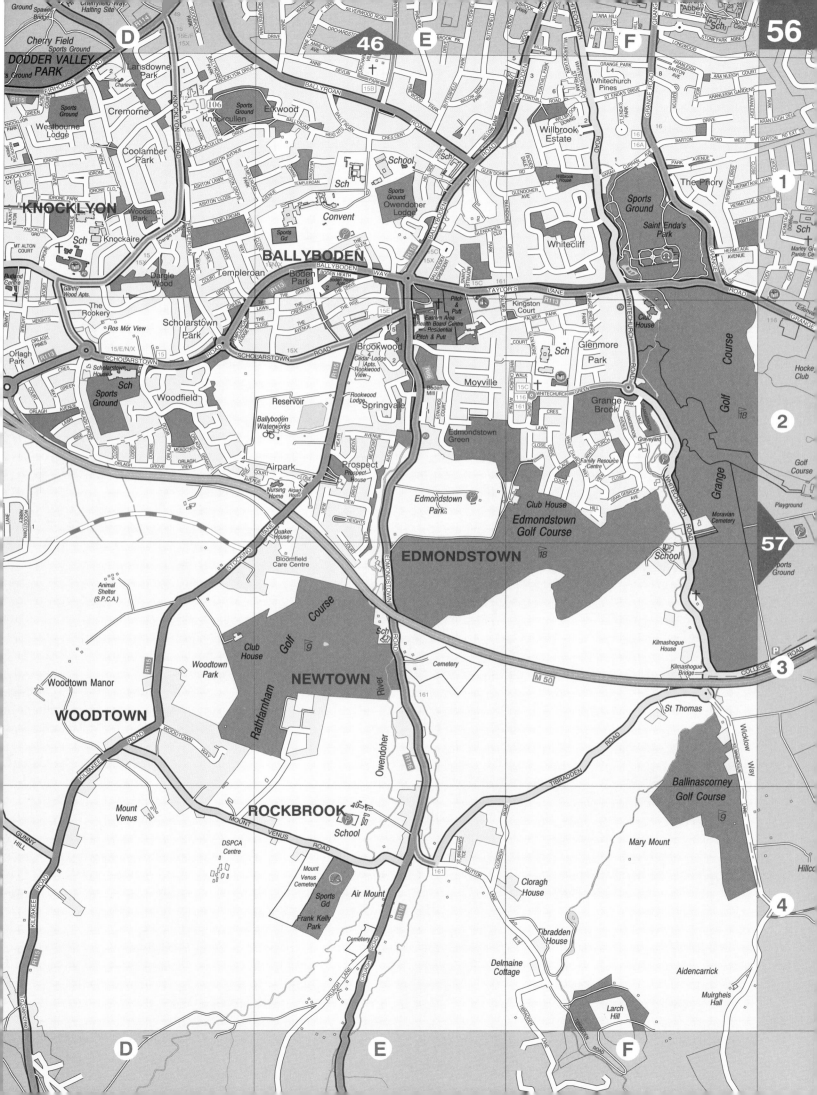

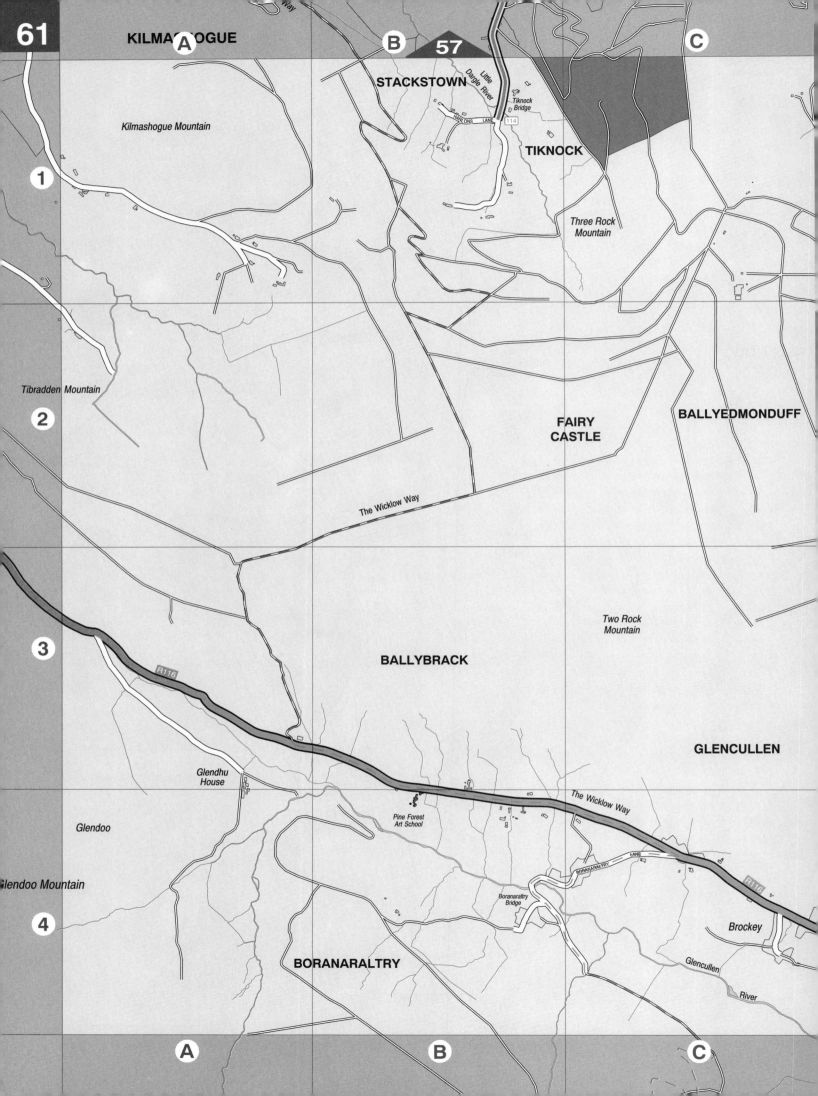

KILMASHOGUE
A
B
57
C

STACKSTOWN

Little Dargle River

Tiknock Bridge

HANLONS LANE

114

TIKNOCK

Kilmashogue Mountain

1

Three Rock Mountain

Tibradden Mountain

2

FAIRY CASTLE

BALLYEDMONDUFF

The Wicklow Way

Two Rock Mountain

3

R116

BALLYBRACK

GLENCULLEN

Glendhu House

The Wicklow Way

Glendoo

Pine Forest Art School

Glendoo Mountain

BORANARALTRY LANE

Boranaraltry Bridge

R116

Brockey

4

BORANARALTRY

Glencullen River

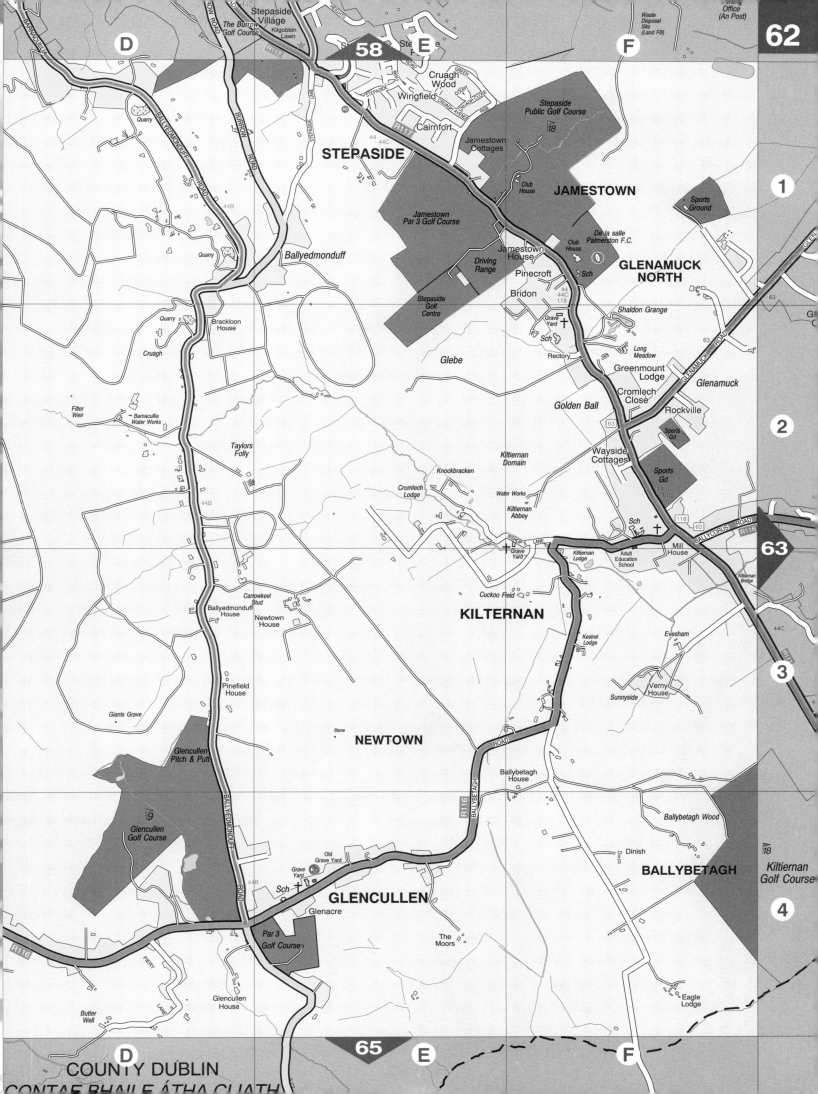

1

2

63

3

4

Waste
Disposal
Site
(Land Fill)

Office
(An Post)

Stepaside
Village
The Burrow
Golf Course
Kilgobbin
Lawn
R117

Cruagh
Wood
Wingfield
Cairnfort
R117
44
44C

STEPASIDE

Quarry

BALLYEDMONDUFF ROAD

BURROW ROAD

BARNACULLIA

STEPASIDE LANE

Stepaside
Public Golf Course
18

Jamestown
Cottages

JAMESTOWN

Club
House

Sports
Ground

Quarry

44B

Ballyedmonduff

Jamestown
Par 3 Golf Course

Driving
Range

Jamestown
House

Pinecroft

Bridon

Stepaside
Golf Centre

Club
House

Sch

De la salle
Palmerston F.C.

**GLENAMUCK
NORTH**

Shaldon Grange

63

GLENAMUCK ROAD

Quarry

Brackloon
House

Grave
Yard

Sch

Rectory

Long
Meadow

Greenmount
Lodge

Cromlech
Close

Glenamuck

Cruagh

Glebe

Filter
Weir

Barnacullia
Water Works

Taylors
Folly

Golden Ball
63

Rockville

Sports
Gd

2

Knockbracken

Kiltiernan
Domain

Wayside
Cottages

Sports
Gd
44
44C

Cromlech
Lodge

Water Works

Kiltiernan
Abbey

44B

Sch

118
63

Mill
House

BALLYCORUS ROAD

R116

BISHOP'S LANE

Grave
Yard

Grave
Yard

Kiltiernan
Lodge

Adult
Education
School

Kiltiernan
Bridge

Carrowkeel
Stud

Ballyedmonduff
House

Newtown
House

Cuckoo Field

KILTERNAN

Kestrel
Lodge

Evesham

44C

Pinefield
House

Sunnyside

Verny
House

3

Giants Grave

Stone

NEWTOWN

ROAD

Ballybetagh
House

Glencullen
Pitch & Putt

R116

BALLYBETAGH

Ballybetagh Wood

BALLYEDMONDUFF ROAD

9

Glencullen
Golf Course

Old
Grave Yard

Dinish

BALLYBETAGH

18

Kiltiernan
Golf Course

Grave
Yard

Sch

GLENCULLEN

Glenacre

The
Moors

4

44B

R116

Par 3
Golf Course

Eagle
Lodge

FIERY LANE

Butter
Well

Glencullen
House

COUNTY DUBLIN
CONTAE BHAILE ÁTHA CLIATH

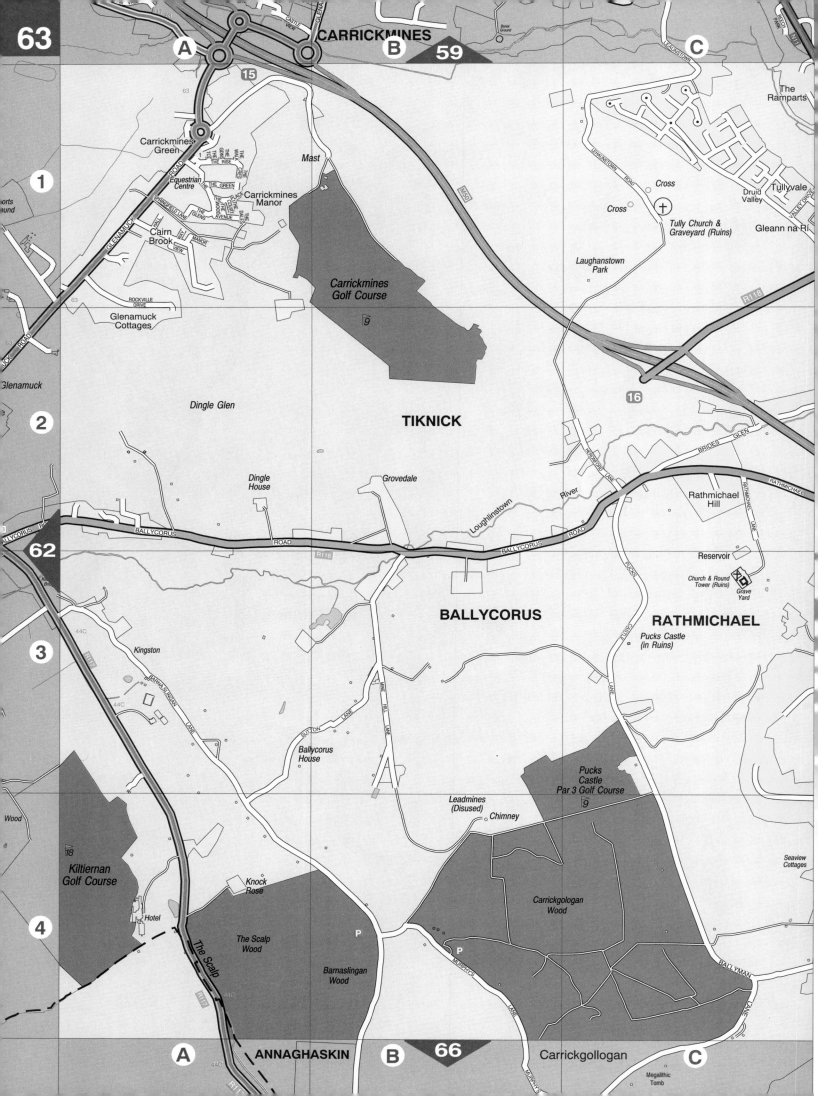

A

B 59 C

15

The Ramparts

1

Carrickmines
Green

Equestrian
Centre

THE GREEN

THE WALK
THE CRES
THE GDNS
THE RISE

Carrickmines
Manor

Mast

Cross

Druid
Valley

Tullyvale

SPRINGFIELD LANE

THE PLACE
THE GLENS
THE CLOSE
THE DALES
AVENUE

Cross

Gleann na Rí

Cairn
Brook

GLENAMUCK ROAD

MANOR
VIEW

Cross

Tully Church &
Graveyard (Ruins)

Laughanstown
Park

LEHAUNSTOWN ROAD

Glenamuck
Cottages

ROCKVILLE
DRIVE

Carrickmines
Golf Course

9

R118

ROAD

Glenamuck

2

Dingle Glen

Grovedale

TIKNICK

Loughlinstown

River

16

BRIDES   GLEN

Rathmichael
Hill

RATHMICHAEL LANE
RATHMICHAEL

Dingle
House

62

BALLYCORUS   ROAD

ROAD

R116

BALLYCORUS   ROAD

Reservoir

Church & Round
Tower (Ruins)

Grave
Yard

PUCKS

BALLYCORUS ROAD

BARNASLINGAN LANE

3

R117

44C

Kingston

SUTTON   LANE

MINE   HILL   LANE

BALLYCORUS

RATHMICHAEL

Pucks Castle
(in Ruins)

CASTLE LANE

Ballycorus
House

Leadmines
(Disused)

Chimney

Pucks
Castle
Par 3 Golf Course

9

Seaview
Cottages

Wood

18

Kiltiernan
Golf Course

Knock
Rose

The Scalp
Wood

P

Carrickgologan
Wood

4

Hotel

The Scalp

R117

44C

Barnaslingan
Wood

P

MURPHY'S   LANE

BALLYMAN LANE

A

B 66

Carrickgollogan

C

Megalithic
Tomb

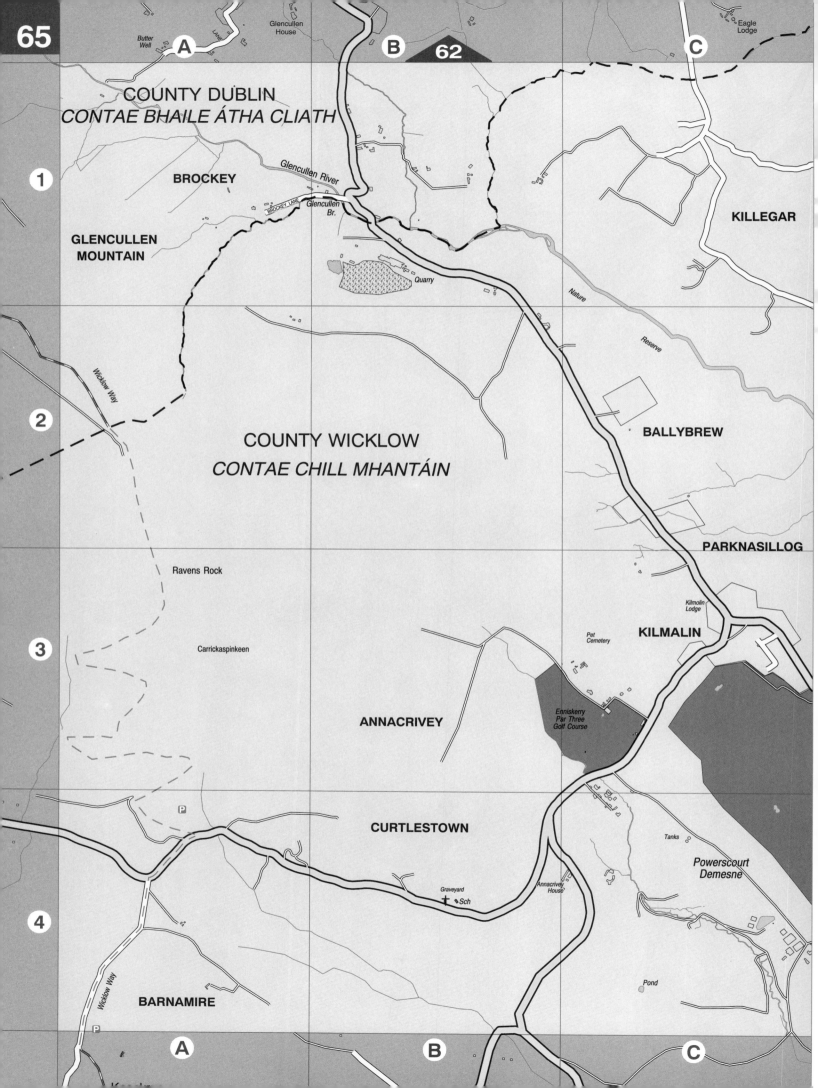

A

C

Eagle
Lodge

*Glencullen
House*

*Butter
Well*

COUNTY DUBLIN
CONTAE BHAILE ÁTHA CLIATH

Glencullen River

1

BROCKEY

BROCKEY LANE

*Glencullen
Br.*

KILLEGAR

**GLENCULLEN
MOUNTAIN**

Quarry

Nature

2

Wicklow Way

COUNTY WICKLOW
CONTAE CHILL MHANTÁIN

Reserve

BALLYBREW

PARKNASILLOG

Ravens Rock

*Kilmolin
Lodge*

3

Carrickaspinkeen

*Pet
Cemetery*

KILMALIN

*Enniskerry
Par Three
Golf Course*

ANNACRIVEY

P

Tanks

CURTLESTOWN

*Powerscourt
Demesne*

Graveyard

*Annacrivey
House*

✝ ◆ Sch

4

Wicklow Way

BARNAMIRE

Pond

P

A

B

C

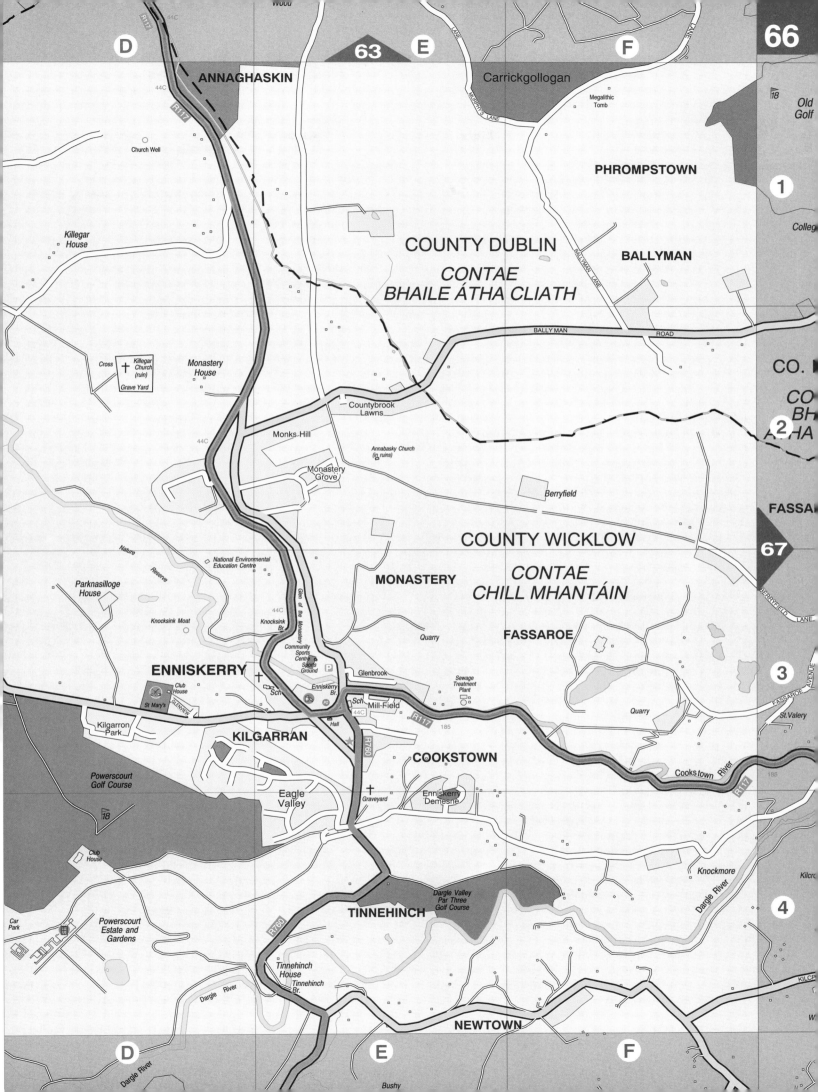

1

BRAY

National
Sea Life
Aquarium

2

Naylor's Cove

Fontenoy
Terrace

RAHEEN PARK

AVENUE

Raheenacluig Church
(in Ruins)

Golf Course

3

Briar
Wood

Tunnel

*Bray
Head*

NEWCOURT

4

84X
84
184

COUNTY WICKLOW

*CONTAE
CHILL MHANTÁIN*

Tunnel

Tunnel
Tunnel

EAST POINT
Business Park

EAST WALL

M50

R131

Entrance to
Port Tunnel

John McCormack
Bridge

Portside
Business
Centre

Harbour
Police

Port
Centre

DRY
DOCKS

ALEXANDRA QUAY

Port & Docks
Centre

The
Point
Depot

NORTH WALL

ALEXANDRA BASIN

National College
of Ireland

North Quay Extension

RIVER

LIFFEY

Lighthouse

East Link
Toll Bridge

SIR JOHN ROGERSON'S QUAY

Port View
House

Toll
Plaza

Poolbeg Marina
and Clubhouse

Thorncastle
Court

R131

GRAND CANAL
DOCK

RINGSEND

RINGSEND
PARK

MacMahon
Bridge

Charlotte Quay

Waterways
Visitor's
Centre

Ringsend
Bridge

Irishtown
Stadium

Grand Canal
Dock Station
DART

Shelbourne
Greyhound
Race Track

National
Maternity
Hospital

Beggar's
Bush Buildings

Print
Museum

IRISHTOWN

SEAN
MOORE
PARK

Geological
Survey of
Ireland

Lansdowne
Village

Czech
Republic
Embassy

Lansdowne
Rugby Gd

Royal City
of Dublin Hosp

Lansdowne Rd
Station
DART

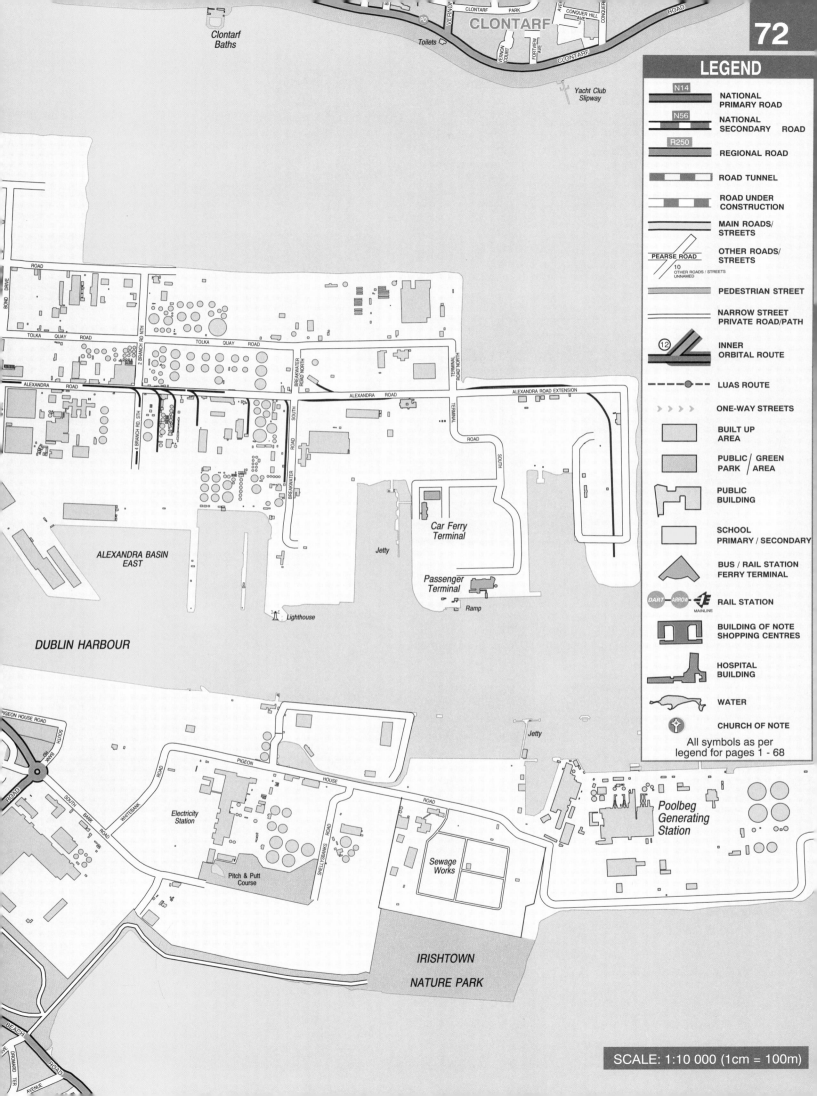

CLONTARF

Clontarf Baths

Toilets

Yacht Club Slipway

LEGEND

N14	NATIONAL PRIMARY ROAD
N56	NATIONAL SECONDARY ROAD
R250	REGIONAL ROAD
	ROAD TUNNEL
	ROAD UNDER CONSTRUCTION
	MAIN ROADS/ STREETS
PEARSE ROAD / 10 OTHER ROADS / STREETS UNNAMED	OTHER ROADS/ STREETS
	PEDESTRIAN STREET
	NARROW STREET PRIVATE ROAD/PATH
12	INNER ORBITAL ROUTE
	LUAS ROUTE
> > > >	ONE-WAY STREETS
	BUILT UP AREA
	PUBLIC / GREEN PARK / AREA
	PUBLIC BUILDING
	SCHOOL PRIMARY / SECONDARY
	BUS / RAIL STATION FERRY TERMINAL
DART – ARROW – MAINLINE	RAIL STATION
	BUILDING OF NOTE SHOPPING CENTRES
	HOSPITAL BUILDING
	WATER
	CHURCH OF NOTE

All symbols as per legend for pages 1 - 68

BOND DRIVE

ROAD

TOLKA QUAY ROAD

2 BRANCH RD NTH

TOLKA QUAY ROAD

BREAKWATER ROAD NORTH

TERMINAL ROAD NORTH

ALEXANDRA ROAD

ALEXANDRA ROAD

ALEXANDRA ROAD EXTENSION

4 BRANCH RD STH

BREAKWATER ROAD SOUTH

TERMINAL ROAD SOUTH

ALEXANDRA BASIN EAST

Car Ferry Terminal

Jetty

Passenger Terminal

Ramp

Lighthouse

DUBLIN HARBOUR

PIGEON HOUSE ROAD

SOUTH BANK ROAD

PIGEON HOUSE ROAD

WHITEBANK ROAD

Jetty

Electricity Station

SHELLYBANKS ROAD

Poolbeg Generating Station

Pitch & Putt Course

Sewage Works

BEACH

DRUMARD TER

AVENUE

IRISHTOWN

NATURE PARK

SCALE: 1:10 000 (1cm = 100m)

PLACES TO VISIT

Phoenix Park Visitor Centre

Located in the Phoenix Park, 5kms from the City Centre. The Tower House possibly dates from the 17th Century, and nearby is the visitor centre. There are exhibitions, a film show, and visitors can view a colourful and realistic historical interpretation of the past.

Visiting times:

Mid March - end of March:	daily	10.00 a.m. - 5.30 p.m.
April - September:	daily	10.00 a.m. - 6.00 p.m.
October:	daily	10.00 a.m. - 5.30 p.m.
November - Mid March:	Sat.-Sun.	10.00 a.m. - 5.00 p.m.

Last admission 45 minutes before closing.
Free guided tours to Áras an Uachtaráin Saturdays only. Phone 670 9155.

23 C4

Phoenix Park Visitor Centre

Bank of Ireland: (former Parliament House)
College Green.
Origins: Built between 1729 and 1739.
Designed by Sir Edward Lovatt Pearce (1699-1733) and enlarged by James Gandon and Robert Parke between 1785 and 1794.
The Bank of Ireland took over this building in 1804. It had been the scene of many dramatic events in Irish politics up to the passing of the Act of Union in 1800.
Visiting times:

Monday, Tuesday, Wednesday and Friday.	10.00 a.m. - 4.00 p.m.
Thursday	10.00 a.m. - 5.00 p.m.

Bank of Ireland Arts Centre

Tuesday to Friday	9.30 a.m. - 4.00 p.m.

38 D2

Castletown House
Located in Celbridge, Co. Kildare. Castletown House, designed by Italian architect Alessandro Galilei and Irish architect Sir Edward Lovett Pearce for the speaker of the Irish House of Commons, William Connolly.
Building commenced in 1722, and Castletown House was continuously used by the Connolly family until 1965 when the house and lands were sold.
Castletown House came into state ownership in 1979 under the management of the Office of Public Works.
Visiting times:

April to September:	Monday to Friday	10.00 a.m. – 6.00 p.m.
	Saturday/Sunday/	
	Bank Holidays	1.00 p.m. – 6.00 p.m.
October:	Monday to Friday	10.00 a.m. – 5.00 p.m.
	Sunday/	
	Bank Holidays	1.00 p.m. – 5.00 p.m.
November:	Sundays only	1.00 p.m. – 5.00 p.m.

Last admission one hour before closing.

32 D2

Celbridge Abbey
Located 12 miles from Dublin, Celbridge Abbey was built by Bartholomew Van Homrigh, Lord Mayor of Dublin in 1697.
The Abbey grounds contain many colourful attractions and are open to the public at the following times.
Visiting times:

Monday to Saturday	10.00 a.m. - 6.00 p.m.
Sunday/Bank Holidays	11.00 a.m. - 6.00 p.m.

31 C4

Castletown House

Custom House
Custom House Quay
Origins: Designed by James Gandon and built between 1781 and 1791.
The building was reduced to a shell when it was gutted by fire during the War of Independence. It was restored by the Office of Public Works after the Irish Free State was established.

38 E2

Custom House

Casino Marino
Malahide Road
Located just 4kms from the city centre, off the Malahide Road, Dublin 3. The Casino, has been described as one of the finest 18th century classical buildings in Ireland. Access is by Guided Tour only.
Visiting times:

January Closed		
February / March	Saturday / Sunday 12 noon	- 4.00 p.m.
April	Saturday / Sunday 12 noon	- 5.00 p.m.
May and October	daily	10.00 a.m. - 5.00 p.m.
June - September	daily	10.00 a.m. - 6.00 p.m.
November / December	Saturday / Sunday 12 noon	- 4.00 p.m.

26 D3

Casino Marino

City Hall
Cork Hill, Dame Street.
Origins: Formerly the Royal Exchange, designed by Thomas Cooley (1740 – 1784) and completed between 1769 and 1779.
This is the headquarters of Dublin's municipal government. Archives dating back to the twelfth century are stored in the Muniment Room. It also houses the mace and sword of the city, along with 102 Royal Charters, including the original charter of 1171 by which Dublin was granted to the men of Bristol by Henry II.

Mon - Sat	10.00a.m. - 5.15p.m.
Sunday and Bank Holidays	2.00p.m. - 5.00p.m.

38 D2

Dublinia – Christ Church,
St. Michael's Hill, Dublin 8.
The realistic and novel exhibition that is Dublinia is situated in the old Synod Hall on St. Michael's Hill, alongside of Christ Church Cathedral, to which it is connected by an ornate pedestrian archway over St. Michael's Hill.
The exhibition heralds the arrival of the Anglo-Normans in 1170 through a broad spectrum of Dublin life to the closure of the Monasteries in 1540.
Visiting times:
April - September: daily   10.00 a.m. - 5.00 p.m.
October - March: Monday to Friday   11.00 a.m. - 4.00 p.m.
Saturday, Sunday/Bank Holiday   10.00 a.m. - 4.30 p.m.

38 D3

Dublin Castle
The main entrance is located at the junction of Cork Hill and Castle Street. Dating from the 13th Century, the site, once a Viking stronghold, has served as a military fortress, prison, courts of law, and the core of British Administration in Ireland until 1922. Dublin Castle is now used for State functions. Guided tours of State Apartments, Chapel Royal and Undercroft.

Visiting times:
Monday/Friday   10.00 a.m. - 5.00 p.m.
Saturday,Sunday and Public Holidays   2.00 p.m. - 5.00 p.m.
Closed 24th. - 26th. December, 1st. January and Good Friday

38 D3

The Throne Room, Dublin Castle

St. Patrick's Hall, Dublin Castle

Dunsink Observatory
Dunsink Lane, near Castleknock.
Origins: Founded in 1783, this is one of the world's oldest observatories. It formerly belonged to Trinity College but is now the centre of the school of Astronomical Physics of the Dublin Institute for Advanced Studies.
Visiting times: Open to the public on the first and third Wednesday of each month from October to March, at 8.00 p.m.
Admission free on written application to the secretary enclosing stamp-addressed envelope.

23 B2

General Post Office

General Post Office
O'Connell Street.
Origins: Designed by Francis Johnston and built between 1814 and 1818.
The GPO became the focal point of the 1916 Insurrection and the Proclamation of the Irish Republic took place there. Destroyed by fire, it was restored in 1929. In the public office is a noteworthy statue representing the Death of Cuchulainn, the work of Oliver Sheppard R.H.A.

38 D2

Kilmainham Jail
Inchicore Road, Dublin 8.
One of the largest decommissioned jails in Europe, it played its part in some of the most patriotic and tragic episodes that light the path of Ireland's journey to modern nationhood, from the 1780's to 1924.
Featuring many exhibitions and a multi-lingual audio-visual show. Access by guided tour only.
Visiting times:

October - March:	Monday to Saturday	9.30 a.m. - 5.30 p.m.
	Sunday	10.00 a.m. - 6.00 p.m.
April - September:	daily	9.30 a.m. - 6.00 p.m.

Closed 24th. - 26th. December
Last admission 1hr 15min before closing.

37 A3

Four Courts

Four Courts
Inns Quay.
Origins: Designed by James Gandon and built between 1785 and 1802. This building, dominated by a great domed central mass, is one of Gandon's masterpieces. The Irish Law Courts and Law Library are housed here. Like the Custom House, Gandon's other great building, it was also destroyed by fire during the struggle for Irish independence. Although significantly altered, the building was completely restored by 1932.

38 D2

Leinster House

Leinster House
Kildare Street.
Origins: Designed by Richard Cassells, building commenced on this fine Georgian mansion in 1745. Originally the residence of the Duke of Leinster, the building became the property of the Royal Dublin Society in 1815. In 1922 it was purchased by the first Irish Free State Government to serve as a Parliament House. Presently it is the meeting place of the Dail (Chamber of Deputies) and Seanad (Senate).

38 E3

Waterways Visitor Centre
Grand Canal Quay, Dublin 2
Located at Grand Canal Docks, beside McMahon Bridge, Pearse Street. The centre houses an exhibition outlining the history of Ireland's Inland Waterways and the activities and experiences currently available. Featuring an audio-visual show and working models of various engineering features.
Visiting times:

| October - May: | Wednesday to Sunday 12.30 p.m. - 5.00 p.m. |
| June - September: | daily | 9.30 a.m. - 6.30 p.m |

Last admission 45 minutes before closing.
Closed until July 2007

38 F3

Royal Hospital and Irish Museum of Modern Art

Royal Hospital and Irish Museum of Modern Art
Military Road, Kilmainham.
The most important 17th century building in Ireland has been restored. Guided tours available of the Master's Quarters, the Great Hall with the portrait collection, and the chapel which contains outstanding woodcarving by Tabary and a magnificent Baroque ceiling.

Visiting Times:	Tues,Thurs, Fri, & Sat	10.00 a.m. - 5.30 p.m.
	Wed	10.30 a.m. - 5.30 p.m.
	Sunday and Bank Holidays	12noon - 5.30 p.m.

Closed Mondays Good Friday and 24-26th. Dceember
Last admission 5.15p.m

37 B3

Trinity College

Trinity College

Main entrance, College Green.
Origins: Trinity College is the sole college of the University of Dublin. Founded by Queen Elizabeth I in 1592, it is built on the site of the Augustinian priory of All Hallows which was founded by Dermot McMurrough. The oldest buildings now surviving are the Rubrics, a range of brick apartments dating from 1700. The Palladian facade was added in 1759. In the same year the Provost's house (facing the northern end of Grafton Street) was built. This is the only great Georgian house in Dublin still being used for its original purpose. Many world-famous men have attended this college over the centuries.
Visiting Times: Monday to Saturday   10.00 a.m. - 5.00 p.m.
                    See also 'Trinity College Library'.

38 E2

Mansion House
Dawson Street.
Origins: This Queen Anne house was built in 1705, the round room having been added in 1821 as the venue for a function to honour King George IV. Built in brick, the building underwent changes during the Victorian era.
Since 1715 the Mansion House has been the residence of Dublin's Lord Mayor. In 1919 the Declaration of Independence was adopted here and here also was signed the truce which ended Anglo-Irish hostilities in 1921.

38 E3

Swords Castle
Built in 1183 as a summer palace for the first Norman Archbishop of Dublin, Swords Castle was designed both as a residence and as a place of defence. In 1324 Archbishop de Bicknor left Swords and the castle fell into disrepair. Despite many attempts at renovation over the centuries, it has remained so. Currently in the ownership of Fingal Council, and now in the process of being restored.
Visiting times:
       Monday, Wednesday and Thursday 10.00 a.m. - 4.00 p.m.
       Friday   10.00 a.m. - 3.00 p.m.

2 D2

Howth Castle
The great English architect Sir Edwin Lutyens restyled this 14thcentury castle overlooking Dublin Bay. The grounds are also noted for its wild rhododendron gardens. The grounds are open daily from 8.00 a.m. to sunset.

29 C1

Howth Transport Museum
This Museum is located in the grounds of Howth Castle. It features lorries, trucks, fire engines and tractors. Also exhibited is the restored Hill of Howth No.9 Tram.
Visiting times:
June - August: Monday to Saturday   10.00 a.m. - 5.00 p.m.
September - May: Sat., Sun. and Bank Holiday   2.00 p.m. - 5.00 p.m.
       26th.Dec. to 1st. Jan.   2.00 p.m. - 5.00 p.m.

29 C1

Malahide Castle
Built by Sir Richard de Talbot about 1200 and developed over the centuries into the imposing architectural achievement that it is today. The castle houses part of the National Portrait Collection in the Great Hall.
The extensive grounds are open from 9 a.m. - 9 p.m.daily and incorporate the 20 acre Talbot Botanic Garden, which is open to all from 2 p.m. to 5 p.m. daily.
Visiting times:
Jan - Dec   Mon to Sat   10.00 a.m. - 5.00 p.m.
Apr - Sept   Sun./B.Holiday   10.00 a.m. - 6.00 p.m.
Oct - Mar   Sun./B.Holiday   11.00 p.m. - 5.00 p.m.
                    Closed daily from   12.45 p.m. - 2.00 p.m.
Also included is the Fry Model Railway Museum, which contains a unique collection of hand-made models showing the history of Irish railways from its inception to the modern day period.

3 A3

Bray Courthouse
Located on Main Street between Quinsborough Road and Seapoint Road, this building was designed by William Murray, and built in 1841. It is now the location of Bray Heritage Museum, and Bray Tourist Office.
Visiting times: daily   10.00 a.m. – 5.00 p.m.

67 C2

Bray Town Hall
Located on Main Street at the junction of Killarney Road and Vevay Road is the jewel in Bray's architectural crown. Designed by Edward G. Dawber for architects Thomas Newenham Deane & Son, it was built in 1884 at the request of Lord and Lady Brabazon for the people of Bray. Currently the seat of Bray Urban District Council.

67 C2

St Patrick's College, Maynooth
St Patrick's College, Maynooth was founded in 1795 as the National Seminary for Ireland. In 1896, it was granted a Pontifical Charter which empowered it to confer degrees in Theology, Philosophy and Canon Law.
The Universities Act (1997) resulted in the creation of a new university, National University of Ireland, Maynooth. St.Patrick's College, which consists of the Pontifical University and the National Seminary, continues to exist side by side with NUI Maynooth. The two institutions share the same campus and work in close co-operation with each other.
Visiting times:
May - September: Monday to Friday   11.00 a.m. - 5.00 p.m.
                    Saturday and Sunday   2.00 p.m. - 6.00 p.m.
Groups welcome.

17 C3

Powerscourt Gardens
Powerscourt Gardens, situated 12 miles south of Dublin is a blend of formal gardens, sweeping terraces, statuary and ornamental lakes together with secret hollows, rambling walks, walled gardens and over 200 variations of trees and shrubs. Facilities include tea rooms, craft shop, garden centre, play area and riverside picnic spots.
Visiting times:
              9.30 a.m. - 5.30 p.m.
       Waterfall open daily 9.30 a.m. - 7.00 p.m.
              Closes Winter at dusk

66 D4

CHURCHES AND CATHEDRALS

Christ Church Cathedral
Main entrance, Christchurch Place.
Origins: The original church was built about 1030 by Sigtryggr Silkenbeard, Norse King of Dublin. A new church was built in 1173 by Strongbow. The present structure dates mainly from the nineteenth century, although the wonderful medieval crypt still remains. Christ Church contains many interesting historical remains.
Visiting times:

June-August	Mon to Fri	9.45 a.m. - 6.00 p.m.
Sept-May	Mon to Fri	9.45 a.m. - 5.00 p.m.
	Saturday	10.00 a.m. - 4.30 p.m.
	Sunday	12.45 a.m. - 2.45 p.m.
	Closed St. Stephens Day	

Group tours available on request / application.

38 D3

St. Audoen's Church
High Street
Origins: St. Audoen's dates from medieval times and is the oldest of Dublin's parish churches. The tower houses Ireland's three most ancient bells, dating from 1423. There's a font in the nave dating from 1124. St. Audoen's Arch stands nearby. This is Dublin's only surviving city gate. Built in 1240 it originally led to a strand on the River Liffey.
Visiting times: June - September: 9.30 a.m. - 5.00 p.m.

37 C3

St. Mary's Church
Mary Street.
Origins: Dating from 1627, this was the first Dublin church to be built with galleries. Theobald Wolfe Tone was baptised here in 1763 and Sean O'Casey the playwright in 1880. The Church is now a retail outlet.

38 D2

St. Michan's Church
Church Street
Origins: Founded by the Norse in 1096, the present building dates from 1685-6, having been much restored in 1828. The Church's Harris organ is said to have been used by Handel during his visit to Dublin. Dry magnesium limestone vaults beneath the church contain mummified corpses which may be seen by the public.
Visiting times: Church and Vaults:

March - October	Monday to Friday	10.00 a.m. - 4.30 p.m.
	Closed 12.30 p.m. - 2.00 p.m.	
November - March	Monday to Friday	12.30 p.m. - 3.30 p.m.
	Saturday	10.00 a.m. - 12.45 p.m.
	Vaults closed on Sundays.	

37 C2

St. Mary's Pro-Cathedral
Marlborough Street.
Origins: Designed by John Sweetman and built between 1815 and 1825. Originally intended for O'Connell Street but erected on this less suitable site to satisfy Protestant opposition at the time. The interior reveals the inspiration of Chalgin's Church of St. Philippe de Roule, Paris. Some interesting monuments may be seen inside. The metropolitan church of the diocese, it is used for State functions. A Latin Mass is sung each Sunday at 11 a.m. by the Palestrina Choir of which the famous tenor John McCormack was once a member.
Visiting times:

Monday to Friday	7.30 a.m. - 6.45 p.m.
Saturday	7.30 a.m. - 7.15 p.m.
Sunday	9.00 a.m. - 1.45 p.m.
	and 5.30 p.m. - 7.45 p.m.

38 D2

St. Werburgh's Church
Werburgh Street, off Christchurch Place.
Origins: Erected in 1715 on the site of the medieval successor to pre-Norman St. Werburgh's. Destroyed by fire in 1754, the church was re-opened in 1759. A spire was added in 1768 but removed in the early nineteenth century by the fearful authorities of Dublin castle, which it overlooked. Until 1790 St. Werburgh's was the Chapel Royal. In the vaults beneath is buried Lord Edward Fitzgerald. His captor Town Major Sirr, is buried in the nearby churchyard.
This fine Georgian building, now well restored, contains many interesting features including an attractive pulpit designed by Francis Johnston and carved by Richard Stewart, as well as a sixteenth-century Fitzgerald tomb located in the porch.
Visiting times: By appointment only. Tel. 478 3710
Monday to Friday   10.00 a.m. - 4.00 p.m.
Entrance: North Door, 8 Castle Street.
Main Sunday Service: 10.00 a.m.

38 D3

St. Patrick's Cathedral
Patrick Street.
Origins: St. Patrick's, Ireland's largest church, was built on the site of the pre-Norman parish church of St. Patrick. The church was rebuilt in 1191 by Archbishop Comyn. In 1213 it gained cathedral status, but later, in 1300 a papal decree gave Christ Church precedence. At the Reformation it became a parish church, but under the Catholic restoration of Philip and Mary it once again became a cathedral.
A university was established there in 1320 but was suppressed later by Henry VIII. The square tower dates from the fourteenth century.
During the wars of the seventeenth century the Cromwellians used the ruinous cathedral as a stable for their horses. But the future saw a great improvement in the fabric of the building. A spire was added by the architect John Semple in 1749 and a general restoration was undertaken between 1844 and 1869 being financed by Sir Benjamin Lee Guinness. Jonathan Swift was Dean of St. Patrick's from 1713 to 1745. His pulpit may still be seen and his tomb, with its famous epitaph is in the south aisle. Buried nearby is Esther (Stella) Johnston one of Swift's two great lovers.
Visiting times:

Monday to Friday		9.00 a.m.- 6.00 p.m.
Saturday	March - October:	9.00 a.m. - 5.00 p.m.
	November - February:	9.00 a.m. - 5.00 p.m.
Sunday	March - October:	9.00 a.m. - 11.00 a.m.
	12.45 a.m. - 3.00 p.m.	4.15 p.m. - 6.00 p.m.
Sunday	November - February:	10.00 a.m. - 11.00 a.m.
	12.45 p.m. - 3.00 p.m.	

38 D3

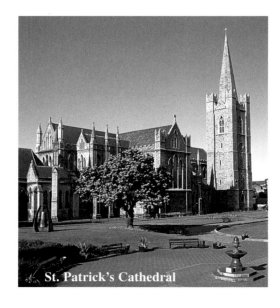
St. Patrick's Cathedral

LIBRARIES

Chester Beatty Library
Dublin Castle.

One of the world's most valuable private collections of oriental manuscripts and miniatures can be seen here. There are manuscripts of the New Testament, Manichean papyri and Eastern miniatures, as well as picture scrolls, albums and jades from the Far East.

The library is located in the Clock Tower building and is open daily. Admisson free.

Visiting Times:

May - September:	Monday to Friday	10.00 a.m. - 5.00 p.m.
October - April:	Tuesday to Friday	10.00 a.m. - 5.00 p.m.
	Saturday	11.00 a.m. - 5.00 p.m.
	Sunday	1.00 p.m. - 5.00 p.m.

Closed Jan 1st./ Good Friday/24,25,26 Dec/Monday Public Holidays
For guided tours phone 407 0750.

38 D3

Trinity College Library

Trinity College Library
Main entrance to college from College Green.

Dating from the late sixteenth century, Trinity College Library is Ireland's oldest library. It contains over 1,000,000 volumes and Ireland's most extensive collection of manuscripts and early printed books. Its greatest treasure is the Book of Kells (probably eighth century). This is considered to be the most beautiful illuminated manuscript in existence today. Manuscripts in the library include State letters of Queen Elizabeth I, diaries of Wolfe Tone and manuscripts of the Irish dramatist, John Millington Synge.

The library is housed in two buildings – the Old Library (completed in 1732) and the New Library (1967). Trinity College Library has the right to a copy of any book printed in Ireland or Britain.

Visiting hours:	Monday to Saturday	9.30 a.m. - 5.00 p.m.
May - September:	Sunday	9.30 a.m. - 4.30 p.m.
October - April:	Sunday	12 noon - 4.30 p.m.

38 E2

Royal Irish Academy Library
19 Dawson Street.

A very extensive collection of ancient Irish manuscripts can be seen in this library. These include the 'Book of the Dun Cow', the 'Book of Ballymote', the 'Speckled Book' and the 'Stowe Missal'. Also to be seen is the Cathach or Battle Book, believed to be the actual copy of the Psalms made in the sixth century by St. Colmcille. An autograph copy of the Annals of the Four Masters made in Donegal between 1632 and 1636 is also there.

Visiting hours: Monday to Thursday 10.00 a.m. - 5.30 p.m.
Friday 10.00 a.m. - 5.00 p.m.
Closed Bank Holidays Tuesday after Easter and last week in December
Admission free.

38 E3

Marsh's Library
St. Patrick's Close.

This is Ireland's oldest public library, founded in 1701 by Archbishop Narcissus Marsh. The collection consists mainly of theological, medical, ancient historical, Hebrew, Syriac, Greek, French and Latin literature. Still to be seen are the original carved bookcases and the cages into which readers were locked to prevent theft.

Visiting Hours:
Weekdays 10.00 a.m. - 1.00 p.m. and 2.00 p.m. - 5.00 p.m.
Saturday 10.30 a.m. - 1.00 p.m.
Closed Tuesdays, Sundays and Bank Holidays.

38 D3

National Library
Kildare Street.

Founded in 1877, the National Library is the largest public library in Ireland. Over 500,000 books as well as maps, prints and manuscripts are housed there. Its huge newspaper collection provides a rich source of historical reference. An extensive collection of historical and literary manuscripts relating to Ireland and microfilms of documents from overseas libraries and archives are available for reference. The public service counter is manned by helpful officials.

Visiting hours: (Main Reading Room)
Monday to Wednesday 10.00 a.m. - 9.00 p.m.
Thursday / Friday 10.00 a.m. - 5.00 p.m.
Saturday 10.00 a.m. - 1.00 p.m. *38 E3*

National Library

Dublin City Libraries

There are twenty-eight public libraries maintained by the Corporation of Dublin.

The administrative headquarters for the Dublin Public Libraries is at Fenian Street. It houses special reference collections, including the Gilbert Library of manuscripts and books relating to Dublin. And there are extensive collections of books on Ireland. A collection of W. B. Yeats material contains a full edition of Mosada.

Other Dublin Libraries

Other libraries of note are the King's Inn Library, Henrietta Street; University College Library, Belfield; the Worth Library, Steeven's Hospital; the Franciscan Library, Franciscan House of Studies, Killiney; the Central Catholic Library at 74 Merrion Square; the Royal Dublin Society's Library at Ballsbridge and the library in the Ilac Centre, Henry Street.

ART GALLERIES

Hugh Lane Municipal Gallery of Modern Art.
Charlemont House, Parnell Square.
This building, dating from 1762, was formerly the residence of Lord Charlemont. The collection was originally housed in Harcourt Street, the present gallery dating from 1908. It was Sir Hugh Lane who contributed the nucleus of this collection of pictures. Lane was drowned in the sinking of the Lusitania in 1915. Before his death he left his continental collection to the National Gallery in London but had stipulated in his will that they should return to Dublin. Unfortunately an unwitnessed codicil of his will caused complications and his intentions were declared invalid.

After many years it was agreed in 1959 to divide the pictures between Dublin and London in two groups. The two groups are exchanged every five years. This gallery has an interesting collection of works by nineteenth and twentieth-century artists.

National Gallery
Merrion Lawn, Merrion Square West.
The gallery was officially opened in 1864. It then consisted of only 100 pictures donated by William Dargan and George Mulvany. Dargan was a railway entrepreneur who died in 1867. His statue may be seen on the lawn outside the gallery.

There are now over 2000 pictures in the gallery, representing all the European schools. Donors of pictures include Lady Milltown, Sir Hugh Lane, Edward Martyn, the Friends of the National Collections and Sir Alfred Chester Beatty. Famous works by Poussin, Goya and Gainsborough, may be seen. Irish artists are well represented, in a comprehensive collection which includes works by Ashford, Barry, Barrett, John Butler Yeats, Hone, Osborne, Lavery and Orpen. Part of the National Portrait Gallery provides an interesting survey of personalities spanning 300 years. This is housed under the same roof.

National Gallery

Visiting times:
Monday to Saturday   9.30 a.m. - 5.30 p.m.
Thursday   9.30 a.m. - 8.30 p.m.
(Except Holy Thursday   9.30 a.m. - 5.30 p.m.)
Sunday   12 noon   - 5.30 p.m.
Closed Good Friday and 24th - 26th December
Restaurant open during gallery hours.

Art Reference Library open Monday to Friday: 10.00 a.m. - 5.00 p.m.
Free public lectures Sundays at 3.00 p.m. and Tuesdays at 10.30 a.m.
Conducted tours of gallery on Saturdays at 3.00 p.m. and Sundays at 2.00 p.m., 3.00 p.m. and 4.00 p.m. Admission free.

38 E3

Royal Hospital and Irish Museum of Modern Art
Military Road, Kilmainham.
The Irish Museum of Modern Art was established in 1991 and exhibits Irish and International Art of the 20th century

Visiting times:
Tuesday to Saturday   10.00 a.m. – 5.30 p.m.
Wednesday   10.30 a.m. – 5.30 p.m.
Sunday/Bank Holidays   12 noon   – 5.30 p.m.
Closed Mondays, Good Friday and 24th. to 26th. December

37 B3

Hugh Lane Municipal Gallery of Modern Art.

Visiting times: Tuesday to Thursday 10.00 a.m. to 6.00p.m.
Friday and Saturday 10.00 a.m. to 5.00p.m.
Sunday   11.00 a.m. to 5.00 p.m.
Closed Monday.   Admission free.

38 D1

MUSEUMS

National Museum of Ireland
Kildare Street/Merrion Street.
The contents of this museum comes under three headings – Irish Antiquities, Art and Industrial and Natural History. The Irish Antiquities division holds one of Europe's most impressive collections of antiquities. Items displayed cover every age from the Stone Age to medieval times. Gold lunulae, torques and fibulae from the Bronze Age are of particular interest, as well as famous items like the Tara Brooch, the Cross of Cong and the Ardagh Chalice from the early Christian period.
The main entrance is from Kildare Street but part of the Natural History division is approached from Merrion Street.
Visiting times: Tuesday to Saturday   10.00 a.m. - 5.00 p.m.
                     Sunday   2.00 p.m. - 5.00 p.m.
                     Closed Mondays, Christmas Day and Good Friday.
                                                              38 E3

National Museum of Ireland
Collins Barracks, Benburb Street.
Collins Barracks which was acquired by the National Museum in 1994 is Europe's oldest military barracks and the world's oldest continuously occupied barracks .
It houses exhibits of the decorative arts and of the economic, social, political and military history of the state.
Among the exhibits are: Etruscan vases; a pocket book carried by Wolfe Tone during his imprisonment in the barracks in 1798; gauntlets worn by King William at the Battle of the Boyne and a life-belt and oar from the wreckage of the Lusitania.
Visiting Times: Tuesday to Saturday   10.00 a.m. - 5.00 p.m.
                     Sunday   2.00 p.m. - 5.00 p.m.
                     Closed Mondays, Christmas Day and Good Friday.
                                                              37 C2

Dublin Civic Museum
South William Street.
Occupying the former City Assembly House, this museum was opened in 1953. It contains a permanent collection of exhibits of antiquarian and historical interest, pertaining to Dublin city. Newspapers and cuttings, as well as maps, prints, and various unique items provide a vivid record of Dublin's past.
Visiting times:

 Closed until further notice. For information Tel 6794260.   *38 D3*

The Writer's Museum

The Writer's Museum
18/19 Parnell Square North.
Opened in 1991 in two restored Georgian houses. It features a display of paintings, photographs, manuscripts and other memorabilia relating to Irish writers such as Shaw, Yeats, Beckett, Wilde, O'Casey, Joyce, Behan and Swift.
Opening hours: Monday to Saturday   10.00 a.m. - 5.00 p.m.
                   Sundays and Bank Holidays 11.30 a.m. - 5.00 p.m.
Late Opening June, July and August: Mon-Fri 10.00 a.m. - 6.00 p.m.

Closed 24th - 26th December
                                                              38 D1

Genealogical Office and Heraldic Museum
2 Kildare St. Dublin 2.
   The oldest office of state in Ireland, founded in 1552. It contains the unique Heraldic Museum with its colourful display of coats of arms, banners and facility.
The Consultancy Service on ancestry tracing is designed to enable you to undertake on your own the task of uncovering your Irish roots.
Opening Hours: Monday to Wednesday   10.00 a.m. - 8.30 p.m.
                   Thursday to Friday   10.00 a.m. - 4.30 p.m.
                   Saturday   10.00 a.m. - 12.30 p.m.
                                                              38 E3

Genealogical Office and Heraldic Museum

National Print Museum
Garrison Chapel, Beggars Bush, Dublin 4.
This Museum houses a unique collection of implements, artefacts and machines from all sectors of the printing industry in Ireland. Many of them are still in full working order.
Visiting times:

Monday to Friday   9.00 a.m. - 5.00 p.m.
Saturday, Sunday   2.00 p.m. - 5.00 p.m.

                                                              38 F3

National Wax Museum
Smithfield.
On display are life-size figures of prominent Irish historical, political, theatrical, literary and sporting personalities. Taped narrations on each scene, guide one along. The Chamber of Horrors is a must for all the family.

                          Opening late 2006   *37 C2*

FAMOUS PEOPLE ASSOCIATED WITH DUBLIN

Dublin has produced an amazing number of well-known writers, scientist and scholars. Many of these personalities not only distinguished themselves in their native city, but through their work established their names world - wide. The following is a brief guide to some of the most famous people who were born in Dublin and/or lived there for a considerable period of time.

THE WORLD OF LETTERS

Samuel Beckett, (1906-1989). Novelist and dramatist, born in Dublin. Novels include 'Murphy','Mollag and Malone Dies'. Plays include 'Waiting for Godot', 'Va et Vient', and 'Silence'. Awarded the Nobel Prize for Literature in 1969.

Brendan Behan, (1923-1964). Dublin-born dramatist.

Plays include 'The Quare Fellow' and 'The Hostage'.

Edmund Burke, (1729-1797). Son of a Dublin attorney. Orator, political philosopher and champion of American liberties.

Anna Maria Hall (née Fielding) (1800 - 1881).Author, born Dublin. Published Sketches of Irish Character (1829); further Sketches followed, and nine novels. She had four plays produced successfully. With her husband, published Ireland, its Scenery, Characters, etc. (1840), her best-known work and a valuable record of pre-Famine conditions.

James Joyce, (1882-1941). Poet and writer, born and educated in Dublin. Works include 'A Portrait of the Artist as a Young Man', 'Ulysses' and 'Finnegan's Wake'. The Martello Tower where Joyce lived outside Dublin is now a museum in his memory.

Mary Lavin (1912 - 1996). Writer, born 1912, Massachusetts of Irish parents. She was educated at Loreto College, St Stephen's Green, Dublin, and UCD. Amongst her achievements are the Katherine Mansfield Prize, the Éire Society Gold Medal (1974), and two Guggenheim fellowships. She was elected MIAL, was president 1972-74, and received its Gregory Medal in 1975.

William E.H. Lecky, (1838 - 1903). Famous Dublin-born historian.

Joseph Sheridan Le Fanu, (1814-1873). Nineteenth-century Dublin novelist, author of 'The House by the Churchyard', among others.

Charles Jones Lever, (1806-1872). A native of Dublin. His novels include 'Harry Lorrequer' and 'Charles O'Malley'.

Edmund Malone, (1741-1812). This great scholar specialised in the study of Shakespeare.

James Clarence Mangan, (1803-1849). Son of a Dublin grocer. His poetry includes 'Dark Rosaleen', 'O'Hussey's Ode to the Maguire' and the autobiographic ballad 'The Nameless One'.

Annie M P Smithson (1873 - 1948). Nurse and writer, Born in Dublin. Secretary and organiser of the Irish Nurses' Organisation between 1929 and 1942. In 1917 she published her first novel, Her Irish Heritage. It became a best-seller. In 1944 she published her autobiography, Myself-and Others. One of the earliest members of the Old Dublin Society.

Lady Jane Francesca Wilde (née Elgee) 'Speranza', (1826 - 1896). Writer, born in Dublin. As an ardent nationalist, she contributed verse and prose to the 'Nation' under the pen-name Speranza. In 1851 she married Dr (afterwards Sir) William Wilde. She published a volume of poems in 1864 under her pen-name Speranza, and as Lady Wilde she published a number of works on folklore. She was the mother of Oscar Wilde.

Katharine Tynan (1859 - 1931). Novelist and poet. Born in Dublin. Educated at the Siena Convent, Drogheda, she wrote over a hundred novels, many poems, and an autobiography in five volumes.

Ethna Carbery (pen-name of Anna MacManus, née Johnston) (1866 - 1911). Writer, Born Ballymena, County Antrim. She wrote many poems for the Nation, United Ireland and other papers.

Theodora Fitzgibbon (née Rosling) (1916 - 1991). Cookery expert, author, and lecturer, born in London of Irish parents.. She specialised in cookery and published more than thirty books. From 1960 to 1976 she worked on her encyclopaedia, The Food of the Western World (1976). Her novel Flight of the Kingfisher (1968) was turned into a play and broadcast by the BBC.

Thomas Moore, (1779-1852). Like Mangan this poet was also a grocer's son. He distinguished himself as an adaptor of traditional airs and as a writer of biographies. Works include 'Moore's Melodies', 'The Twopenny Post Bag' and 'Lalla Rookh'.

Sean O'Casey, (1880-1964). Originally a labourer, O'Casey became one of Ireland's most famous dramatists. Plays include 'The Shadow of a Gunman', 'Juno and the Paycock', 'The Plough and the Stars', 'The Silver Tassie' and 'Purple Dust'.

George Bernard Shaw, (1856-1950). Shaw, a world-famous playwright and wit spent the first twenty years of his life in Dublin, his birthplace. Works include 'John's Bull's Other Island', 'Candida', 'The Doctor's Dilemma', 'Man and Superman', 'Pygmalion', 'Heartbreak House' and 'Saint Joan'. In 1925 he won the Nobel Prize for Literature.

Richard Brinsley Sheridan, (1751-1816). Dramatist and distinguished parliamentary orator. Born in Upper Dorset Street. His three great comedies were 'The Rivals', 'The School for Scandal' and 'The Critic'.

James Stephens, (1882-1950). Novelist and poet. His novels include 'The Crock of Gold', 'The Charwoman's Daughter', 'The Demigods' and 'In the Land of Youth'. Poems include 'The Goat Paths' and 'The Snare'.

Jonathan Swift, (1667-1745). Known mainly as a satirist. Became Dean of St. Patrick's in 1713. Probably best known for 'The Tale of a Tub', the 'Drapier's Letters' and 'Gulliver's Travels'.

John Millington Synge, (1871-1909). Although a Dubliner, this dramatist's first love was the West of Ireland. This is reflected in his work. Best known are 'Playboy of the Western World', 'Riders to the Sea' and 'Deirdre of the Sorrows'.

Sir James Ware, (1594-1666). As an historian and antiquary, Ware is one of Dublin's most distinguished great scholars.

Oscar Wilde, (1854-1900). Born in Dublin and educated at Trinity College, Wilde moved to London when he was twenty-five. His outstanding works are the novel 'The Picture of Dorian Gray', and 'The Importance of being Earnest', his dramatic masterpiece. Also of note is his long letter 'De Profundis' and 'The Ballad of Reading Gaol'.

William Butler Yeats, (1865-1939). Born in London and educated in Dublin, Yeats contributed much to the cultural life of Dublin. He was awarded the Nobel Prize for Literature in 1923. Published works include 'Responsibilities', 'The Tower' and 'The Winding Stair'. This great literary personality played a major part in the establishment of the Abbey Theatre in 1904.

THE WORLD OF MUSIC

Michael William Balfe, (1808-1870). Balfe was famous as a conductor and composer of operas. Works include 'The Bohemian Girl' and 'Il Talismano'.

Michele Esposito (1855 - 1929). Composer, pianist, teacher, conductor, editor and music publisher. Born Naples. Came to Dublin 1882. Senior Professor of Piano at the RIAM for 46 years. He died in Florence in 1929.

John Field, (1782-1837). Outstanding as a pianist and romantic composer. His nocturnes are said to have inspired Chopin. Glinka, founder of the Russian school, was taught by Field.

Catherine Hayes (1825 - 1861). Soprano, born Patrick Street, Limerick. She studied under Antonio Sapio in Dublin and then in Paris and Milan under Felici Ronconi. She appeared at La Scala, in 1845, and successfully toured the world.

Margaret Sheridan (1889 - 1958). Soprano, born, Castlebar, Co. Mayo, educated at Dominican Convent, Eccles Street, Dublin. Studied at the Royal Academy of Music, London and in Rome. In 1936 she retired and returned to Ireland.

Sir Charles Villiers Stanford, (1852-1924). Composer of opera, songs, symphonies and chamber music.

THE WORLD OF VISUAL ARTS

Beatrice Behan (1925 - 1993). Artist, widow of Brendan Behan, Born Dublin. She studied painting in Italy and her work was exhibited at the RHA. In 1974 she published her memoirs, My Life With Brendan Behan.

Muriel Brandt (1909 - 1981). Painter, Born Belfast. Her first important commission was a set of panels in the Church of the Immaculate Conception ('Adam and Eve's'), Merchants' Quay, Dublin. She painted portraits of Sir Alfred Chester Beatty, George O'Brien, and other notables. Her picture of Micheál Mac Liammóir, Christine Longford and Hilton Edwards, directors of the Gate hangs in the foyer of the theatre.

Máire de Paor (neé MacDermott) (1925 - 1994). Archaeologist and activist in the contemporary arts, born Buncrana, Co. Donegal. Elected MRIA in 1960 and represented the academy on the Board of Visitors of the National Museum. Founder-member of Cumann Merriman in 1967. Member of the Arts Council between 1973 and 1993. Early in 1994 she was appointed to the Cultural Relations Committee of the Department of Foreign Affairs.

Willhelmina Geddes (1888 - 1955). Stained-glass artist, born Drumreilly, County Leitrim. Her stained glass is on view in the Hugh Lane Municipal Gallery, Dublin, and the Victoria and Albert Museum, London, and over thirty of her designs are in the National Gallery, Dublin.

Evie Hone (1894 - 1955). Artist. Her best-known works are My Four Green Fields for the CIE offices, Upper O'Connell Street, Dublin (now in Government Buildings), five windows for the Jesuit college of Tullabeg at Rahan, County Offaly, and a large window depicting the Last Supper and the Crucifixion for the chapel of Eton College.

Nathaniel Hone I, (1718-1784). Portrait painter and a founder member of the Royal Academy, London.

Nathaniel Hone II, (1831-1917). Painter of landscapes and seascapes. Hone II was a member of the Barbizon Group. He was also a founder of the modern school of Irish painting.

Mary Harriet (Mainie) Jellett, (1897 - 1944). artist, born 36 Fitzwilliam Square, Dublin. In 1943 with Evie Hone and others she founded the Irish Exhibition of Living Art. Examples of her austere abstract paintings are in the Municipal Gallery of Modern Art, Dublin. Died in Dublin.

James Arthur O'Connor, (1791 - 1841). Landscape painter.

Sir. William Orpen, (1870 - 1931). Orpen specialised in portrait painting.

Sarah Purser (1848-1943). Sarah Purser established herself as a portrait painter. In 1923, Purser was the first woman to be admitted as an associate member of the Royal Hibernian Academy, Dublin, and the following year she was elected a member.

Jack Butler Yeats, (1871-1957). This modern artist painted in a highly original style, his work distinguished by a heavy, unmistakeable texture. His brother was William Butler Yeats.

John Butler Yeats, (1839-1922). Well known as a portrait painter. Father of Jack and William Butler Yeats.

Harry Clarke, (1889-1931) **Michael Healy,** (1893-1941), Renowned for their Stained Glass creations.

John Henry Foley, (1818-1874). **Thomas Kirk,** (1777-1845).

Andrew O'Connor, (1874-1941). **Edward Smyth,**(1749-1812). Well known for their sculptures.

THE WORLD OF MEDICINE AND SCIENCE

Sir Robert Stawell Ball, (1840-1913). Noted astronomer and mathematician.

Abraham Colles, (1773-1843). In the medical world Colles is remembered for 'Colles' Law', 'Colles' fracture' and 'Colles' Fuchsia'.

Sir Dominic Corrigan, (1802-1880). Corrigan specialised in diseases of the aorta. Remembered for 'Corrigan's Disease', 'Corrigan's Pulse'. He also invented 'Corrigan's Button'.

Sir Philip Crampton, (1778-1858). This famous Dublin surgeon played an important role in establishing the fame of the Dublin medical school in the early nineteenth century. He was co-author of a book on bedside teaching with Robert Graves.

George Francis Fitzgerald, (1851-1901). Fitzgerald made a valuable contribution to the study of physics.

Robert Graves, (1796-1853). The concept of bedside teaching was introduced in medical education by Robert Graves. His book 'Clinical Lectures' became an international textbook for medical students.

Sir William Rowan Hamilton, (1805-1865). Hamilton was the discoverer of quaternions. Through his pioneering work he achieved international fame by foreshadowing the quantum theory and later important discoveries in nuclear physics.

Richard Kirwan, (1735-1812). The first systematic textbook in English on mineralogy was written by Kirwan.

Francis Rynd, (1801-1861). A major contribution was made to medical science by Rynd, through his invention of the hypodermic syringe.

George Salmon, (1819-1904). Dublin-born mathematician.

William Stokes, (1804-1878). Stokes is remembered for 'Stokes-Adam Syndrome' and 'Cheyne-Stokes Respiration'. He was the author of 'Diseases of the Chest and Diseases of the Heart and Aorta'.

Sir William Wilde, (1815–1876). Wilde was noted as an ophalmologist, otologist, and archaeologist. In the medical field he is associated with 'Wilde's Incision' and 'Wilde's Cord'. He was Oscar Wilde's father.

Ellen Hutchins (1785-1815). Botanist, born in Ballylickey, Co.Cork. The major part of her botanical collection lies in Kew Botanical Gardens, London.

Mary Ward (1827-1869). Microscopist, artist, entomologist and author. Born in Ballylin, Co Offaly. Two of her books were selected to be displayed at the international exhibition at the Crystal Palace in 1862.

THE WORLD OF HUMANITIES

Louie Bennett (1870 - 1956). Irish trade unionist. Born in Dublin. She helped to start the Irishwomen's Suffrage Federation in 1913 and co-founded the Irish Women's Reform League. She was the first woman President of the Irish Trades Union Congress in 1931-2 and again in 1947-8.

Leslie de Barra (née Price) (1893 - 1984). Revolutionary and Red Cross official. After marriage, she devoted the rest of her life to the relief of human suffering at home and abroad. Chairwoman of the Irish Red Cross from 1950.

Catherine McAuley (1778 - 1841). Founded the Order of Mercy which became one of the largest religious congregations ever founded, is buried at the convent in Baggot Street.

Helena Molony (1884 - 1967). Actress and trade unionist. She became secretary of the Irish Women Workers' Union in 1915 and was subsequently honoured with presidency of the Irish Trade Union Congress.

DUBLIN'S PARKS AND GARDENS

Garden of Remembrance
Parnell Square East Dublin 1.
The Garden of Remembrance was designed by Daithí Hanly and is dedicated to the memory of those who died in the cause of Irish freedom.The central theme is peaceful remembrance and reflection, and the sculpture by Oisen Kelly, "Children of Lir" reflects this.

Opening Hours:	March - April/October:	11.00 a.m. - 7.00 p.m.
	May - September:	9.30 a.m. - 8.00 p.m.
	November - February:	11.00 a.m. - 4.00 p.m.

38 D1

St. Anne's Park and Gardens
Mount Prospect Avenue, Clontarf.
In a pleasant setting adjacent to Dollymount Strand, the rose gardens in this park cover over three acres alone. The Park and Gardens are open all year round. Admission free. Entrance Howth Road/All Saints Road .

27 A3

Marlay Park
Rathfarnham.
This is the largest park on the south side of Dublin. It covers three hundred acres in a highly picturesque setting at the foot of the Dublin mountains. It is the starting point of the 'Wicklow Way' long distance signposted walk. A craft centre, including workshops, is situated within the area of the park.

57 A2

Merrion Square Park
Merrion Square.
Formerly only for the use of the residents of Merrion Square, this public park is surrounded on all sides by some of Dublin's finest Georgian architecture. Open all year, daylight hours.

38 E3

National Botanic Gardens

National Botanic Gardens
Botanic Road, Glasnevin.
Covering 19.5 hectares, these beautiful gardens contain a huge assortment of trees, plants and shrubs. Rare blooms and palms are housed in the huge Victorian conservatories. These gardens were founded in 1795 when the estate, on which the gardens now stand, was purchased from the Ticknell family by the Royal Dublin Society.
Open all year except Christmas Day.

Visiting times:	Summer:	Monday - Saturday	9.00 a.m. – 6.00 p.m.
		Sunday	10.00 a.m. – 6.00 p.m.
	Winter :	Monday - Saturday	10.00 a.m. – 4.30 p.m.
		Sunday	11.00 a.m. – 4.30 p.m.
	Admission free.		

25 A3

Herbert Park
Ballsbridge.
A charming mature park, well laid out with interesting trees, shrubs and flower beds. An attractive feature is the large pond on the eastern side of the park.

38 F4

St. Enda's Park

St. Enda's Park
Grange Road, Rathfarnham.
One of Dublin's most attractive suburban public parks. The park occupies the grounds of St. Enda's, the former school where the patriot Padraic Pearse once taught. The well-restored estate house has been opened as a museum to Pearse's memory.

Visiting hours:

November - January:	10.00 a.m. – 4.00 p.m.
February - April, September - October:	10.00 a.m. – 5.00 p.m.
May - August:	10.00 a.m. – 5.30 p.m.

56 F1

St. Stephen's Green
Covering twenty-two acres at the top of Grafton Street, St. Stephen's Green is right in the heart of the city. The varied landscaping of this delightful park includes trees, flower beds, a waterfall and an artificial lake. Several notable monuments and sculptures may also be seen.

Opening Times:	During daylight hours.	
	Monday to Friday	8.00 a.m. - Dusk.
	Sat./Sun./Bank Holidays	10.00 a.m. - Dusk.
	Christmas Day	10.00 a.m. - 1.00 p.m.

38 D3

Irish National War Memorial Park.
Islandbridge.
Designed by the English architect Sir Edward Lutyens, these gardens are dedicated to the memory of 49,400 Irish soldiers who died in the First World War.

Opening Times:	During daylight hours only.	
	Monday - Friday from	8.00 a.m.
	Saturday and Sunday from	10.00 a.m.

37 A2

National War Memorial Gardens.

Phoenix Park
North-western edge of city.
Acknowledged as one of the largest enclosed urban parks in the world, it covers 1,760 acres, with a circumference of seven miles.
Close to the main entrance at Parkgate Street are the People's Gardens and the Zoological Gardens (see separate entry). Within the park are the residence of the President of Ireland (Aras an Uachtarain), the American Ambassador's residence and the Ordnance Survey Office.
In the south-western part of the park is 'The Fifteen Acres', an area of playing fields actually covering two hundred acres. In eighteenth-century Dublin this was used as a duelling ground. During the visit of Pope John Paul II in 1979 it was the site of an outdoor Mass.
Visiting times: Phoenix Park is open to the public at all times but the People's Gardens have their own opening times.

Monday to Friday	8.30 a.m. - 9.00 p.m.	in summer.
	8.30 a.m. - 4.00 p.m.	in winter.
Saturday	10.00 a.m. - 9.00 p.m.	in summer.
	10.30 a.m. - 4.00 p.m.	in winter.
Sunday	10.30 a.m. - 9.00 p.m.	in summer.
	10.30 a.m. - 4.00 p.m.	in winter.

Admission free.

37 B2

Zoological Gardens
Phoenix Park
In these outstanding attractive gardens may be seen a large collection of wild animals and birds from all over the world. Spacious houses and outdoor enclosures add to the total effect. Lion breeding has a long and distinguished history at Dublin Zoo. Two natural lakes house pelicans, flamingos, ducks and geese.
Visiting hours:

Weekday	Opening 9.30 a.m. - 6.00 p.m.
Sunday	Opening 10.30 a.m. - 6.00 p.m.

The grounds close at varying times throughout the year. Last admission 1 Hour before closing.

37 A1

Furry Glen, Phoenix Park

Other public parks
Most notable are Corkagh Demesne in Clondalkin, Palmerston Park Dartry, Bushy Park, Terenure, Mountjoy Square Park, Griffeen Valley Park in Lucan and Ward River Valley Park, Swords.

Phoenix Monument, Phoenix Park

Apostolic Nunciature
183 Navan Road
Dublin
Tel: 838 0577
24 D4

Argentine Embassy
15 Ailesbury Drive
Dublin 4
Tel: 269 1546 / 269 1713
48 D1

Australian Embassy
7th Floor,
Fitzwilton House
Wilton Terrace, Dublin 2
Tel: 664 5300
38 E4

Austrian Embassy
15 Ailesbury Court Apts.
93 Ailesbury Road
Dublin 4
Tel: 269 4577 / 269 1451
48 D1

Belgian Embassy
2 Shrewsbury Road
Dublin 4
Tel: 269 2082 / 269 1588
48 D1

Embassy of the Federative Republic of Brazil
Europa House
Block 9. Harcourt Centre
41-49 Harcourt House,
Dublin 2.
Tel: 475 6000 / 416 1202
38 D4

British Embassy
29 Merrion Road
Dublin 4
Tel: 205 3700
48 D1

Bulgarian Embassy
22 Burlington Road
Dublin 4
Tel: 660 3293
38 E4

Canadian Embassy
4th Floor
65/68 St.Stephen's Green S.
Dublin 2
Tel: 417 4100
38 E3

Chilean Embassy
44 Wellington Road
Ballsbridge
Dublin 4
Tel: 667 5094
38 F4

Embassy of the People's Republic of China
40 and 77 Ailesbury Road
Dublin 4
Tel: 269 1707 / 260 1119
48 D1

Embassy of the Republic of Croatia
Adelaide Chambers
Peter Street
Dublin 8
Tel: 476 7181
38 D3

Embassy of the Republic of Cuba
2 Adelaide Court,
Adelaide Road,
Dublin 2
Tel: 475 0899 / 475 2999
38 E4

Embassy of Cyprus
71 Lower Leeson Street
Dublin 2
Tel: 676 3060
38 E3

Czech Embassy
57 Northumberland Road
Dublin 4
Tel: 668 1135 / 668 1343
38 F4

Royal Danish Embassy
121/122
St. Stephen's Green West,
Dublin 2
Tel: 475 6404 / 475 6405
38 D3

Embassy of the Arab Republic of Egypt
12 Clyde Road
Ballsbridge, Dublin 4
Tel: 660 6566 / 660 6718 / 667 6150 (Visas)
38 F4

Estonia Embassy
Ailesbury Road
Dublin 4
Tel: 219 6730
48 D1

Embassy of the Federated Democratic Republic of Ethiopia
Suite 2
1-3 Merrion House,
Fitzwilliam Street Lower,
Dublin 2
Tel: 678 7062 / 678 7063
38 E3

Finnish Embassy
Russell House
Stokes Place
St. Stephen's Green South
Dublin 2
Tel: 478 1344
38 D3

French Embassy
36 Ailesbury Road
Dublin 4
Tel: 277 5000
48 D1

Embassy of the Federal Republic of Germany
31 Trimleston Avenue
Booterstown, Co. Dublin
Tel: 269 3011 / 269 3123
48 E2

Greek Embassy
1 Upper
Pembroke Street
Dublin 2
Tel: 676 7254 / 676 7255
38 E3

Embassy of the Republic of Hungary
2 Fitzwilliam Place
Dublin 2
Tel: 661 2902 / 661 2905
38 E4

Indian Embassy
6 Leeson Park
Dublin 6
Tel: 496 6792 /497 0959
38 E4

Embassy of the Islamic Republic of Iran
72 Mount Merrion Avenue
Blackrock, Co. Dublin
Tel: 288 0252 / 288 2967 / 288 5881
48 F3

Israel Embassy
122 Pembroke Road
Dublin 4
2309400
38 F4

Italian Embassy
63/65 Northumberland Road
Ballsbridge,
Dublin 4
Tel: 660 1744 / 664 2300 /664 2301
38 F4

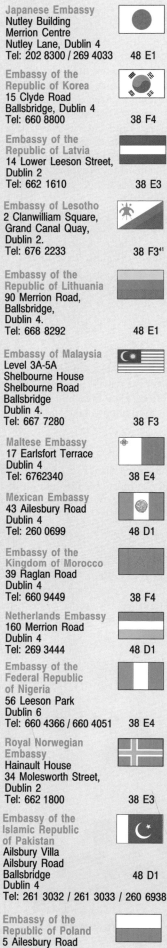

Japanese Embassy
Nutley Building
Merrion Centre
Nutley Lane, Dublin 4
Tel: 202 8300 / 269 4033
48 E1

Embassy of the Republic of Korea
15 Clyde Road
Ballsbridge, Dublin 4
Tel: 660 8800
38 F4

Embassy of the Republic of Latvia
14 Lower Leeson Street,
Dublin 2
Tel: 662 1610
38 E3

Embassy of Lesotho
2 Clanwilliam Square,
Grand Canal Quay,
Dublin 2.
Tel: 676 2233
38 F3[41]

Embassy of the Republic of Lithuania
90 Merrion Road,
Ballsbridge,
Dublin 4.
Tel: 668 8292
48 E1

Embassy of Malaysia
Level 3A-5A
Shelbourne House
Shelbourne Road
Ballsbridge
Dublin 4.
Tel: 667 7280
38 F3

Maltese Embassy
17 Earlsfort Terrace
Dublin 4
Tel: 6762340
38 E4

Mexican Embassy
43 Ailesbury Road
Dublin 4
Tel: 260 0699
48 D1

Embassy of the Kingdom of Morocco
39 Raglan Road
Dublin 4
Tel: 660 9449
38 F4

Netherlands Embassy
160 Merrion Road
Dublin 4
Tel: 269 3444
48 D1

Embassy of the Federal Republic of Nigeria
56 Leeson Park
Dublin 6
Tel: 660 4366 / 660 4051
38 E4

Royal Norwegian Embassy
Hainault House
34 Molesworth Street,
Dublin 2
Tel: 662 1800
38 E3

Embassy of the Islamic Republic of Pakistan
Ailsbury Villa
Ailsbury Road
Ballsbridge
Dublin 4
Tel: 261 3032 / 261 3033 / 260 6938
48 D1

Embassy of the Republic of Poland
5 Ailesbury Road
Dublin 4
Tel: 283 0855
48 D1

Portuguese Embassy
Knocksinna Mews
7 Willow Park /
Westminster Park
Foxrock, Dublin 18
Tel: 289 4416 / 289 3375
59 A2

Embassy of Romania
26 Waterloo Road
Dublin 4
Tel: 668 1085
48 D1

Embassy of the Russian Federation
184/186 Orwell Road
Rathgar, Dublin 14
Tel: 492 2048(Embassy)
492 3492 (Consular Section)
47 B3

Embassy of the Slovak Republic
20 Clyde Road
Dublin 4
Tel: 660 0012 / 660 0008
38 F4

Embassy of the Republic of Slovenia
Morrison Chambers
2nd Floor,
32 Nassau Street
Dublin 2
Tel: 670 5240
38 E3

Embassy of South Africa
Alexandra House,
Earlsfort Centre,
Earlsfort Terrace, Dublin 2
Tel: 661 5553
38 E3

Spanish Embassy
17A Merlyn Park
Dublin 4
Tel: 283 9900 / 269 1640
48 E1

Swedish Embassy
Sun Alliance House
13-17 Dawson Street
Dublin 2
Tel: 474 4400
38 E3

Swiss Embassy
6 Ailesbury Road
Ballsbridge
Dublin 4
Tel: 218 6382
48 D1

Embassy of the Republic of Turkey
11 Clyde Road
Ballsbridge, Dublin 4
Tel: 668 5240 / 660 1623
38 F4

Embassy of Ukraine
16 Elgin Road,
Ballsbridge,
Dublin 4.
Tel: 668 8601 / 668 5189
38 F4

Embassy of the United States of America
42 Elgin Road
Ballsbridge, Dublin 4
Tel: 668 8777
38 F4

For further information contact:
Dept of Foreign Affairs,
80 St. Stephen's Green, Dublin 2.
Tel: 478 0822 / www.foreignaffairs.gov.

Introduction

Dublin Bus is the main provider of public transport in Dublin. We have a fleet of over 1,200 blue and yellow buses with over 150 routes serving the greater Dublin area. To date, over half of our fleet is operated by low floor, wheelchair accessible buses.

How to use the bus

All our services* are exact fare only and will not accept Euro notes. Please ensure that you have the correct change when paying for your fare. Change is not given however the driver will issue you with a 'change receipt'. This receipt can be redeemed at our Head Office.

Dublin Bus prepaid tickets are the smartest choice for bus travel around Dublin. We have a range of flexible ticket options to suit your needs. Prepaid tickets give unlimited travel on most Dublin Bus services. All tickets must be inserted into the ticket reader machines (validators) when boarding.

Contact Information

Our Head Office is located at 59 Upper O'Connell Street, Dublin 1 and our opening hours are as follows:
Monday: 0830 – 1730hrs
Tuesday to Friday:
0900 – 1730hrs
Saturday: 0900 – 1300hrs
Please note that the Dublin Bus Head Office is closed Sundays and Bank Holidays.

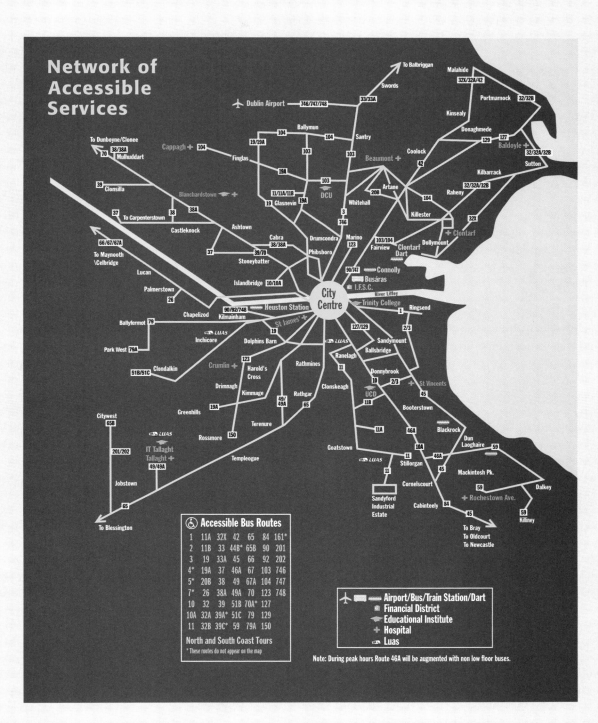

For more information on our services, contact our Information Bureau and Customer Service line on (01) 873 4222, phone lines open 9am to 7pm, Monday to Saturday or visit www.dublinbus.ie

*Airlink service accepts notes and coins.

Airlink

Airlink is a direct bus service from Dublin Airport to the City Centre, Central Bus Station (Busaras), Connolly Rail Station and Heuston Rail Station. The route maps below outline the express bus stops along Airlink routes 746 and 747.

A single Airlink ticket cost €5 and a return ticket is €9. You can get Airlink tickets from Dublin Bus Head Office, the CIE desk in Dublin Airport and the Tourist Office in Suffolk Street. Airlink tickets are also available from the vending machines located on the Arrivals Road in Dublin Airport.

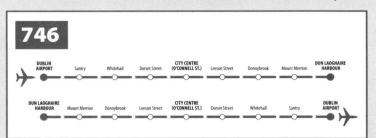

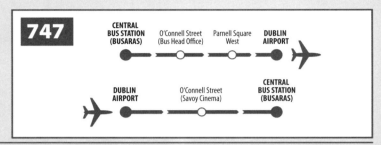

Nitelink

Our late night bus service operates every night from Monday to Saturday. There is no Sunday service, however occasionally a Sunday service operates before a Bank Holiday Monday. The cost of a single ticket is €4.00 or €6.00 for longer routes. Tickets can be bought from the driver when you board the bus (exact fare, coin only) or from the ticket buses which operate on Friday and Saturday nights only.

Nitelink Departure Points

How to find your Nitelink route

Nitelink services depart from College Street, Westmoreland Street and D'Olier Street. Some services operate on a Friday and Saturday night only and are indicated on the map below by an asterisk. To find your Nitelink route visit www.dublinbus.ie

Dublin City Hop On Hop Off Tour

What better way to take in Dublin's sights than by the comfort of an open-top bus. Our native guides will entertain you on a 1 hr 15 min tour. Your ticket is valid for 24 hours, so you can hop off at any of the 20 stops to further explore our city.

South Coast & Gardens Tour

From the charming coastal village of Dublin Bay's Dun Laoghaire, to the beauty of the Wicklow mountains and the magnificent Powerscourt Estate, the scenery on this journey is simply a joy to behold. Free admission to Powerscourt Gardens included.

North Coast & Castle Tour

Take a trip to visit the splendour of Malahide Castle, home of the Talbot Family. Situated in the heritage coastal town of Malahide the castle is located on acres of landscaped gardens and parks. Drive along the coast past Portmarnock before taking in the beautiful fishing village of Howth. On the way back catch breathtaking views of Dublin Bay from Howth Head. Free admission to Malahide Castle included.

GhostBus Tour

Prepare for some spine chilling stories on the world's only Ghost Bus. Let us regale you with ghoulish tales of the felons, fiends and phantoms that walked Dublin's streets. This theatrical experience is conducted by professional actors, is not for the faint of heart. This tour is not suitable for children under 14.

These tours start and end at Dublin Bus Head Office, 59 Upper O'Connell Street, Dublin 1.

For more information on Dublin Sightseeing Tours visit www.dublinsightseeing.ie

Dublin Bus
Serving the entire community

Name	Phone Number	Page	Grid Ref.
Beaumont Hospital	809 3000	**26**	D1
Blackrock Clinic	283 2222	**48**	F3
Bloomfield Hospital (Donnybrook)	495 0021	**47**	B1
Bon Secours Private (St. Joseph's Glasnevin)	806 5300	**25**	A3
Cappagh National Orthopaedic (Finglas)	834 1211	**23**	C1
Central Mental Hospital (Dundrum)	215 7400	**47**	C3
Cheeverstown (Templeogue)	490 4681	**46**	D4
Cheery Orchard (Ballyfermot)	620 6000	**35**	C3
Children's University Hospital (Temple Street)	878 4200	**38**	D1
City of Dublin Skin and Cancer (Hume Street)	676 6935	**38**	E3
Clonskeagh (Vergemount)	268 0500	**47**	C2
Connolly Hospital (Blanchardstown)	821 3844	**22**	F1
Coombe Women's Hospital (Dolphin's Barn)	408 5200	**37**	C4
Dublin Dental School & Hospital (Lincoln Place)	612 7200	**38**	E3
Gascoigne Home (Camden Row)	496 9399	**38**	D4
Highfield Private Hospital (Whitehall)	837 4444	**25**	B3
Leopardstown Park (Foxrock)	295 5055	**58**	E3
Mater Misericordiae University Hospital Ltd (Eccles Street)	803 2000	**38**	D1
Mount Carmel (Braemor Park)	492 2211	**47**	A3
National Maternity (Holles Street)	637 3100	**38**	E3
National Rehabilitation Hospital (Dun Laoighaire)	235 5000	**59**	C2
Orthopaedic Hospital of Ireland (Clontarf)	833 2521	**26**	E4
Our Lady's Hospital for Sick Children (Crumlin)	409 6100	**46**	D1
Our Lady's Hospice (Harold's Cross)	406 8700	**37**	C4
Rotunda (Maternity), (Parnell Street)	873 0700	**38**	D1
Royal City of Dublin (Baggot Street)	668 1577	**38**	F4
Royal Hospital (Donnybrook)	497 2844	**47**	B1
Royal Victoria Eye and Ear (Adelaide Road)	664 4600	**38**	E4
St. Bricin's Military (Infirmary Road)	677 6112	**37**	B2
St. Brigid's Home (Crooksling)	458 2123	**53**	A4
St. Clare's Home (Griffith Avenue)	837 3619	**25**	A2
St. Edmundsbury Hospital (Lucan)	621 8200	**34**	E1
St. James Hospital (James's Street)	410 3000	**37**	B3
St. John of God (Stillorgan)	277 1400	**58**	F1
St. Joseph's (Clonsilla)	821 7177	**21**	B2
St. Joseph's (Raheny)	847 8433	**27**	A2
St. Luke's (Oakland, Highfield Road)	406 5000	**47**	A2
St. Mary's Orthopaedic (Baldoyle)	832 3056	**15**	A4
St. Mary's Hospital (Phoenix Park)	677 8132	**36**	E2
St. Michael's Public Hospital (Dun Laoighaire)	280 6901	**50**	D4
St. Patrick's (James Street)	249 3200	**37**	B3
St. Paul's (Beaumont)	837 7673	**25**	C1
St. Vincent's University Hospital (Elm Park, Merrion Road)	221 4000	**48**	E1
St. Vincent's (Richmond Road)	884 2400	**25**	B4
Simpson's Hospital (Dundrum)	298 4322	**57**	B2
Stewart's Hospital (Palmerston)	626 4444	**35**	C1
Tallaght Hospital	414 2000	**54**	F1
Verville Retreat (Vernon Avenue)	833 2598	**26**	E4

Name	Page	Grid Ref.	No.
Abbey Business Park	14	F4	112
Advance Business Park	12	F3	179
Airport Business Park	13	A1	213
Airport Industrial Campus	12	E4	1
Airside Business Park Swords	2	D3	266
Airside Retail Park	1	C3	295
Airton Business Park	45	A4	2
Airton Business Park	45	A4	3
Airton Business Park	45	A4	4
Airways Industrial Estate	12	F4	5
Allied Industrial Estate	36	E4	6
Alltech Technology Park	6	E2	307
Ardee Court	67	B2	7
Ashgrove Ind Est Dun Laoghaire	59	C1	8
Aughrim Lane Ind Est	37	C1	268
Avonbeg Ind Est	45	B1	277
Avondale	49	A4	167
Baldonnel Business Park	43	A4	241
Baldoyle Ind Est	27	C1	10
Balfe Road Ind Est	45	C1	196
Balheary Ind Park	2	D1	11
Ballyboggan Ind Est	24	D3	12
Ballycoolin Business Park	10	D4	13
Ballymount Business Centre	45	B2	14
Ballymount Court Business Centre	45	B2	72
Ballymount Cross Ind. Est.	45	A2	15
Ballymount Ind Est	45	B2	16
Ballymount Road Ind. Est.	45	B2	17
Ballymount Trading Centre	45	B2	18
Ballymun Ind Est	12	D4	19
Barbeque Poultry Business Pk	64	E3	300
Base Park Industrial Est	9	A4	301
Beech Hill Office Campus, Clonskeagh	47	C2	228
Beechlawn Ind Complex	45	B2	20
Beechwood Close Ind Est	67	C4	21
Belfield Office Park	47	C2	229
Belgard Ind Est	44	F4	22
Benson St. Enterprise Centre	38	F2	24
Blackhorse Ind Est	37	B1	25
Blackrock Business Park	49	A3	169
Blanchardstown Corporate Park	9	C3	165
Blanchardstown Ind Park (off Snugborough)	9	C4	26
Bluebell Business Centre	36	E4	273
Bluebell Business Park	36	E4	27
Bluebell Ind Est	36	D4	28
Bracetown Business Park	7	C1	29
Bray Business Park, Kilruddery	67	C4	255
Bray Ind Est	67	C4	30
Bridges Ind Est	45	A1	32
Bridgewater Business Centre	37	B2	31
Brookfield Enterprise Centre	54	D1	247
Broombridge Ind Est	24	E3	33
Broomfield Business Park Malahide	3	B4	271
Broomhill Bus Pk Close	45	A4	35
Broomhill Bus Pk Drive	45	A4	36
Broomhill Bus Pk Road	45	A4	37
Broomhill Bus Pk Tce	45	A4	38
Broomhill Business Park	45	A4	84
Burton Hall Campus	58	E2	39
Butterly Business Park	26	D2	66
Calmount Business Park	45	B2	197
Carrigalea Ind Est	45	B1	40
Cashel Business Centre	46	E2	293
Castleforbes Ind Est	38	F2	41
Cedar Ind Park, Bray	67	B4	258
Celbridge Ind Est	31	C3	238
Central Park Business Park	58	E2	253
Century Business Park	11	B4	206
Chapelizod Ind Est	36	E2	90
Charlestown Centre	11	A4	160
Cherry Orchard Ind Est	35	C2	42
Cherrywood Business Park	64	D1	251
Churchtown Business Park	47	B4	225
Cian Park Ind Est	25	B4	43
City Junction Business Park	13	C4	212
City Link Business Park	36	E4	215
City West Business Campus	53	B1	44
Clondalkin Business Centre	35	B4	46
Clondalkin Commercial Park	35	B4	45
Clondalkin Enterprise Centre	35	A3	177
Clonshaugh Ind Est	13	A4	47
Clonskeagh House Office Pk	47	C2	226
Clonskeagh Square Office Pk	47	C2	227
Cloverhill Ind Est	35	B4	48
College Business and Technology Park	9	C4	200
Collinstown Cross Ind Est, Cloghran	12	F2	49
Collinstown Ind Est	12	F3	50
Collinstown Ind Park (Intel)	19	B3	92
Concord Ind Est, Naas Road	36	E4	272
Cookstown Business Centre	44	F4	245
Cookstown Enterprise Park	44	F4	51
Cookstown Ind Est	44	F4	52
Cookstown Ind Est, The Extension	44	E4	243
Cookstown Square	44	F4	244
Coolmine Ind Est	22	D2	53
Courtyard Business Park, The Nangor Rd	43	B2	269
Crag Avenue Ind Centre	35	B4	219
Cranford Centre, Stillorgan	48	D2	274
Croke Park Ind Est	38	E1	55
Crosbie Business Centre	38	F1	262
Crossbeg Ind Est	45	A2	56
Crosslands Business Park	45	A2	297
Crosslands Ind Park	45	A2	57
Cruiserath Business Park	9	C3	199
Crumlin Business Park, Stanaway Drive	46	E1	292
Damastown Ind Est	8	F3	58
Damastown Ind Park	8	F3	166
Damastown Business Centre	9	A3	302
Dartmouth House Ind Centre	36	E3	217
Deansgrange Business Park	59	B2	59
Docklands Innovation Park	39	A1	155
Donnelly Centre, The Cork Street	37	C3	275
Dublin Ind Est Glasnevin/Broombridge	24	E3	61
Dun Laoghaire Ind Est	59	B2	63
Dunboyne Ind Est	7	B2	62
Dundrum Business Park	47	C3	231
Earlscourt Industrial Estate	47	B4	224
Earlsfort Centre	38	E3	276
East Point Business Park	39	A1	263
East Road Ind Est	38	F1	64
Elmfield Ind Est, Ninth Lock Rd	44	E1	65
Fashion City	45	A3	69
Feltrim Ind Park, Swords	2	E3	67
Finches Industrial Park	45	B1	68
Finglas Business Centre	11	B4	140
Finglas Business Park	24	E3	23
Finglas Business Park	9	C3	210
Fonthill Retail Park, Clondalkin	35	A2	176
Frank Fahey Centre, Naas Road	45	B1	9
Furry Park Ind Est, Santry	12	E3	181
Gaywood Ind Est, Mulhuddart	9	B3	70
Glasnevin Business Centre	24	D3	220
Glasnevin Business Park	24	D3	221
Glen Abbey Complex	44	F4	71
Glen Ind Est	24	E3	73
Glenageary Office Park	60	D2	291
Glenview Ind Est	37	B4	74
Glenville Ind Est, Mount Merrion	48	E3	75
Goldenbridge Ind Est	36	F4	76
Grange Castle Business Park	34	D4	218
Grange Castle International Business Park	43	B1	239
Great Keppel Business Centre	15	A1	296
Green Isle Business Park	44	D3	242
Greenhills Business Centre, Greenhills Rd	45	B4	193
Greenhills Business Park	45	B4	192
Greenhills Centre	45	B4	191
Greenhills Ind Est	45	A4	77
Greenmount Ind Est	37	C4	78
Greenogue Business Park	42	E4	235
Grove Ind Est Dubber Cross	11	B3	79
Grove Ind Est, Finglas	24	E1	80
Harbour Ind Est	67	C1	81
Harcourt Centre, The	38	D4	278
Henley Ind Park	36	D4	216
Hewlett Packard Ind Park	32	F2	234
Hibernian Industrial Estate	45	A4	82
Hillcrest Industrial Estate	45	B2	93
Hills Ind Est	34	D1	83
Hollywood Business Park	9	C3	303
Horizon Logistics	11	B2	204
Howth Junction Business Pk	27	B1	270
I.D.A. Enterprise Centre	38	F3	85
I.D.A. Ind Centre	37	C1	86
I.D.A. Small Ind Centre	13	A4	88
I.D.A. Small Ind Centre	38	F1	87
I.D.A. Tallaght Business Park	54	F2	89
Industrial Yarns Complex	67	C1	91
International Financial Services Centre (IFSC)	38	E2	279
Irish Life Centre	38	E2	280

Name	Page	Grid Ref.	No.
J.F.K. Ave	45	A1	96
J.F.K. Drive	45	B1	97
J.F.K. Park	36	D4	98
J.F.K. Road	36	D4	99
Jamestown Business Park	11	A4	208
Jamestown Ind Centre	36	F4	95
Jamestown Industrial Estate	36	E4	94
Jamestown Little Ind Est	11	A4	298
KCR Ind Est	46	E2	100
Kilbarrack Ind Est	27	B1	101
Kilcarberry Ind Park, Clondalkin	43	A1	283
Killarney Road Business Park	67	B3	257
Killinardin Enterprise Park	54	F2	246
Kinsealy Business Park	14	D1	281
Knockmitten Business Park	44	F1	282
Kylemore Ind Est	36	D4	102
Kylemore Park North	36	D3	103
Kylemore Park South	36	E4	104
Kylemore Park West	36	D4	105
Landys Ind Est	56	D1	106
Lansdown Valley	45	C1	107
Leopardstown Office Park	58	E2	261
Leopardstown Retail Park	58	E2	108
Liberties Craft & Small Industries Centre	37	C3	109
Liffey Trust Enterprise Centre, The	38	F2	150
Lilmar Ind Est	12	F4	110
Loughlinstown Ind Est	64	D1	111
Maltings Business Park, The Marrowbone Lane	37	C3	259
Maynooth Business Campus	17	C4	211
Merrywell Business Park	45	A2	188
Merrywell Ind Est	45	A2	182
Metropolitan Ind Est	37	A3	113
Mill Lane Business Park, Leixlip	33	B1	232
Millenium Business Park	10	E3	202
Monarch Ind Est	44	F4	114
Montone Business Park, Oak Road	44	F1	248
Mount Pleasant Ind Est	47	A1	284
Mulcahy Keane Est	45	C2	115
Mygan Industrial Estate	11	B4	207
Naas Road Business Park	36	F4	132
Naas Road Ind Park	36	E4	170
Nangor Road Business Centre	35	C4	174
Newcastle Business Centre	42	E1	308
Newcourt Business Park	11	A2	205
Newlands Business Centre	44	E2	116
Newtown Ind Est	13	C4	117
North Park Business & Office Park	11	A4	209
North Richmond Ind Est	38	E1	118
North Ring Business Park, Santry	12	F3	180
Northern Cross Business Park	11	A4	285
Northwest Business Park	10	D3	201
Nutgrove Enterprise Park	57	A1	252
Nutgrove Office Park	47	A4	223
Oak Road Business Park	44	F1	250
Oakfield Ind Est	44	E1	119
Old Court Ind Est	67	B4	120
Old Sawmills Ind Est	45	B2	121
Ossory Ind Est	38	F1	122
Palmgrove Ind Est	25	B2	265
Park West Business Park	35	C4	173
Park West Enterprise Centre	35	C4	172
Park West Ind Park	36	D4	171
Parkmore Ind Est	45	B1	123
Parkway Business Centre	45	A2	183
Phoenix Ind Est	23	B3	124
Pineview Ind Est, Firhouse Road	55	C1	125
Pinewood Close Ind Est	67	C4	126
Plato Business Park	9	A3	198
Poppintree Ind Est	11	B4	127
Portside Business Centre	38	F1	128
Red Cow Business Park	45	A1	184
Red Cow Interchange Estate, The	44	F2	233
Richmond Road Ind Est	25	B4	129
Richview Park	47	C2	230
Riversdale Ind Est	36	E4	130
Riverview Business Centre, Clondalkin	35	C4	175
Robinhood Business Park	45	A1	294
Robinhood Ind Est	45	B1	131
Rock Enterprise Centre	43	B3	240
Rosemount Business Park	10	D4	133
Royal Liver Retail Park	36	E4	214
S.P.A.D.E. Unemployment Enterprise Centre	37	C2	287
Sandyford Business Centre	58	E2	137
Sandyford Ind Est	58	E2	135
Sandyford Office Park	58	E2	136
Sandyford Park	58	E2	163
Santry Avenue Ind Est	12	E4	138
Santry Hall Ind Est	25	B1	139
Shankhill Business Centre	64	E2	141
Shanowen Ind Est, Santry	25	B1	142
Sitecast Ind Est	45	B4	194
Solas Retail Park, Bray	67	C1	254
South City Business Park	54	F2	306
South City Executive Park	46	E1	288
South County Business Park	58	F2	143
Southern Cross Business Park	67	B4	256
Square Ind Complex, The	54	F1	289
St Joan's Ind Est	45	A2	134
St John's Court Office Park	25	B1	264
St Margaret's Business Park	11	A4	286
St. Anthony's Business Park	45	A2	309
Stadium Ind Est	10	E4	203
Stillorgan Ind Park	58	D2	144
Sunbury Ind Est	45	B2	145
Sunshine Ind Est	37	A4	146
Swanward Business Centre	45	A2	185
Swiftbrook Ind Est	53	A2	147
Swords Business Campus	2	D1	267
Swords Business Park	2	E1	148
Tallaght Enterprise Centre	55	A1	149
Taurus Business Park, Greenhills Road	45	B4	195
Terenure Business Park	46	F2	290
Terenure Enterprise Centre	46	F2	304
Tolka Ind Park	24	D3	34
Tolka Valley Business Park	24	D3	222
Turnpike Ind Est see Ballymount Cross	45	A2	151
Unidare/Jamestown Business Pk	24	E1	152
Weatherwell Ind Est	35	A4	153
West Pier Business Campus, Dun Laoghaire	49	C4	168
Western Business Park	44	F1	249
Western Ind Est	45	A1	156
Western Office Park	22	E1	236
Western Parkway Business Centre Ballymount Rd	45	B2	157
Western Parkway Business Park	45	B2	190
Western Retail Park	22	E2	237
Westgate Business Park	45	A3	186
Westland Sq Business Park	38	E2	260
Westlink Ind Est	36	E3	154
Westpoint Business Park	8	F4	164
Westway Centre	45	B2	189
White Heather Ind Est	37	B4	158
White Swan Business Park	37	C4	159
Whitestown Industrial Estate	54	F1	305
Willow Business Park, Knockmitten Lane	45	A1	187
Woodford Business Park, Santry	12	F3	178
Woodlawn Ind Est	12	F3	162

Due to the limitations imposed by scale it has not been possible to include all street names on the maps. Unnamed streets have been given small numbers which appear after their grid reference in this index. A list of such streets, by grid reference, is given on page 130.
Streets not named or indicated by number on map pages are prefixed by * and are given their approximate location and grid reference.

STREET NAME	PAGE/GRID REFERENCE		STREET NAME	PAGE/GRID REFERENCE		STREET NAME	PAGE/GRID REFERENCE		STREET NAME	PAGE/GRID REFERENCE	
A			Adare Avenue	26	E1	Albert Walk	67	C2	Amber Vale	44	E4
1 Branch Road North	39	A2	Adare Drive	26	E1	Aldborough House	38	E1 [72]	Amberwood	9	A4
1 Branch Road South	39	A2	Adare Green	26	E1	Aldborough Parade	38	E1 [17]	Amiens Street	38	E2
2 Branch Road North	39	B2	Adare Park	26	E1	Aldborough Place	38	E1	Anastasia Lane	60	F2 [3]
2 Branch Road South	39	A2	Adare Road	26	E1	*Aldborough Square (off	38	E1	Anglers Rest	47	C1
3 Branch Road South	39	A2	Addison Drive	24	F3	Aldborough Place)			Anglesea Avenue	49	A3
4 Branch Road South	39	B2	Addison Lane	24	F3	Aldemere	21	B2	Anglesea Lane	50	D4 [20]
A.W. Pugin House	46	F4 [19]	Addison Park	24	F3	Alden Drive	27	C1	Anglesea Park	60	E2
Abberley	64	E1	Addison Place	25	A3 [9]	Alden Park	27	C1	Anglesea Road	47	C1
Abbey Cottages	38	D2 [43]	Addison Road	25	C4	Alden Road	27	C1	Anglesea Row	38	D2 [7]
Abbey Court (Celbridge)	31	C4	Adelaide Court	38	D4 [57]	Alder Court	4	D4 [1]	Anglesea Street	38	D2
Abbey Court (Killester)	26	E3	Adelaide Mews	48	E1	Alder Lodge	23	A4	Anley Court	34	E1
Abbey Court (Monkstown)	59	B1 [7]	Adelaide Road (Bray)	67	C2	Alderpark Court	54	F1	Ann Devlin Avenue	46	E4
Abbey Drive	24	D4	Adelaide Road (Dun Laoghaire)	60	E1	Alderwood Avenue	54	E1	Ann Devlin Drive	46	E4
Abbey Green	31	C4	Adelaide Road (Leeson Street)	38	D4	Alderwood Close	54	E1	Ann Devlin Park	56	E1
Abbey Lane	31	C4	Adelaide Street	50	D4	Alderwood Court	54	E1	Ann Devlin Road	46	E4
Abbey Park (Baldoyle)	27	C1	Adelaide Terrace	60	E1 [28]	Alderwood Drive	54	F1	Anna Villa	47	B1
Abbey Park (Kill o' the Grange)	59	B1	(Dun Laoghaire)			Alderwood Green	54	E1	Annabeg	60	D4 [1]
Abbey Park (Killester)	26	E3	*Adelaide Terrace	37	B3	Alderwood Grove	54	F1	Annacrivey	65	B3
Abbey Road	59	B1	(off Brookfield Road)			Alderwood Lawn	54	E1	Annadale	47	B4 [16]
Abbey Street (Howth)	30	D1	Adelaide Villas (Bray)	67	C2	Alderwood Park	54	F1	Annadale Avenue	25	C4 [1]
Abbey Street Lower	38	E2	Adelaide Villas (Dun Laoghaire)	60	E1 [27]	Alderwood Rise	54	E1	Annadale Crescent	25	C3
Abbey Street Middle	38	D2	Admiral Court	15	A4 [9]	Alderwood Way	54	F1	Annadale Drive	25	C3
Abbey Street Old	38	E2 [19]	Admiral Park	15	A4	Aldrin Walk	26	E1	Annagh Court	22	F1
Abbey Street Upper	38	D2	Adrian Avenue	46	F1	*Alen Hall (Belgard Square)	54	F1	Annaghaskin	66	D1
Abbey Terrace	30	D1 [11]	*Aengus Hall (Belgard Square)	54	F1	Alexander Terrace (Bray)	67	C2 [43]	Annaly Close	21	B1
Abbey View	59	B1	Affollus	5	C3	Alexander Terrace (North Wall)	38	F2 [11]	Annaly Court	21	B1
Abbeydale	34	F3	Aideen Avenue	46	E2	Alexandra Court	47	C4	Annaly Drive	21	B1
Abbeydale Close	34	F3	Aideen Drive	46	E2	Alexandra Quay	39	A2 [2]	Annaly Grove	21	B1
Abbeydale Crescent	34	F3	Aideen Place	46	E2	Alexandra Road	39	A2	Annaly Road	24	F4
Abbeydale Gardens	34	F3	Aikenhead Terrace	39	A3	Alexandra Road Extension	39	C2	Annaly Terrace	21	B1
Abbeydale Park	34	F3	Aiken's Village	58	D3	Alexandra Terrace (Dundrum)	47	C4	Annamoe Drive	37	C1
Abbeydale Rise	34	F3	Ailesbury	25	B1 [1]	Alexandra Terrace (Portobello)	38	D4 [45]	Annamoe Parade	37	C1 [2]
Abbeydale Walk	34	F3	Ailesbury Close	48	D1 [4]	Alexandra Terrace (Terenure)	46	F2	Annamoe Park	37	C1
Abbeyfarm	31	C4	Ailesbury Drive	48	D1	Alexandra Villas	47	C4 [3]	Annamoe Road	37	B1
Abbeyfield (Clonskeagh)	47	B2	Ailesbury Gardens	48	E1	Alfie Byrne Road	38	F1	Annamoe Terrace	37	C1
Abbeyfield (Killester)	26	E3	Ailesbury Grove (Donnybrook)	48	D1	All Hallows Green	25	B3	Annaville Avenue	59	A1
Abbeylea Avenue	1	C1	Ailesbury Grove (Dundrum)	57	B1	All Hallows Lane	25	B3 [7]	Annaville Close	47	C4
Abbeylea Close	1	C1	*Ailesbury Lane	48	D1	All Saint's Close	27	A3	Annaville Grove	47	C3 [1]
Abbeylea Drive	1	C1	(off Ailesbury Road)			All Saints Drive	27	A3	Annaville Lodge	47	C4
Abbeylea Green	1	C1	Ailesbury Lawn	57	B1	All Saints Park	27	A3	Annaville Park	47	C4
Abbeyvale Avenue	1	B1	Ailesbury Mews	48	E1	All Saints Road	26	F3	Annaville Terrace	47	C3
Abbeyvale Close	1	B1	Ailesbury Park	48	E1	Allen Park Drive	58	E1	Anne Street North	38	D2 [5]
Abbeyvale Court	1	B1	Ailesbury Road	48	D1	Allen Park Road	58	E1	Anne Street South	38	D3
Abbeyvale Crescent	1	B1	Ailesbury Wood	48	D1	*Allen Terrace	37	C1	Anner Road	37	A3
Abbeyvale Drive	1	B2	Airfield Court	48	D2	(off Avondale Avenue)			Anne's Lane	38	D3 [33]
Abbeyvale Green	1	B2	Airfield Drive	47	B4 [13]	Allendale Close	21	B2	Annesley Avenue	38	F1 [9]
Abbeyvale Grove	1	B1	Airfield Park	48	D2	Allendale Copse	21	B1	Annesley Bridge Road	38	F1
Abbeyvale Lawn	1	B1	Airfield Road	46	F2	Allendale Court	21	B1	Annesley Park	47	B1
Abbeyvale Place	1	B1	Airlie Heights	33	B2	Allendale Drive	21	B1	Annesley Place	38	F1
Abbeyvale Rise	1	B1	Airpark Avenue	56	E2	Allendale Elms	21	B1	Annfield	22	D3
Abbeyvale View	1	B2	Airpark Close	56	E2	Allendale Glen	21	B1	Annfield Court	22	D3
Abbeyvale Way	1	B2	Airpark Court	56	E2	Allendale Green	21	B1	Annfield Crescent	22	D3
Abbeywood	34	F3	Airpark House	56	E2	Allendale Grove	21	B1	Annfield Drive	22	D3
Abbeywood Avenue	34	F3	Airpark Rise	56	D2	Allendale Heath	21	B1	Annfield Lawn	22	D4
Abbeywood Close	34	F3	Airpark Rise	56	D2	Allendale Lawn	21	B1	Annsbrook	47	C2
Abbeywood Court	34	E3	Airside	2	D3	Allendale Place	21	B1	Annville Drive	58	E1
Abbeywood Crescent	34	F3	Airton Close	45	A4	Allendale Rise	21	B1	Apollo Way	26	D1
Abbeywood Park	34	F3	Airton Road	45	A4	Allendale Square	21	B2	*Appian Close (on Leeson Park)	38	E4
Abbeywood Way	34	F3	Airton Terrace	45	A4	Allendale Terrace	21	B1	Apples Road	58	D2
Abbots Hill	3	C3	(off Greenhills Rd)			Allendale View	21	B1	Aranleigh Court	56	F1
Abbotstown Avenue	23	C2	Albany Avenue	49	B4	Allendale Walk	21	B1	Aranleigh Dell	57	A1
Abbotstown Drive	23	C1	Albany Court	64	E1	Allenton Avenue	55	A3	Aranleigh Gardens	56	F1
Abbotstown Road	24	D2	Albany Road	47	B1	Allenton Crescent	55	A2 [3]	Aranleigh Mount	56	F1
Abby Well	14	D1	Albert Avenue	68	D2	Allenton Drive	55	A3	Aranleigh Park	57	A1
Abercorn Road	38	F2	Albert College Avenue	25	A2	Allenton Gardens	55	A3	Aranleigh Walk	56	F1
Abercorn Square	36	F3 [19]	Albert College Court	25	A2	Allenton Green	55	A3	Arás na Cluaine	35	B4
Abercorn Terrace	36	F3 [10]	Albert College Crescent	25	A2	Allenton Lawns	55	A2	Aravon Court	68	D2
Aberdeen Street	37	B2	Albert College Drive	25	A2	Allenton Park	55	A2	Arbour Hill	37	C2
Abington	2	F3	Albert College Grove	25	A2	Allenton Road	55	B3 [1]	Arbour Place	37	C2
Accommodation Road	19	C4	Albert College Lawn	25	A2	Allenton Way	55	A3	Arbour Terrace	37	B2 [6]
Achill Road (Drumcondra)	25	B3	Albert College Park	25	A2	Allies River Road	67	A1	Arbutus Avenue	37	C4 [8]
Achill Road (Loughlinstown)	64	E1	Albert Court (Grand Canal St. Lower)	38	F3 [30]	Allingham Street	37	C3 [15]	Arbutus Grove	67	B1 [4]
Acorn Drive	57	B1	Albert Court (Sandycove Road)	60	E1	Alma Park	49	C4 [30]	Arbutus Place	38	D4 [51]
Acorn Road	57	B1	*Albert Court	38	F4	Alma Place	49	C4 [14]	Ard Gréine (Ballymorris)	67	B4
Acres Road	36	F2	(off Grand Canal St)			Alma Road	49	B4	Ard Lorcain	58	F1
Adair	39	A4 [14]	Albert Park	60	E1 [3]	Alma Terrace	47	A1 [13]	Ard Lorcain Villas	58	F1 [2]
*Adair Lane (off Dorset Street)	38	D1	Albert Place East	38	F3 [14]	Almeida Avenue	37	B3 [26]	Ard Mhacha	54	F2
*Adair Terrace	38	D1	Albert Place West	38	D4 [15]	Almeida Terrace	37	B3 [27]	Ard Mhuire Park	60	E2
(on St Joseph's Parade)			Albert Road Lower	60	E1	Alone Walk	26	E2	Ard Mor Avenue	53	C1
*Adam Court (off Grafton Street)	38	D3	Albert Road Upper	60	E1	Alpine Heights	44	D1	Ard Mor Close	53	C1
Adamstown Avenue	33	C4	Albert Terrace	38	D4 [18]	Alpine Rise	44	E4	Ard Mor Court	53	C1
Adamstown Road	34	D2	(Charlemont Street)			Altadore	60	D2	Ard Mor Crescent	53	C1
			Albert Terrace (Dún Laoghaire)	50	D4 [27]	Altamont Hall	47	C4	Ard Mor Dale	53	C1
						Alverno	39	B1 [1]	Ard Mor Drive	53	C1

STREET NAME	PAGE/GRID REFERENCE	STREET NAME	PAGE/GRID REFERENCE	STREET NAME	PAGE/GRID REFERENCE	STREET NAME	PAGE/GRID REFERENCE
Ard Mor Green	53 C1	Arran Close	64 E1	Ashleigh Green	22 F3	Aulden Grange	12 F4
Ard Mor Lawn	53 C1	Arran Court	22 F1	Ashleigh Grove	22 F3	Aungier Lane	38 D3 [23]
Ard Mor Park	53 C1	Arran Drive	64 E1	(Blanchardstown)		Aungier Place	38 D3 [10]
Ard Mor Walk	53 C1	Arran Green	67 C2	Ashleigh Grove (Maynooth)	17 B4	Aungier Street	38 D3
Ard Na Gréine	47 A3 [11]	Arran Quay	37 C2	Ashleigh Lawn	3 B3	Austin's Cottages	38 F1 [23]
Ard na Mara	3 A3	Arran Quay Terrace	37 C2 [10]	Ashley Avenue	2 D2	Avalon	59 A3 [3]
Ard na Meala	12 D4	Arran Road	25 B3	Ashley Drive	2 D2	Avalon Apts.	29 B1 [2]
Ard Ri Road	37 C2	Arran Street East	38 D2	Ashley Grove	2 D2	Ave Maria Road	37 B3 [18]
Ard Righ Place	37 C2 [27]	Arran Street West	37 C2 [17]	Ashley Heights	67 B2 [4]	Avenue Road	38 D4 [26]
Ardagh Avenue	59 A1	Arranmore Avenue	38 D1 [36]	Ashley Rise	4 D4	Avila Apts	59 A1 [10]
Ardagh Close	59 A1 [6]	Arranmore Road	47 C1	Ashling Close	37 B4	Avila Park	23 C1
Ardagh Court	58 F1	Artane	26 E2	Ashling Court	47 B1	Avila Park Gardens	23 C1
Ardagh Crescent	59 A1	Artane Cottages Lower	26 E2 [2]	Ashling Heights	22 E1	Avoca Apartments	32 D3
Ardagh Drive	59 A1	Artane Cottages Upper	26 E2 [3]	Ashmount	9 A4 [1]	Avoca Avenue (Dun Laoghaire)	67 C3
Ardagh Grove	59 A1	Arthur Griffith Court	34 D2 [1]	Ashmount Court	37 A3 [23]	Avoca Avenue (Stillorgan)	48 F4
Ardagh Park	59 A1	Arthur Griffith Park	34 D3	Ashton Avenue	56 D1	Avoca Hall	49 A4 [10]
Ardagh Park Road	59 A1	Arundel	49 B4 [19]	Ashton Close	56 D1	Avoca Park	48 F4
Ardagh Road	37 B4	*Asdill's Row (off Temple Bar)	38 D2	Ashton Grove	56 D1	Avoca Place	49 A3
Ardara Avenue	14 D4	Asgard Apts.	30 D1	Ashton Lawn	56 D1	Avoca Road	48 F4
Ardbeg Crescent	26 E2	Asgard Park	30 D2	Ashton Park	49 B4	Avoca Terrace	48 F4
Ardbeg Drive	26 E2	Asgard Road	30 D2	Ashton Wood	67 A3	Avoca Wood	48 F4
Ardbeg Park	26 E2	Ash Grove (Meath Street)	37 C3	Ashtown	23 C3	Avonbeg Court	55 A1 [3]
Ardbeg Road	26 E2	Ash Park Avenue	34 E3	Ashtown Court	23 C4	Avonbeg Drive	55 A1
Ardbrugh Close	60 F2 [31]	Ash Park Court	34 E3	Ashtown Gate Road	23 B4	Avonbeg Gardens	55 B1
Ardbrugh Road	60 F2	Ash Park Grove	34 E2	Ashtown Grove	23 C4	Avonbeg Park	55 A1
Ardbrugh Villas	60 F2 [21]	Ash Park Heath	34 E2	Ashtown Lodge	23 C4 [4]	Avonbeg Road	55 B1
Ardcian Park	1 C1	Ash Street	37 C3	Ashtown Road	23 B3	Avondale	20 D4
Ardcollum Avenue	26 E2	Ashberry	34 D3	Ashtowngate	23 C3	Avondale Avenue	37 C1
Ardee Grove	38 D4	Ashbrook (Ashtown)	23 C3	Ashurst	60 E4	Avondale Court (Blackrock)	49 A4
Ardee Road	38 D4	Ashbrook (Bray)	67 C2	Ashurst (Ballybrack)	64 E1	Avondale Court (Dalkey)	60 E1 [31]
Ardee Row	37 C3 [34]	Ashbrook (Clontarf)	26 D4	Ashurst (Mount Merrion)	48 E4 [3]	Avondale Crescent	60 E2
Ardee Street (Bray)	67 B2	*Ashbrook Terrace (Ranelagh)	47 B1	Ashville Close	34 E1	Avondale House	38 E1 [63]
Ardee Street (The Coombe)	37 C3	*Ashbrook Villas (Ranelagh)	47 B1	Ashwood Avenue	43 C1	Avondale Lawn	49 A4
Ardeen	33 C2	Ashbury Park	67 C2	Ashwood Close	43 C1	Avondale Park (Blackrock)	49 A4 [1]
Ardeevin Avenue	33 C2	Ashcroft	27 A2	Ashwood Drive	44 D1	Avondale Park (Bray)	67 B3
Ardeevin Court	33 C2	Ashcroft Grove	22 D1 [4]	Ashwood Lawns	44 D1	Avondale Park (Dalkey)	60 E2
Ardeevin Drive	33 C2	Ashdale Avenue	46 F2	Ashwood Park	44 D1	Avondale Park (Raheny)	27 A2
Ardeevin Road	60 F2	Ashdale Close	2 E3	Ashwood Road	44 D1	Avondale Road (Dalkey)	60 D2
*Ardeevin Terrace	60 F2	Ashdale Gardens	46 F2	Ashwood Way	44 D1	Avondale Road (Phibsborough)	37 C1
(off Ardeevin Road)		Ashdale Park	46 F2 [1]	*Ashworth Place (off Mount	37 C4	Avondale Square	7 B2 [2]
Ardenza Park	49 B3 [3]	Ashdale Road (Swords)	2 E3	Drumond Avenue)		Avondale Terrace	45 C2
Ardenza Terrace	49 B3 [1]	Ashdale Road (Terenure)	46 F2	Aspen Drive	2 E3	Avonmore	59 A2
Ardglas Estate	57 C1	Ashe Court	2 E3	Aspen Park (Kill O'The Grange)	59 C1 [11]	Avonmore Avenue	55 B1 [5]
Ardilaun	14 F1	Ashfield	46 D4	Aspen Park (Kinsealy Court)	2 E3	Avonmore Close	55 B1
Ardilaun Road	38 E1 [3]	Ashfield Avenue (Clondalkin)	44 F3	Aspen Road	2 E3	Avonmore Drive	55 B1
*Ardilaun Square	38 E1	Ashfield Avenue (Ranelagh)	47 B1	Aspen Wood	22 D2	Avonmore Grove	55 B1
(off Sackville Avenue)		Ashfield Close (Clondalkin)	44 F3	Assumpta Park	64 E3	Avonmore Park	55 B1
Ardilea Downs	48 D4	Ashfield Court (Ballymorris)	67 B4	Aston Place	38 D2 [39]	Avonmore Road	55 B1
Ardilea Wood	48 D4	Ashfield Court (Mulhuddart)	9 A4	Aston Quay	38 D2	Aylesbury	55 A2
Ardlea Road	26 E2	Ashfield Drive	44 F3	Athgoe	51 C1	Aylmer Ave	42 D4
Ardlui Park	59 A1	Ashfield Gardens	9 A4	Athgoe Drive	64 E2 [4]	Aylmer Road	42 D4
Ardmeen Park	59 A1	Ashfield Green	8 F4	Athgoe North	51 B1	Ayrefield Avenue	26 F1
Ardmore Avenue	37 B1 [4]	Ashfield Grove	9 A4	Athgoe Road (Newcastle)	41 C4	Ayrefield Court	26 F1
Ardmore Close	26 D2	Ashfield Lawn	8 F4	Athgoe Road (Shankill)	64 E2	Ayrefield Drive	26 F1
Ardmore Crescent (Artane)	26 D2	Ashfield Park (Booterstown)	48 E2	Athgoe South	51 B2	Ayrefield Grove	26 F1
Ardmore Crescent (Bray)	67 B2	Ashfield Park (Clondalkin)	44 F3	Atlumney Villas	38 D4 [12]	Ayrefield Park	26 F1 [1]
Ardmore Drive	26 D1	Ashfield Park (Huntstown Way)	9 A4 [2]	Atmospheric Road	60 E1 [29]	Ayrefield Place	26 F1
Ardmore Grove	26 D1	Ashfield Park (Terenure)	46 F2	Aubrey Grove	64 E3	Ayrefield Road	26 F1
Ardmore Lawn	67 B3	Ashfield Road (Ranelagh)	47 B1	Aubrey Park	64 E3	Ayward Green	24 D2
Ardmore Park (Artane)	26 D2	Ashfield Way	9 A4	Auburn	26 D4		
Ardmore Park (Bray)	67 B2	Ashfield Way	8 A4	Auburn Avenue (Cabinteely)	60 D3	**B**	
Ardmore Park	59 C1	Ashford Cottages	37 B1 [17]	Auburn Avenue (Castleknock)	23 A3		
(Kill o' the Grange)		Ashford Place	37 B1 [16]	Auburn Avenue (Donnybrook)	47 C1	Bachelor's Walk	38 D2
Ardmore Wood	67 B3	Ashford Street	37 B1 [10]	Auburn Close (Cabinteely)	60 D3	Bachelors Way	38 D2 [30]
Ardpatrick Road	24 D4	Ashgrove (Baskin Lane)	13 C1	Auburn Close (Castleknock)	23 A3	Back Lane (Baldoyle)	15 A4 [3]
Ardtona Avenue	47 B4 [6]	Ashgrove (Celbridge)	31 C2	Auburn Drive (Cabinteely)	60 D3	Back Lane (High Street)	38 D3
Arena Road	58 E2	Ashgrove (Kill o' the Grange)	59 C1	Auburn Drive (Castleknock)	23 A3	Back Lane (Maynooth)	17 C3
Argus House	37 C4 [41]	Ashgrove (Tallaght)	54 E1	Auburn Green	23 A3	*Back Lane (off Sandwith St Upr)	38 E3
Argyle Road	38 F4	Ashgrove Court	57 C1 [8]	Auburn Grove	3 A3	Back Road	3 B4
Arkendale Court	60 E1 [26]	Ashgrove Terrace	57 C1 [2]	Auburn Road (Cabinteely)	60 D3	Baggot Close	38 E3
Arkendale Road	60 E1	Ashington Avenue	24 D3	Auburn Road (Cabinteely)	60 D3 [1]	Baggot Court	38 E3 [9]
Arkendale Woods	60 E1 [25]	Ashington Close	24 D3	Auburn Road (Donnybrook)	47 C1 [11]	Baggot Lane	38 F4
Arkle Road	58 E2	Ashington Court	24 D3	Auburn Street	38 D1	Baggot Road	23 C4
Arkle Square	58 F2 [6]	Ashington Crescent	23 C3	*Auburn Terrace (Old	37 B3	Baggot Street Lower	38 E3
Arklow Street	37 B1 [13]	Ashington Dale	24 D3	Kilmainham)		Baggot Street Upper	38 F4
Armagh Road	46 D1	Ashington Gardens	24 D3	Auburn Villas (Bray)	67 B2 [1]	Baggot Terrace	23 C4 [1]
Armstrong Street	37 C4 [37]	Ashington Green	24 D3	Auburn Villas (Rathgar)	47 A2	Baggotrath Place	38 E3 [28]
*Armstrong Street	37 C4	Ashington Grove	24 D3	Auburn Walk	37 B1 [18]	Bailey Green Road	30 E3
(off Harold's Cross Road)		Ashington Heath	24 D3	Aughavannagh Road	37 C4	Bailey View	60 F1 [15]
Armstrong Walk	26 E1	Ashington Mews	24 D3	Aughrim Court	37 C1 [21]	Bailey's Row	38 E1 [11]
Army Road	37 A2	Ashington Park	24 D3	Aughrim Lane	37 C1 [1]	Balally Avenue	58 D1
Arnold Grove	60 D2	Ashington Rise	23 C3	Aughrim Place	37 B1 [8]	Balally Close	58 D1
Arnold Park	60 D2	Ashlawn	57 C1	Aughrim Street	37 B1	Balally Drive	58 D1
Arnott Street	38 D3	Ashlawn Court	67 B2	Aughrim Villas	37 B1 [12]	Balally Grove	58 D2
Arran Avenue	64 E1	Ashlawn Park	60 D4	Augustine Villas	67 C2 [30]	Balally Hill	58 D2

STREET NAME	PAGE	GRID
Balally Park	58	D1
Balally Road	57	C1
Balally Terrace	58	D2 [1]
Balbutcher Drive	11	C4
Balbutcher Lane	11	C4
Balbutcher Lane Lower	11	C4
Balbutcher Way	11	C4
Balcurris Close	12	D4
Balcurris Gardens	12	D4
Balcurris Park East	12	D4
Balcurris Road	12	D4
Baldoyle	15	A4
Baldoyle Road	28	D1
Balfe Avenue	45	C1
Balfe Gardens	32	D4 [1]
Balfe Road	45	C1
Balfe Road East	46	D1
Balfe Street	38	D3 [29]
Balgaddy Road	34	F3
Balglass Road	30	D2
Balgriffin	14	D3
Balgriffin Cottages	14	D3
Balgriffin Road	14	D3
Balheary Road	2	D1
Balkill Park	30	D2
Balkill Road	30	D2
Ballawley Court	57	C2
Ballentree	9	B2
Ballentree Avenue	9	B2
Ballentree Close	9	B2
Ballentree Crescent	9	B2
Ballentree Drive	9	B2
Ballentree Grove	9	B3
*Ballentree Lodge Apts.	9	B2
Ballentree Villa	9	B3
Ballinclea Heights	60	E3
Ballinclea Road	60	D3
Ballinteer	57	B2
Ballinteer Avenue	57	B2
Ballinteer Close	57	B2
Ballinteer Court	57	B2 [2]
Ballinteer Crescent	57	B2
Ballinteer Drive	57	B2
Ballinteer Gardens	57	C2
Ballinteer Grove	57	B2
Ballinteer Park	57	B2
Ballinteer Road	57	C1
Ballintrane Wood	1	C2
Ballintyre Demesne	57	B2
Ballintyre Downs	57	B2
Ballintyre Lane	57	B2
Ballintyre Meadows	57	B2
Ballintyre Square	57	B2
Ballintyre Terrace	57	B2
Ballintyre Walk	57	B2
Ballintyre Woods	57	B2
Ball's Lane	38	D2 [23]
Ballsbridge	38	F4
Ballsbridge Avenue	39	A4 [26]
Ballsbridge Gardens	39	A4 [25]
Ballsbridge Park	39	A4 [23]
Ballsbridge Terrace	38	F4 [14]
Ballsbridge Wood	39	A4 [27]
Ballybetagh	62	F4
Ballybetagh Road	62	E4
Ballyboden	56	E1
Ballyboden Crescent	56	E1
Ballyboden Road	56	E1
Ballyboden Way	56	E1
Ballyboggan Road	24	E3
Ballybough Avenue	38	E1 [42]
Ballybough Court	38	E1 [43]
Ballybough Lane	38	E1 [4]
Ballybough Road	38	E1
Ballybrack	60	E4
Ballybrack (Two Rock Mountain)	61	B3
Ballybrew	65	C2
Ballybride	64	D3
Ballybride Road	64	D3
Ballycoolin Road	10	D4
Ballycorus	63	B3
Ballycorus Road	63	A2
Ballycorus Road	62	F2
Ballycullen Avenue	55	B2
Ballycullen Drive	55	B2
Ballycullen Road	55	C1
Ballydowd Grove	34	E1
Ballydowd Manor	34	E2
Ballyedmonduff	61	C2
Ballyedmonduff Road	62	D1
Ballyfermot	36	D3
Ballyfermot Avenue	36	D3
Ballyfermot Crescent	36	D3
Ballyfermot Drive	36	D3
Ballyfermot Parade	36	D3
Ballyfermot Road	35	C3
Ballyfermot Road	36	E3
Ballygall Avenue	24	E1
Ballygall Crescent	24	E2
Ballygall Parade	24	E2
Ballygall Place	24	E2 [1]
Ballygall Road East	24	F2
Ballygall Road West	24	E1
Ballygihen Avenue	60	E1
Ballygihen Villas	60	E1 [20]
Ballygoran	18	E4
Ballygoran Court	31	C2
Ballygoran View	31	C2
Ballyhoy Avenue	27	A3
Ballymacartle	13	C1
Ballymace Green	46	E4
Ballymacoll	6	D3
Ballymadrough Road	2	F1
Ballymakeally Lawns	31	C4
Ballymakealy Grove	31	C4
Ballyman	66	F1
Ballyman Lane	66	F1
Ballyman Lane	63	C4
Ballyman Road	66	F2
Ballymana	54	E4
Ballymanagin Lane	35	A4 [1]
Ballymorris	67	B4 [2]
Ballymorris	67	B4
Ballymoss Parade	58	F2 [5]
Ballymoss Road	58	E2
Ballymount Avenue	45	B2
Ballymount Cottages	45	B3 [2]
Ballymount Drive	45	B2
Ballymount Road	44	F3
Ballymount Road Lower	45	B2
Ballymount Road Upper	45	A2
Ballymount Square	45	B2
Ballymun	25	A1
Ballymun Main Street	12	D4
Ballymun Road	25	A1
Ballymun Road	25	A3
Ballynakelly	42	D4
Ballyneety Road	36	F3
Ballynoe Court	67	B3 [1]
Ballyogan Avenue	58	F4
Ballyogan Close	58	F4
Ballyogan Court	58	F4
Ballyogan Crescent	58	F4
Ballyogan Drive	58	F4
Ballyogan Estate	58	F4
Ballyogan Green	58	F4
Ballyogan Lawn	58	F4
Ballyogan Park	58	F4 [1]
Ballyogan Road	58	F4
Ballyogen Vale	59	A4
Ballyogen Wood	59	A4
Ballyolaf Manor	57	C1 [6]
Ballyoulster Park	32	E3
Ballyowen Avenue	34	F1
Ballyowen Court	34	F1
Ballyowen Crescent	34	F1
Ballyowen Drive	34	F1
Ballyowen Green	34	F1
Ballyowen Grove	34	F1
Ballyowen Hall	34	F2
Ballyowen Lane	34	F2
Ballyowen Lawn	34	F1
Ballyowen Road	34	F1
Ballyowen Square	34	F2
Ballyowen View	34	F1
Ballyowen Way	34	F1
Ballyroan Court	56	D1 [3]
Ballyroan Crescent	56	E1
Ballyroan Heights	56	E1
Ballyroan Park	56	D1
Ballyroan Road	56	E1
Ballyshannon Avenue	25	C1
Ballyshannon Road	26	D1
Ballytore Road	46	F3
Ballywaltrim Cottages	67	B4 [1]
Ballywaltrim Heights	67	B4
Ballywaltrim Lane	67	A4
Ballywaltrim Road	67	B4
Ballywilliam Close	67	B4
Balnagowan	47	B2 [4]
Balrothery Cottages	55	C1 [5]
Balrothery Estate	45	B4
Balscadden Road	30	E1
Balscott	41	C1
Bancroft Avenue	55	A1
Bancroft Close	55	B1
Bancroft Crescent	45	B4
Bancroft Downs	45	A4
Bancroft Grove	55	B1
Bancroft Park	55	A1
Bancroft Road	55	B1
Bangor Circle	46	E1
Bangor Drive	37	B4
Bangor Road	46	E1
Bankside Cottages	47	B2
Bann Road	24	E3
Bannaville	38	D4 [41]
Bannow Road	24	E4
Banshee	51	A2
Bantry Road	25	A3
Banville Avenue	36	D4
Barberstown Lane	1	A4
Barclay Court	49	A3
Bargy Road	38	F1
Barnacoille Park	60	F1
Barnamire	65	A4
Barnamore Crescent	24	D3
Barnamore Grove	24	D3
Barnamore Park	24	D3
Barnaslingan Lane	63	A3
Barneville Green	35	C3
Barneville Walk	35	C4
Barnhall Drive	32	F1
Barnhill Avenue	60	E2
Barnhill Cross Road	34	D1
Barnhill Grove	60	F2 [7]
Barnhill Lawn	60	E2 [1]
Barnhill Park	60	E2 [3]
Barnhill Road	60	E2
*Barnhill Villas (on Barnhill Road)	60	F2
Barnville Park	35	C4
Barnwell Drive	24	F1
Baroma	46	E2 [10]
Barrack Court	52	F2
*Barrack Lane (off Irishtown Road)	39	A3
Barrett Street	49	C4 [2]
Barrogstown East	18	F4
Barrogstown West	18	E4
Barron Place	25	A3 [4]
Barrow Road	24	E3
Barrow Street	38	F3
Barry Avenue	24	D1
Barry Close(off Barry Drive)	24	D1
Barry Drive	24	D1
Barry Green	24	D1
Barry Park	24	D1
Barry Road	24	D1
Barry's Park	2	D2
Barryscourt Road	26	E1
Barton Avenue	56	F1
Barton Court	57	A1 [3]
Barton Drive	56	F1
Barton Road East	57	B1
Barton Road East Extension	57	A1
Barton Road Extension	57	A1
Barton Road West	56	F1
Bartra Rock Apts.	60	F1 [18]
Basin Grove	37	B3
Basin Street Lower	37	B3
Basin Street Upper	37	B3
*Basin View (off Basin Street Upper)	37	B3
Baskin Cottages	13	C1
Baskin Lane	13	B1
Bass Place	38	E3 [3]
Bath Avenue (Malahide)	3	C2
Bath Avenue (Sandymount)	38	F3
Bath Avenue Gardens	38	F3
Bath Avenue Place	38	F3 [10]
Bath Lane	38	D1 [42]
Bath Place	49	A3 [8]
Bath Street	39	A3
Bawnlea Avenue	54	D2
Bawnlea Close	54	D2
Bawnlea Crescent	54	D2
Bawnlea Drive	54	D2
Bawnlea Green	54	D2
Bawnogue Cottages	43	C1 [1]
Bawnogue Road	43	C1
Bawnville Avenue	55	A2
Bawnville Close	55	A2
Bawnville Drive	55	B2
Bawnville Park	55	B2
Bawnville Road	55	A2
Baymount Park	27	A4
Bayshore Lane	64	E1
Bayside Boulevard North	27	C1
Bayside Boulevard South	27	C1
Bayside Crescent	27	C1 [1]
Bayside Park	27	C1
Bayside Square East	27	C1
Bayside Square North	27	C1
Bayside Square South	27	C1
Bayside Square West	27	C1
Bayside Walk	27	C1
Bayswater Terrace	60	F1 [7]
Baytownpark	6	E1
Bayview (Bray)	67	C2 [51]
Bayview (Loughlinstown)	64	E1
*Bayview (On Seapoint Road)	67	C2
Bayview Avenue	38	E1
Bayview Close	64	E1
Bayview Court	64	E1
Bayview Crescent	64	E1
Bayview Drive	64	E1
Bayview Glade	64	E1 [12]
Bayview Glen	64	E1
Bayview Green	64	E1
Bayview Grove	64	E1
Bayview Lawn	64	E1
Bayview Park	64	E1
Bayview Rise	64	E1
Beach Avenue	39	A3
Beach Drive	39	A3
Beach Park	15	A1
Beach Road	39	A3
Beach View	27	C2
Beacon Court	58	D2
*Beacon Hill (off Nerano Road)	60	F2
Beaconsfield Court	37	A3 [18]
Bealing	9	B2
Bealing Avenue	9	B2
Bealing Close	9	B3
Bealing Crescent	9	B2
Bealing Grove	9	B2
Bealing Mews	9	B2
Bealing View	9	B2
Bealing Village	9	B3
Bealing Walk	9	B2
Bealing Wood	9	B3
Bearna Park	58	D3
Beatty Grove	32	D2
Beatty Park	32	D3
Beatty's Avenue	38	F4 [8]
Beaucourt	25	B3 [4]
Beaufield	17	C4
Beaufield Ave	17	C4
Beaufield Close	17	C4
Beaufield Crescent	17	C4
Beaufield Drive	17	C4
Beaufield Gardens	17	C4
Beaufield Green	17	C4
Beaufield Grove	17	C4
Beaufield Lawn	17	C4
Beaufield Manor	48	E4
Beaufield Mews	48	E4 [2]
Beaufield Park	48	E4

STREET NAME	PAGE/GRID REFERENCE
Beaufort	60 E1 [19]
Beaufort Court	46 F4 [10]
Beaufort Downs	46 F4
Beaufort Villas	46 F4 [3]
Beaumont	26 D1
Beaumont Avenue	47 B4
Beaumont Close	47 B4 [3]
Beaumont Cottages	34 D2
Beaumont Court	25 C1 [2]
Beaumont Crescent	26 D2
Beaumont Drive	47 B4
Beaumont Gardens	48 F4
Beaumont Grove	25 C2
Beaumont Hall	25 C2 [7]
Beaumont House	46 F2 [25]
Beaumont Road	25 C2
Beaumont Wood	25 C1 [3]
Beaupark Downs	49 B4 [15]
Beaupark Avenue	14 E4
Beaupark Close	14 E4
Beaupark Crescent	14 E4
Beaupark Mews	14 E4
Beaupark Place	14 E4
Beaupark Road	14 E4
Beaupark Row	14 E4
Beaupark Square	14 E4
Beaupark Street	14 E4
Beaupark Terrace	14 E4
Beauvale Park	26 D2
Beaver Close	38 E1 [51]
Beaver Row	47 C1
Beaver Street	38 E1
Beckett Hall	59 B4
Beckett Way	35 C4
Bedford Court	46 E1 [5]
*Bedford Lane (off Aston Quay)	38 D2
*Bedford Row (off Aston Quay)	38 D2
Beech Drive	57 B1
Beech Grove (Blackrock)	48 F2
Beech Grove (Lucan)	34 E2
Beech Hill	47 C2
Beech Hill Avenue	47 C2
Beech Hill Court	47 C1
Beech Hill Crescent	47 C2 [3]
Beech Hill Drive	47 C2
Beech Hill Road	47 C2
Beech Hill Terrace	47 C2 [4]
Beech Hill Villas	47 C2 [2]
Beech Lawn	57 B1
Beech Lodge	23 A4
Beech Park (Cabinteely)	59 C4
Beech Park (Castleknock)	22 F3
Beech Park (Lucan)	34 E1
Beech Park Avenue (Castleknock)	23 A3
Beech Park Avenue (Deans Grange)	59 B2
Beech Park Crescent	23 A3 [1]
Beech Park Drive	59 B2
Beech Park Grove	59 B2
Beech Park Lawn	23 A3
Beech Park Road	59 B2
Beech Road (Bray)	67 B1
Beech Road (Fox & Geese)	45 A1
Beech Row (Nangor Road)	44 D1 [3]
Beech Row (Newlands Road)	35 A4
Beech Walk	56 E2 [4]
Beechbrook Grove	14 D4 [4]
Beechcourt	60 D3
Beechdale	7 B3
Beechdale Avenue	55 B3
Beechdale Close	55 B3 [6]
Beechdale Court	55 B3
Beechdale Crescent	55 B3
Beechdale Lawn	55 B3
Beechdale Mews	47 B1 [19]
Beechdale Park	55 B3
Beechdale Place	55 C3
Beechdale Road	55 C3
Beechdale Way	55 B3
Beeches Park	60 E1
Beeches Road	58 D1
Beechfield	8 D4
Beechfield Avenue (Clonee)	8 D4
Beechfield Avenue (Walkinstown)	45 C2
Beechfield Close (Clonee)	8 D4
Beechfield Close (Walkinstown)	46 D2
Beechfield Court	8 D4
Beechfield Drive	8 D4
Beechfield Green	8 D4
Beechfield Haven	64 E2 [3]
Beechfield Heights	8 D4
Beechfield Lawn	8 E4
Beechfield Manor	64 E2
Beechfield Meadows	8 E4
Beechfield Mews	46 D2 [4]
Beechfield Place	8 E4
Beechfield Rise	8 E4
Beechfield Road (Clonee)	8 D4
Beechfield Road (Walkinstown)	45 C2
Beechfield View	8 E4
Beechfield Way	8 E4
Beechlawn	48 F3
Beechlawn Avenue (Ballinteer)	57 B1
Beechlawn Avenue (Coolock)	26 E1
Beechlawn Close	26 E1
Beechlawn Green	26 E1
Beechlawn Grove	26 E1
Beechlawn Manor	46 F2 [20]
Beechlawn Mews	46 F2 [21]
Beechmount Drive (Bird Avenue)	47 C3
Beechmount Drive (Windy Arbour)	47 C3
Beechpark Avenue	26 E1
Beechpark Close	23 A3 [3]
Beechpark Court	26 E1
Beechpark Orchard	23 A3
Beechurst	67 B2
Beechview	56 E2 [1]
Beechwood Avenue Lower	47 B1
Beechwood Avenue Upper	47 B1
Beechwood Close (Boghall Road)	67 C4
Beechwood Close (Hartstown)	21 C1
Beechwood Court	58 F1
Beechwood Downs	21 C1
Beechwood Grove	60 D1 [11]
Beechwood House	64 E2 [10]
Beechwood Lawn	60 D2
Beechwood Lawns	52 F2
Beechwood Park (Dun Laoghaire)	60 D1
Beechwood Park (Rathmines)	47 B1 [7]
Beechwood Road	47 B1
Beggar's Bush Buildings	38 F3
Beggars Bush Court	38 F3 [48]
Belarmine	58 D4
Belarmine Avenue	58 D4
Belarmine Close	58 D4
Belarmine Court	58 D4
Belarmine Drive	58 D4
Belarmine Grange	58 D4
Belarmine Heath	58 D4
Belarmine Park	58 D4
Belarmine Place	58 D4
Belarmine Square	58 D4
Belarmine Vale	58 D4
Belarmine Way	58 D4
Belcamp Avenue	13 B4
Belcamp Crescent	13 B4
Belcamp Gardens	13 B4
Belcamp Green	13 B4
Belcamp Grove	13 B4
Belcamp Lane	13 C4
Belclare Avenue	11 C4
Belclare Crescent	11 C4
Belclare Drive	11 C4
Belclare Green	11 C4
Belclare Grove	11 C4
Belclare Lawns	11 C4
Belclare Park	11 C4
Belclare Terrace	11 C4
Belclare View	11 C4
Belclare Way	11 C4
Belfield Close	47 C3 [8]
Belfield Court	48 D2
Belfield Downs	47 C4
Belfield Park Apts.	48 E3
Belfry Avenue	53 C2
Belfry Close	53 C2
Belfry Dale	53 C2
Belfry Gardens	53 C2
Belfry Green	53 C2
Belfry Hall	53 C2
Belfry Lawn	53 C2
Belfry Manor	53 C2
Belfry Meadows	53 C2
Belfry Park	53 C2
Belfry Place	53 C2
Belfry Rise	53 C2
Belfry Square	53 C2
Belfry Terrace	53 C2
Belfry Walk	53 C2
Belfry Way	53 C2
Belgard Close	44 F3 [2]
Belgard Green	44 E4
Belgard Heights	44 F4
Belgard Road	44 E3
Belgard Square	54 F1
Belgard Square East	54 F1
Belgard Square North	54 F1
Belgard Square South	54 F1
Belgard Square West	54 F1
Belgrave Avenue	47 B1
Belgrave Place (Monkstown)	49 B4 [10]
Belgrave Place (Rathmines)	47 A1 [15]
Belgrave Road (Monkstown)	49 B4
Belgrave Road (Rathmines)	47 A1
Belgrave Square (Monkstown)	49 B4
Belgrave Square (Rathmines)	47 A1
Belgrave Square East (Monkstown)	49 B4
Belgrave Square East (Rathmines)	47 A1
Belgrave Square North (Monkstown)	49 B4
Belgrave Square North (Rathmines)	47 A1
Belgrave Square South (Monkstown)	49 B4
Belgrave Square South (Rathmines)	47 A1
Belgrave Square West (Monkstown)	49 B4
Belgrave Square West (Rathmines)	47 A1
Belgrave Terrace (Bray)	68 D2 [10]
Belgrave Terrace (Monkstown)	49 B4 [11]
Belgrave Villas (Bray)	68 D2 [9]
Belgrave Villas (Rathmines)	47 B1 [16]
Belgree	9 B2
Belgree Avenue	9 B2
Belgree Close	9 B2
Belgree Court	9 B2
Belgree Drive	9 B2
Belgree Green	9 B2
Belgree Grove	9 B2
Belgree Heights	9 B2
Belgree Lawns	9 B2
Belgree Rise	9 B2
Belgree Square	9 B2
Belgree Walk	9 B2
Belgree Woods	9 B2
Belgrove Lawn	36 D2
Belgrove Park (Chapelizod)	36 D2
Belgrove Park (Vernon Avenue)	26 F4
Belgrove Road	26 F4
*Bella Avenue (off Bella St)	38 E1
*Bella Place (off Bella St)	38 E1
Bella Street	38 E1 [27]
Belleview Maltings	37 A2
Belleville	23 C4
Belleville Avenue	47 A2
Bellevue	37 C3
Bellevue Ave (Merrion)	48 E2
Bellevue Avenue (Dalkey)	60 E2
Bellevue Copse	48 E2
Bellevue Cottages	24 F3 [4]
Bellevue Court	48 E2 [2]
Bellevue Park	48 E2
Bellevue Park Avenue	48 E2
Bellevue Road	60 D2
Bellman's Walk	38 F2 [2]
Bell's Lane	1 C2
Bell's Lane	38 E3 [30]
Belmont (Irishtown)	67 C4
Belmont (Stillorgan)	59 A1
Belmont Avenue	47 C1
*Belmont Court (off Belmont Ave)	47 C1
Belmont Gardens	47 C1
Belmont Green	58 F1
Belmont Grove	58 F1
Belmont Lawn	58 F1
Belmont Park (Donnybrook)	47 C1 [3]
Belmont Park (Raheny)	27 A2
*Belmont Place (off Gardiner St Middle)	38 E1
Belmont Square	27 A2
*Belmont Terrace (off Stillorgan Road)	58 F1
Belmont Villas	47 C1
Belmount Court	25 C4 [18]
Belton Park Avenue	26 D3
Belton Park Gardens	26 D3
Belton Park Road	26 D3
Belton Park Villas	26 D3
Belton Terrace	67 C2 [44]
Belvidere Avenue	38 E1 [19]
Belvidere Court	38 D1 [11]
Belvidere Place	38 E1
Belvidere Road	38 D1
Ben Edar Road	37 B1
Ben Inagh Park	49 A3 [3]
Benbulbin Avenue	37 A4
Benbulbin Road	37 A4
Benburb Street	37 C2
Beneavin Court	24 F2
Beneavin Drive	24 F2
Beneavin Park	24 F1
Beneavin Road	24 F2
Bengal Terrace	24 F4 [4]
Benmadigan Road	37 A4
Benson Street	38 F2
Bentley Avenue	67 C4 [3]
Bentley Park	67 C4
Bentley Road	67 C4
Bentley Villas	49 C4 [17]
Beresford	25 B3
Beresford Avenue	25 B3
Beresford Green	25 B3
Beresford Lane	38 E2 [9]
Beresford Lawn	25 B3
Beresford Place	38 E2
Beresford Street	38 D2
Berkeley Avenue	38 D1 [55]
Berkeley Place	38 D1 [57]
Berkeley Road	38 D1
Berkeley Street	38 D1
Berkeley Terrace	38 F3 [36]
Bernard Curtis Court	36 F4
Bernard Curtis House	36 F4 [2]
Berryfield	34 D3
Berryfield Crescent	24 D2
Berryfield Drive	24 D2
Berryfield Lane	67 A3
Berryfield Road	24 D2
Berwick Avenue	1 B1
Berwick Court	1 B1
Berwick Crescent	1 B1
Berwick Drive	1 B1
Berwick Grove	1 B1
Berwick Hall	47 A4
Berwick Lawn	1 B1
Berwick Place	1 B1
Berwick Rise	1 B2
Berwick View	1 B1
Berwick Walk	1 B1
Berwick Way	1 B1
Berystede	38 E4 [25]
Bessborough Avenue	38 F1
Bessborough Parade	38 D4 [9]
Besser Drive	35 B4
Bethany House	39 B4 [4]
Bethesda Place	38 D1 [58]
Bettyglen	27 B2
Bettysford	44 E1 [3]

STREET NAME	PAGE/GRID REFERENCE
Bettystown Avenue	26 F3
Beverly Avenue	56 D1
Beverly Court	26 F4
Beverly Crescent	55 C2
Beverly Downs	55 C2
Beverly Drive	56 D2
Beverly Green	55 C2
Beverly Grove	56 D1
Beverly Heights	56 D2
Beverly Lawns	56 D2
Beverly Park	55 C1
Beverly Rise	55 C2
Bewley	34 E2
Bewley Avenue	34 E2
Bewley Drive	34 E2
Bewley Grove	34 E2
Bewley Lawn	34 E2
Bianconi Ave	53 B1
Big Lane	32 D3
Bigger Road	45 C2
Bill Shelly Park	23 C2
Binn Eadair Court	29 A1
Binn Eadair Crescent	29 A1
Binn Eadair View	29 A1
Birch Avenue	58 D2
Birch Dale (Foxrock)	59 A2 [9]
Birch Dale (Kill O'The Grange)	59 C1 [12]
Birch Grove	59 C1
Birchdale Close	2 E3
Birchdale Drive	2 E3
Birchdale Park	2 F3
Birchdale Road	2 E3
Birches Road	58 D1
Birchfield Avenue	47 C4
Birchfield Court	47 C4
Birchfield Heights	47 C4
Birchfield Lawn	47 C4
Birchfield Park	47 C4
Birch's Lane	47 C4
Birchview Avenue	45 A4
Birchview Close	45 A4
Birchview Court	45 A4
Birchview Drive	45 A4
Birchview Heights	45 A4
Birchview Lawn	45 A4
Birchview Rise	45 A4
Birchwood Close	44 E4
Birchwood Drive	54 E1
Birchwood Heights	54 E1
Bird Avenue	47 C3
Biscayne	3 C3
Bishop Street	38 D3
Bishops Lane	62 F2
Bishop's Orchard	9 B2
Bishop's Orchard Boulevard	9 B2
*Bishop's Orchard House Apts.	9 B2
Bisset's Strand	3 B2
Bissett's Loft Apts.	3 B2
Black Street	37 B2 [9]
Blackberry Lane (Portmarnock)	15 A1
Blackberry Lane (Rathmines)	38 D4 [8]
Blackberry Rise	15 A1
Blackburn Square	46 F4 [15]
Blackcourt Road	22 E1
Blackditch Drive	35 C3
Blackditch Road	35 C3
Blackglen Court	58 D3
Blackglen Road	57 C3
Blackhall Green	37 C2
Blackhall Little	5 B1
Blackhall Parade	37 C2 [4]
Blackhall Place	37 C2
Blackhall Street	37 C2 [13]
Blackheath Avenue	26 F4
Blackheath Court	26 F4
Blackheath Drive	26 E4
Blackheath Gardens	26 E4
Blackheath Grove	26 E4
Blackheath Park	26 E4
Blackhorse Avenue	37 B1
Blackhorse Avenue	23 C4
Blackhorse Grove	37 B1
Blackpitts	37 C3
Blackrock	49 A3
Blackthorn Avenue	58 E2

STREET NAME	PAGE/GRID REFERENCE
Blackthorn Close (Portmarnock)	4 D4
Blackthorn Close (Sandyford)	58 D2 [7]
Blackthorn Court	58 D2 [4]
Blackthorn Drive	58 D2
Blackthorn Green	58 D2 [6]
Blackthorn Grove	58 D2 [3]
Blackthorn Hill Avenue	52 E2
Blackthorn Hill Close	52 E2
Blackthorn Hill Crescent	52 E2
Blackthorn Hill Drive	52 E2
Blackthorn Hill View	52 E2
Blackthorn Road	58 D2
Blackwater Road	24 E3
Blackwood Close	21 A1
Blackwood Crescent	21 A1
Blackwood Drive	21 A1
Blackwood Lane	3 C4
Blackwood Lawn	21 A1
Blackwood Mews	21 A1
Blackwood Park	21 A1
Blackwood Place	21 A1
Blackwoods	3 B4
Blakeney House	2 E2
Blakeney House (Mews)	30 E3
*Blakes Villas (on Grangegorman Lower)	37 C1
Blakesfield	21 C1
Blakestown Cottages	22 D1
Blakestown Drive	22 D1
Blakestown Road	22 D1
Blakestown Way	22 D1
Blanchardstown	22 F2
Blanchardstown ByPass	22 F2
Blanchardstown Road North	9 B4
Blanchardstown Road South	22 D2
Blanchardstown Roundabout	22 F2
Blarney Park	46 E1
Blasket Square	22 F1
Blessington Court	38 D1 [56]
Blessington Lane	38 D1 [53]
*Blessington Place (off St Joseph's Parade)	38 D1
Blessington Road	53 C2
Blessington Street	38 D1
Bloomfield Avenue (Donnybrook)	38 E4
Bloomfield Avenue (Portobello)	38 D4
Bloomfield Cottages	38 D4 [49]
Bloomfield Park (Ballsbridge)	38 F4
Bloomfield Park (Rathmines)	38 D4 [46]
Bluebell	36 E4
Bluebell Avenue	36 E4
Bluebell Road	36 E4
Blundelstown	42 E3
Blunden Drive	13 C4
Blythe Avenue	38 F2 [4]
*Boardman's Lane (off Cork Street)	37 C3
Boden Dale	56 F1
Boden Heath	56 E1
Boden Heath Apts.	56 E1
Boden Mill	56 E2
Boden Park	56 E1
Boden Wood	46 F4
Boeing Road	12 F4
Boghall Road	67 B4
Boherboy	53 B2
Boherboy Road	53 B2
Bohernabreena Road	55 A3
Bolbrook Avenue	55 B1 [3]
Bolbrook Close	55 B1 [4]
Bolbrook Drive	55 B1 [1]
Bolbrook Grove	55 B1
Bolbrook Park	55 B1
Bolbrook Villas	55 B1
Bolton Green	1 A2
Bolton Street	38 D2
Bond Drive	39 A1
Bond Road	39 A1
Bond Street	37 C3
Bonham Street	37 C2
Boolavogue Road	38 F1 [13]
Boot Road	44 D2
Booterstown	48 E2
Booterstown Avenue	48 F3

STREET NAME	PAGE/GRID REFERENCE
*Booterstown Grove (off Booterstown Avenue)	48 F2
Booterstown Park	48 F3
Boranaraltry	61 B4
Boranaraltry Lane	61 C4
Boroimhe Alder	1 C3
Boroimhe Ash	1 C3
Boroimhe Aspen	1 C3
Boroimhe Beech	1 C3
Boroimhe Birches	1 C3
Boroimhe Blackthorn	1 C3
Boroimhe Cedars	1 C3
Boroimhe Cherry	1 C3
Boroimhe Elms	1 C3
Boroimhe Hawthorns	1 C3
Boroimhe Hazel	1 C3
Boroimhe Laurels	1 C3
Boroimhe Maples	1 C3
Boroimhe Oaks	1 C3
Boroimhe Pines	1 C3
Boroimhe Poplars	1 C3
Boroimhe Rowan	1 B3
Boroimhe Willows	1 C3
Botanic Avenue	25 A4
Botanic Hall	24 F3
Botanic Park	25 A4 [14]
Botanic Road	25 A4
Botanic Villas	25 A4 [10]
Bottle Works	39 A3
Boulevard Mount Eustace	9 B2
Boundary Road	39 A1
Bow Bridge	37 B3
*Bow Bridge Place	37 B3
Bow Lane East	38 D3 [37]
Bow Lane West	37 B3
Bow Street	37 C2
Boyne Court	37 C4 [31]
Boyne Lane	38 E3 [2]
Boyne Road	24 E3
Boyne Street	38 E3
Brabazon Cottages	67 C2 [16]
Brabazon House	37 C3
Brabazon Place	37 C3 [35]
Brabazon Row	37 C3 [18]
Brabazon Square	37 C3 [40]
Brabazon Street	37 C3 [17]
Bracken Drive	4 D4
Bracken Hill	57 C3
Bracken Road	58 D2
Brackenbush Park	60 D4
Brackenbush Road	60 D4
Bracken's Lane	38 E2 [28]
Brackenstown Avenue	1 C2
Brackenstown Road	1 C2
Braemor Avenue	47 A3
Braemor Drive	47 A3
Braemor Grove	47 A3
Braemor Park	47 A3
Braemor Road	47 A3
Braithwaite Street	37 C3
Bramblefield Court	8 F4
Bramblefield Crescent	8 F4
Bramblefield Drive	8 F4
Bramblefield Park	8 F4
Bramblefield View	8 F4
Bramblefield Walk	8 F4
Bramley Avenue	22 E3
Bramley Court	22 E3
Bramley Crescent	22 E3
Bramley Garth	22 E3
Bramley Green	22 E3
Bramley Grove	22 E3
Bramley Heath	22 E3
Bramley Park	22 E3
Bramley Road	22 E3
Bramley View	22 E3
Bramley Walk	22 E3
Bramley Way	22 E3
Brandon Road	45 C1
Brandon Road	36 F4
Brandon Terrace	37 B3 [32]
Bray	68 D1
Bray Commons	67 B2
Bray Head Terrace	67 C3 [20]
Bray Road	59 B2

STREET NAME	PAGE/GRID REFERENCE
Bray Road	59 C4
Bray Southern Cross Road	67 B4
Breakwater Road North	39 B1
Breakwater Road South	39 B2
Breffini Terrace	60 E1
Breffni Gardens	15 A4 [5]
Breffni Road	60 E1
Bregia Road	24 F4
Brehon Field Road	57 B2
Brehon's Chair	57 A3
Bremen Avenue	39 A3
Bremen Grove	39 A3
Bremen Road	39 A3
Brendan Behan Court	38 E1 [33]
Brendan Road	47 C1
Brennans Parade	68 D2 [14]
Brennans Terrace	68 D2 [4]
Brennanstown Avenue	59 C4
Brennanstown Road	59 B4
Brennanstown Square	59 C4
Brennanstown Vale	59 B4
Brewery Road	58 F2
Brian Avenue	25 C4
Brian Boru Avenue	39 C1
Brian Boru Street	39 C1
Brian Road	25 C4
Brian Terrace	25 C4
Briansboro Terrace	37 C4 [23]
Briar Walk	4 D4
Briar Wood	68 D3
Briarfield Grove	27 B1
Briarfield Road	27 B2
Briarfield Villas	27 B1 [5]
Briarly Court	47 B4 [4]
Briarsfield Walk	27 B1 [4]
Briarwood Avenue	22 D1
Briarwood Close	9 A4
Briarwood Gardens	22 D1
Briarwood Green	22 D1
Briarwood Lawn	22 D1
Briarwood Park	22 D1 [1]
Briarwood Road	22 D1 [3]
Brickfield	67 B3
Brickfield Drive	37 B4
Brickfield Lane	37 C3 [48]
Bride Close	38 D3 [55]
Bride Road	38 D3
Bride Street	38 D3
Bride Street New	38 D3
Brides Glen	63 C2
Bridge Street (Ringsend)	39 A3
Bridge Street (Swords)	2 D2
Bridge Street Lower	37 C2
Bridge Street Upper	37 C3
Bridgefoot Street	37 C2
Bridgeview	35 B3
Bridgewater Quay	37 A2
Bridon	62 F1
Brighton Avenue (Carrickmines)	59 A4
Brighton Avenue (Clontarf)	26 D4 [1]
Brighton Avenue (Monkstown)	49 B4
Brighton Avenue (Rathgar)	46 F2
Brighton Cottages	59 A3 [1]
Brighton Court	59 A4
Brighton Gardens	46 F2
Brighton Green	46 F2 [13]
Brighton Hall	59 A4
Brighton Lane	49 B4 [22]
Brighton Lodge	59 A3 [4]
Brighton Place	59 A4
Brighton Road (Foxrock)	59 A3
Brighton Road (Terenure)	46 F2
Brighton Square	46 F2
Brighton Terrace (Dun Laoghaire)	60 E1 [13]
Brighton Terrace (Monkstown)	49 B4 [9]
Brighton Vale	49 B3
Britain Place	38 D1 [47]
Britain Quay	38 F2
Broadfield Avenue	52 E2
Broadfield Close	52 E2
Broadfield Court	52 E2
Broadfield Heath	52 E2
Broadfield Manor	52 E2
Broadfield Meadows	52 E2

STREET NAME	PAGE/GRID REFERENCE	STREET NAME	PAGE/GRID REFERENCE	STREET NAME	PAGE/GRID REFERENCE	STREET NAME	PAGE/GRID REFERENCE
Broadfield Park	52 E2	Brookview Close	54 D1	Burnell Park Green	22 E4	Camac Court	37 A3 [10]
Broadford Avenue	57 B2	Brookview Court	54 D1	Burnell Square	14 D4	Camac Park	36 E4
Broadford Close	57 B2	Brookview Crescent	54 D1	Burren Court	11 C4	Camaderry Road	68 D3
Broadford Crescent	57 B2	Brookview Drive	54 D1	*Burris Court (off High Street)	38 D3	Camberley Oaks	47 B4
Broadford Drive	57 B2	Brookview Gardens	54 D1	Burrow Court (Poppintree)	11 C4	Cambridge Avenue	39 A3 [7]
Broadford Hill	57 B2	Brookview Green	54 D1	Burrow Court (Portmarnock)	15 A1	Cambridge Court	39 A3 [24]
Broadford Lawn	57 B2	Brookview Grove	54 D1	Burrow Road (Stepaside)	62 D1	Cambridge Park	39 A3
Broadford Park	57 B2	Brookview Lawns	54 D1	Burrow Road (Stepaside)	58 D4	Cambridge Road (Rathmines)	47 A1
Broadford Rise	57 B2	Brookview Park	54 D1	Burrow Road (Sutton)	29 B1	Cambridge Road (Ringsend)	39 A3
Broadford Road	57 B2	Brookview Rise	54 D1	Burrowfield Road	28 D1	*Cambridge Square	39 A3
Broadford Walk	57 B2	Brookview Terrace	54 D1	Burton Court	58 E2	(off Thorncastle St.)	
Broadmeadow	1 C1	Brookview Way	54 D1	Burton Hall Avenue	58 E2	Cambridge Street	39 A3 [1]
Broadstone Avenue	38 D1 [68]	Brookville	24 D1	Burton Hall Road	58 E2	Cambridge Terrace	49 C4 [24]
*Broadstone Avenue	38 D1	Brookville Crescent	26 E1 [2]	Burton Road	60 F2	(Dun Laoghaire)	
(off Royal Canal Bank)		Brookville Park (Artane)	26 E2	Bushfield Avenue	47 B1 [8]	Cambridge Terrace	38 E4 [7]
*Broadstone Place	38 D1	Brookville Park (Coolock)	26 E1	Bushfield Drive	44 D2	(Ranelagh)	
(off Royal Canal Bank)		Brookville Park (Dean's Grange)	59 B1	Bushfield Green	44 D2	Cambridge Villas	47 A1 [16]
Broadway Drive	22 E2	Brookwood	56 E2	Bushfield Grove	44 D3	Camden Avenue	23 C3
Broadway Grove	22 E2	Brookwood	67 B2 [29]	Bushfield Lawns	44 D2	Camden Buildings	38 D3 [54]
Broadway Park	22 E2	Brookwood Avenue	26 E2	Bushfield Place	47 B1 [17]	Camden Court	38 D4 [30]
Broadway Road	22 E2	Brookwood Crescent	26 F2	Bushfield Square	25 C4 [15]	Camden Lock	38 F3 [39]
Brockey	65 A1	Brookwood Drive	26 E2	Bushfield Terrace	47 B1	Camden Market	38 D4 [28]
Brockey	61 C4	Brookwood Glen	26 F3	Bushy Park Gardens	46 F3	Camden Place	38 D3
Brockey Lane	65 A1	Brookwood Grove	26 E2	Bushy Park House	46 E3	Camden Row	38 D3
Brodin Row	37 B2 [15]	Brookwood Hall	26 E3	Bushy Park Road	46 F3	Camden Street Lower	38 D3
Brompton Court	22 E3	Brookwood Heights	26 F2	Bustyhill	51 B3	Camden Street Upper	38 D4
Brompton Green	22 E2	Brookwood Lawn	26 F2	Buttercup Close	13 C4	Camden Villas	38 D3 [22]
Brompton Grove	22 E2	Brookwood Meadow	26 E2	Buttercup Drive	13 C4	Cameron Square	37 B3 [5]
Brompton Lawn	22 E2	Brookwood Park	26 E3	Buttercup Park	13 C4	Cameron Street	37 C3
Brook Court	49 B4	Brookwood Rise	26 F3	Buttercup Square	13 C4	Camogie Road	37 A2
Brookdale	55 A2	Brookwood Road	26 E2	Buttercup Terrace	13 C4	Campbell Court	30 D2 [16]
Brookdale Avenue	1 B3	Broombridge Road	24 E4	Butterfield Avenue	46 E4	Campbell's Court	38 D2 [34]
Brookdale Close	1 B2	Broomfield	21 B4	Butterfield Close	46 E4	Campbell's Lane	38 E1 [71]
Brookdale Court	1 B3	Broomfield (Malahide)	3 B4	Butterfield Court	46 F4	(off Belvidere Ave)	
Brookdale Drive	1 B2	Broomfield Court	64 E2	Butterfield Crescent	46 F4	Campbell's Row	38 E1 [69]
Brookdale Green	1 B2	Broomfield Mews	3 B4	Butterfield Drive	46 F4	(off Portland Street N)	
Brookdale Grove	1 B2	Broomhill Close	45 A4	Butterfield Grove	46 E4	Campfield Terrace	57 C1
Brookdale Lawns	1 B2	Broomhill Drive	45 A4	Butterfield Meadow	46 E4 [1]	Canal Road	38 D4
Brookdale Park	1 B2	Broomhill Road	45 A4	Butterfield Orchard	46 E4	Canal Terrace	36 E4
Brookdale Road	1 B2	Broomhill Terrace	45 A4	Butterfield Park	46 E4	Canal Turn	35 B4
Brookdale Walk	1 B2	(Off Broomhill Road)		*Byrne's Cottages (Francis Street)	37 C3	Cannon Mews East	38 F3 [47]
Brookdale Way	1 B2	Brown Street North	37 C2 [5]	Byrne's Lane (Jervis St)	38 D2 [31]	Cannon Rock Estate	30 E2
Brookdene	64 E2	Brown Street South	37 C3	*Byrne's Lane (Pearse Sq West)	38 F2	Cannon Rock View	30 E2 [1]
Brookfield (Blackrock)	48 F3	Brownrath	5 B1			Cannonbrook	34 D2
Brookfield (Coolock)	26 F2	Brownsbarn	43 C4	**C**		Cannonbrook Avenue	34 D2
Brookfield (Donnybrook)	47 C1 [19]	Brownsbarn Court	43 C4			Cannonbrook Court	34 D2
Brookfield (Lucan)	34 D3	Brownsbarn Garden	43 C4	Cabinteely	59 C4	Cannonbrook Lawn	34 D2
Brookfield (Milltown)	47 B2	Brownsbarn Orchard	43 C4	Cabinteely Avenue	59 C3	Cannonbrook Park	34 D2
Brookfield Avenue (Blackrock)	49 A4	Brownstown	42 D1	Cabinteely Bypass	59 C3	Canon Lillis Avenue	38 F1
Brookfield Avenue (Bray)	68 D3 [4]	Brownstown (Kilcloon)	5 B2	Cabinteely Close	59 C3	Canon Mooney Gardens	39 A3 [15]
Brookfield Avenue (Maynooth)	17 C4	Bruce's Terrace	67 B2	Cabinteely Court	59 C3 [2]	Capel Street	38 D2
Brookfield Court (Blackrock)	49 A4 [12]	Brug Chroimlinn	46 D1 [6]	Cabinteely Crescent	59 C3	Cappagh Avenue	24 D1
Brookfield Court (Kimmage)	46 E2 [6]	Brunswick Place	38 F3 [22]	Cabinteely Drive	59 C3	Cappagh Drive	24 D2
Brookfield Court (Tallaght)	54 D1 [1]	Brunswick Street North	37 C2	Cabinteely Green	59 C3	Cappagh Green	24 D1
Brookfield Estate	46 E2	Brunswick Villas (Pearse Street)	38 E2 [30]	Cabinteely Park	59 C3 [3]	Cappagh Road	24 D1
Brookfield Green	46 E2 [5]	Brusna Cottages	49 A3 [12]	Cabinteely Way	59 C3	Cappagh Road	10 E4
Brookfield Grove	49 A4 [11]	Buckingham St Lower	38 E1	Cabra	24 E4	Cappaghmore Estate	35 A4
Brookfield Park	17 C4	Buckingham St Upper	38 E1	Cabra Drive	37 B1	Cappoge	10 F4
Brookfield Place	49 A4	Buckingham Village	38 E1 [56]	Cabra Grove	37 B1	Cappoge Cottages	10 E4
Brookfield Road (Kilmainham)	37 B3	Buckleys Lane	33 A1	Cabra Park	24 F4	Captain's Avenue	46 D1
Brookfield Road (Tallaght)	54 D1	Bulfin Court	37 A3 [26]	Cabra Road	37 B1	Captain's Drive	46 D2
Brookfield Street	37 B3	Bulfin Gardens	37 A3	Caddell	14 F2	Captain's Hill	20 D4
Brookfield Terrace	49 A4	Bulfin Road	37 A3	Cadogan Road	25 C4	Captain's Road	46 D2
Brookhaven Drive	22 E1	Bull Alley Street	38 D3	Cairn Brook	63 A1	Cara Park	13 B3
Brookhaven Grove	22 E1	Bull Lane	67 C2 [59]	Cairn Brook Hall	63 A1	Caragh Court	25 C4 [12]
Brookhaven Lawn	22 E1	*Bull Lane (Off Main Street)	67 C2	Cairn Brook Manor	63 A1	Caragh Road	37 B1
Brookhaven Park	22 E1	Bull Wall	40 D1	Cairn Brook View	63 A1	Carberry Road	25 C3
Brookhaven Rise	22 E1	Bull Wall Cottages	40 D1	Cairn Brook Way	63 A1	Carbury Place	49 A3 [20]
Brooklands	48 E1	Bullock Steps	60 F1 [8]	Cairn Court	12 D4	Carbury Terrace	38 F2 [9]
Brooklawn (Blackrock)	48 F3	Bunratty Avenue	26 E1	Cairn Hill	59 B2	Cardiff Castle Road	24 D2
Brooklawn (Clontarf)	26 D4	Bunratty Drive	26 E1	Cairnfort	62 E1	Cardiff Lane	38 F2
Brooklawn (Lucan)	34 D3	Bunratty Road	26 E1	Cairnwood Avenue	44 E4	Cardiffs Bridge	24 D3
Brooklawn Avenue	49 B4 [12]	Bunting Road	45 C1	Cairnwood Court	44 E4	Cardiffsbridge Avenue	24 D2
Brooklawn Wood	49 B4 [13]	Burdett Avenue	60 E1	Cairnwood Green	44 E4	Cardiffsbridge Grove	24 D1 [1]
Brookmount Avenue	55 C1	Burg an Rí Glen	34 F3	Calderwood Avenue	25 C3	Cardiffsbridge Road	24 D2
Brookmount Court	46 E4 [2]	Burg an Rí Terrace	34 F3	Calderwood Grove	25 C3 [3]	Card's Lane (Pearse St)	38 E2 [13]
Brookmount Lawns	55 C1 [1]	Burgess Lane	37 C2 [18]	Calderwood Road	25 C3	Careys Lane	2 F4
Brookpark	34 D3	Burgh Quay	38 E2	Caledon Court	38 F1 [25]	Carfdiff Castle Road	24 D1
Brookstone Lane	15 A4 [6]	Burke Place	37 B3 [42]	Caledon Road	38 F1	Carleton Road	25 C4
Brookstone Road	15 A4	*Burke Place (off Mount Brown)	37 B3	Callary Road	48 D3	Carlingford Parade	38 F3 [4]
Brookvale	34 D1 [8]	Burleigh Court	38 E4 [34]	Calmount Avenue	45 B2	Carlingford Road	25 A4
Brookvale Downs	46 F3	Burlington Gardens	38 E4 [33]	Calmount Park	45 B2	Carlisle Avenue	47 B1
Brookvale Road (Donnybrook)	47 C1 [8]	Burlington Road	38 E4	Calmount Road	45 B2	Carlisle Court	46 F2 [23]
Brookvale Road (Rathfarnham)	46 F3	Burmah Close	60 F2 [22]	Camac Close	37 A3 [6]	Carlisle Street	38 D4
Brookview Avenue	54 D1	Burnell Park Avenue	22 E4				

STREET NAME	PAGE/GRID REFERENCE	STREET NAME	PAGE/GRID REFERENCE	STREET NAME	PAGE/GRID REFERENCE	STREET NAME	PAGE/GRID REFERENCE
Carlisle Terrace (Dún Laoghaire)	60 D1 [17]	Carriglea View	55 B2	Castle Grove (Clondalkin)	44 E1	Castlegate Square	33 C4
Carlisle Terrace (Malahide)	3 B3	Carriglea Walk	55 B2	Castle Grove (Clontarf)	26 E4	Castlegate Walk	33 C3
*Carlisle Terrace (Off N C Rd)	37 C1	Carrigmore Avenue	53 B2	Castle Grove (Stepaside)	58 E4	Castlegate Way	34 C3
*Carlisle Terrace (On Seymour Road)	67 C2	Carrigmore Close (Oldbawn)	54 F3	Castle Grove (Swords)	2 D2	Castlegrange	21 B1
*Carlisle Terrace (on Tivoli Road)	60 D1	Carrigmore Close (Saggart)	53 B2	Castle Lawn	58 E4	Castlegrange Avenue (Clonsilla)	21 B1
Carlton Court (Clontarf)	26 D4	Carrigmore Court	53 C2	Castle Lawns (Malahide)	2 F2	Castlegrange Avenue (Swords)	2 D1
Carlton Court (Swords)	2 D2	Carrigmore Crescent	53 C1	Castle Lawns (Tallaght)	45 B4	Castlegrange Close (Clondalkin)	43 B1
Carlton Terrace	67 C2 [41]	Carrigmore Dale	53 B2	*Castle Market (off Drury Street)	38 D3	Castlegrange Close (Swords)	2 D1
Carlton Villas (Ballsbridge)	38 F4 [6]	Carrigmore Downs	53 B1	Castle Park (Clondalkin)	44 E1	Castlegrange Court (Clondalkin)	43 C1
Carlton Villas (Clontarf)	67 C2 [42]	Carrigmore Drive	54 F2	Castle Park (Leixlip)	33 A1	Castlegrange Court (Clonsilla)	21 B1
Carmanhall Court	58 E2	Carrigmore Elms	53 B2	Castle Park (Monkstown)	49 C4	Castlegrange Dale	21 B1
Carmanhall Road	58 E2	Carrigmore Gardens	53 B1	Castle Park (Swords)	2 D2	Castlegrange Drive (Clondalkin)	43 B1
Carman's Hall	37 C3	Carrigmore Glen	53 B1	Castle Park (Tallaght)	45 B4	Castlegrange Drive (Clonsilla)	21 B1
Carna Road	35 C3	Carrigmore Green	53 B2	Castle Park Estate (Tallaght)	55 B1	Castlegrange Gardens	21 B1
Carndonagh Drive	27 B1	Carrigmore Grove (Oldbawn)	54 F3	*Castle Place (on Breffni Road)	60 F1	Castlegrange Green (Clondalkin)	43 B1
Carndonagh Lawn	27 B1	Carrigmore Grove (Saggart)	53 B2	Castle Riada Avenue	34 E3	Castlegrange Green (Clonsilla)	21 B1
Carndonagh Park	27 B1	Carrigmore Lawns	53 B1	Castle Riada Crescent	34 E2	Castlegrange Green (Swords)	2 D1
Carndonagh Road	27 B1	Carrigmore Manor	53 B2	Castle Riada Drive	34 E3	Castlegrange Grove	8 E4
Carne Court	8 F4	Carrigmore Meadows	53 B2	Castle Riada Grove	34 E2	Castlegrange Grove	8 E4
Carnegie Court	2 D1	Carrigmore Oak	53 B2	Castle Road	34 F3	Castlegrange Heights	2 D1
Carnew Street	37 B1 [9]	Carrigmore Park	54 F3	Castle Road (Clontarf)	26 E4	Castlegrange Hill	2 D1
Carnlough Road	24 E4	Carrigmore Place	53 B2	Castle Road (Lucan)	34 E2	Castlegrange Lawn (Clondalkin)	43 C1
Caroline Row	39 A3 [16]	Carrigmore Road	54 F2	Castle Rosse	14 F4	Castlegrange Lawn (Clonsilla)	21 B1
Carpenterstown	22 D3	Carrigmore Terrace	53 B2	*Castle Steps (off Castle St)	38 D3	Castlegrange Park	21 B1
Carpenterstown Avenue	22 E3	Carrigmore View	54 F3	Castle Street (Bray)	67 C2	Castlegrange Road (Clondalkin)	43 C1
Carpenterstown Manor	22 E3	Carrigmore Way	53 C2	Castle Street (Cork Hill)	38 D3 [3]	Castlegrange Road (Swords)	2 D1
Carpenterstown Park East	22 E3	Carrigwood	55 C2	Castle Street (Dalkey)	60 F2	Castlegrange Row	21 B1
Carpenterstown Road	22 E4	Carrow Road	36 F4	Castle Terrace (Malahide)	3 B2	Castlegrange Square (Clondalkin)	43 C1
Carraig Close	11 C4	Carton Avenue	18 D2	*Castle Terrace (off Ulverton Road)	60 F1	Castlegrange Square (Clonsilla)	21 B1
Carraig Glen	59 C4	Carton Court	18 D4	Castle Terrace (Phibsborough Ave)	37 C1 [17]	Castlegrange Terrace	21 B1
Carraig Grennane	60 E4	Carton Court	17 C4	Castle View (Carrickmines)	59 A4	Castlegrange Way	2 D1
Carraroe Avenue	27 A1	Carwell Court	2 E2	Castle View (Clondalkin)	44 E1	Castleheath	3 A3
Carrick Court	14 F1	Carysfort Avenue	49 A4	Castle Village	31 C2	Castlekevin Road	26 D1
Carrick Lawn	58 D1 [2]	Carysfort Downs	58 F1	Castle Village Avenue	31 C2	Castleknock	22 F3
Carrick Terrace	37 B3 [29]	Carysfort Downs	59 A1	Castle Village Close	31 C2	Castleknock Avenue	22 F3
Carrickaspinkeen	65 A3	Carysfort Drive	60 F1 [1]	Castle Village Court	31 C2	Castleknock Brook	22 F3
Carrickbrack	30 D4	Carysfort Grove	59 A1	Castle Village Crescent	31 C2	Castleknock Close	22 E3
Carrickbrack Heath	29 B2	Carysfort Hall	49 A4	Castle Village Drive	31 C2	Castleknock Court	22 F3 [2]
Carrickbrack Hill	29 B2	Carysfort Park	49 A4	Castle Village Green	31 C2	Castleknock Crescent	22 F3
Carrickbrack Lawn	29 B2	Carysfort Road	60 F1	Castle Village Lawns	31 C2	Castleknock Dale	22 F3
Carrickbrack Park	29 B2	Carysfort Woods	59 A1	Castle Village Park	31 C2	Castleknock Downs	22 E3
Carrickbrack Road	29 B2	Casana View	30 E2	Castle Village Place	31 C2	Castleknock Drive	22 F3
Carrickbrennan Lawn	49 C4	Casement Close (off Barry Road)	24 D1 [2]	Castle Village Rise	31 C2	Castleknock Elms	22 F3
Carrickbrennan Road	49 C4	Casement Drive	24 D1	Castle Village Walk	31 C2	Castleknock Gate	23 B4 [1]
Carrickfoyle Terrace	37 A3 [15]	Casement Green	24 D1	Castle Village Way	31 C2	Castleknock Glade	22 F3
Carrickhill Close	4 D4	Casement Grove	24 D1	Castle Village Woods	31 C2	Castleknock Grange	22 F3
Carrickhill Drive	15 A1	Casement Park	24 D1	Castle Villas	60 F2	Castleknock Green	23 A3
Carrickhill Heights	15 A1	Casement Road	24 D1	Castlebridge	18 D3	Castleknock Grove	22 F3
Carrickhill Rise	4 D4	Casement Road	24 D2	Castlebrook	57 C1	Castleknock Laurels	22 F3
Carrickhill Road	15 A1	Casement Villas	59 B1	Castlebyrne Park	49 A4	Castleknock Lodge	23 A4
Carrickhill Road Middle	15 A1	Cashel Avenue	46 E2	Castlecurragh Heath	9 A4	Castleknock Manor	23 A3 [5]
Carrickhill Road Upper	3 C4	Cashel Road	46 D1	Castlecurragh Park	9 B4	Castleknock Meadows	22 F3
Carrickhill Walk	4 D4	Casimir Avenue	46 F1	Castlecurragh Vale	9 B4	Castleknock Oaks	22 F3
Carrickmines	59 B4	Casimir Court	46 F1 [17]	Castledawson Avenue	48 F3	Castleknock Park	23 A3
Carrickmines Avenue	59 B4	Casimir Road	46 F1	Castlefarm	1 C1	Castleknock Rise	22 E3
Carrickmines Chase	59 B4	Casino Park	26 D3	Castlefield Avenue	55 C1	Castleknock Road	22 F3
Carrickmines Dale	59 B4	Casino Road	25 C4	Castlefield Court (Clonsilla)	21 C2	Castleknock Road	23 A4
Carrickmines Garth	59 B4	Cassian Court	24 D3 [2]	Castlefield Court (Firhouse)	55 C1	Castleknock Vale	22 F3
Carrickmines Green	63 A1	Castaheany	8 E4	Castlefield Drive	55 C2	Castleknock View	22 F3
Carrickmines Little	59 A4	Castilla Park	26 F4	Castlefield Green	55 C2	Castleknock Walk	22 E3
Carrickmines Manor	63 A1	Castle Avenue (Clondalkin)	44 E1	Castlefield Grove	55 C2	Castleknock Way	22 F3
Carrickmines Oaks	59 B4	Castle Avenue (Clontarf)	26 E4	Castlefield Lawn	55 C1	Castleknock Wood	22 F3
Carrickmount Avenue	57 B1	Castle Avenue (Swords)	2 D2	Castlefield Manor (Firhouse)	55 C1	Castlelands	60 F1 [16]
Carrickmount Drive	57 A1	Castle Close (Clondalkin)	44 E1	Castlefield Manor (Malahide)	3 B3	Castlelands Grove	60 F1 [12]
Carrig Road	11 C4	Castle Close (Dalkey)	60 F1	Castlefield Orchard	55 C1	Castlemoyne	14 D3
Carrigallen Drive	24 E3	Castle Court (Booterstown)	48 F2	Castlefield Park ((Firhouse)	55 C1	Castlepark Court	60 E2 [9]
Carrigallen Park	24 E3	Castle Court (Clontarf)	26 D4	Castlefield Park (Clonsilla)	21 C2	Castlepark Road	60 E1
Carrigallen Road	24 E3	Castle Court (Dundrum)	57 C1 [4]	Castlefield Way	55 C2	Castlerosse Crescent	14 F4
Carrigeen	52 D3	Castle Court (Loughlinstown)	64 E1	Castlefield Woods	21 C2	Castlerosse Drive	14 F4
Carriglea Avenue (Kill O'The Grange)	59 C2	*Castle Court (off Cypress Lawn)	46 D4	Castleforbes Road	38 F2	Castlerosse View	14 F4
Carriglea Avenue (Tallaght)	55 B2	Castle Court (Rathfarnham)	46 F4 [18]	Castlegate (Lucan)	33 C1	Castleside Drive	46 F3
Carriglea Court (Kill O'The Grange)	59 C1 [14]	Castle Court (Rathfarnham)	47 A4 [1]	Castlegate (Monkstown)	59 C1	Castletimon Avenue	25 C1
Carriglea Court (Tallaght)	55 B2	Castle Cove (Dalkey)	60 F2 [32]	Castlegate (Shankill)	64 D3	Castletimon Drive	25 C1
Carriglea Downs (Kill O'The Grange)	59 C2	Castle Cove (Malahide)	3 A2	Castlegate Chase	33 C3	Castletimon Gardens	25 C1
Carriglea Downs (Tallaght)	55 B2	Castle Crescent	44 E1 [4]	Castlegate Close	33 C3	Castletimon Green	25 C1
Carriglea Drive	55 B2	Castle Dawson	17 B3	Castlegate Crescent	33 C3	Castletimon Park	25 C1
Carriglea Gardens	59 C1	Castle Down Croft	2 F2	Castlegate Dene	33 C4	Castletimon Road	25 C1
Carriglea Grove	55 B2	Castle Down Grove	2 F2	Castlegate Drive	33 C3	Castletown	32 F1
Carriglea Rise	55 B2	Castle Down Road	2 F2	Castlegate Elms	33 C3	Castletown Court	32 D3
		Castle Drive (Clondalkin)	44 E1	Castlegate Green	33 C3	Castletown Drive	32 D3
		Castle Drive (Swords)	2 D2	Castlegate Grove	33 C3	Castletown Grove	32 D3
		Castle Elms	26 E1	Castlegate Park	33 C4	Castletown Lawn	32 D3
		Castle Farm	64 E3	Castlegate Place	33 C4	Castletymon Court	45 B4
		Castle Farm Wood	64 E3			Castletymon Gardens	45 B4

STREET NAME	PAGE/GRID REFERENCE		STREET NAME	PAGE/GRID REFERENCE		STREET NAME	PAGE/GRID REFERENCE		STREET NAME	PAGE/GRID REFERENCE	
Castletymon Green	45	B4	Chanel Avenue	26	E2	Cherrington Drive	64	E3	Church Avenue (Rathmines)	47	A1
Castleview	26	E4	Chanel Grove	26	E1	Cherrington Road	64	E3	Church Avenue South (Dolphin's Barn)	37	B3 22
Castleview (Artane)	26	E2	Chanel Road	26	E2	Cherry Avenue (Carpenterstown)	22	E3			
Castleview (Dunboyne)	7	B3	*Chapel Avenue (off Bath St)	39	A3	Cherry Avenue (Swords)	1	C3	Church Avenue West (Church Street)	37	C2 25
Castleview (Dundrum)	57	C1 7	Chapel Crescent	24	D3	Cherry Court (Loughlinstown)	64	D1 2	*Church Avenue (off Irvine Street)	38	F2
Castleview Park	3	A3	Chapel Lane (Bray)	67	B1	Cherry Court (Terenure)	46	F2			
Castlewarden	51	A3	Chapel Lane (Parnell Street)	38	D2 13	Cherry Drive	22	E3	Church Court (Castleknock)	22	F3
Castlewarden North	51	A3	Chapel Lane (Swords)	2	D2	Cherry Garth (Stillorgan)	48	E4	Church Court (East Wall)	38	F1
Castlewood	21	C1	Chapel Road	14	D1	Cherry Garth (Swords)	1	C2	Church Gardens	47	A1
Castlewood Avenue	47	A1	Chapel View Apts.	34	D1	Cherry Grove (Crumlin)	45	C2	Church Green	46	F1
Castlewood Close	47	A1 24	Chapelizod	36	E2	Cherry Grove (Swords)	1	B3	Church Grove	55	A2
Castlewood Park	47	A1	Chapelizod Bypass	36	E2	Cherry Lawn	22	E3	Church Lands	67	C3
Castlewood Place	47	A1 6	Chapelizod Court	36	E2	Cherry Lawns	33	C2	Church Lane (College Green)	38	D2 41
Castlewood Terrace	47	A1 5	Chapelizod Hill Road	36	E2	Cherry Lodge	23	A4	Church Lane (Rathfarnham)	46	F3
Cathal Brugha Street	38	D2	Chapelizod Road	36	F2	Cherry Orchard Avenue	35	C3	Church Lane South	38	D3 53
Cathedral Lane	38	D3 5	Charlemont	25	C3	Cherry Orchard Court	35	C4	*Church Lane South (off Kevin Street)	38	D3
Cathedral Street	38	D2	Charlemont Avenue	50	D4 5	Cherry Orchard Crescent	35	C4			
Cathedral View Court	38	D3 43	Charlemont Gardens	38	D4 20	Cherry Orchard Drive	35	C4	Church Park	46	F1
Cathedral View Walk	38	D3 44	Charlemont Mall	38	D4	Cherry Orchard Green	35	C3	Church Park Avenue	46	F1
*Catherine Court (off William Street N)	38	E1	Charlemont Parade	38	E1 5	Cherry Orchard Grove	35	C4	Church Park Court	46	F1
			Charlemont Place	38	E4	Cherry Orchard Parade	35	C4	Church Park Drive	46	F1
Catherine Lane	37	C2 22	Charlemont Road	26	D4	Cherry Orchard Way	35	C4 1	Church Park Lawn	46	F1
Catherine Street (Swift's Alley)	37	C3 45	Charlemont Street	38	D4	Cherry Park (Carpenterstown)	22	E3	Church Park Way	46	F1
Cats Ladder	60	F2 5	Charlemont Terrace	50	D4 18	Cherry Park (Swords)	1	B3	*Church Place (off Irvine Terrace)	38	F2
Causeway Road	27	B3	Charles Lane	38	E1	Cherry Tree Drive	67	C3 1			
Cavendish Row	38	D1 21	*Charles Sheils Houses	58	F2	Cherry Wood	64	D1	Church Road (Ballybrack)	60	E4
*Ceannt Fort (off Mount Brown)	37	B3	Charles Street Great	38	E1	Cherryfield Avenue	45	C2	Church Road (Bray)	67	C3
Cecil Avenue	26	D4	*Charles Street West (off Ormond Quay Upper)	38	D2	Cherryfield Avenue Lr	47	B1	Church Road (Celbridge)	32	D4
*Cecilia Street (off Temple Bar)	38	D2				Cherryfield Avenue Upr	47	B1	Church Road (Dalkey)	60	F1
Cedar Avenue	45	A3	Charleston Avenue	47	B1	Cherryfield Close	21	C1	Church Road (East Wall)	38	F1
*Cedar Brook	35	C4	Charleston Court Flats	47	B1 9	Cherryfield Court	21	B1	Church Road (Finglas)	24	D2
Cedar Brook Avenue	35	B3	Charleston Road	47	B1	Cherryfield Drive	45	C2	Church Road (Killiney)	60	D3
Cedar Brook Place	35	B3	Charlestown Avenue	11	B4	Cherryfield Lawn	21	C1	Church Road (Malahide)	3	B3
Cedar Brook Walk	35	B3	Charlestown Avenue	11	A4	Cherryfield Park	21	C1	Church Road (Mulhuddart)	9	A4
Cedar Court (Loughlinstown)	64	D1	Charlestown Court	11	B4	Cherryfield Road	45	C2	Church Road (Rathcoole)	52	E2
Cedar Court (Terenure)	46	F2	Charlestown Drive	11	B4	Cherryfield View	21	B1	Church Road (Sutton)	29	B1
Cedar Drive (Dunboyne)	7	B2	Charlestown Green	11	B4	Cherryfield Walk	21	B1	Church Road (Swords)	2	D2
Cedar Drive (Palmerstown)	35	B2	Charlestown Park	11	B4	Cherryfield Way	46	D4	Church Street (Finglas)	24	E2
Cedar Grove	21	C2 2	Charlestown Way	11	B4	Cherrymount Crescent	26	D3 1	Church Street (Four Courts)	37	C2
Cedar Hall	47	C1 16	Charleville	47	B4	Cherrymount Grove	26	D3 2	Church Street (Howth)	30	D1
Cedar Lodge	23	A4	Charleville Avenue	38	E1	Cherrymount Park	37	C1 3	Church Street East	38	F2
Cedar Lodge Apts	56	E2	Charleville Close	47	A1	Cherrywood	32	D3	Church Street New	37	C2 11
Cedar Park (Donaghmede)	27	A1	Charleville Mall	38	E1	Cherrywood Avenue	44	D1	Church Street Upper	37	C2
Cedar Park (Leixlip)	19	C4	Charleville Road (Phibsborough)	37	C1	Cherrywood Crescent	43	C1	Church Terrace (Bray)	67	C2 45
Cedar Square (Stillorgan)	48	F4 4	Charleville Road (Rathmines)	47	A1	Cherrywood Drive	43	C1	Church Terrace (Finglas)	24	E2
Cedar Square (Swords)	1	B3	Charleville Square	46	E4	Cherrywood Grove	44	D1	*Church Terrace (off Church Street)	37	C2
Cedar Walk	27	B2	*Charleville Terrace(on Charleville Rd)	37	C1	Cherrywood Lawn	43	C2			
Cedarhurst Green	23	B3				Cherrywood Park (Clondalkin)	43	C2	Church View (Clondalkin)	44	D2 1
Cedarhurst Road	23	B3	Charlotte Quay	38	F3	Cherrywood Park (Loughlinstown)	64	D1	Church View (Drumcondra)	25	B3
Cedarmount Road	48	E4	Charlotte Terrace	60	F2 18				Church View (Finglas)	24	D2 7
Cedarwood	32	D3	Charlotte Way	38	D4 32	Cherrywood Road	64	D2	Church View (Harold's Cross)	46	F1
Cedarwood Avenue	24	F1	Charlton Lawn	48	D4	Cherrywood Villas	43	C1	Church Villas	59	C4 2
Cedarwood Close	24	F1	Charnwood (Bray)	67	C3	Cherrywood Villas	44	D1 6	Church Walk	24	D4
Cedarwood Green	24	F1	Charnwood (Clonsilla)	21	C2	Chester Downs	60	D1	Churchfields	47	C2
Cedarwood Grove	24	F1	Charnwood Avenue	21	C2	Chester Road	47	B1	Churchgate Avenue	39	C1 1
Cedarwood Park	24	F1	Charnwood Court	21	C2	Chester Square	60	E1 23	Churchill Mews	60	F1 17
Cedarwood Rise	24	F1	Charnwood Dale	21	C2	Chesterfield Avenue (Castleknock)	23	C1	Churchill Terrace	39	A4 6
Cedarwood Road	24	F1	Charnwood Gardens	21	C2				Churchland's	58	D3 1
Ceder Park	1	B3	Charnwood Green	21	C2	Chesterfield Avenue (Phoenix Park)	23	B4	Churchtown	47	B4
Ceder View	1	B3	Charnwood Grove	21	C2				Churchtown Avenue	47	B3
Celbridge	32	D3	Charnwood Heath	21	C2	Chesterfield Avenue (Phoenix Park)	36	F1	Churchtown Close	47	B3
Celbridge Abbey	31	C4	Charnwood Meadows	21	C2				Churchtown Drive	47	B3
Celbridge Road (Leixlip)	32	F2	Charnwood Park	21	C2	Chesterfield Close	23	B4	Churchtown Road Lower	47	B3
Celbridge Road (Lucan)	33	B2	Charter House	17	C3 7	Chesterfield Copse	23	B3	Churchtown Road Upper	47	A4
Celbridge Road (Maynooth)	18	D4	*Chatham Court (on Chatham Street)	38	D3	Chesterfield Grove	23	B4	Churchtown Road Upper	47	B4
*Celestine Avenue (off Dermot O'Hurley Ave)	39	A3				Chesterfield Park	23	B3	Churchview Avenue	60	D3
			*Chatham Lane (off Chatham Street)	38	D3	Chesterfield View	23	B3	Churchview Drive	60	D3
Celtic Park Avenue	25	C2	Chatham Row	38	D3 35	Chestnut Court	25	C2 1	Churchview Park	60	D3
Celtic Park Road	25	C2	Chatham Street	38	D3	Chestnut Grove (Ballinteer)	57	B2	Churchview Road	60	D3
Cenecle Grove	64	E1	*Chaworth Terrace (Hanbury Lane)	37	C3	Chestnut Grove (Celbridge)	32	D3	Cian Park	25	B4
Chalet Gardens	34	E1				Chestnut Grove (Clondalkin)	44	F3	Cianlea	1	B1
Chalfont Avenue	3	B2	Cheeverstown Road	54	D1	Chestnut Grove (Dunboyne)	7	B3	Cill Cais	54	F2
Chalfont Park	3	B2	Chelmsford Avenue	38	E4 8	Chestnut Park	59	A2 5	Cill Eanna	26	F2
Chalfont Place	3	B2	Chelmsford Lane	47	B1 15	Chestnut Road (Clondalkin)	45	A1	Cill Manntan Park	67	C2 9
Chalfont Road	3	A2	Chelmsford Road	47	B1	Chestnut Road (Mount Merrion)	48	E3	Cill Sarain	67	B3
*Chamber Court (off Chamber St)	37	C3	Chelsea Gardens	26	F4	Christchurch Place	38	D3	City Quay	38	E2
			Cheltenham Place	38	D4 13	Christchurch Square	38	D3 51	Citywest Avenue	53	C1
Chamber Street	37	C3	Cherbury Court	48	F3	Church Avenue (Blanchardstown)	22	F2	Citywest Road	53	C1
Chamley Park	2	F3	Cherbury Gardens	48	F3	Church Avenue (Drumcondra)	25	B3	Claddagh Green	35	C3
Champions Avenue	38	E2 32	Cherbury Mews	48	F3 4	Church Avenue (Glasnevin)	25	A3 2	Claddagh Road	35	C3
Chancel Mews	24	D4	Cherbury Park Avenue	34	D2	Church Avenue (Irishtown)	39	A4	Claddagh Terrace	68	D2 15
Chancery Lane	38	D3	Cherbury Park Road	34	D2	Church Avenue (Killiney)	60	E4	*Claddagh Terrace (On Strand Road)	67	C2
Chancery Place	38	D2	Cherries Road	58	D2	Church Avenue (Portmarnock)	14	F2 2			
Chancery Street	38	D2	Cherrington Close	64	E3				Clanawley Road	26	E3

STREET NAME	PAGE/GRID REFERENCE
Clanboy Road	26 E3
Clanbrassil Close	37 C4 [17]
Clanbrassil Street Lower	37 C4
Clanbrassil Street Upper	37 C4
Clancarthy Road	26 D3
Clancy Avenue	24 E1
Clancy Road	24 E1
Clandonagh Road	26 D3
Clane Road	31 B4
Clanfadda Wood	48 F3
Clanhugh Road	26 E3
Clanmahon Road	26 E3
Clanmaurice Road	26 D3
Clanmawr	64 E2
Clanmoyle Road	26 D3
Clanranald Road	26 D3
Clanree Road	26 D3
Clanwilliam Place	38 F3
Clanwilliam Square	38 F3 [41]
Clanwilliam Terrace	38 F3 [40]
Clare Hall	14 D4
Clare Lane	38 E3 [14]
Clare Park Villas	25 B3 [3]
Clare Road	25 B3
Clare Street	38 E3
Claremont Avenue	25 A3 [1]
Claremont Close	24 F4
Claremont Court (Finglas)	24 F4
Claremont Court (Sandymount)	39 A4 [21]
Claremont Crescent	24 F4
Claremont Drive	24 F2
Claremont Grove	60 E3
Claremont Lawn	24 F4
Claremont Mews	29 C1
Claremont Park	39 A4
Claremont Road (Carrickmines)	59 B4
Claremont Road (Killiney)	60 E3
Claremont Road (Sandymount)	39 A4
Claremont Road (Sutton)	29 B1
Claremont Terrace	47 C4 [7]
Claremont Villas	60 E1 [4]
Claremount	64 E3
Claremount Pines	59 B4
Claremount Terrace	68 D2 [11]
Clarence Mangan Road	37 C3
*Clarence Mangan Square (off John Dillon St)	38 D3
Clarence Place Great	38 F3 [1]
Clarence St Great North	38 E1 [67]
Clarence Street	49 C4
*Clarendon Market (off William St)	38 E1
*Clarendon Row (off King St South)	38 D3
Clarendon Street	38 D3
Clareville Court	24 F4 [7]
Clareville Grove	24 F4
Clareville Road	46 F1
Clarinda Manor	60 D1
Clarinda Park East	60 D1
Clarinda Park North	50 D4
Clarinda Park West	50 D4
Clarke Terrace	37 B3 [16]
Clarkeville Terrace	35 C1 [3]
Claude Road	25 A4
Clayton Terrace	36 E2 [8]
Clearwater Court	24 D3 [1]
Clearwater Cove	49 C4 [31]
Cleggan Avenue	35 C3
Cleggan Park	35 C3
Cleggan Road	35 C3
Clifden Drive	35 C3
Clifden Road	36 D3
Cliff Terrace	60 E1 [18]
Clifford's Lane	2 E2
Clifton Avenue	49 C4 [11]
Clifton Lane	49 C4 [10]
Clifton Park	64 E2
Clifton Terrace	49 C4 [13]
Cliftonville Road	25 A4
Clinch's Court	38 E1 [7]
Clogher Road	46 E1
Cloghran	1 C4
Cloghran Roundabout	1 C4
Cloister Avenue	49 A4

STREET NAME	PAGE/GRID REFERENCE
Cloister Close	48 F4
Cloister Court	24 D3
Cloister Gate	49 A4
Cloister Green	49 A4
Cloister Grove	49 A4
Cloister Park	49 A4
Cloister Square	49 A4
Cloister Way	49 A4
Clonallen	46 E2 [11]
Clonard Avenue	57 C2
Clonard Close	57 C2
Clonard Court	46 E2 [8]
Clonard Drive	57 C2
Clonard Grove	57 C2
Clonard Lawn	57 C2
Clonard Park	57 C2
Clonard Road (Crumlin)	46 D1
Clonard Road (Sandyford)	57 C2
Clonasleigh	64 E2 [2]
Cloncourt Apts.	8 D3
Clondalkin	44 D1
Clonee	8 D3
Clonee Bypass	8 D3
Clonfert Road	46 E1
Clongriffin	14 E4
Clonkeen Court	59 B3
Clonkeen Crescent	59 B2
Clonkeen Drive	59 B2
Clonkeen Grove	59 B2
Clonkeen Lawn	59 B3 [5]
Clonkeen Road	59 B3
Clonkeen Road	59 B2
Clonlara Avenue	43 A4
Clonlara Road (Naas Road)	43 A4
Clonlara Road (Ringsend)	39 A3 [12]
Clonlea	57 C2
Clonlea Wood	57 C2 [1]
Clonliffe Avenue	38 E1
Clonliffe Gardens	25 B4
Clonliffe Road	25 B4
Clonmacnoise Grove	46 E1 [4]
Clonmacnoise Road	46 E1
Clonmel Road	25 A2
Clonmel Street	38 D3 [18]
Clonmellon Grove	14 D4 [3]
Clonmore Court	25 A3 [11]
Clonmore Road (Ballybough)	38 E1
Clonmore Road (Goatstown)	48 E4
Clonmore Terrace	38 E1 [6]
Clonmore Villas	38 E1 [39]
Clonrosse Court	26 F1
Clonrosse Drive	26 F1
Clonrosse Park	26 F1
Clonshaugh Avenue	13 A4
Clonshaugh Close	13 B4
Clonshaugh Court	13 B4 [4]
Clonshaugh Crescent	13 A4
Clonshaugh Drive	13 B4
Clonshaugh Glen	13 B4
Clonshaugh Green	13 B4
Clonshaugh Grove	13 B4
Clonshaugh Heights	13 A4
Clonshaugh Lawns	13 B4
Clonshaugh Meadow	13 A4
Clonshaugh Park	13 B4
Clonshaugh Rise	13 B4 [2]
Clonshaugh Road	13 A4
Clonshaugh Walk	13 B4
Clonsilla	21 C2
Clonsilla Close	22 E2
Clonsilla Park	22 E2
Clonsilla Road	22 E2
Clonskeagh	47 C2
Clonskeagh Drive	47 C2 [6]
Clonskeagh Road	47 C2
Clonskeagh Square	47 C2 [7]
Clontarf	39 C1
Clontarf Park	39 C1
Clontarf Road	26 D4
Clonturk Avenue	25 B3 [1]
Clonturk Court	25 B3 [6]
Clonturk Gardens	25 B4 [3]
Clonturk Park	25 B4
Cloonlara Crescent	24 E3
Cloonlara Drive	24 E2

STREET NAME	PAGE/GRID REFERENCE
Cloonlara Road	24 E3
Cloonmore Avenue	54 D2
Cloonmore Close	54 D2
Cloonmore Crescent	54 D2
Cloonmore Drive	54 D2
Cloonmore Gardens	54 D2
Cloonmore Green	54 D2
Cloonmore Grove	54 D2
Cloonmore Lawn	54 D2
Cloonmore Park	54 D2
Cloonmore Road	54 D2
Cloragh Road	56 E4
Clover Hill	67 B3
Clover Hill Drive	36 D3
Clover Hill Road	36 D4
Cloverhill Road	35 A4
Cloyne Road	46 E1 [2]
Cluain Aoibhinn	17 C4
Cluain Mhuire	60 D1
Cluain Rí	34 F2
Club Road	45 A1
Clune Road	24 E1
Cluny Grove	60 D3
Cluny Park	60 E2
Clutterland	42 F1
Clyde Court	38 F4 [19]
Clyde Lane	38 F4
Clyde Road	38 F4
Cnoc Aoibhean	33 B2
Coast Road (Baldoyle)	15 A4
Coast Road (Malahide)	3 C2
Coates Lane	17 C3 [3]
Coburg	67 B2
Coburg Place	38 E1
*Coghill's Court (off Dame Street)	38 D2
Cois Cairn	67 B1
Cois Coillte	64 D1 [3]
Cois Eala	38 D4
Cois Na hAbhann	54 F2
Cois Sleibhe	67 B4
Coke Lane	37 C2 [42]
Coke Ovens Cottages	24 F4
Coke Ovens Cottages	24 F4
Coke Ovens Cottages	24 F4
*Colbert's Fort (off St James Walk)	37 B3
Colbert's Fort (Tallaght)	44 F4
Coldcut Road	35 B2
Coldwater Lakes	53 B2
Coldwell Street	60 D1
Colepark Avenue	36 D3
Colepark Drive	36 D3
Colepark Green	36 D3
Colepark Road	36 D3
Coleraine Street	38 D2
Colganstown	41 B2
Coliemore Road	60 F2
Coliemore Road	60 G2
Coliemore Villas	60 F2 [14]
College Crescent	46 D3
College Drive	46 E3
College Fort	22 F4
College Gate	22 F3
College Green	38 D2
College Green (Maynooth)	17 C4
College Grove	22 F4
College Lane (Rathcoole)	52 F1
College Lane (Trinity College)	38 E3 [19]
College Manor	25 B4 [8]
College Mews	25 B4 [11]
College Park (Castleknock)	23 A4
College Park (Kimmage)	46 E3
College Park Avenue	57 C2
College Park Close	57 C2
College Park Court	57 C2 [2]
College Park Drive	57 C2 [3]
College Park Grove	57 C2
College Park Way	57 C2
College Road (Castleknock)	22 F4
College Road (Whitechurch Road)	57 A3
College Street (Baldoyle)	15 A4 [8]
College Street (Baldoyle)	15 A4
College Street (Trinity College)	38 E2
College View (Drumcondra)	25 B3
College View (Tallaght)	55 A1 [6]

STREET NAME	PAGE/GRID REFERENCE
College Wood	22 F4
Collegeland	42 F4
Collier's Avenue	47 B1 [3]
Colliersland	6 F2
Collindale	25 C2 [6]
Collins Avenue	25 C2
Collins Avenue East	26 D3
Collins Avenue Extension	25 A2
Collins Avenue West	25 B2
Collins Close	25 C3 [8]
Collins Court (Blackrock)	49 A3 [13]
Collins Court (Collins Avenue)	25 C3 [6]
Collins Drive	24 E1
Collins Green	24 E1
Collins Park	26 D3
Collins Place	24 E1
Collins Row	24 E2 [6]
Collinstown Crescent	35 A3 [3]
Collinstown Grove	35 B3
Collinstown Road	35 A3
Collinswood	25 C2
Colmanstown	51 C2
Colmanstown Lane	51 C2
Colmcille Court	2 D2 [3]
Colthurst Close	34 F2
Colthurst Crescent	34 F2
Colthurst Gardens	34 F2
Colthurst Green	34 F2
Colthurst Mews	34 F2
Colthurst Park	34 F2
Colthurst Rise	34 F2
Colthurst Road	34 F2
Colthurst Way	34 F2
Comeragh Road	36 F4
Common Little	42 D4
Commons (Hazelhatch)	41 C2
Commons (Rathcoole)	52 E1
Commons East	2 D3
Commons Lower	41 A1
Commons Road (Loughlinstown)	64 E2
Commons Road (St. John's Gate)	44 D2
Commons Street	38 E2
Compass Court	23 C3
Comyn Place	25 A3 [5]
Con Colbert Road	37 A3
Confey	20 D4
Congress Gardens	60 E1 [2]
Congress Hall	7 B3
Congress Park	7 B3 [1]
Connaught Parade	24 F4 [6]
Connaught Place	50 D4 [26]
Connaught Street	24 F4
Connawood Copse	67 B1
Connawood Crescent	67 B1
Connawood Drive	67 B1
Connawood Green	67 B1
Connawood Grove	67 B1
Connawood Lawn	67 B1
Connawood Walk	67 B1
Connawood Way	67 B1
Connolly Avenue (Kilmainham)	37 A3
Connolly Avenue (Malahide)	3 A4
Connolly Gardens	37 A3 [3]
Connolly's Folly	18 E4
Conor Clune Road	23 C4
Conquer Hill Avenue	39 C1
Conquer Hill Road	39 C1
Constellation Road	12 F4
Constitution Hill	38 D2
Convent Avenue (Bray)	68 D2
Convent Avenue (Marino)	25 B4
Convent Close	38 E3 [40]
Convent Court	58 E1 [4]
Convent Lane (Maynooth)	17 C3
Convent Lane (Portmarnock)	4 D4
Convent Lane (Willbrook)	46 F4
Convent Lawns	36 E3 [4]
Convent Lodge	26 F2
Convent Place	38 E4 [12]
Convent Road (Blackrock)	49 A4
Convent Road (Clondalkin)	44 E2
Convent Road (Dalkey)	60 F2
Convent Road (Dun Laoghaire)	50 D4
Convent View (Bray)	68 D2 [23]

STREET NAME	PAGE/GRID REFERENCE	STREET NAME	PAGE/GRID REFERENCE	STREET NAME	PAGE/GRID REFERENCE	STREET NAME	PAGE/GRID REFERENCE
Convent View (Oldcourt)	67 C3	Corbawn Lane	64 E2	Cranford Court	48 D2	Croydon Park Avenue	25 C4
Convent View Cottages (Cabra)	24 D4 [2]	Corbawn Lawn	64 E3	(Stillorgan Road)		Croydon Terrace	25 C3 [4]
Convent View Cottages	44 D2	Corbawn Wood	64 E2	Cranmer Lane	38 F3 [19]	Cruagh Avenue	62 E1
(St. John's Gate)		Corduff	22 F1	Crannagh	47 C2 [9]	Cruagh Close	62 E1
Convent View Crescent	24 D4 [3]	Corduff Avenue	22 F1	Crannagh Castle	46 F3 [9]	Cruagh Court	62 E1
Convent Way	24 D4	Corduff Close	22 F1	Crannagh Court	46 F3 [10]	Cruagh Green	62 E1
Conway Court	38 F3 [23]	Corduff Cottages	22 E1	Crannagh Grove	47 A3	Cruagh Lane	56 E4
Conyngham Road	37 B2	Corduff Crescent	22 F1	Crannagh Hall	47 A3	Cruagh Rise	62 E1
Cook Street	38 D2	Corduff Gardens	22 F1	Crannagh Park	46 F3	Cruagh Road	56 E4
Cooks Road	1 A4	Corduff Green	22 F1	Crannagh Road	46 F3	Cruagh Wood	62 E1
Cookstown	66 E3	Corduff Grove	9 B4	Crannagh Way	47 A3 [8]	Cruise Park	9 A2
Cookstown Court	44 F4	Corduff Park	9 B4	Crannogue Close	11 C4	Cruise Park Avenue	9 A2
Cookstown Road	44 F4	Corduff Place	22 F1	Crannogue Road	11 C4	Cruise Park Close	9 A2
Cookstown Road	44 E4	Corduff Way	22 F1	Crawford Avenue	25 A4	Cruise Park Court	9 A2
Cookstown Way	44 E4	*Cork Hill (off Dame St)	38 D2	*Crawford Terrace	38 E1	Cruise Park Crescent	9 A2
Coolamber Court	56 D1 [1]	Cork Street	37 C3	(off Kings Avenue)		Cruise Park Drive	9 A2
Coolamber Drive	52 F2	Corkagh View	44 D2	Creighton Street	38 E2	Cruise Park Hall	9 A2
Coolamber Park	56 D1	Corke Abbey	67 C1	Cremona Road	36 E3	Cruise Park Rise	9 A2
Coolamber Road	52 F2	Corke Abbey Avenue	67 B1	Cremore Avenue	24 F3	Cruise Park Square	9 A2
Coolatree Close	25 C2	Cormac Terrace	46 F2	Cremore Crescent	24 F3	Cruise Park Walk	9 A2
Coolatree Park	25 C2	Corn Exchange Place	38 E2 [24]	Cremore Drive	24 F3	Crumlin	46 D1
Coolatree Road	25 C2	Cornelscourt	59 B3	Cremore Heights	24 F2	Crumlin Park(off Crumlin Road)	46 D1
Cooldrinagh Lane	33 B1	Cornelscourt Hill Road	59 B3	Cremore Lawn	24 F3	Crumlin Road	37 B4
Cooldrinagh Terrace	33 B1	Cornelstown	6 D2	Cremore Park	25 A3	Cuala Grove	68 D3
Cooldríona Court	2 D2	Cornerpark	42 D3	Cremore Road	24 F3	Cuala Road (Bray)	68 D3
Cooleen Avenue	25 C1	Cornmarket	37 C3	Cremore Villas	24 F3 [5]	Cuala Road (Cabra)	24 F4
Coolevin (Ballybrack)	60 D4	Corr Castle	29 B1	Cremorne (Knocklyon)	56 D1	Cuan na Mara	30 D1 [13]
Coolevin Road	38 D3 [49]	Corr Castle Apts	29 B1 [3]	Cremorne (Terenure Road East)	46 F2	Cuckoo Lane	38 D2
Cooley Close	36 F4	Corrbridge Terrace	29 B1 [1]	Crescent Gardens	38 F1 [11]	Cuffe Lane	38 D3
Cooley Road	36 F4	(off Claremont Road)		Crescent House	26 D4 [6]	Cuffe Street	38 D3
Coolgariff Road	25 C1	Corrib Road	46 E2	Crescent Place	26 D4	Cuilenn Park	24 F1
Coolgreena Close	25 C2	Corrib Road	46 F2	Crescent Villas	25 A4	Cul na Greine	54 F2
Coolgreena Road	25 C1	Corrig Avenue	50 D4	Crestfield Avenue	25 B2	Cullen's Cottages	49 A4 [7]
Coolkill	58 D3	Corrig Close	45 B3	Crestfield Close	25 B2	Cullen's Wood House	38 E4 [37]
Coolmine	52 F3	Corrig Park	50 D4	Crestfield Drive	25 B2	*Cullenswood Court (off	47 B1
Coolmine Boulevard	22 E2	Corrig Road (Dalkey)	60 F1	Crestfield Park	25 B2	Cullenswood Park)	
Coolmine Close	22 D2	Corrig Road (Dun Laoghaire)	60 D1	Crestfield Road	25 B2	Cullenswood Gardens	47 B1
Coolmine Cottages	9 A4	Corrig Road (Stillorgan)	58 E2	Crewhill	17 B1	Cullenswood Park	47 B1
Coolmine Court	22 E2	Corrybeg	46 D4	Crinan Strand	38 E2 [31]	Cullenswood Road	47 B1 [11]
Coolmine Green	22 D3	Cosy Lodge	47 A1 [26]	Crinken Glen	64 E3	Culmore Park	35 C2 [1]
Coolmine Lawn	22 D2	Coulson Avenue	46 F2	Crinken Lane	64 D4	Culmore Road	35 C2
Coolmine Mews	22 D2 [1]	Coultry Avenue	25 B1	Crinstown	17 A4	*Cumberland Place North	37 C1
Coolmine Park	22 E2	Coultry Close	25 A1	Croaghpatrick Road	24 D4	(on North Circular Road)	
Coolmine Road	22 E3	Coultry Court	12 D4	Crockshane	52 E3	Cumberland Road	38 E4
Coolmine Woods	22 E2	Coultry Crescent	12 D4	Crodaun Court	31 C2 [1]	Cumberland Street	49 C4
Coolnevaun	58 E1	Coultry Drive	12 D4	Crodaun Forest Park	32 D2	Cumberland Street North	38 E1
Coolock	26 E1	Coultry Gardens	12 D4	Crofton Avenue	50 D4	Cumberland Street South	38 E3 [1]
Coolock Drive	26 E1	Coultry Green	12 D4	Crofton Mansions	50 D4 [28]	Cunningham Drive	60 F2
Coolock Lane (Santry)	12 F4	Coultry Grove	12 E4	Crofton Road	50 D4	Cunningham Road	60 F2
Coolock Village	26 E1	Coultry Lawn	12 E4	Crofton Terrace	50 D4 [25]	Curlew Road	36 F4
Coolock Village Close	26 E1 [3]	Coultry Park	12 E4	Croftwood Crescent	35 C3	Curracloe Drive	27 A1 [4]
Coolrua Drive	25 C1	Coultry Road	12 D4	Croftwood Drive	35 C3	Curragh Hall	9 B3
Coombe Court	37 C3 [62]	Coultry Terrace	12 D4	Croftwood Gardens	35 C3	Curragh Hall Avenue	9 B3
Cope Street	38 D2 [22]	Coultry Way	25 B1	Croftwood Green	36 D3	Curragh Hall Close	9 B3
Copeland Avenue	26 D4	Coundon Court	60 E4	Croftwood Grove	35 C3	Curragh Hall Court	9 B3
Copeland Grove	26 D4	Countybrook Lawns	66 E2	Croftwood Park	36 D3	Curragh Hall Crescent	9 B3
Copper Alley	38 D2 [49]	Court House Square	17 C3 [5]	Croke Villas	38 E1 [68]	Curragh Hall Drive	9 B3
Copper Beech Grove	67 B2 [6]	Courthill Drive	7 B2	Cromcastle Avenue	26 D1	Curragh Hall Gate	9 B3
Coppinger	49 A4	Courtlands	59 C3	Cromcastle Close	26 D1 [2]	Curragh Hall Green	9 B3
Coppinger Close	48 F4	Courtney Place	38 F1 [8]	Cromcastle Court	26 D1 [6]	Curragh Hall Grove	9 B3
Coppinger Glade	48 F4	Courtview Apts.	23 C3	Cromcastle Drive	26 D1	Curragh Hall House	9 B3
Coppinger Row	38 D3 [34]	Cow Parlour	37 C3 [24]	Cromcastle Green	26 D1	Curragh Hall Lane	9 B3
Coppinger Walk	49 A4	Cowbooter Lane	30 E2	Cromcastle Park	26 D1	Curragh Hall Lodge	9 B3
Coppinger Wood	48 F4	Cowper Downs	47 A1	Cromcastle Road	26 D1	Curragh Hall Road	9 B3
Corbally	53 C3	Cowper Drive	47 B2	Cromlech Close	62 F2	Curragh Hall View	9 B3
Corbally Avenue	53 C2	Cowper Gardens	47 B2	Cromlech Court	11 C4	Curragh Hall Way	9 B3
Corbally Close	53 C2	Cowper Mews	47 A2 [4]	Cromlech Fields	64 E1	Curragh Hall Wood	9 B3
Corbally Down	53 C2	Cowper Road	47 A2	Cromwell's Quarters	37 B3 [3]	Curtlestown	65 B4
Corbally Drive	53 C2	Cowper Street	37 B1	Cromwellsfort Road	45 C2	Curved Street	38 D2 [49]
Corbally Glade	53 C2	Cowper Village	47 A2	Crooksling	53 B4	Curzon Street	38 D4
Corbally Green	53 C2	Cows Lane	38 D2 [48]	Crosbie House	38 E4 [35]	Cushinstown	6 F1
Corbally Heath	53 C2	Crag Avenue	35 B4	Cross Avenue (Booterstown)	48 F3	Cushlawn Avenue	54 F2
Corbally Lawn	53 C2	Crag Crescent	35 B4	Cross Avenue (Dun Laoghaire)	50 D4	Cushlawn Close	54 F3
Corbally Park	53 C2	Crag Terrace	35 B4	Cross Lane	17 C3	Cushlawn Dale	54 F3
Corbally Rise	53 C2	Craigford Avenue	26 E3	Crosstrees Court	30 D2 [13]	Cushlawn Drive	54 F2
Corbally Square	53 C2	Craigford Drive	26 E3	Crosthwaite Park East	60 D1	Cushlawn Grove	54 F2
Corbally Vale	53 C2	Craiglands	60 F2 [26]	Crosthwaite Park South	60 D1	Cushlawn Park	54 F2
Corbally Way	53 C2	Craigmore Gardens	49 A3 [5]	Crosthwaite Park West	60 D1	Cushlawn Walk	54 F3
Corbawn Avenue	64 E2	Crampton Avenue	38 F4 [16]	Crosthwaite Terrace	50 D4 [15]	Cushlawn Way	54 F3
Corbawn Close	64 F2	*Crampton Court (off Dame St)	38 D2	*Crostick Alley (off Meath St)	37 C3	Custom House Harbour	38 E2 [27]
Corbawn Court	64 F2	Crampton Quay	38 D2 [40]	Crotty Avenue	45 C1	Custom House Quay	38 E2
Corbawn Dale	64 F2	*Crane Lane (off Dame Street)	38 D2	*Crow Street (off Dame St)	38 D2	Cymric Road	39 A3
Corbawn Drive	64 F2	Crane Street	37 C3	*Crown Alley (Off Temple Bar)	38 D2	Cypress Avenue	56 E2 [2]
Corbawn Glade	64 E3	Cranfield Place	39 A3	Croydon Gardens	25 C4	Cypress Court	64 E1
Corbawn Grove	64 F2	Cranford Court (Kimmage)	46 E2 [12]	Croydon Green	25 C4	Cypress Drive	46 D3

STREET NAME	PAGE/GRID REFERENCE	STREET NAME	PAGE/GRID REFERENCE	STREET NAME	PAGE/GRID REFERENCE	STREET NAME	PAGE/GRID REFERENCE
Cypress Garth	46 D4	Darling Estate	23 C4	Deerpark Road	23 A3	Dodder View Cottages	38 F4 [9]
Cypress Grove North	46 D3	Dartmouth Lane	38 E4 [6]	(Castleknock Road)		Dodsboro Cottages	33 B2
Cypress Grove Road	46 D3	Dartmouth Place	38 E4 [4]	Deerpark Road (Kiltipper)	54 F3	Dodsboro Road	33 C2
Cypress Grove South	46 D4	Dartmouth Road	38 E4	Deerpark Road	48 D4	D'Olier Street	38 E2
Cypress House	28 D1	Dartmouth Square East	38 E4	(Mount Merrion)		Dollymount	27 A4
Cypress Lawn	46 D4	Dartmouth Square North	38 E4	Deerpark Square	54 F3	Dollymount Avenue	27 A4
Cypress Park	46 D4	Dartmouth Square South	38 E4	Deerpark Terrace	54 F3	Dollymount Grove	26 F4
Cypress Road	48 E3	Dartmouth Square West	38 E4	Deerpark Walk	54 F3	Dollymount Park	27 A4
Cypress Springs	20 D4 [1]	Dartmouth Terrace	38 E4 [5]	Deerpark Way	54 F3	Dollymount Rise	27 A4
		Dartry Cottages	47 B3 [1]	Del Val Avenue	27 C2	Dolly's Grove	5 C2
D		Dartry Park	47 A2	Del Val Court	27 C2 [2]	Dolmen Court	12 D4
		Dartry Road	47 A2	Delaford Avenue	55 C1	Dolphin Avenue	37 C4
*Daisy Market (on Parnell Street)	38 D2	David Park	25 A4	Delaford Drive	55 C1	Dolphin Court	37 B4 [7]
Dakota Avenue	12 F4	David Road	25 A4	Delaford Grove	55 C1	Dolphin House	37 B4 [1]
Dakota Court	25 A4	*Davis Place	37 C3	Delaford Lawn	55 C1	*Dolphin Market	37 B4
Dal Riada	3 C4	(off Thomas Davis St Sth)		Delaford Park	55 C1	(off Dolphin's Barn St)	
Dalcassian Downs	24 F4	Davitt House	37 A4	Delbrook Manor	57 C2	Dolphin Park	37 B4 [5]
Dale Close	58 E1 [1]	Davitt Park	60 D4	Delbrook Park	57 C2	Dolphin Road	37 B4
Dale Drive	58 E1	Davitt Road (Bray)	67 C2	Delhurst Avenue	21 B1	Dolphin's Barn	37 B4
Dale Road	58 E1	Davitt Road (Inchicore)	36 F4	Delhurst Close	21 B1	Dolphin's Barn Street	37 B4
Dale View	60 E4	Dawson Court	48 F3	Delhurst Mews	21 B1	Dominick Lane	38 D2 [35]
Dale View Park	60 E4 [2]	*Dawson Court	38 D3	Delhurst Terrace	21 B1	Dominick Place	38 D2
Dalepark Road	55 A2	(off Stephen St Lower)		Delville Road	25 A2	Dominick Street	50 D4
Daletree Avenue	55 B2	Dawson Lane	38 E3 [18]	Delvin Road	24 F4 [3]	Dominick Street Lower	38 D2
Daletree Close	55 C3	Dawson Street	38 E3	Delwood Close	22 E3	Dominick Street Upper	38 D1
Daletree Court	55 C3	De Bret House	46 F4 [24]	Delwood Drive	22 E3	Domville Drive	46 D4
Daletree Crescent	55 C2	De Burgh Road	37 B2 [14]	Delwood Grove	22 E3	Domville Green	46 D4
Daletree Drive	55 C2	De Courcy Square	25 A4 [2]	Delwood Lawn	22 E3	Domville Grove	64 E1 [9]
Daletree Park	55 C3	De Selby	54 D2	Delwood Park	22 E3	Domville Road	46 D4
Daletree Place	55 C3	De Selby Close	54 D2	Delwood Road	22 E3	Donaghmede	14 E4
Daletree Road	55 C3	De Selby Court	54 D2	Delwood Walk	22 E3	Donaghmede Avenue	27 B1
Daletree Terrace	55 C3	De Selby Crescent	54 D2	Demesne	26 E3	Donaghmede Drive	27 B1
Daletree View	55 B3	De Selby Downs	54 D2	Denmark Street Great	38 D1	Donaghmede Park	27 B1
Daleview Road	1 C1	De Selby Drive	54 D2	Denville Court	60 D4	Donaghmede Road	27 B1
Dalkey	60 F1	De Selby Green	54 D2	Denzille Lane	38 E3	Donaghmore	18 F3
Dalkey Avenue	60 F2	De Selby Lane	54 D2	*Derby Square (off Werburgh St)	38 D3	Donard Road	36 F4
Dalkey Court	60 F2 [23]	De Selby Lawns	54 D2	Dermot O'Hurley Avenue	39 A3	Donnellan Avenue	37 B3 [7]
Dalkey Grove	60 F2 [6]	De Selby Park	53 C2	Derravaragh Road	46 E2	Donnybrook	47 C1
Dalkey Park	60 E2	De Selby Rise	54 D2	Derry Drive	46 D1	Donnybrook Castle	47 C1 [24]
Dalkey Rock	60 F2	De Selby Road	54 D2	Derry Park	46 D1	Donnybrook Close	48 D2 [2]
Dalton Mews	3 B3	De Velara Place	38 D1 [19]	Derry Road	46 D1	Donnybrook Court	47 C2
Dalymount	37 C1	*De Vesci Court (off Sloperton)	49 C4	Derrynane Gardens	39 A3	Donnybrook Green	48 D2 [3]
Damastown Avenue	8 F3	De Vesci Terrace	49 C4	Derrynane Parade	38 D1 [33]	Donnybrook Manor	47 C1
Damastown Close	8 F3	Dean Street	38 D3	Desmond Avenue	50 D4 [3]	Donnybrook Mews	47 C1
Damastown Court	9 A3	Dean Swift Green	25 A2	Desmond Cottages	60 F2 [20]	Donnybrook Road	47 C1
Damastown Drive	8 E3	Dean Swift Road	25 A2	Desmond Street	38 D4 [2]	Donnycarney	26 D3
Damastown Green	8 F3	Dean Swift Square	37 C3	Devenish Road	46 E1	Donnycarney Road	26 D3
Damastown Road	8 F3	Deans Court	59 B1 [10]	Deverell Place	38 E2 [5]	Donomore Avenue	54 E2
Damastown Walk	8 E3	Deans Grange	59 B2	Devery's Lane	25 A4 [4]	Donomore Crescent	54 E2
Damastown Way	8 F3	Dean's Grange Road	59 B1	Devitt Villas	60 E1 [8]	Donomore Green	54 E2
Dame Court	38 D3 [16]	Deansrath Avenue	34 F4	Devlin's Place	38 E3 [22]	Donomore Park	54 E2
Dame Lane	38 D3 [7]	Deansrath Crescent	43 C1	Devon Close	59 B1 [11]	Donore Avenue	37 C3
Dame Lane	38 D2 [42]	Deansrath Green	43 C1	Devoy Road	37 A3	Donore Road	37 C3
Dame Street	38 D2	Deansrath Grove	34 F4	Dewberry Park	4 D4	Donore Terrace	37 C3 [55]
Damer House	2 E2	Deansrath Lawn	34 F4	Dexter Terrace	38 E4 [29]	Donovan Lane	37 C4 [21]
Dane Close	11 C4	Deansrath Park	43 C1	Diamond Terrace	67 B2 [15]	Doon Avenue	37 B1 [6]
Dane Road	11 C4	Deansrath Road	43 C1	Diamond Valley Apts.	67 B2	Doon Court	11 C4
Danes Court	27 A4	Deanstown Avenue	24 D2	Digges Lane	38 D3 [38]	Doonamana Road	60 D3
Danesfort	39 B1	Deanstown Drive	24 D2	Digges Street Upper	38 D3	Doonanore Park	60 D3
Daneswell Road	25 A4	Deanstown Green	24 D2	*Dillon Place South	38 D3	Doonsalla Drive	60 D3
Dangan	41 A2	Deanstown Park	24 D2	(off John Dillon St)		Doonsalla Park	60 D3
Dangan Avenue	46 D2	Deanstown Road	24 D2	Dillon's Row	17 C2	Doris Street	38 F3
Dangan Drive	46 D2	Decies Road	36 E3	Dingle Road	24 E4	Dornden Park	48 E2
Dangan Park	46 D2	Deepdales	67 B4	Dispensary Lane (Lucan)	34 D1 [6]	Dorney Court	64 E3
Daniel Street	38 D3	Deerhaven	8 F4	Dispensary Lane (Willbrook)	46 F4	Dorset Lane	38 D1
Danieli Drive	26 E2	Deerhaven Avenue	8 F4	Distillery House Apts.	36 E2 [14]	Dorset Place	38 D1 [63]
Danieli Road	26 E2	Deerhaven Close	8 F4	Distillery Lane	20 D4	Dorset Street Lower	38 D1
Dara Court	32 D3	Deerhaven Crescent	8 F4	Distillery Road	25 B4	Dorset Street Upper	38 D1
Dara Crescent	32 D3	Deerhaven Green	8 F4	Diswellstown Cottages	22 E4	Double Lane	17 C3
Dargan Court	68 D2 [6]	Deerhaven Park	8 F4	Diswellstown Road	22 D3	Dowland Road	46 D1
Dargan Street	67 B2 [10]	Deerhaven View	8 F4	Dixon Villas	60 E1 [9]	Dowling's Court	38 E2 [15]
Dargle Court	67 B2 [28]	Deerhaven Walk	8 F4	Doctor's Lane	17 C3	Downpatrick Road	37 B4
Dargle Crescent	67 B2 [5]	Deerpark	67 B4	Dodder Avenue	55 B2	Downpatrick Road	46 E1
Dargle Drive	57 A1	Deerpark Avenue (Castleknock)	23 A4	Dodder Bank	47 B2 [10]	Dowth Avenue	24 F4
Dargle Heights	67 B2	Deerpark Avenue (Kiltipper)	54 F3	Dodder Court	55 B2	Drapier Green	24 F2 [1]
Dargle Road (Dean's Grange)	59 A1	Deerpark Close (Castleknock)	23 A3	Dodder Crescent	55 B2	Drapier Road	24 F2
Dargle Road (Drumcondra)	25 A4	Deerpark Close (Kiltipper)	54 F3	Dodder Dale	46 F4	Drayton Close	49 B4 [16]
*Dargle Terrace	67 B2	Deerpark Downs	54 F3	Dodder Green	55 B2	Drimnagh	36 F4
(On Lower Dargle Road)		Deerpark Drive (Castleknock)	23 A3	Dodder Lawn	55 B2	Drimnagh Road	45 C1
Dargle Valley	57 A1	Deerpark Drive (Kiltipper)	54 F3	Dodder Park Drive	46 F3 [3]	Drinagh Park	58 F4
Dargle View	57 A1	Deerpark Green	54 F3	Dodder Park Grove	46 F3	Drinaghmore	58 F4
Dargle Wood	56 D1	Deerpark Lawn	23 B3	Dodder Park Road	46 F3	Drinaghmore Avenue	58 F4
Darley Cottages	67 C2 [15]	Deerpark Lodge	54 F3	Dodder Road Lower	47 A3	Drinaghmore Close	58 F4
Darley Street	37 C4 [40]	Deerpark Place	54 F3	Dodder Terrace	39 A3 [18]	Drinaghmore Court	58 F4
Darley's Terrace	37 C3 [9]	Deerpark Rise	54 F3	Dodder Vale	47 A3 [13]	Droim na Coille Avenue	34 F2

STREET NAME	PAGE/GRID REFERENCE
Droim na Coille Court	34 F2
Droim na Coille Place	34 F2
Dromard Road	36 F4
Dromard Terrace	39 A4 [17]
Dromawling Road	25 C2
Drombawn Avenue	25 C2
Dromcarra Avenue	54 E2
Dromcarra Drive	54 E2
Dromcarra Green	54 D2
Dromcarra Grove	54 E2
Dromeen Avenue	25 C2
Dromheath Avenue	9 B4
Dromheath Drive	9 B4
Dromheath Gardens	9 B4
Dromheath Grove	9 B4
Dromheath Park	9 B4
Dromlee Crescent	25 C2
Dromnanane Park	25 C2 [3]
Dromnanane Road	25 C2 [2]
Dromore Road	37 A4
Druid Court	11 C4
Druid Valley	64 D1
Drumahill	58 D1
Drumalee Avenue	37 B1
Drumalee Court	37 B1 [14]
Drumalee Drive	37 B1
Drumalee Grove	37 B1
Drumalee Park	37 B1
Drumalee Road	37 B1
Drumcairn Avenue	54 E1
Drumcairn Drive	54 D1
Drumcairn Gardens	54 D1
Drumcairn Green	54 E1
Drumcairn Park	54 E1
Drumcliffe Drive	24 E4
Drumcliffe Road	24 E4
Drumcondra	25 A4
Drumcondra Park	38 E1 [18]
Drumcondra Road Lower	25 B4
Drumcondra Road Upper	25 B3
Drumderg Court	25 C4
Drumfinn Avenue	35 C2
Drumfinn Park	36 D3
Drumfinn Road	36 D2
Drumkeen Manor	60 D3
Drummartin Close	48 D4
Drummartin Crescent	58 D1 [1]
Drummartin Park	58 D1
Drummartin Road	48 D4
Drummartin Terrace	48 D4
*Drummond Place (off Mount Drummond Ave)	37 C4
Drumnigh Road	14 E3
Drumnigh Wood	14 E2
Drury Street	38 D3
Drynam Avenue	2 E3
Drynam Close	2 E4
Drynam Copse	2 E4
Drynam Court	2 D2
Drynam Crescent	2 E3
Drynam Drive	2 E3
Drynam Glen	2 E3
Drynam Green	2 E3
Drynam Grove	2 E3
Drynam Hall	2 E3
Drynam Mews	2 E4
Drynam Place	2 E4
Drynam Rise	2 E4
Drynam Road	2 D2
Drynam Square	2 E3
Drynam View	2 E3
Drynam Walk	2 E3
Drynam Way	2 E3
Drysdale Close	55 A2
Dualla Court	48 E4
Dublin Airport	12 E1
Dublin Road (Bray)	67 B1
Dublin Road (Celbridge)	32 D3
Dublin Road (Donaghmore)	18 F3
Dublin Road (Dunboyne)	7 C3
Dublin Road (Kilbarrack)	27 C2
Dublin Road (Malahide)	3 A3
Dublin Road (Maynooth)	18 D3
Dublin Road (Shankill)	64 E3
Dublin Road (Sutton)	29 A1
Dublin Road (Swords)	1 C3

STREET NAME	PAGE/GRID REFERENCE
Dublin Street (Baldoyle)	15 A4
Duck Lane	37 C2
Dufferin Avenue	37 C4
Duke Lane Lower	38 E3 [17]
Duke Lane Upper	38 D3 [32]
Duke Row	38 E1 [57]
Duke Street	38 D3
Dun Aengus	54 F2
Dun an Oir	54 F2
Dun Emer Drive	57 C1
Dun Emer Park	57 C1
Dun Emer Road	57 C1
Dun Laoghaire	50 D4
Dunard Avenue	37 A1
Dunard Court	37 B1
Dunard Drive	37 B1
Dunard Park	37 B1
Dunard Road	37 B1 [11]
Dunard Road	37 B1
Dunard Walk	37 B1
Dunawley Avenue	44 D1
Dunawley Drive	44 D1
Dunawley Grove	44 D1
Dunawley Way	44 D1
Dunbo Hill	30 D1 [4]
Dunbo Terrace	30 D1 [1]
Dunboy	59 A4
Dunboyne	7 B2
Dunboyne Castle	7 B3
Dunbro Lane	11 C1
Dunbur Terrace	67 C2 [21]
Duncairn Avenue	67 C2
Duncairn Terrace	67 C2
Duncarraig	29 B2
Dundaniel Road	26 D1
Dundela Avenue	60 E1
Dundela Crescent	60 E1
Dundela Haven	60 E1 [24]
Dundela Park	60 E1
Dundrum	57 C1
Dundrum By Pass	57 C1
Dundrum Gate Apts	57 C1 [9]
Dundrum Road	47 C3
Dundrum Wood	57 B1
Dunedin Court	59 C1
Dunedin Drive	59 C1 [8]
Dunedin Park	59 C1
Dunedin Terrace	59 C1
Dungar Terrace	50 D4 [12]
Dungriffan Road	30 D2
Dungriffan Villas	30 D2 [8]
Dunleary Hill	49 C4
Dunleary Road	49 C4
Dunluce Road	26 E3
Dunmanus Road	24 E4
Dunmore Grove	44 F2
Dunmore Lawn	44 F3
Dunmore Park	44 F2
Dunne Street	38 E1
Dunree Park	26 F1
Dunsandle Court	23 A3
Dunsandle Grove	23 A3
Dunseverick Road	26 E4
Dunsink Avenue	24 D2
Dunsink Drive	24 D2
Dunsink Gardens	24 D2
Dunsink Green	24 D2
Dunsink Lane	23 A2
Dunsink Park	24 D2
Dunsink Road	24 D2
Dunsoghly	23 C1
Dunsoghly Avenue	23 C1
Dunsoghly Close	23 C1
Dunsoghly Court	23 C1
Dunsoghly Drive	23 C1
Dunsoghly Green	23 C1
Dunsoghly Grove	23 C1
Dunsoghly Park	23 C1
Dunstaffnage Hall Apts	58 F1 [6]
Dunville Avenue	47 B1
Durham Place	60 D1 [18]
Durham Road	39 B4
Durrow Road	46 E1
Dursey Row	22 F1
Dwyer Park	67 C1

E

STREET NAME	PAGE/GRID REFERENCE
Eagle Hill	49 A3 [15]
Eagle Hill Avenue	46 F2 [4]
Eagle Park	26 D1
Eagle Terrace (Dalkey)	60 F2
Eagle Terrace (Dundrum)	57 C1 [3]
Eagle Valley	66 E4
Eaglewood Apts	59 C2 [5]
Eaglewood House	59 C2 [7]
Eaglewood Mews	59 C2 [8]
Earl Place	38 D2 [19]
Earl Street North	38 D2
Earl Street South	37 C3
Earls Court (Cabra)	37 B1
Earls Court (Terenure)	46 F2 [15]
Earlscroft	67 C4
Earlsfort	34 F3
Earlsfort Avenue	34 F3
Earlsfort Close	34 F3
Earlsfort Court	34 F3
Earlsfort Drive	34 F3
Earlsfort Gardens	34 F2
Earlsfort Green	34 F3
Earlsfort Grove	34 F3
Earlsfort Lane	34 F3
Earlsfort Lawn	34 F3
Earlsfort Meadows	34 F2
Earlsfort Park	34 F2
Earlsfort Rise	34 F3
Earlsfort Road	34 F2
Earlsfort Terrace	38 E4
Earlsfort Vale	34 F3
Earlsfort View	34 F3
Earlsfort Way	34 F3
East Pier (Dun Laoghaire)	50 E3
East Pier (Howth)	30 D1
East Road	38 F2
East Wall	39 A1
East Wall Road	38 F1
Eastmoreland Lane	38 F4 [2]
Eastmoreland Place	38 F4 [1]
Easton Park	19 C4
Easton Road	19 B4
Eastwood	23 C2 [1]
Eaton Brae (Orwell Road)	47 A3
Eaton Brae (Shankill)	64 E2
Eaton Close	52 F2
Eaton Court (Bray)	68 D3 [1]
Eaton Court (Terenure)	46 F2 [22]
Eaton Green	52 F2
Eaton Hall	46 F2 [18]
Eaton House	52 F2 [1]
Eaton Place	49 B4
Eaton Road	46 F2
Eaton Square (Monkstown)	49 B4
Eaton Square (Terenure)	46 F2
Eaton Terrace	52 F2
Eaton Way	52 F2
Eaton Wood Avenue	64 E3
Eaton Wood Court	64 E3
Eaton Wood Green	64 E3
Eaton Wood Grove	64 E3
Eaton Wood Square	64 E2
Ebenezer Terrace	37 C3 [53]
Eblana Avenue	50 D4
Eblana Villas (Lr Grand Canal St)	38 F3 [2]
*Eblana Villas (off Arbour Hill)	37 B2
Eccles Court	38 D1 [20]
Eccles Place	38 D1
Eccles Street	38 D1
Echlin Street	37 C3
Eden Avenue	57 A1
Eden Court	57 A1
Eden Crescent	57 A1
Eden Grove	57 A1
Eden Park	60 D1
Eden Park Avenue	58 D1
Eden Park Drive	48 D4
Eden Park Road	58 D1
Eden Quay	38 E2
Eden Road Lower	60 D1
Eden Road Upper	60 D1

STREET NAME	PAGE/GRID REFERENCE
Eden Terrace (Botanic Ave)	25 A4
Eden Terrace (Dun Laoghaire)	60 D1
Eden Villas	60 D1 [5]
Edenbrook Court	56 F1 [5]
Edenbrook Drive	46 E4
Edenbrook Park	46 E4
Edenmore	26 F2
Edenmore Avenue	26 F1
Edenmore Crescent	27 A2
Edenmore Drive	26 F2
Edenmore Gardens	26 F2
Edenmore Green	26 F2
Edenmore Grove	26 F2
Edenmore Park	26 F2
Edenvale	57 A2
Edenvale Road	47 B1
Edenwood (Goatstown)	48 D4 [1]
Edgewood (Richmond Road)	25 B4 [10]
Edgewood Lawns	22 E1
Edmondsbury Court	34 E1 [1]
Edmondstown	56 E3
Edmondstown Green	56 E2
Edmondstown Road	56 E3
Edward Road	68 D3
*Edward Terrace (Off Nerano Rd)	60 F2
Edwards Court	56 E2
Edwin Court	60 E2 [5]
Effra Road	47 A1
Eglington Road	67 C2 [3]
Eglinton Court	47 C1
Eglinton Park (Donnybrook)	47 C1
Eglinton Road	47 C1
Eglinton Square	47 C1 [13]
Eglinton Terrace (Donnybrook)	47 C1
Eglinton Terrace (Dundrum)	47 C4
*Eglinton Terrace (Royal Canal Bank)	38 D1
Eglinton Wood	47 C1 [22]
Eklad Close	13 C4
Eklad Park	13 C4
Elderberry	34 D3
Elderwood Road	35 B2
*Elford Terrace (off Donore Avenue)	37 C3
Elgin Heights	67 A4
Elgin Road	38 F4
Elgin Wood	67 B4
Elizabeth Street	25 B4
Elkwood	56 E1
Ellenfield Road	25 C2
Ellensborough	54 F3
Ellensborough Avenue	54 F3
Ellensborough Close	54 F3
Ellensborough Copse	54 F3
Ellensborough Court	54 F3
Ellensborough Crescent	54 F3
Ellensborough Dale	54 F3
Ellensborough Downs	54 F3
Ellensborough Grange	54 F3
Ellensborough Green	54 F3
Ellensborough Grove	54 F3
Ellensborough Lane	54 F3
Ellensborough Lawn	54 F3
Ellensborough Meadows	54 F3
Ellensborough Park	54 F3
Ellensborough Rise	54 F3
Ellensborough View	54 F3
Ellensborough Walk	54 F3
Ellensborough Way	54 F3
Ellesmere	58 F2 [4]
Ellesmere Avenue	37 B1
Ellis Court	37 C2 [44]
Ellis Quay	37 C2
Ellis Street	37 C2 [38]
Elm Close	34 E3
Elm Court (Jobstown)	54 D2
Elm Court (Lucan)	34 E3
Elm Dene	34 E3
Elm Drive (Jobstown)	54 D2
Elm Drive (Lucan)	34 E3
Elm Green	34 E3
Elm Grove	49 E1
Elm Grove (Jobstown)	54 D2
Elm Grove (Lucan)	34 E3

STREET NAME	PAGE/GRID REFERENCE			STREET NAME	PAGE/GRID REFERENCE			STREET NAME	PAGE/GRID REFERENCE			STREET NAME	PAGE/GRID REFERENCE		
Elm Mount Avenue	25	C2		Emerald Square	37	B3	[20]	Estate Cottages (Shelbourne Rd)	38	F4	[13]	Father Scully House	38	E1	
Elm Mount Avenue	26	D3		Emerald Street	38	F2	[1]	Estuary Court	2	D1		Fatima Mansions	37	B3	[23]
Elm Mount Close	26	D2		Emerald Terrace	37	C3	[63]	Estuary Road	2	E1		(off James's Walk)			
Elm Mount Court	26	D3		Emmet Court	37	A3		Estuary Road	2	F2		Fatima Terrace	67	C2	
Elm Mount Crescent	26	D2		Emmet Road	37	A3		Estuary Row	3	B2		Faughart Road	46	E1	[3]
Elm Mount Drive	26	D2		Emmet Square	48	F3		Estuary Walk	2	F2		Faulkner's Terrace	37	B3	[37]
Elm Mount Grove	26	D2		Emmet Street (Harold's Cross)	37	C4	[10]	Eugene Street	37	C3		Faussagh Avenue	24	E4	
Elm Mount Heights	26	D2		Emmet Street (Nth Circular Rd)	38	E1		Eustace Street	38	D2		Faussagh Road	24	E4	
Elm Mount Lawn	26	D2		Emmet Street (Sallynoggin)	60	D1	[4]	Everton Avenue	37	B1	[3]	Fawn Lodge	23	A4	
Elm Mount Park	26	D2		Emor Street	38	D4		Evora Crescent	30	D1	[12]	Feltrim	3	A4	
Elm Mount Rise	26	D2		Emorville Avenue	38	D4		Evora Park	30	D1		Feltrim Hall	2	D3	
Elm Mount Road	26	D2		Empress Place	38	E1		Evora Terrace	30	D1	[2]	Feltrim Road	2	F4	
Elm Mount View	26	D2		*Enaville Avenue	38	F1		Ewington Lane	37	B3	[12]	Fenian Street	38	E3	
Elm Park (Celbridge)	32	D3		(off Annesley Place)				*Exchange Street Lower	38	D2		Fergus Road	46	F2	
Elm Park (Nutley Lane)	48	D1		Enaville Road	38	F1	[10]	(off Wood Quay)				Ferguson Road	25	A3	
Elm Park Terrace	46	F2		*Engine Alley (off Meath St)	37	C3		*Exchange Street Upper	38	D2		Fernbrook	67	B1	[6]
Elm Road (Donnycarney)	26	D3		English Row	32	D4		(off Lord Edward St)				Ferncarrig Avenue	58	D3	
Elm Road (Fox & Geese)	45	A1		Ennafort Avenue	26	F2		Exchequer Street	38	D3		Ferncarrig Court	58	D3	
Elm Vale	34	E3		Ennafort Court	26	F3		Eyre Court	2	E3		Ferncarrig Rise	58	D3	
Elm Way (Grange Wood)	57	A2	[3]	Ennafort Drive	26	F3						Ferncourt Avenue	55	B3	
Elm Way (Lucan)	34	E3		Ennafort Grove	26	F2		**F**				Ferncourt Close	55	B3	
Elm Wood	34	E3		Ennafort Park	26	F3						Ferncourt Crescent	55	B3	[5]
Elmbrook	34	E2		Ennafort Road	26	F3		Faber Grove	59	B1	[9]	Ferncourt Drive	55	B3	[4]
Elmbrook Crescent	34	E2		Ennel Avenue	26	F2		Fade Street	38	D3	[39]	Ferncourt Green	55	B3	
Elmbrook Lawn	34	E2		Ennel Court	64	E1	[6]	Fagan's Lane	17	C3	[2]	Ferncourt Park	55	B3	
Elmbrook Walk	34	E2		Ennel Drive	26	F2		Fair Haven	3	B2	[1]	Ferncourt View	55	B3	
Elmcastle Close	45	A3		Ennel Park	26	F2		Fairacre	2	F3		Ferndale (Hartstown)	21	C1	
Elmcastle Court	45	A3		Ennis Grove	39	A3	[19]	Fairbrook Lawn	46	F4		Ferndale (Tallaght)	55	A2	
Elmcastle Drive	45	A3		Enniskerry	66	D3		Fairfield Avenue	38	F1		Ferndale Avenue	24	F2	
Elmcastle Green	45	A3		Enniskerry Road (Phibsborough)	25	A4	[3]	Fairfield House	46	F2	[24]	Ferndale Glen	64	D3	
Elmcastle Park	45	A3		Enniskerry Road (Sandyford)	58	D4		Fairfield Park	47	A2		Ferndale Hill	64	D4	
Elmcastle Walk	45	A3		Erne Place	38	F3	[21]	Fairfield Road	25	A4		Ferndale Road (Bray)	67	A1	
Elmdale Crescent	35	C3		Erne Place Little	38	E3	[4]	Fairgreen	53	A2		Ferndale Road (Glasnevin)	24	F2	
Elmdale Drive	35	C3		Erne Place Lower	38	E2	[2]	Fairgreen Court	67	C2	[50]	Ferndale Road (Shankill)	64	D3	
Elmdale Park	35	C3		Erne Street Lower	38	E2		Fairgreen Road	67	B2	[11]	Fernhill Avenue	45	C3	
Elmfield	14	E4		Erne Street Upper	38	E3		Fairgreen Terrace	67	C2	[32]	Fernhill Park	45	C3	
Elmfield Avenue	14	D4		Erne Terrace Front	38	E3	[20]	Fairlawn Park	24	E2		Fernhill Road	45	C2	
Elmfield Close	14	D4	[2]	Erne Terrace Rere	38	E3	[21]	Fairlawn Road	24	E2		Fernleigh	22	D3	
Elmfield Court	14	D4		Errigal Gardens	45	C1		Fairlawns	60	E2	[6]	Fernleigh Close	22	D3	
Elmfield Court (Clondalkin)	44	E1		Errigal Road	45	C1		Fairview	25	C4		Fernleigh Court	22	D3	
Elmfield Crescent	14	E4		Errigal Road	36	F4		Fairview Avenue Lower	25	C4		Fernleigh Crescent	22	D3	
Elmfield Drive	14	E4		Erris Road	24	E4		Fairview Avenue Upper	25	C4		Fernleigh Dale	22	D3	
Elmfield Green	14	D4		Esker Drive	34	D2		Fairview Court	25	C4	[14]	Fernleigh Dene	22	D4	
Elmfield Grove	14	D4		Esker Glebe	34	D2		Fairview Green	25	C4	[7]	Fernleigh Drive	22	D3	
Elmfield Lawn	14	E4		Esker Lane	34	E2		Fairview Lawn	64	D1		Fernleigh Grange	22	D4	
Elmfield Park	14	E4		Esker Lane	34	E1		Fairview Passage	25	C4	[10]	Fernleigh Green	22	D3	
Elmfield Rise	14	D4		Esker Lawns	34	D1		Fairview Strand	25	C4		Fernleigh Grove	22	D4	
Elmfield Vale	14	E4		Esker Lodge	34	E2		Fairview Terrace	25	C4	[11]	Fernleigh Heath	22	D4	
Elmfield Walk	14	D4		Esker Lodge Avenue	34	E2		Fairways	46	E4		Fernleigh Lawn	22	D3	
Elmfield Way	14	D4		Esker Lodge Close	34	E2		Fairway's Avenue	24	F2		Fernleigh Park	22	D3	
Elmgrove	60	D4		Esker Lodge View	34	E2		Fairway's Green	24	F2		Fernleigh Place	22	D3	
Elmgrove Terrace	67	C2	[22]	Esker Manor	34	E2		Fairways Grove	24	E2		Fernleigh Vale	22	D3	
Elmpark Apts.	48	E2		Esker Meadow	34	E2		Fairway's Park	24	F2		Fernleigh View	22	D4	
Elmpark Avenue	47	B1		Esker Meadow Close	34	E2		Fairy Castle	61	B2		Fernley Court	38	D3	
Elms	48	F3		Esker Meadow Court	34	E2		Fairyhill (Oldcourt)	67	B3		Ferns Road	46	E1	
Elmwood Avenue Lower	47	B1		Esker Meadow Green	34	E2		Fairyhill (Stillorgan)	59	A1		Fernvale Drive	46	D1	
Elmwood Avenue Upper	47	B1		Esker Meadow Grove	34	E2		Faith Avenue	38	F1		Fernwood Avenue	54	E1	
Elmwood Close	21	B1		Esker Meadow Lawn	34	E2		Falcarragh Road	25	B2		Fernwood Close	54	E1	
Elmwood Court	1	C1	[1]	Esker Meadow Rise	34	E2		Falls Road	64	D2		Fernwood Court	54	E1	
Elmwood Drive	1	C1		Esker Meadow View	34	E2		Farmhill Drive	47	C4		Fernwood Lawn	54	E1	
Elmwood Park	1	C1		Esker Park	34	E2		Farmhill Park	47	C4		Fernwood Park	54	E1	
Elmwood Road	1	C1		Esker Pines	34	E1		Farmhill Road	47	C4		Fernwood Way	54	E1	
Elner Court	4	D4		Esker Road	34	D2		Farmleigh Avenue (Castleknock)	23	A4		Ferrard Road	46	F2	
Elton Court (Coolock)	26	F1	[1]	Esker South	34	D3		Farmleigh Avenue (Stillorgan)	58	F1		Ferrycarrig Avenue	13	B4	
Elton Court (Dalkey)	60	E1		Esker Villas	47	A1	[11]	Farmleigh Close (Castleknock)	23	A4		Ferrycarrig Drive	13	B4	
Elton Court (Dunboyne)	7	B3		Esker Woods	34	E2		Farmleigh Close (Stillorgan)	58	F1		Ferrycarrig Green	13	B4	[3]
Elton Court (Leixlip)	32	F1		Esker Woods Close	34	E2		Farmleigh Court	23	A4		Ferrycarrig Park	13	B4	
Elton Court (Marino)	25	C4	[17]	Esker Woods Court	34	E2		Farmleigh Park (Castleknock)	23	A4		Ferrycarrig Road	13	B4	
Elton Drive (Coolock)	27	A1		Esker Woods Drive	34	E2		Farmleigh Park (Stillorgan)	58	F1		Ferryman's Crossing	38	F2	[14]
Elton Drive (Dunboyne)	7	B2		Esker Woods Grove	34	E2		Farmleigh View	23	A4		Fertullagh Road	24	F4	[5]
Elton Grove (Dunboyne)	7	B3		Esker Woods Rise	34	E2		Farmleigh Woods	23	A4		Fettercairn	44	E4	
Elton Park (Coolock)	27	A1		Esker Woods View	34	E2		Farney Park	39	A4		Fettercairn Road	44	E4	
Elton Park (Dalkey)	60	E1		Esker Woods Walk	34	E2		Farnham Crescent	24	E2		Fey Yerra	58	F2	[8]
Elton Walk	27	A1	[1]	Esmond Avenue	25	C4		Farnham Drive	24	E2		Fforester	34	E2	
Ely Close	55	B3		Esmonde Terrace	67	B2	[18]	Farrenboley Cottages	47	B3		Fforester Close	34	E2	
Ely Crescent	55	B3	[1]	Esplanade Terrace	68	D2	[3]	Farrenboley Park	47	B3		Fforester Court	34	E2	
Ely Drive	55	B3		Esposito Road	45	C1	[5]	Fassaroe	67	A2		Fforester Drive	34	E2	
Ely Green	55	B3	[3]	*Essex Gate (off Essex Quay)	38	D2		Fassaroe	66	F3		Fforester Lawn	34	E2	
Ely Grove	55	B3	[2]	Essex Quay	38	D2		Fassaroe Avenue	67	A3		Fforester Park	34	E2	
Ely Place	38	E3		Essex Street East	38	D2		Fassaroe Glen	67	A2		Fforester Walk	34	E2	
Ely Place Upper	38	E3	[31]	*Essex Street West	38	D2		Fassaroe Lane	67	A3		Fforester Way	34	E2	
Ely View	55	B3		(off Fishamble St)				Father Colohan Terrace	67	C2	[11]	Field Avenue	45	C1	[1]
Embassy Lawn	47	C2		Estate Avenue	48	E1		Father Kitt Court	46	D1	[3]	Field's Terrace	47	B1	[5]
Emerald Cottages	38	F3	[34]	Estate Cottages	38	F3	[16]	Father Lemass Court	36	D3		Fieldview Cottages	49	A4	[6]
Emerald Place	38	E2	[23]	(Northumberland Rd)				Father Mathew Square	37	C2	[26]	Findlater Building Apts.	30	D1	[3]

STREET NAME	PAGE/GRID REFERENCE
Findlater Place	38 D2 [25]
Findlater Street (Dun Laoghaire)	60 E1 [7]
Findlater Street (Nth Circular Rd)	37 B2 [10]
Fingal Place	37 C1 [5]
Fingal Street	37 C3 [11]
Finglas	24 D2
Finglas East	24 E1
Finglas Park	24 E1
Finglas Place	24 E2
Finglas Road	24 E2
Finglas Road Old	24 F3
Finglas South	24 D2
Finglas Square	48 D3 [2]
Finglas West	24 D1
Finglaswood Road	24 D1
Finn Street	37 B2 [12]
Finneber Fort	24 E2
Finneber Fort Square	24 E2
Finnscourt	34 D3
Finnsgreen	34 D3
Finnsgrove	34 D3
Finnslawn	34 D3
Finnspark	34 D3
Finnstown Fairways	34 D3
Finnstown Hall	34 D3
Finnsvale	34 D3
Finnsview	34 D3
Finnswalk	34 D3
Finnswood	34 D3
Finsbury Green	47 B4
Finsbury Park	47 B4
Firgrove	60 E4 [7]
Firhouse	55 C1
Firhouse Road	55 B2
Firhouse Road West	55 A2
First Avenue (Belgard Heights)	44 F4
First Avenue (Sarsfield Road)	36 F3
First Avenue (Seville Place)	38 F2 [3]
Fishamble Street	38 D2
Fishermans Wharf	39 A2 [1]
Fitzgerald Park	59 C1 [6]
Fitzgerald Street	38 D4 [1]
Fitzgibbon Lane	38 E1 [21]
Fitzgibbon Street	38 E1
Fitzmaurice Road (Glasnevin)	24 F2
Fitzmaurice Road (Rathcoole)	52 F2
Fitzpatrick's Cottages	46 F1 [6]
Fitzroy Avenue	25 B4
Fitzwilliam Court (Fitzwilliam Road)	38 E3 [38]
Fitzwilliam Court (Stillorgan Road)	48 E3
Fitzwilliam Lane	38 E3
Fitzwilliam Place	38 E4
Fitzwilliam Place North (Grangegorman)	37 C2 [23]
Fitzwilliam Quay	39 A3
Fitzwilliam Square East	38 E3
Fitzwilliam Square North	38 E3
Fitzwilliam Square South	38 E3
Fitzwilliam Square West	38 E3
Fitzwilliam Street (Ringsend)	39 A3 [2]
Fitzwilliam Street Lower	38 E3
Fitzwilliam Street Upper	38 E3
Fitzwilliam Terrace	68 D2 [21]
Fleet Street	38 D2
Fleming Road	25 A3
Fleming's Place	38 E4
Flemingstown Park	47 B4
Flemming House	38 E4 [39]
Fleurville	49 A4
Floraville Avenue	44 E1
Floraville Drive	44 E2
Floraville Estate	44 E1
Floraville Lawn	44 E1
Florence Road	67 C2
Florence Street	38 D4 [17]
Florence Terrace (Bray)	67 C2 [39]
*Florence Terrace (Leeson Park Avenue)	38 E4
Florence Villas (Bray)	67 C2 [40]
*Florence Villas (Sandymount)	39 A4
Flower Grove	60 D2
Foley Street	38 E2

STREET NAME	PAGE/GRID REFERENCE
Fontenoy Street	38 D1
Fontenoy Terrace	68 D3
Fonthill Abbey	56 F1 [3]
Fonthill Park	56 F1
Fonthill Road (Clondalkin)	35 A2
Fonthill Road (Rathfarnham)	56 F1
Fonthill Road North	35 A3
Fonthill Road South	44 D2
Forbes Lane	37 C3
Forbes Street	38 F2
Forest Avenue (Kilnamanagh)	45 A3
Forest Avenue (Swords)	1 B3
Forest Boulevard	1 B3
Forest Close	45 A3
Forest Court	1 B2
Forest Crescent	1 B3
Forest Dale	1 B2
Forest Drive (Kilnamanagh)	45 A3
Forest Drive (Swords)	1 B3
Forest Green (Kilnamanagh)	45 A3
Forest Green (Swords)	1 B3
Forest Grove	1 B3
Forest Hills (Rathcoole)	52 E2
Forest Hills (Swords)	1 C3
Forest Lawn	45 A2
Forest Park (Kilnamanagh)	45 A3
Forest Park (Leixlip)	32 F1
Forest Park (Swords)	1 B2
Forest Road	1 B4
Forest View	1 B3
Forest Walk	1 C3
Forest Way	1 C3
Forestfields Road	1 C3
Forestwood Avenue	12 D4
Forestwood Close	12 E4
Forge Court	30 D2 [15]
Forster Way	2 D2
Fort Ostman	37 B4
Fortescue Lane	38 D4
Fortfield Avenue	46 E3
Fortfield Court	46 E3 [2]
Fortfield Drive	46 E3
Fortfield Gardens	47 A2
Fortfield Grove	46 E3
Fortfield Park	46 E3
Fortfield Road	46 E2
Fortfield Road	46 E3
Fortfield Square	46 E3
Fortfield Terrace	47 A2
Forth Road	38 F1
Forthill Court	56 F1 [6]
Fortlawn Avenue	22 D1
Fortlawn Drive	22 D1
Fortlawn Park	22 D1
Fortlawns	60 E2
Fortrose Park	46 E4
Fortunestown	53 C1
Fortunestown Close	53 C1
Fortunestown Crescent	53 C1
Fortunestown Lane	53 B1
Fortunestown Road	54 D2
Fortunestown Way	54 D1
Fortview Avenue	39 C1
Fortwilliam	48 E4
Foster Place North	38 E1 [41]
Foster Place South (College Green)	38 D2 [38]
Foster Terrace	38 E1
Fosterbrook	48 E2
Fosters Avenue	48 D3
Fountain Place	37 C2
Fountain Road	37 B2
Fourth Avenue (Seville Place)	38 F2 [8]
Fourth Avenue (Tallaght)	44 F4
*Fownes Street Lower (off Temple Bar)	38 D2
Fownes Street Upper	38 D2 [47]
Fox and Geese	45 A1
Fox Hill	55 A4
Foxborough Avenue	34 E3
Foxborough Close	34 F3
Foxborough Court	34 F3
Foxborough Crescent	34 F3 [2]
Foxborough Downes	34 E3
Foxborough Drive	34 E3

STREET NAME	PAGE/GRID REFERENCE
Foxborough Gardens	34 F3
Foxborough Glade	34 F3
Foxborough Glen	34 F3
Foxborough Green	34 F3
Foxborough Hall	34 F3 [1]
Foxborough Heights	34 F3
Foxborough Hill	34 E3
Foxborough Lane	34 F3
Foxborough Lawn	34 F3
Foxborough Manor	34 F3
Foxborough Meadows	34 E3
Foxborough Park	34 E3
Foxborough Place	34 E3
Foxborough Rise	34 E3
Foxborough Road	34 F3
Foxborough Road	34 E3
Foxborough Row	34 F3
Foxborough Walk	34 F3
Foxborough Way	34 F3
Foxdene Avenue	34 F3
Foxdene Drive	34 F3
Foxdene Gardens	34 F3
Foxdene Green	34 F3
Foxdene Grove	34 F3
Foxdene Park	34 F3
Foxes Grove	64 E3
Foxe's Lane	27 B2
Foxfield	34 D3
Foxfield Avenue	27 B2
Foxfield Crescent	27 B2
Foxfield Drive	27 B2
Foxfield Green	27 B2
Foxfield Grove	27 B2
Foxfield Heights	27 B2
Foxfield Lawn	27 B2
Foxfield Park	27 B2
Foxfield Road	27 B2
Foxfield St John	27 B2
Foxford	34 F2
Foxhill Avenue	27 A1
Foxhill Close	27 A1
Foxhill Court	27 A1
Foxhill Crescent	27 A1
Foxhill Drive	27 A1
Foxhill Green	14 D4
Foxhill Grove	27 A1
Foxhill Lawn	27 A1
Foxhill Park	27 A1
Foxhill Way	27 A1
Foxpark	34 D3
Foxrock	59 A3
Foxrock Avenue	59 A2
Foxrock Close	59 B2
Foxrock Court	59 A2
Foxrock Crescent	59 B2
Foxrock Green	59 A2
Foxrock Grove	59 B2
Foxrock Manor	58 F2
Foxrock Mount	59 A2 [4]
Foxrock Park	59 A2
Foxrock Wood	59 B2
Foxwood (Lucan)	34 D3
Foxwood (Swords)	2 D2
Foyle Road	25 C4
Frances Ball House	46 F4 [23]
Francis Street	37 C3
Frankfort	47 B4 [10]
Frankfort Avenue	47 A2
Frankfort Cottages	38 E1
Frankfort Court	46 F2 [8]
Frankfort Flats	46 F2 [9]
Frankfort Mews	47 B4
Frankfort Park	47 B4
Frascati Court	49 A3 [23]
Frascati Hall	49 A3 [24]
Frascati Park	49 A3
Frascati Road	49 A3
Frederick Court	38 D1 [46]
Frederick Lane North	38 D1 [14]
Frederick Street North	38 D1
Frederick Street South	38 E3
French Park	9 B2
Frenchman's Lane	38 E2 [20]
Friar's Walk	44 E1 [5]
Friarsland Avenue	47 C3 [3]

STREET NAME	PAGE/GRID REFERENCE
Friarsland Crescent	47 C3
Friarsland Road	47 C3
Friary Avenue	37 C2 [6]
Friary Grove	37 C2 [41]
Friel Avenue	36 D4
Fumbally Lane	38 D3
Furry Park Court	26 E3
Furry Park Road	26 E3
Furze Road (Phoenix Park)	36 E1
Furze Road (Sandyford)	58 E2

G

STREET NAME	PAGE/GRID REFERENCE
Gables	27 A1 [6]
Gaelic Street	38 F1 [6]
Gainsborough	2 F3
Gainsborough Avenue	2 F3
Gainsborough Close	2 F3
Gainsborough Court	2 F3
Gainsborough Crescent	2 F3
Gainsborough Downs	2 F3
Gainsborough Green	2 F3
Gainsborough Lawn	2 F3
Gainsborough Park	2 F3
Gallaun Road	11 C4
Gallery Quay	38 F3
Galloping Green	59 A1 [9]
Galloping Green	58 F1
Gallows Hill	1 C2
Galmoy Road	24 F4
Galtrim Park	67 C2
Galtrim Road	67 C2
Galtymore Close	36 F4
Galtymore Drive	37 A4
Galtymore Park	36 F4
Galtymore Road	37 A4
Gandon Close	46 F1 [9]
Gandon Mews	34 D1 [10]
Garden Lane	37 C3 [21]
*Garden Terrace (off Clanbrassil St Upper)	37 C4
Garden View	38 D4 [42]
Gardiner Lane	38 E1
Gardiner Place	38 D1
Gardiner Row	38 D1 [40]
Gardiner St Middle	38 E1
Gardiner Street Lower	38 E1
Gardiner Street Upper	38 D1
Garnett Hall	7 A2
Garnett Vale	7 A2
Garnish Square	22 F1
Garrison Mews	64 D1
Garrynisk Close	44 F3
Garrynisk Road	44 F3
Garrynure	47 B2
Garryowen Road	36 E3
Gartan Avenue	25 A4
Gartan Court	2 E1
Gartan Drive	2 E1
Garter Lane	53 B1
Garthy Wood Apts.	56 D1
Garville Avenue	47 A2
Garville Avenue Upper	46 F2
Garville Court	47 A2 [10]
Garville Drive	47 A2 [6]
Garville Lane	47 A2
Garville Place	47 A2 [5]
Garville Road	47 A2
Gas Yard Lane	3 B2
Gateway Avenue	25 A1
Gateway Court	25 A1
Gateway Crescent	25 A1
Gateway Gardens	25 A1
Gateway Mews	25 A1
Gateway Place	25 A1
Gateway View	25 A1
Gaybrook Lawns	3 A3
Gazelle Avenue	9 B2
Gazelle Lane	9 B2
Gazelle Mews	9 B2
Gazelle Terrace	9 B2
Gazelle Walk	9 B2
Geoffrey Keating Road	37 C3 [30]
*George Reynolds Flats (off Oliver Plunkett Ave)	39 A3

STREET NAME	PAGE/GRID REFERENCE	STREET NAME	PAGE/GRID REFERENCE	STREET NAME	PAGE/GRID REFERENCE	STREET NAME	PAGE/GRID REFERENCE
George's Avenue (Blackrock)	49 A3	Glen Ellan Pines	1 C1	Glencairn Park	58 E3	Glenlyon Grove	55 C2
George's Dock	38 E2 [36]	Glen Ellan Walk	1 C1	Glencairn Place	58 E4	Glenlyon Park	55 C2
George's Hill	38 D2 [6]	Glen Garth	59 B3	Glencairn Rise	58 E3	Glenmalure Park	37 B3 [13]
George's Lane	37 C2 [3]	Glen Grove	59 B3	Glencairn Road	58 E3	Glenmalure Square	47 B2
George's Place (Blackrock)	49 A3 [6]	Glen Lawn Drive	59 B3	Glencairn Thicket	58 F3	*Glenmalure Villas	37 B3
George's Place (Dun Laoghaire)	50 D4	Glen na Smol	67 C4	Glencairn View	58 E3	Glenmaroon Park	35 C2
George's Place (Temple Street)	38 D1 [43]	Glen Terrace	60 E1 [10]	Glencairn Walk	58 E3	Glenmaroon Road	35 C2
George's Quay	38 E2	Glen Walk	59 B3	Glencairn Way	58 E3	Glenmore Court	56 F2
Georges Road	24 E1 [1]	Glenaan Road	25 B2	Glencar Road	37 B1 [2]	Glenmore Park	56 F2
George's Street Great North	38 D1	Glenabbey Road	48 E4	Glencarr Court	64 E1 [8]	Glenmore Road	37 B1 [1]
George's Street Great South	38 D3	Glenacre	62 E4	Glencarr Lawn	64 E1	Glenmurry Park	45 C3
George's Street Lower	50 D4	Glenageary Avenue	60 D2	Glencarraig	29 B1	Glenomena Grove	48 E2
George's Street Upper	50 D4	Glenageary Court	60 D2	Glencarrig Court	55 B2	Glenomena Park	48 E2
Georgian Hamlet	15 A4	Glenageary Hall	60 E2	Glencarrig Drive	55 B2	Glenpark Close	35 B1
Georgian Village	23 A4	Glenageary Lodge	60 D2	Glencarrig Green	55 B2	Glenpark Drive	35 B1
Gerald Street	38 F3 [9]	Glenageary Park	60 D2	Glencarthy Court Apts.	26 D3	Glenpark Road	35 B1
Geraldine Court	17 C3 [4]	Glenageary Road Lower	60 D1	Glencloy Road	25 B2	Glenshane Close	54 D1
Geraldine Street	38 D1	Glenageary Road Upper	60 D1	Glencorp Road	25 C2	Glenshane Crescent	54 D1
*Geraldstown Woods Apts	12 D4	Glenageary Woods	60 D1	Glencourt Estate	67 C3	Glenshane Drive	54 D1
Gertrude Terrace	67 B2 [25]	Glenagerry Road	50 D4	Glencullen	62 E4	Glenshane Gardens	54 D1
Gilbert Road	37 C4 [12]	Glenalbyn Road	58 F1	Glencullen	61 C3	Glenshane Green	54 D1
Gilford Avenue	39 B4	Glenalua Heights	60 E3	Glendale	20 D4	Glenshane Grove	54 D1
Gilford Court	39 A4 [10]	Glenalua Road	60 E3	Glendale Drive	67 C3	Glenshane Lawns	54 D1
Gilford Drive	39 A4	Glenalua Terrace	60 E3	Glendale Meadows	20 E4	Glenshane Park	54 D1
Gilford Park	39 A4	Glenamuck Cottages	63 A2	Glendale Park	46 D3	Glenshesk Road	25 C2
Gilford Place	38 E1 [30]	Glenamuck North	62 F1	Glendalough Road	25 A4 [6]	Glenside Villas	35 C1 [2]
Gilford Road	39 A4	Glenamuck Road	63 A1	*Glendenning Lane	38 D3	Glenthorn	67 B4
Gilford Terrace	39 B4 [1]	Glenamuck Road	62 F2	(off Wicklow Street)		Glenties Drive	24 D2
Giltspur Heights	67 B4	Glenamuck Road	59 B4	Glendhu Park	23 C3	Glenties Park	24 D2
Giltspur Lane	67 B4	Glenann	46 F4 [4]	Glendhu Road	23 C3	Glentow Road	25 B2
Giltspur Wood	67 B3	Glenanne	46 E2	Glendoher Avenue	56 F1	Glentworth Park	27 A1 [2]
Glandore Park	59 C1	Glenard Avenue (Bray)	67 C2	Glendoher Close	56 F1	Glenvale	34 E3
Glandore Road	25 C3	Glenard Avenue (Cabra)	37 B1 [5]	Glendoher Drive	56 F1	Glenvar Park	48 F3
Glasanaon Court	24 E2	Glenard Hall	47 C3 [7]	Glendoher Park	56 E1	Glenvara Park	55 C2
Glasanaon Park	24 E2	Glenarm Avenue	25 B4	Glendoher Road	56 E1	Glenview (Enniskerry)	66 D3
Glasanaon Road	24 E2	Glenarriff Road	23 C3	Glendoo Close	45 B3	Glenview (Rochestown Avenue)	60 D3
Glasaree Court	24 E2	Glenart Avenue	48 F4	Glendown Avenue	46 D3	Glenview Drive	55 B1
Glasaree Road	24 E2	Glenaulin	36 D2	Glendown Close	46 D3	Glenview Lawns	55 B1
Glasilawn Avenue	24 F2	Glenaulin Drive	36 D2	Glendown Court	46 D3	Glenview Park	55 B1
Glasilawn Road	24 F2	Glenaulin Green	35 C2 [2]	Glendown Crescent	46 D3	Glenville Avenue	22 E2
Glaslyn	26 D4	Glenaulin Park	36 D2	Glendown Drive	46 D3	Glenville Court	22 E3
Glasmeen Road	24 F2	Glenaulin Road	35 C2	Glendown Green	46 D3	Glenville Drive	22 E3
Glasmore Park	1 C1	Glenavon Park	64 D1	Glendown Grove	46 D3	Glenville Garth	22 E3
Glasnamana Place	24 F2 [2]	Glenavy Park	46 E2	Glendown Lawn	46 D3	Glenville Green	22 E2
Glasnamana Road	24 F2	Glenayle Road	26 F1	Glendown Park	46 D3	Glenville Grove	22 E2
Glasnevin	24 F3	Glenayr Road	46 F2	Glendown Road	46 D3	Glenville Lawn	22 E2
Glasnevin Avenue	24 F1	Glenbeigh Park	37 B1	Glendun Road	25 B2	Glenville Road	22 E3
Glasnevin Court	24 E3	Glenbeigh Road	37 B1	Glenealy Downs	8 F4	Glenville Terrace	47 C4 [8]
Glasnevin Downs	24 F3	Glenbourne Avenue	58 F4	Glenealy Road	37 B4	Glenville Way	22 E2
Glasnevin Drive	25 A1	Glenbourne Close	58 F4	Gleneaston	19 B4	Glenwood	67 B2
Glasnevin Hill	25 A3	Glenbourne Crescent	58 F4	Gleneaston Avenue	19 B4	Glenwood Road	26 F1
Glasnevin North	24 F1	*Glenbourne Drive	58 F4	Gleneaston Close	19 B4	Glin Avenue	13 B4
Glasnevin Oaks	24 F3 [3]	Glenbourne Green	58 F4	Gleneaston Court	19 B4	Glin Crescent	13 B4
Glasnevin Park	24 F1	Glenbourne Grove	58 F4	Gleneaston Crescent	19 B4	Glin Drive	13 B4
Glasnevin Woods	24 E3	Glenbourne Park	58 F4	Gleneaston Drive	19 B4	Glin Grove	13 B4
Glasson Court	47 B3	Glenbourne Road	58 F4	Gleneaston Gardens	19 B4	Glin Park	13 B4
Glasthule Buildings	60 E1 [11]	Glenbourne View	58 F4	Gleneaston Green	19 B4	Glin Road	13 B4
Glasthule Road	60 E1	Glenbourne Walk	58 F4	Gleneaston Grove	19 B4	Glitspur Brook	67 C3
Gleann na Rí	63 C1	Glenbourne Way	58 F4	Gleneaston Lawns	19 B4	Gloucester Diamond	38 E1 [52]
Gleann na Smol (Monkstown)	49 B4	Glenbower Park	47 B4 [1]	Gleneaston Manor	19 B4	*Gloucester Lane (off	38 E1
Gleann na Smol (Tallaght)	54 F2	Glenbrae	64 E2	Gleneaston Park	19 B4	Sean McDermott Street Lower)	
Glebe (Airport)	13 B1	Glenbrian Hall	26 D4 [8]	Gleneaston Rise	19 B4	Gloucester Place	38 E1 [25]
Glebe (Newcastle)	41 C3	Glenbrook	66 E3	Gleneaston Square	19 B4	Gloucester Place Lower	38 E1 [53]
Glebe (Rathcoole)	52 D3	Glenbrook	67 B3	Gleneaston View	19 B4	Gloucester Place Lower	38 E1 [54]
Glebe Hall	59 C1	Glenbrook Park	46 F4	Gleneaston Way	19 B4	Gloucester Place Upper	38 E1 [24]
Glebe View (Finglas)	24 E2	Glenbrook Road	23 C3	Gleneaston Woods	19 B4	Gloucester Street South	38 E2
Glebe View (Finglas)	24 E2 [7]	Glenburgh Terrace	67 B2 [2]	Glenfarne Road	26 F1	Glovers Alley	38 D3 [28]
Gledswood Avenue	47 C3	Glencairn	58 E3	Glenfield Avenue	35 A2	*Glovers Court (off York Street)	38 D3
Gledswood Close	47 C3	Glencairn Avenue	58 E3	Glenfield Close	35 A2	Goatstown	48 D4
Gledswood Drive	47 C3 [5]	Glencairn Chase	58 E3	Glenfield Drive	35 A2	Goatstown Avenue	47 C4
Gledswood Park	47 C3	Glencairn Close	58 E3	Glenfield Grove	35 A2	Goatstown Road	47 C4
Glen Avenue	59 B3	Glencairn Copse	58 E4	Glenfield Park	35 A2	Gobán Saor	58 E4
Glen Close	59 B3	Glencairn Court	58 E4	Glengara Close	60 D1 [15]	*Godfrey Place	37 B1
Glen Dale	59 B3	Glencairn Crescent	58 E4	Glengara Park	60 D1	(off Oxmanstown Road)	
Glen Drive	59 B3	Glencairn Dale	58 E3	Glengariff Parade	38 D1 [64]	Gofton Hall	24 E1 [2]
Glen Druid	64 E1	Glencairn Drive	58 E3	Glengarriff Crescent	38 D1 [18]	Golden Ball	62 F2
Glen Ellan Avenue	1 C1	Glencairn Garth	58 E3 [1]	Glengarriff Parade	38 D1	Golden Lane	38 D3
Glen Ellan Close	1 C1	Glencairn Glade	58 E4	Glenhill Avenue	24 E2	Goldenbridge Avenue	37 A3
Glen Ellan Court	1 C1	Glencairn Glen	58 F4	Glenhill Court	24 E2	Goldenbridge Gardens	37 A3 [4]
Glen Ellan Crescent	1 C1	Glencairn Green	58 E3	Glenhill Drive	24 E2	Goldenbridge Terrace	37 A3 [5]
Glen Ellan Drive	1 C1	Glencairn Grove	58 F4	Glenhill Grove	24 E2	Goldenbridge Walk	36 F4
Glen Ellan Gardens	1 C1	Glencairn Heath	58 E3	Glenhill Road	24 E2	Goldenbridge Walk	37 A3 [16]
Glen Ellan Green	1 C1	Glencairn Heights	58 E3	Glenhill Villas	24 E2 [2]	Goldsmith Street	38 D1
Glen Ellan Grove	1 C1	Glencairn Lawn	58 E3	Glenlucan	67 B2	Goldsmith Terrace	67 C2 [25]
Glen Ellan Park	1 C1	Glencairn Oaks	58 E4	Glenlyon Crescent	55 C2	Golf Links Road	15 A2

STREET NAME	PAGE/GRID REFERENCE
Gordon Avenue	59 A3
Gordon Place	38 D4 [23]
Gordon Street	38 F3
Gorsefield Court	26 F2 [1]
Gort na Mona Drive	59 B3
Gortbeg Avenue	24 E3
Gortbeg Drive	24 E3
Gortbeg Park	24 E3
Gortbeg Road	24 E3
Gortmore Avenue	24 E2
Gortmore Drive	24 E2
Gortmore Park	24 E3
Gortmore Road	24 E3
Gosworth Park	60 E1
Gowrie Park	60 D1
Grace O'Malley Drive	30 D2
Grace O'Malley Road	30 D2
Grace Park Avenue	25 B4
Grace Park Court	25 C2
Grace Park Gardens	25 B4
Grace Park Heights	25 C3
Grace Park Manor	25 B3
Grace Park Meadows	25 C3
Grace Park Road	25 C3
Grace Park Terrace	25 C3
Gracefield Avenue	26 F2
Gracefield Road	26 E2
Grafton Street	38 D3
Graham Court	38 D1 [13]
Graham's Row	38 D1 [54]
Graigue Court	11 C4
Granby Lane	38 D1
Granby Place	38 D2
Granby Row	38 D1
Grand Canal Docks	38 F3
Grand Canal Place	37 C3 [2]
Grand Canal Quay	38 F3
Grand Canal Street Lower	38 F3
Grand Canal Street Upper	38 F3
Grand Canal View	37 A3
Grand Parade	38 E4
Grange (Malahide)	14 E1
Grange (Meath)	6 E4
Grange Abbey Crescent	14 E4
Grange Abbey Drive	14 E4
Grange Abbey Grove	14 E4
Grange Abbey Road	14 E4
Grange Avenue	14 F4
Grange Brook	56 F2
Grange Close (Kilbarrack)	27 C1
Grange Close (Pottery Road)	59 C3
Grange Cottages	58 F1 [3]
Grange Court	57 A1
Grange Crescent	59 B2
Grange Downs	57 A1
Grange Drive	27 C1
Grange Grove	59 B1 [2]
Grange Hall	57 B3
Grange Hall Apts.	27 A2
Grange Lodge Avenue	14 E4
Grange Lodge Court	14 E4
Grange Manor	34 D3
Grange Manor Avenue	57 A1
Grange Manor Close	57 A1
Grange Manor Drive	57 A1
Grange Manor Grove	57 A1
Grange Manor Road	57 A1
Grange Parade	27 C1
Grange Park (Baldoyle)	14 F4
Grange Park (Cornelscourt)	59 B2
Grange Park (Willbrook)	56 F1
Grange Park Avenue	27 A2
Grange Park Close	27 B2
Grange Park Crescent	27 B2
Grange Park Drive	27 A2
Grange Park Green	27 B2
Grange Park Grove	27 A2
Grange Park Rise	27 B1
Grange Park Road	27 A2
Grange Park View	27 B1
Grange Park Walk	27 A2
Grange Rise	14 F4
Grange Road (Baldoyle)	14 F4
Grange Road (Marley Park)	57 A2
Grange Road (Rathfarnham)	46 F4

STREET NAME	PAGE/GRID REFERENCE
Grange Road (The Priory)	56 F1
Grange Terrace	59 B1 [6]
Grange View Close	43 B1
Grange View Court	43 B1
Grange View Green	43 B1
Grange View Grove	43 B1
Grange View Lawn	43 B1
Grange View Park	43 B1
Grange View Road	43 B1
Grange View Walk	43 B1
Grange View Way	43 B1
Grange View Wood	43 B1
Grange Way	27 C1
Grange Wood (Ballinteer)	57 A2
Grangebrook Avenue	56 F2
Grangebrook Close	56 F2
Grangebrook Park	56 F2
Grangebrook Vale	56 F2
Grangefield	57 B3
Grangegorman Lower	37 C2
Grangegorman Upper	37 C1
*Grangegorman Villas	37 C1
(Grangegorman Upper)	
Grangemore	14 E4
Grangemore Avenue	14 D4
Grangemore Court	14 D4
Grangemore Crescent	14 D4
Grangemore Drive	14 E4
Grangemore Grove	14 E4
Grangemore Lawn	14 E4
Grangemore Park	14 E4
Grangemore Rise	14 D4
Grangemore Road	14 D4
Grangewood	59 C1
Granite Hall	60 D1 [7]
Granite Place	38 F4 [10]
Granite Terrace	36 F3 [11]
Granitefield	59 C3
Granitefield	60 D3
Granitefield Manor	59 C3
Grantham Place	38 D4
Grantham Street	38 D4
Grant's Row	38 E3 [5]
Granville Close	60 D3
Granville Crescent	60 D3 [2]
Granville Park	59 A1
Granville Road (Cabinteely)	59 C3
Granville Road (Deans Grange)	59 A2
Grattan Court	31 C4
Grattan Court East	38 F3 [28]
Grattan Crescent	36 F3
Grattan Hall	14 E4
Grattan Lodge	14 E4
Grattan Parade	25 A4
Grattan Place	38 F3 [29]
Grattan Street	38 F3
Gray Square	37 C3 [41]
*Gray Street (off Meath St)	37 C3
Great Western Avenue	37 C1 [18]
Great Western Square	37 C1 [8]
Great Western Villas	37 C1 [9]
Greeg Court	38 D2
Greek Street	38 D2
Green Acre Court	56 D1
Green Isle Court	44 D2 [2]
Green Isle Road	43 C3
Green Lane (Celbridge)	31 A2
Green Lane (Leixlip)	19 C4
Green Lane (Rathcoole)	52 E2
Green Park (Rathgar)	47 B3
Green Park Road	67 B2
Green Road (Blackrock)	48 F3
Green Street	38 D2
Green Street East	38 F2
Green Street Little	38 D2 [8]
Greencastle Avenue	26 E1
Greencastle Crescent	26 E1
Greencastle Drive	13 B4
Greencastle Parade	26 F1
Greencastle Park	13 B4
Greencastle Road	13 B4
Greendale Avenue	27 C2
Greendale Court	27 B2 [2]
Greendale Road	27 B2
Greenfield Close	17 C4

STREET NAME	PAGE/GRID REFERENCE
Greenfield Crescent	48 D2
Greenfield Drive	18 D4
Greenfield Manor	48 D2 [4]
Greenfield Park	55 C2
(Ballycullen Road)	
Greenfield Park	48 D2
(Stillorgan Road)	
*Greenfield Place	37 C4
(off Mount Drummond Ave)	
Greenfield Road	48 E4
(Mount Merrion)	
Greenfield Road (Sutton)	29 B1
Greenfort Avenue	35 A2
Greenfort Close	35 A2
Greenfort Crescent	35 A2
Greenfort Drive	35 A2
Greenfort Gardens	35 A2
Greenfort Lawns	35 A2
Greenfort Park	35 A2
Greenfort Walk	35 A2
Greenhills	45 B3
Greenhills Court	55 A1
Greenhills Road	45 A4
Greenlands	58 D2
Greenlawns	13 B4 [1]
Greenlea Avenue	46 E2
Greenlea Drive	46 E2
Greenlea Grove	46 E2
Greenlea Park	46 E3
Greenlea Place	46 F2 [12]
Greenlea Road	46 E3
Greenmount Avenue	37 C4 [9]
Greenmount Court	37 C4 [19]
Greenmount Lane	37 C4
Greenmount Lawns	46 F2
Greenmount Lodge	62 F2
Greenmount Road	46 F2
Greenmount Square	37 C4 [14]
Greenoge	42 E4
Greenogue Drive	52 F2
Greenore Terrace	38 F3 [26]
Greenpark Road	33 C2
Greenridge Court	22 E1
Greentrees Drive	45 C2
Greentrees Park	45 C2
Greentrees Road	45 C2
Greenview	14 E2
Greenville Avenue	37 C4 [11]
*Greenville Parade (Blackpitts)	37 C3
Greenville Place	37 C4 [35]
Greenville Road	49 B4
Greenville Terrace	37 C4
Greenwood	13 C1
Greenwood Avenue	14 D4
Greenwood Close	14 D4
Greenwood Court	14 D4
Greenwood Drive	14 D4
Greenwood Park	14 D4
Greenwood Walk	14 D4
Greenwood Way	14 D4
Grenville Lane	38 D1 [15]
Grenville Street	38 D1
Greygates (Fitzwilliam Court)	48 E3
Greygates (Sycamore Crescent)	48 E4 [1]
Grey's Lane	30 D2
Greythorn Park	60 D1
Griffeen	34 E3
Griffeen Avenue	34 D3
Griffeen Glen Avenue	34 E3
Griffeen Glen Boulevard	34 E3
Griffeen Glen Chase	34 E3
Griffeen Glen Close	34 E3
Griffeen Glen Court	34 E3
Griffeen Glen Court Yard	34 E3
Griffeen Glen Crescent	34 E3
Griffeen Glen Dale	34 E3
Griffeen Glen Dene	34 E3
Griffeen Glen Drive	34 E3
Griffeen Glen Green	34 E3
Griffeen Glen Grove	34 E3
Griffeen Glen Lawn	34 E3
Griffeen Glen Park	34 E3
Griffeen Glen Place	34 E3
Griffeen Glen Road	34 E3
Griffeen Glen Vale	34 E3

STREET NAME	PAGE/GRID REFERENCE
Griffeen Glen View	34 E3
Griffeen Glen Way	34 E3
Griffeen Glen Wood	34 D3
Griffeen Road	34 E3
Griffeen Way	34 E2
Griffin Rath Hall	18 D4
Griffin Rath Manor	18 D4
Griffin Rath Road	18 D4
Griffith Avenue	25 B3
Griffith Close	24 F2
Griffith Court	25 C4
Griffith Crescent	24 F2
Griffith Downs	25 B3
Griffith Drive	24 F2
Griffith Hall	25 C3
Griffith Heights	24 F2
Griffith Lawns	25 A3
Griffith Parade	24 F2
Griffith Road	24 F2
Griffith Square	37 C4 [22]
Grosvenor Avenue	68 D3 [3]
Grosvenor Court (Clontarf)	26 E4
Grosvenor Court	46 D3
(Templeville Road)	
Grosvenor Lane	47 A1
Grosvenor Lodge	47 A1
Grosvenor Park	47 A1 [7]
Grosvenor Place	47 A1
Grosvenor Road	47 A1
Grosvenor Square	47 A1
Grosvenor Terrace (Dalkey)	60 F2 [17]
Grosvenor Terrace	49 C4 [9]
(Dun Laoghaire)	
*Grosvenor Villas	60 F2
(Off Sorrento Rd)	
Grosvenor Villas (Rathmines)	47 A1
Grotto Avenue	48 F2
Grotto Place	48 F2
Grove Avenue (Finglas)	24 E1
Grove Avenue (Harold's Cross)	38 D4 [47]
Grove Avenue (Malahide)	3 C3
Grove Avenue (Mount Merrion)	48 F4
Grove Court (Bluebell)	36 F4 [4]
Grove Court	1 A2 [1]
(Brackenstown Road)	
Grove Court Apts.	22 D1
*Grove House Apts.	59 A3
Grove House Gardens	48 F4 [5]
Grove Lane	13 C4
Grove Lawn (Stillorgan)	48 F4
Grove Lawns (Malahide)	3 C3
Grove Paddock	48 F4
Grove Park (Coolock)	13 C4
Grove Park (Rathmines)	38 D4
Grove Park Avenue	24 F1
Grove Park Crescent	24 F1
Grove Park Drive	24 F1
Grove Park Road	24 F1
Grove Road (Blanchardstown)	22 D2
Grove Road (Finglas)	24 E1
Grove Road (Malahide)	3 C3
Grove Road (Rathmines)	38 D4
Grove Wood (Finglas)	24 E1
Grove Wood (Foxrock)	59 A3
Grovedale	63 B2
Guild Street	38 F2
Guilford Terrace	64 E3 [1]
Gulistan Cottages	47 A1
Gulistan Place	47 A1
Gulistan Terrace	47 A1
Gunny Hill	55 C3
Gurteen Avenue	36 D3
Gurteen Park	36 D3
Gurteen Road	36 D2

H

STREET NAME	PAGE/GRID REFERENCE
Hacketsland	64 E1
Haddington Lawns	60 E2
Haddington Park	60 E2
Haddington Place	38 F3 [18]
Haddington Road	38 F3
Haddington Terrace	50 D4 [7]
Haddon Court	39 B1 [2]
Haddon Park	26 D4 [5]
Haddon Road	26 E4

STREET NAME	PAGE/GRID REFERENCE		
Hadleigh Court	23	A3	
Hadleigh Green	23	A3	[2]
Hadleigh Park	23	A3	
Hagan's Court	38	E3	[39]
Haigh Terrace	50	D4	
Hainault Drive	59	B3	
Hainault Grove	59	B3	
Hainault Lawn	59	B3	
Hainault Park	59	A3	
Hainault Road	59	A3	
Halliday Road	37	C2	
Halliday Square	37	B2	[2]
Hallscourt	67	C2	
Halston Street	38	D2	
Hamilton Court (Dunboyne)	7	B3	[3]
*Hamilton Court (off Strand St Little)	38	D2	
Hamilton Hall	7	B3	
Hamilton Street	37	C4	[1]
Hammond Lane	37	C2	
Hammond Street	37	C3	[56]
Hampstead Avenue	25	A2	
Hampstead Court	25	A2	
Hampstead Park	25	A3	
Hampton Court (Clontarf)	26	F4	
Hampton Court (Tyreconnell Road)	36	F3	[16]
Hampton Crescent	48	E3	
Hampton Green	37	A1	
Hampton Park	48	E3	
Hampton Square	37	B1	
Hampton Wood	11	C4	
Hampton Wood Avenue	11	B4	
Hampton Wood Court	11	C4	
Hampton Wood Crescent	11	B4	
Hampton Wood Drive	11	C4	
Hampton Wood Green	11	B4	
Hampton Wood Lawn	11	C4	
Hampton Wood Park	11	B4	
Hampton Wood Road	11	B4	
Hampton Wood Square	11	C4	
Hampton Wood Way	11	C4	
Hamwood	6	F3	
Hanbury Lane (Lucan)	34	D1	[3]
Hanbury Lane (The Coombe)	37	C3	
Hanlon's Lane	61	B1	
Hannaville Park	46	F2	
Hanover Lane	38	D3	[1]
Hanover Quay	38	F2	
Hanover Square	38	D3	[47]
Hanover Street East	38	E2	
Hanover Street West	37	C3	[47]
Hansfield	8	E4	
Hanstead Close	34	D4	
Hanstead Dale	34	D5	
Hanstead Drive	34	D6	
Hanstead Place	34	D7	
Hanstead Way	34	D9	
Hansted Crescent	34	D4	
Hansted Park	34	D4	
Hansted Road	34	D4	
Harbour Court	38	E2	[18]
Harbour Crescent	60	F1	
Harbour Master Place	38	E2	[34]
Harbour Road (Dalkey)	60	F1	
Harbour Road (Dun Laoghaire)	50	D4	
Harbour Road (Howth)	30	D1	
Harbour Square	50	D4	
Harbour Terrace	49	C4	[8]
Harbour View (Dún Laoghaire)	50	D4	
Harbour View (Howth)	30	D1	[6]
Harcourt Lane	38	D4	[14]
Harcourt Lodge	37	A3	[22]
Harcourt Road	38	D4	
Harcourt Street	38	D3	
Harcourt Terrace	38	E4	
*Harcourt Villas (off Dundrum Rd/Mulvey Pk)	47	C3	
Hardebeck Avenue	45	C1	
Hardiman Road	25	A3	
*Hardwicke Arch (off Hardwicke St)	38	D1	
Hardwicke Lane	38	D1	[45]
Hardwicke Place	38	D1	[12]
Hardwicke Street	38	D1	

STREET NAME	PAGE/GRID REFERENCE		
Harelawn Avenue	35	A3	
Harelawn Crescent	35	A3	
Harelawn Drive	35	A2	
*Harelawn Green	35	A2	
Harelawn Grove	35	A2	
Harelawn Park	35	A2	
Harlech Crescent	48	D3	
Harlech Downs	47	C3	
Harlech Grove	48	D3	
Harlech Villas	47	C3	[4]
Harmac Court	46	F2	
Harman Street	37	C3	[54]
Harmonstown Road	26	F2	
Harmony Avenue	47	C1	[5]
Harmony Court	47	C1	[20]
Harmony Row	38	E3	[23]
Harold Bridge Court	37	C4	[36]
*Harold Crescent (off Eden Rd Lower)	60	E1	
Harold Road	37	C2	
Harold Ville Avenue	37	B3	
Harold's Cross	46	F1	
Harold's Cross Cottages	37	C4	[18]
Harold's Cross Cottages	38	D4	[54]
Harold's Cross Road	46	F1	
Harold's Grange Road	57	B3	
Harrington Street	38	D4	
Harrison Row	46	F2	
Harristown	5	A2	
Harry Street	38	D3	[17]
Hartstown Road	21	C1	
Harty Avenue	45	C1	
Harty Court	45	C1	[8]
*Harty Court (off Daniel Street)	38	D3	
Harty Place	38	D3	
Harvard	48	D3	
Hastings Street	38	F3	[5]
Hastings Terrace	60	E1	[12]
Haven View	3	B2	[2]
Haverty Road	25	C4	
Hawkins Street	38	E2	
Hawthorn Avenue	38	F1	
Hawthorn Drive	57	B1	[2]
Hawthorn Lawn	22	F3	
Hawthorn Lodge	22	F3	
Hawthorn Lodge	23	A4	
Hawthorn Manor	59	A1	[4]
Hawthorn Park	1	C2	
Hawthorn Road (Bray)	67	B1	
Hawthorn Road (Clondalkin)	44	F1	
Hawthorn Terrace	38	F1	
Hawthorn View	32	D2	
Hawthorns Road	58	D2	
Hayden Square	48	D3	[3]
Hayden's Lane	34	D3	
Haydens Park	34	D3	
Haydens Park Avenue	34	D3	
Haydens Park Close	34	D3	
Haydens Park Dale	34	D3	
Haydens Park Drive	34	D3	
Haydens Park Glade	34	D3	
Haydens Park Green	34	D3	
Haydens Park Grove	34	D3	
Haydens Park Lawn	34	D3	
Haydens Park View	34	D3	
Haydens Park Walk	34	D3	
Haydens Park Way	34	D3	
Haymarket	37	C2	
Haymarket House	37	C2	[49]
Hayworth Close	21	A1	[1]
Hayworth Court	21	B1	
Hayworth Drive	21	B1	
Hayworth Mews	21	A1	
Hayworth Place	21	A1	
Hayworth Rise	21	A1	
Hayworth Terrace	21	A1	
Hazel Avenue	58	D1	
Hazel Court	14	F2	[7]

STREET NAME	PAGE/GRID REFERENCE		
Hazel Grove	14	F2	
Hazel Lawn (Blanchardstown)	22	E2	
Hazel Lawn (Kill O'The Grange)	59	C2	[4]
Hazel Park	46	E2	[2]
Hazel Road	26	D3	
Hazel Villas	58	D1	
Hazelbrook (Kilmacud)	58	D1	
Hazelbrook (Malahide)	14	E1	
Hazelbrook (Tymon North)	45	B4	
Hazelbrook Apts.	46	E2	[7]
Hazelbrook Court	46	E2	
Hazelbrook Drive	46	E2	
Hazelbrook Road	46	E2	
Hazelbury Green	8	E4	
Hazelbury Park	8	E4	
Hazelcroft Gardens	24	E2	
Hazelcroft Park	24	E2	
Hazelcroft Road	24	E2	
Hazeldene	47	C1	
Hazeldine	67	C4	
Hazelgrove	54	D2	
Hazelgrove Court	54	E2	
Hazelhatch	41	B1	
Hazelhatch Road	41	C3	
Hazelwood (Bray)	67	B2	
Hazelwood (Shankill)	64	E2	
Hazelwood Avenue	21	C1	
Hazelwood Bank	44	D2	
Hazelwood Close	44	D2	
Hazelwood Court (Beaumont)	26	D1	
Hazelwood Court (Hartstown)	21	C1	
Hazelwood Crescent (Bray)	67	B2	
Hazelwood Crescent (Clondalkin)	44	D2	
Hazelwood Crescent (Hartstown)	21	C1	
Hazelwood Drive	26	D2	
Hazelwood Green	21	C1	
Hazelwood Grove	26	E1	
Hazelwood House	38	D4	[59]
Hazelwood Lane	44	D2	
Hazelwood Park	26	D1	
Hazelwood View	44	D2	
Hazlebury Park	8	E4	
Headford Grove	47	B4	
Healthfield Road	46	F2	
*Healy Street (off Rutland Place North)	38	E1	
Heaney Avenue	35	C4	
Heany Avenue	60	F2	[19]
Heath Square	24	E1	[3]
Heather Close	57	A2	
Heather Drive	57	A2	
Heather Gardens	4	D4	
Heather Grove (Ballinteer)	57	B2	
Heather Grove (Palmerston)	35	B2	
Heather Lawn	57	A2	
Heather Park	57	B2	
Heather Road (Ballinteer)	57	A2	
Heather Road (Burton Hall)	58	E2	
Heather View Avenue	54	F2	
Heather View Close	54	F2	
Heather View Drive	54	F2	
Heather View Lawn	54	F2	
Heather View Park	54	F2	
Heather View Road	54	F2	
Heather Walk	4	D4	
Heatherwood	67	B4	
Heathfield	49	B4	[17]
Heidelberg	48	D3	
Hempenstal Terrace	39	B4	[5]
Hendrick Place	37	C2	[9]
Hendrick Street	37	C2	
Henley Court	47	B4	[8]
Henley Park	47	B4	
Henley Villas	47	B4	
Henrietta Lane	38	D1	
Henrietta Place	38	D2	
Henrietta Street	38	D2	
Henry Place	38	D2	[16]
Henry Road	36	D4	
Henry Street	38	D2	
Herbert Avenue	48	E1	
Herbert Cottages	38	F4	[4]
Herbert Crescent	22	F2	[1]

STREET NAME	PAGE/GRID REFERENCE		
Herbert Lane	38	E3	[41]
Herbert Park (Ballsbridge)	38	F4	
Herbert Park (Oldcourt)	67	B3	
Herbert Park Lane	38	F4	
Herbert Park Mews	47	C1	
Herbert Place (Baggot Street Lower)	38	E3	
*Herbert Place (off Bath St)	39	A3	
Herbert Road (Blanchardstown)	22	F2	
Herbert Road (Oldcourt)	67	B3	
Herbert Road (Sandymount)	39	A4	
Herbert Street	38	E3	
Herbert View	67	B2	[26]
Herberton Drive	37	B4	
Herberton Park	37	B3	[15]
Herberton Road	37	B4	
Hermitage Avenue	56	F1	
Hermitage Close	56	F1	
Hermitage Court	57	A1	
Hermitage Crescent	34	F1	
Hermitage Downs	57	A1	
Hermitage Drive	56	F1	
Hermitage Garden	34	F1	
Hermitage Green	34	F1	
Hermitage Grove	56	F1	
Hermitage Lawn	56	F1	
Hermitage Manor	34	F1	
Hermitage Park (Grange Road)	56	F1	
Hermitage Park (Lucan)	34	F1	
Hermitage Place	34	F1	
Hermitage Road	34	F1	
Hermitage Valley	34	F1	
Hermitage View	56	F1	
Hermitage Way	34	F1	
Heronford Lane	63	C2	
Heuston Square	37	A3	[11]
*Hewardine Terrace (off Killarney Street)	38	E1	
Heytesbury Lane	38	F4	
Heytesbury Street	38	D3	
Hibernian Avenue	38	F1	[5]
Hibernian Terrace	36	E2	[3]
High Park	25	C2	
High Street (Christ Church)	38	D3	
High Street (Tallaght)	55	A1	[2]
Highdownhill	51	C1	
Highfield Avenue (Rathfarnham)	57	A2	
Highfield Close	1	C2	
Highfield Court (Rathgar)	47	A2	[3]
Highfield Court (Rathfarnham)	57	A2	[4]
Highfield Crescent	1	C2	
Highfield Downs	1	C2	
Highfield Drive	57	A2	
Highfield Green	1	C2	
Highfield Grove	47	A2	
Highfield Lawn	1	C2	
Highfield Manor	47	A2	
Highfield Park (Celbridge Road)	33	A1	
Highfield Park (Churchtown)	47	B3	
Highfield Road	47	A2	
Highland Avenue	59	B3	
Highland Grove	59	B3	
Highland Lawn	59	B3	
Highland View	59	B3	
Highridge Green	58	E1	
Highthorn Park	59	C1	
Highthorn Woods	59	C1	[10]
Hill Cottages	60	E3	[1]
Hill Court	14	F1	
Hill Crest	3	C4	
Hill Drive	3	B3	
Hill Street	38	D1	
Hill View	57	B1	
Hillbrook Woods	22	D1	
Hillcourt	47	A2	
Hillcourt Park	60	D2	
Hillcourt Road	60	D2	
Hillcrest (Lucan)	34	D2	
Hillcrest (Malahide)	3	A2	[1]
Hillcrest (Rathgar)	47	A2	
Hillcrest (Templeogue)	46	D4	[1]
Hillcrest Avenue	33	C2	
Hillcrest Close	33	C2	
Hillcrest Court	34	D2	

STREET NAME	PAGE/GRID REFERENCE
Hillcrest Downs	58 D3
Hillcrest Drive	33 C2
Hillcrest Green	33 C2
Hillcrest Grove	34 D2
Hillcrest Heights	33 C2
Hillcrest Lawns	33 C2
Hillcrest Manor	46 D4 [2]
Hillcrest Park (Glasnevin)	24 F2
Hillcrest Park (Lucan)	33 C2
Hillcrest Road (Lucan)	34 D2
Hillcrest Road (Sandyford)	58 D3
Hillcrest View	33 C2
Hillcrest Walk	33 C2
Hillcrest Way	33 C2
Hillsbrook Avenue	46 D2
Hillsbrook Crescent	46 D2
Hillsbrook Drive	46 D2
Hillsbrook Grove	46 D2
Hillside	60 E2
Hillside Drive	47 A3
Hillside Park	56 E1
Hillside Terrace	30 D2 [7]
Hilltop Lawn	64 D3
Hilltown	1 B3
Hilltown Close	1 C2
Hilltown Court	1 C2
Hilltown Crescent	1 A2
Hilltown Green	1 C2
Hilltown Grove	1 C2
Hilltown Lawn	1 C2
Hilltown Park	1 C2
Hilltown Road	1 C2
Hilltown Way	1 C2
Hillview	52 E2
Hillview Cottages	59 C2 [1]
Hillview Court	57 B1 [6]
Hillview Drive	59 C2
Hillview Glade	57 B1 [5]
Hillview Grove	57 B1
Hillview Lawn	59 C2
Hilton Gardens	57 C2
Hoey Close	14 E4
Hoey Court	14 E4
Hoey Place	14 E4
*Hoeys Court (off Werburgh Street)	38 D3
Hogan Avenue	38 F3 [27]
Hogan House	46 F4 [25]
Hogan Place	38 E3
Holles Place	38 E3 [34]
Holles Row	38 E3 [7]
Holles Street	38 E3
Holly Avenue	58 D1
Holly Court	64 D1 [4]
Holly Park	64 E2
Holly Park Avenue	59 A1
Holly Road (Donnycarney)	26 D3
Holly Road (Fox and Geese)	44 F1
Holly Tree Square	11 C4
Holly Tree Terrace	11 C4
Hollybank Avenue Lower	47 B1
Hollybank Avenue Upper	47 B1
Hollybank Road	25 A4
Hollybrook Court	26 D4 [3]
Hollybrook Court Drive	26 D4 [2]
Hollybrook Grove	26 D4
Hollybrook Manor	26 D4 [10]
Hollybrook Mews	26 D4
Hollybrook Park (Clontarf)	26 D4
Hollybrook Park (Irishtown)	67 C4
Hollybrook Road	26 D4
Hollybrook Wood	26 D4 [9]
Hollybrooke	36 E4 [4]
Hollystown	9 B1
Hollystown Park	9 B1
Hollyville Lawn	35 C1
Hollywell	11 C4
Hollywood Drive	48 D4
Hollywood Park	48 D4
*Holme's Cottages (on Church Avenue Rathmines)	47 A1
Holmston Avenue	60 D1
Holmwood	59 B4
Holycross Avenue	25 B4 [5]

STREET NAME	PAGE/GRID REFERENCE
*Holycross Cottages (off Holycross Avenue)	25 B4
Holyrood Park	39 A4
Holywell	58 D1
Holywell Avenue	27 B1
Holywell Crescent	27 B1
Holywell Road	27 B1
Home Farm Park	25 B3
Home Farm Road	25 A3
Home Villas	47 C1
Homelawn Avenue	55 B1
Homelawn Drive	55 B1
Homelawn Gardens	55 B1
Homelawn Road	55 A1
Homelawn Villas	55 A1
Homelee	39 A4 [11]
Homeleigh	22 D4
Homeville	55 C1 [4]
Homeville Court	55 C1 [3]
Honey Park	60 D2 [1]
Hope Avenue	38 F1
*Hope Street (off Gordon Street)	38 F3
Hopkins Square	48 D3 [1]
*Horan Hall (Belgard Square)	54 F1
Horton Court	46 F2
Hospital Lane	37 A2 [2]
Hotel Yard	38 D2 [29]
Houghton Terrace	37 C2 [28]
*Howard Street (off Gordon Street)	38 F3
Howth	30 D2
Howth House Apts	30 D1 [10]
Howth Junction Cottages	27 B1 [1]
Howth Lodge Apts.	29 C1
Howth Peninsula Apts.	30 D1 [14]
Howth Road (Howth)	29 C1
Howth Road (Killester)	26 E3
Howth Road (Marino)	26 D4
Howth Road (Raheny)	26 F3
Howth Road (Raheny)	27 B2
Howth Road (Sutton)	29 B1
Howth Road Apts.	26 E3
Howth Terrace	30 D1 [5]
Howth View Park	27 B1
Huband Road	36 F4
Hudson Road	60 E1
Hughes Road East	45 C1
Hughes Road North	45 C1
Hughes Road South	45 C1
Hume Avenue	35 C4
Hume Street	38 E3
Hunters Avenue	55 C3
Hunters Court	55 C3
Hunters Crescent	55 C3
Hunters Green	55 C3
Hunters Grove	55 C3
Hunters Hall	55 C3 [1]
Hunters Hill	55 C3
Hunters Lane	55 C3
Hunters Meadow	55 C3
Hunters Parade	55 C3
Hunters Place	55 C3
Hunters Road	55 C3
Hunters Run	8 E4
Hunters Run The Close	8 E4
Hunters Run The Drive	8 F4
Hunters Run The Glade	8 E4
Hunters Run The Grove	8 E4
Hunters Run The Park	8 E4
Hunters Run The Rise	8 F4
Hunters Run The View	8 F4
Hunters Run The Way	8 F4
Hunters Walk	55 C3
Hunters Way	55 C3
Huntstown Avenue	21 C1
Huntstown Close	8 F4
Huntstown Court	8 F4
Huntstown Drive	8 F4
Huntstown Glen	8 F4
Huntstown Green	8 F4
Huntstown Grove	8 F4
Huntstown Lawn	22 D1
Huntstown Park	8 F4
Huntstown Rise	9 A4
Huntstown Road	21 C1

STREET NAME	PAGE/GRID REFERENCE
Huntstown Way	9 A4
Huntstown Wood	8 F4
Hutchinson's Strand	2 E1
Huttonread	51 C4
Huxley Crescent	37 C3 [8]
Hyacinth Street	38 F1 [7]
Hybreasal	37 A3 [1]
Hyde Park (Dalkey)	60 E1
Hyde Park (Templeogue)	46 E3
Hyde Park Avenue	48 F3
Hyde Park Gardens	48 F3
Hyde Road	60 F1
Hyde Square (Fosters Avenue)	48 D3 [4]
Hynestown	42 D2

I

STREET NAME	PAGE/GRID REFERENCE
Idrone Avenue	56 D1
Idrone Close	56 D1
Idrone Drive	56 D1
Idrone Mews	49 A3 [11]
Idrone Park	56 D1
Idrone Terrace	49 A3
Imaal Road	37 C1
Inagh Court	64 E1
Inagh Road	36 D3
Inbhir Ide	3 A2
Inbhir Ide Close	3 A2
Inbhir Ide Drive	3 A2
Inchicore	36 F3
Inchicore Road	37 A3
Inchicore Square	36 F3 [13]
Inchicore Terrace North	36 F3 [3]
Inchicore Terrace South	36 F3
Infirmary Road	37 B2
Inglewood Close	21 C2
Inglewood Crescent	21 C2
Inglewood Drive	21 C2
Inglewood Road	21 C2
Ingram Road	37 C4 [2]
Inis Fail	54 F2
Inis Thiar	54 F2
*Inkerman Cottages (off Amiens Street)	38 E2
Innisfallen Parade	38 D1
Innishmaan Road	25 B2
*Innishmore Terrace (St Mary's Road)	46 D1
Innismore	46 D1
*Inns Court (on Winetavern Street)	38 D2
Inns Quay	37 C2
Inver Road	24 E4
Invermore Grove	27 A1 [3]
Inverness Road	25 C4
Iona Avenue	25 A4
Iona Crescent	25 A4
Iona Drive	25 A4
Iona Park	25 A4
Iona Road	25 A4
Iona Villas	25 A4
Iris Grove	48 E3
Irishtown (Bray)	67 C4
Irishtown (Ringsend)	39 A3
Irishtown Road	39 A3
Irvine Cottages	38 F2 [10]
Irvine Terrace	38 F2
Irwin Court	37 B3 [24]
Irwin Street	37 B3 [1]
Island Street	37 C2
Island View (Kilbarrack)	27 C2
Island View (Malahide)	3 C3
Island View Apts.	30 D1 [9]
Island View Court Apts.	27 C2
Island Villa	38 F3 [3]
Islandbridge	37 A2
Islandbridge Court	37 A2 [1]
Islington Avenue	50 E4
Isolda Road	39 A3
Isolde Gardens	36 E2 [6]
Isolde House Apts.	36 E2 [13]
Ivar Street	37 C2
Iveagh Buildings	38 D3 [4]
Iveagh Gardens	37 A4 [1]
Iveagh Gardens	37 A4
Iveleary Road	25 B2

STREET NAME	PAGE/GRID REFERENCE
Iveragh Court	38 F4 [17]
Iveragh Road	25 B2
Ivy Court	25 C1 [1]
Ivy Terrace	37 C3 [61]

J

STREET NAME	PAGE/GRID REFERENCE
James Connolly Park	35 A4
James Connolly Square	67 C2 [5]
James Everett Park	67 B2
James Joyce St	38 E2
James Larkin Road	27 B2
James McCormack Gardens	29 A1 [1]
James Plunkett House	36 F3
James's Place East	38 E3
James's Street	37 B3
James's Street East	38 E3
James's Street North	38 F1 [20]
James's Terrace	3 B2
James's Walk	37 B3
Jamestown	62 F1
Jamestown Avenue	36 F4
Jamestown Cottages	62 E1
Jamestown Court	36 F4
Jamestown Road (Finglas)	24 E1
Jamestown Road (Inchicore)	36 F4
*Jane-Ville (Off Tivoli Road)	50 D4
Jervis Lane Lower	38 D2 [11]
Jervis Lane Upper	38 D2 [10]
Jervis Street	38 D2
Jobstown	54 D2
Jobstown Road	54 D2
Jobstown Village Square	54 D1 [2]
John Dillon Street	38 D3
John F Kennedy Avenue	45 A1
John F Kennedy Drive	45 A1
John F Kennedy Park	36 D4
John F Kennedy Road	36 D4
John Field Road	38 D3 [40]
John MacCormack Avenue	45 C1
*John Street North (off Ellis Quay)	37 C2
John Street South	37 C3
John Street West	37 C3
John's Lane East	38 D3 [52]
John's Lane West	37 C3 [50]
Johnsbridge	34 D3
Johnsbridge Avenue	34 D3
Johnsbridge Close	34 D3
Johnsbridge Green	34 D3
Johnsbridge Grove	34 D3
Johnsbridge Meadows	34 D3
Johnsbridge Park	34 D3
Johnsbridge Walk	34 D3
Johnson Place	38 D3 [36]
Johnson's Court	38 D3 [30]
Johnstown	51 C4
Johnstown Avenue	59 C3
Johnstown Court	59 C2
Johnstown Gardens	24 E2 [5]
Johnstown Grove	59 C3
Johnstown House	24 F2 [3]
Johnstown Lane	59 C3
Johnstown Park (Cornelscourt)	59 C3
Johnstown Park (Glasnevin)	24 F2
Johnstown Road (Cornelscourt)	59 C3
Jones Terrace	68 D2 [18]
Jones's Road	38 E1
Jordanstown	42 F4
Josephine Avenue	38 D1 [25]
*Joy Street (off Gordon Street)	38 F3
Joyce Avenue	59 A3
Joyce Hall	59 B4
Joyce Road	25 A3
Joyce Way	35 C4
Jugback Close	1 C1
Jugback Court	1 C1
Jugback Crescent	1 C1
Jugback Green	1 C1
Jugback Lane	1 C1

K

STREET NAME	PAGE/GRID REFERENCE
Kavanagh Avenue	36 D4
Keadeen Avenue	45 B2
Kearn's Place	37 A3 [7]

STREET NAME	PAGE/GRID REFERENCE
Keatingspark	52 D2
*Keegan's Cottages (off Merrion Rd)	48 E1
Keeloges	42 D3
Keeper Road	37 B4
Kells Road	46 E1
Kelly's Avenue	50 D4
Kelly's Lane (Maynooth)	17 C3 [1]
Kelly's Lane (Phibsborough)	38 D1 [22]
Kelly's Row	38 D1
Kelly's Square	38 D1
Kellystown Lane	19 A3
Kellystown Road	57 B4
Kelston Avenue	59 A2
Kelston Drive	59 A2
Kelston Hall	59 A2 [11]
Kelston Park	59 A2
Kelston View	59 A2
Kelvin Close	4 D4
Kempton	23 C3
Kempton Avenue	23 C3
Kempton Court	23 C3
Kempton Green	23 C3
Kempton Grove	23 C3
Kempton Heath	23 C3
Kempton Lawn	23 C3
Kempton Park	23 C3
Kempton Rise	23 C3
Kempton View	23 C3
Kempton Way	23 C3
Kenah Court	60 E3
Kengar Mews	46 F1 [14]
Kenilworth Lane	46 F1
Kenilworth Lodge	46 F1 [19]
Kenilworth Manor	46 F1 [11]
Kenilworth Park	46 F1
Kenilworth Road	47 A1
Kenilworth Square	46 F1
Kenilworth Square East	47 A1
Kenilworth Square North	46 F1
Kenilworth Square South	46 F1
Kenilworth Square West	46 F1
Kenmare Parade	38 D1 [31]
Kennedy Court	39 A3 [31]
Kennedy Park	67 C3 [5]
Kennelsfort Green	35 B2
Kennelsfort Road Lower	35 C1
Kennelsfort Road Upper	35 C2
Kennington Close	45 C4
Kennington Crescent	45 C4
Kennington Lawn	45 C4
Kennington Road	45 C3
*Kent Terrace(on Barnhill Road)	60 F2
Kentfield	64 E2
Kerlogue Road	39 A3
Kerrygold House	46 F1 [18]
Kerrymount Avenue	59 A4
Kerrymount Close	59 B3 [1]
Kerrymount Green	59 B3
Kerrymount Mall	59 B3
Kerrymount Rise	59 B3
Kettles Drive	2 E4
Kettles Lane	2 E4
Kettles Place	2 E4
*Kevin Barry` (off Church Street Upper)	37 C2
*Kevin Street Cross (on Bride St New)	38 D3
Kevin Street Lower	38 D3
Kevin Street Upper	38 D3
Kew Park	33 C1
Kew Park Avenue	33 B2
Kew Park Crescent	33 B1
Kickham Road	37 A3
Kilakee Close	45 B3
Kilakee Drive	45 B3
Kilakee Road	56 D4
Kilbarrack	27 C1
Kilbarrack Avenue	27 C2
Kilbarrack Gardens	27 C2
Kilbarrack Grove	27 C2
Kilbarrack Parade	27 B1
Kilbarrack Road	27 B1
Kilbarrack Way	27 B1
Kilbarron Avenue	26 D1
Kilbarron Court	26 D1 [1]
Kilbarron Drive	26 D1
Kilbarron Park	26 D1
Kilbarron Road	26 D1
Kilbegnet Close	60 F2 [24]
Kilbogget Grove	59 C4
Kilbogget Villas	59 C4 [1]
Kilbride Grove	67 B3
Kilbride Lane	67 B3
Kilbride Road	26 E3
Kilbrina	7 B2
Kilcarberry Ave	43 C2
Kilcarberry Close	43 C2
Kilcarberry Court	43 C2
Kilcarberry Lawn	43 C2
Kilcarrig Avenue	44 E4
Kilcarrig Close	54 E1
Kilcarrig Crescent	44 E4
Kilcarrig Green	44 E4
Kilclare Avenue	54 E2
Kilclare Crescent	54 E2
Kilclare Drive	54 E2
Kilclare Gardens	54 E2
Kilcloon	5 A2
Kilcloon Lawns	5 A2
Kilcock Maynooth Leixlip ByPass	32 E1
Kilcock Road	17 C3
Kilcolman Court	60 E2 [4]
Kilcronan Avenue	34 E4
Kilcronan Close	34 E4
Kilcronan Court	34 E4
Kilcronan Crescent	34 E4
Kilcronan Grove	34 E4
Kilcronan Lawns	34 E4
Kilcronan View	34 E4
Kilcroney Lane	67 A4
Kilcross Avenue	58 D3
Kilcross Close	58 D3
Kilcross Court	57 C3
Kilcross Crescent	57 C3
Kilcross Drive	57 C3
Kilcross Grove	57 C3
Kilcross Lawn	58 D3
Kilcross Park	57 C3
Kilcross Road	58 D3
Kilcross Square	57 C3
Kilcross Way	57 C3
Kildare Bridge	18 D2
Kildare Park	46 D1
Kildare Place	38 E3 [25]
Kildare Road	46 D1
Kildare Street	38 E3
Kildonan Avenue	24 D1
Kildonan Court	24 D1
Kildonan Drive	24 D1
Kildonan Road	24 D1
Kilfenora Drive	27 A1
Kilfenora Road	46 E1
Kilgarran	66 D3
Kilgarron Park	66 D3
Kilgobbin Heights	58 E4
Kilgobbin Lane	58 D4
Kilgobbin Lawn	58 E4
Kilgobbin Road	58 E3
Kilgobbin Wood	58 E4
Kilgraigue	5 B3
Kilgrastor Court	67 B3 [5]
Kilkieran Court	24 E4 [1]
Kilkieran Road	24 E4
Kill Abbey	59 B1
Kill Abbey	59 B1
Kill Avenue	59 B1
Kill Avenue	59 C1
Kill Lane	59 B2
Kill O' the Grange	59 C1
Killadoon Park	31 C4
Killakee Avenue	55 B2
Killakee Court	55 B2
Killakee Gardens	55 B2
Killakee Green	55 B2
Killakee Grove	55 B2
Killakee Lawns	55 B2
Killakee Park	55 B2
Killakee Rise	55 B2
Killakee View	55 B2
Killakee Walk	55 B2
Killakee Way	55 B2
Killala Road	24 E4
Killan Road	38 F2
Killarney Avenue	38 E1 [13]
Killarney Court	67 B3 [4]
Killarney Glen	67 B2
Killarney Heights	67 B3
Killarney Lane	67 B3
Killarney Parade	38 D1 [30]
Killarney Park	67 B3
Killarney Road	67 B3
Killarney Street	38 E1
Killarney Villas	67 C2 [48]
Killary Grove	27 B1
Killeany	5 A4
Killeck	1 A2
Killeck Lane	1 A3
Killeen	2 F3
Killeen Avenue	2 F3
Killeen Court	2 F3
Killeen Crescent	2 F3
Killeen Mews	3 B3
Killeen Park	2 F3
Killeen Road (Bluebell)	36 D4
Killeen Road (Fox and Geese)	45 A1
Killeen Road (Rathmines)	47 B1
Killeen Terrace	3 B2
Killegar	65 C1
*Killery Terrace (on Upper Dargle Road)	67 B2
Killester	26 E3
Killester Avenue	26 E3
Killester Court	26 E3 [4]
Killester Park	26 E3 [5]
Killester Park	26 E3
Killinardan	54 E3
Killinarden Estate	54 E2
Killinarden Heights	54 E2
Killinarden Road	54 E3
Killiney	60 E3
Killiney Avenue	60 E4
Killiney Court	64 E1 [1]
Killiney Gate	60 E4
Killiney Grove	60 E2
Killiney Heath	60 E4
Killiney Hill Road	64 E1
Killiney Hill Road	60 E3
Killiney Oaks	64 E1 [2]
Killiney Road	60 E2
Killiney Terrace	60 E1 [15]
Killiney Towers	60 E2 [2]
Killiney View	60 E1
Killininny Cottages	55 B2
Killininny Court Apts	55 B2 [2]
Killininny Road	55 B2
Kilmactalway	42 F3
Kilmacud	58 E1
Kilmacud Avenue	58 E1
Kilmacud Park	58 E1
Kilmacud Road Upper	58 E1
Kilmahuddrick Avenue	43 B1
Kilmahuddrick Close	43 B1
Kilmahuddrick Court	43 B1
Kilmahuddrick Crescent	43 B1
Kilmahuddrick Drive	43 B1
Kilmahuddrick Green	43 B1
Kilmahuddrick Grove	43 B1
Kilmahuddrick Lawn	43 B1
Kilmahuddrick Place	43 B1
Kilmahuddrick Road	43 B1
Kilmahuddrick Walk	43 B1
Kilmahuddrick Way	43 B1
Kilmainham	37 A3
Kilmainham Lane	37 B3
Kilmalin	65 C3
Kilmantain Place	67 C2 [10]
Kilmartin Avenue	54 D1
Kilmartin Crescent	44 D4
Kilmartin Drive	54 D1
Kilmartin Gardens	54 D1
Kilmartin Green	54 D1
Kilmartin Park	54 D1
Kilmashogue Close	45 B3
Kilmashogue Drive	45 B3
Kilmashogue Grove	45 B3
Kilmashogue Lane	56 F3
Kilmore	26 D1
Kilmore Avenue (Coolock)	26 E1
Kilmore Avenue (Killiney)	60 E4
Kilmore Close	26 E1
Kilmore Court	26 D1 [5]
Kilmore Crescent	26 E1
Kilmore Drive	26 E1
Kilmore Place Apts.	26 D1
Kilmore Road	26 D1
Kilmorony Close	27 A1
Kilnamanagh	45 A3
Kilnamanagh Court	45 C1
Kilnamanagh Estate	45 A3
Kilnamanagh Road	45 C1
Kilrock Road	30 E2
Kilronan Court	26 D4 [7]
Kilshane	10 E2
Kilshane Avenue	10 D2
Kilshane Cross	10 F2
Kilshane Drive	10 E3
Kilshane Park	10 D2
Kilshane Road (North Road)	10 E3
Kilshane Road (Rathoath Road)	23 C2
Kilshane View	10 D2
Kilshane Way	10 D2
Kiltalown	54 D3
Kiltalown Avenue	54 D2
Kiltalown Close	54 D2
Kiltalown Cottages	54 D2
Kiltalown Court	54 D2
Kiltalown Crescent	54 D2
Kiltalown Drive	54 D2
Kiltalown Green	54 D2
Kiltalown Grove	54 D2
Kiltalown Heights	54 D2
Kiltalown Hill	54 D2
Kiltalown Park	54 D2
Kiltalown Road	54 D2
Kiltalown View	54 D2
Kiltalown Walk	54 D2
Kiltalown Way	54 D2
Kilteel Road	52 E2
Kilteragh Drive	59 A3
Kilteragh Pines	59 A3 [2]
Kilteragh Road	59 A3
Kilternan	62 E3
Kiltipper	54 F3
Kiltipper Avenue	55 A2
Kiltipper Close	55 A2
Kiltipper Drive	55 A2
Kiltipper Gate	54 F3
Kiltipper Rise	54 F3
Kiltipper Road	55 A3
Kiltipper View	54 F3
Kiltipper Way	54 F2
Kiltuck Park	64 E4 [1]
Kilvere	46 E4
Kilwogan Manor	31 C2
Kilworth Road	36 F4
Kimmage	46 D2
Kimmage Court	46 E2 [3]
Kimmage Grove	46 E2
Kimmage Manor Way	46 D2
Kimmage Road Lower	46 F1
Kimmage Road West	46 D2
Kinahan Street	37 B2 [4]
Kincora Avenue	26 E4
Kincora Court	39 C1
Kincora Drive	26 E4
Kincora Grove	26 E4
Kincora Park	26 E4
Kincora Road	26 E4
King Edward Court	67 C2 [53]
King Edward Lawn	67 C2
King Edward Park	67 B2
King Edward Road	67 B2
King Street North	37 C2
King Street South	38 D3
Kingram Place	38 E4
King's Avenue	38 E1
King's Court	37 C1 [19]
King's Hall	36 E2

STREET NAME	PAGE/GRID REFERENCE	STREET NAME	PAGE/GRID REFERENCE	STREET NAME	PAGE/GRID REFERENCE	STREET NAME	PAGE/GRID REFERENCE
Kings Inns	38 D2	Knockmaroon Road	36 D1	Landscape Avenue	47 A3	*Lauderdale Terrace	38 D3
King's Inns Street	38 D2	Knockmeenagh Lane	44 E2	Landscape Crescent	47 A3	(on New Row South)	
Kingsbury	17 C4	Knockmeenagh Road	44 E2	Landscape Gardens	47 B4	Lauder's Lane	29 A1
Kingsland Parade	38 D4 [5]	Knockmitten Close	44 F1 [1]	Landscape Park	47 A4	Laundry Lane	46 F1
Kingsland Park Avenue	38 D4 [4]	Knockmitten Lane	45 A1	Landscape Road	47 A3	Laurel Avenue (Ballybrack)	64 E1
Kingsmill Road	67 C2	Knockmitten Lane North	44 F1 [2]	Landsdown Valley Place	45 C1	Laurel Avenue (Dundrum)	57 B1
Kingston	57 B3	Knockmore Avenue	54 E2	Landsdowne Valley	45 C1 [6]	Laurel Bank	59 C1
Kingston Avenue	57 B3	Knockmore Crescent	54 E2	Landsdowne Valley Park	36 F4 [5]	Laurel Court	22 E3
Kingston Close	57 B3	Knockmore Drive	54 E2	Lanesborough Avenue	11 B4	Laurel Drive	57 B1
Kingston Court	56 F2	Knockmore Gardens	54 E2	Lanesborough Court	11 B4	Laurel Hill	60 D1 [6]
Kingston Crescent	57 B3	Knockmore Green	54 E2	Lanesborough Drive	11 B4	Laurel Lodge Road	22 F3
Kingston Drive	57 C3	Knockmore Grove	54 E2	Lanesborough Gardens	11 B4	Laurel Park	44 E1
Kingston Green	57 B3	Knockmore Park	54 E2	Lanesborough Grove	11 B4	Laurel Place	46 F2
Kingston Grove	57 B3	Knock-na-Cree Grove	60 F2	Lanesborough Mews	11 B4	Laurel Road	57 B1
Kingston Hall	57 B3	Knock-na-Cree Park	60 F2	Lanesborough Park	11 B4	Laurelton (Rathbeale Road)	1 C1
Kingston Heights	57 C3	Knock-na-Cree Road	60 F2	Lanesborough Road	11 B4	Laurelton (Terenure)	46 F3
Kingston Lawn	57 B3	Knocknagow	49 B4 [23]	Lanesborough Square	11 B4	Laurence Brook	36 E2
Kingston Lodge	25 B4 [4]	Knocknarea Avenue	37 A4	Lanesborough Terrace	11 B4	Laurence Court	46 F1
Kingston Park	57 B3	Knocknarea Road	37 A4	Lanesborough View	11 B4	Laurence Place East	38 F2 [5]
Kingston Rise	57 B3	Knocknarrow Terrace	37 B3 [34]	Lanesville	59 B1	Laurleen	58 F1
Kingston View	57 B3	Knocknashee	47 C4	Lanesville Terrace	59 B1	Lavarna Grove	46 E2
Kingston Walk	57 B3	Knocknashee	48 D4	Langrishe Place	38 E1 [23]	Lavarna Road	46 E2
Kingswood	43 C4	Knocksedan Drive	1 A2	Lanndale Lawns	54 E1	Laverna Avenue	22 E3
Kingswood Avenue (Citywest)	43 C4	Knocksedan Wood	1 A2	Lansdowne Crescent	38 F3 [43]	Laverna Dale	22 E3
Kingswood Avenue (Kilnamanagh)	44 F3	Knocksinna	59 A2	Lansdowne Gardens	38 F4 [7]	Laverna Grove	22 E3
Kingswood Castle	45 A2	Knocksinna Court	59 A2 [2]	Lansdowne Hall	39 A3 [25]	Laverna Way	22 E3
Kingswood Drive (Citywest)	43 C4	Knocksinna Crescent	59 A2	Lansdowne Lane	38 F3 [20]	Lavery Avenue	35 C4
Kingswood Drive (Kilnamanagh)	44 F3	Knocksinna Grove	59 A2 [1]	Lansdowne Park (Ballsbridge)	38 F3	Lavista Avenue	26 E3
Kingswood Heights	44 F3	Knocksinna Park	59 A2	Lansdowne Park (Templeogue)	56 D1	Lawnswood Park	58 F1
Kingswood Road	43 C4	Knowth Court	11 C4	Lansdowne Road	38 F4	Lawrence Grove	26 D4
Kingswood View	44 F3	Kyber Road	36 F2	Lansdowne Square	39 A4 [24]	Lawrence's Avenue	18 D4
Kinsaley	14 D1	Kyle-Clare Road	39 A3 [13]	Lansdowne Terrace	38 F3 [37]	Lawson Spinney	3 A3
Kinsaley Lane	3 A4	Kylemore	45 B2	Lansdowne Village	39 A3	Lawson Terrace	60 E1 [14]
Kinsealy Court	2 E3	Kylemore Avenue	36 D3	Lansdowne Villas	38 F3 [44]	Le Bas Terrace	46 F1 [2]
Kinsealy Downs	2 E3	Kylemore Drive	36 D3	Lapwing Apts.	48 E3	Le Brett Terrace	46 F3 [7]
Kinsealy Lane	14 D1	Kylemore Park North	36 D4	Lar Foley House	14 E4	Le Brocquy Avenue	36 D4
Kinvara Avenue	24 D4	Kylemore Park South	36 D4	Laracor Gardens	27 A1 [5]	Le Fanu Drive	36 D3 [1]
Kinvara Drive	23 C4	Kylemore Park West	36 D4	Laragh	60 E4	Le Fanu Road	36 D3
Kinvara Grove	23 C4	Kylemore Road	36 D2	Laragh Close	27 A1	Le Vere Terrace	37 C4 [38]
Kinvara Park	24 D4			Laragh Flats	25 C2 [5]	Lea Crescent	39 B4
Kinvara Road	23 C4	**L**		Laragh Grove	27 A1	Lea Road	39 B4
Kippure Avenue	45 B3			Laraghbryan East	17 B2	Leahy's Terrace	39 A3
Kippure Park	24 D3	La Touche Court (Ballinteer)	57 A2	Laraghbryan West	17 A2	Lealand Avenue	43 C1
Kirkfield	22 D2 [2]	La Touche Court (Bluebell)	36 F4 [3]	Laraghcon	34 D1	Lealand Close	43 C1
Kirkpatrick Avenue	22 D3	La Touche Drive	36 E4	Larch Drive	56 E2 [3]	Lealand Crescent	43 C1
Kirkpatrick Drive	22 D3	La Touche Road	36 F4	Larch Grove	21 C2	Lealand Drive	43 C1
Kirkwood	39 A4	La Vallee	67 A3	Larch Grove	47 B1	Lealand Gardens	43 C1
Kirwan Street	37 C2	La Vista Avenue	29 B2	Larch Hill	12 F4	Lealand Grove	43 C1
Kirwan Street Cottages	37 C1 [10]	Labre Park	36 E4	Larchfield	7 C3	Lealand Road	43 C1
Kitestown Road	30 E3	Laburnum Road	47 C2	Larchfield	47 C4	Lealand Walk	43 C1
Knapton Court	49 C4 [21]	Laburnum Walk	35 B2	Larchfield Park	47 C4	Leaunstown	59 C4
Knapton Lawn	49 C4 [22]	Lad Lane	38 E3	Larchfield Road	47 C4	Ledwidge Crescent	67 B1
Knapton Road	49 C4	Lad Lane Upper	38 E4	Larkfield	34 F2	Lee Road	24 E3
Knapton Terrace	49 C4 [27]	Lady's Lane	37 A3 [13]	Larkfield Avenue (Harold's Cross)	46 F1	Leeson Close	38 E4 [1]
*Knapton Villas	49 C4	Lady's Well Road	9 A4	Larkfield Avenue (Liffey Valley)	34 F2	Leeson Lane	38 E3 [16]
(on Knapton Road)		Lagan Road	24 E3			Leeson Park	38 E4
Knights Bridge	26 E4 [4]	Lake Drive	53 C1	Larkfield Close	34 F2	Leeson Park Avenue	38 E4
Knights Wood	12 F4	Lakelands Avenue	58 D1	Larkfield Court	34 F2	Leeson Place	38 E4 [3]
Knock Riada	36 D2	Lakelands Close	58 D1	Larkfield Gardens	46 F1	Leeson Street Lower	38 E3
Knockaire	56 D1	Lakelands Crescent	58 E1	Larkfield Green	34 F2	Leeson Street Upper	38 E4
Knockandinny	52 E4	Lakelands Drive	58 D1	Larkfield Grove (Harold's Cross)	46 F1	Leeson Village	38 E4 [30]
Knockaulin	20 D4	Lakelands Grove	58 D1	Larkfield Grove (Liffey Valley)	34 F2	Leeson Walk	38 E4 [19]
Knockcullen	56 D1	Lakelands Lawn	58 D1	Larkfield Mews	32 D3	Lehaunstown Road	63 C1
Knockcullen Drive	56 D1	Lakelands Park	46 E3	Larkfield Park	46 F1	Leicester Avenue	47 A1
Knockcullen Lawn	56 D1	*Lakelands Place	58 D1	Larkfield Place	34 F2	Leighlin Road	46 E1
Knockcullen Park	56 D1	Lakelands Road	58 E1	Larkfield Rise	34 F2	Lein Gardens	26 F2
Knockcullen Rise	56 D1	Lakeshore Drive	2 D3	Larkfield Square	34 F2	Lein Park	26 F2
Knockdara	3 C3	Lakeview Drive	2 D3	Larkfield View	34 F2	Lein Road	26 F2
Knockfield Manor	55 C1	Lally Road	36 E3	Larkfield Way	34 F2	Leinster Avenue	38 F1
Knocklyon	56 D1	Lamb Alley	37 C3	Larkhill Road	25 B2	Leinster Cottages	17 C3 [6]
Knocklyon Avenue	55 C1	Lambay Close	64 E1	Larrisa Court	46 E1 [7]	Leinster Court	18 D3 [2]
Knocklyon Close	56 D1	Lambay Court	3 C3	Latchford	21 B1	Leinster Lane	38 E3 [13]
Knocklyon Court	56 D1	Lambay Drive	64 E1	Latchford Close	21 B1	Leinster Lawn	47 C3
Knocklyon Drive	56 D1	Lambay Road	25 A3	Latchford Court	21 B1	Leinster Lodge Apts.	18 D3 [1]
Knocklyon Gate Apts	55 C2 [3]	Lambourne Avenue	21 C2	Latchford Green	21 B1	Leinster Market	38 E2 [11]
Knocklyon Green	56 D1	Lambourne Court	21 C2	Latchford Park	21 B1	Leinster Park (Harold's Cross)	46 F1
Knocklyon Grove	56 D1	Lambourne Drive	21 C2	Latchford Row	21 B1	Leinster Park (Maynooth)	18 D3
Knocklyon Heights	55 C1	Lambourne Park	21 C2	Latchford Square	21 B1	Leinster Place	46 F1
Knocklyon Mews	55 C1 [2]	Lambourne Road	21 C2	Latchford Terrace	21 B1	Leinster Road	47 A1
Knocklyon Park	55 C1	Lambourne Village	26 E4 [3]	Latouka Apts.	34 F1	Leinster Road West	46 F1
Knocklyon Road	55 C1	Lambourne Wood	59 C4	Lauderdale Estate	67 C3	Leinster Square	47 A1 [1]
Knockmaree Apartments	36 E2	Lamb's Brook	58 D3	Lauderdale Terrace	67 C3 [16]	Leinster Street	17 C3
Knockmaroon Hill	36 D1	*Lamb's Court (off James Street)	37 B3			Leinster Street East	38 F1 [21]
		Landen Road	36 E3			Leinster Street North	24 F4
		Landore	47 A3 [9]			Leinster Street South	38 E3

STREET NAME	PAGE/GRID REFERENCE	STREET NAME	PAGE/GRID REFERENCE	STREET NAME	PAGE/GRID REFERENCE	STREET NAME	PAGE/GRID REFERENCE
Leinster Terrace	44 D1 [2]	Limewood Avenue	26 F1	Llewellyn Grove	57 A1	Loughoreen Hills	30 D3
Leitrim Place	38 F3 [33]	Limewood Park	26 F1	Llewellyn Lawn	57 A1	Loughtown Lower	41 C1
Leix Road	37 B1	Limewood Road	27 A1	Llewellyn Park	57 A1	Loughtown Upper	42 D1
Leixlip	33 B1	Lincoln House	37 C2	Llewellyn Way	57 A1	Louis Lane	47 A1 [23]
Leixlip Park	32 F1	Lincoln Lane	37 C2 [43]	Lock Road	34 D3	Louisa Vally	19 C4
Leixlip Road	33 B1	Lincoln Place	38 E3	Lockkeeper's Walk	24 D3	Lourdes House	38 E1 [61]
Lemon Street	38 D3 [31]	Linden Grove	48 F4	*Loftus Hall	54 F1	Lourdes Road	37 B3
Lennox Place	38 D4	Linden Lea Park	58 F1	Loftus Lane	38 D2	Louvain	48 D3
Lennox Street	38 D4	Linden Square	48 F4	Loftus Square	46 F4 [14]	Louvain Glade	48 D3
Lennox Terrace	38 D4 [31]	Lindenvale	49 A4 [4]	Lohunda Close	22 D2	Love Lane East	38 F3 [15]
Lentisk Lawn	27 A1	Lindisfarne Avenue	43 C1	Lohunda Court	22 D2	Lower Dargle Road	67 B2
Leo Avenue	38 D1 [24]	Lindisfarne Drive	43 C1	Lohunda Crescent	21 C2	Lower Glen Road	36 D1
Leo Street	38 D1	Lindisfarne Green	43 C1	Lohunda Dale	22 D2	Lower Kilmacud Road	48 D4
Leonard's Court	37 C4 [34]	Lindisfarne Grove	43 C1	Lohunda Downs	22 D2	(Goatstown)	
Leopardstown	58 F3	Lindisfarne Lawns	43 C1	Lohunda Drive	22 D2	Lower Kilmacud Road	58 D1
Leopardstown Abbey	58 F4	Lindisfarne Park	34 F4	Lohunda Green	22 D2	(Stillorgan)	
Leopardstown Avenue	58 F2	Lindisfarne Vale	43 C1	Lohunda Grove	22 D2	Lower Lucan Road	21 C4
Leopardstown Court	58 F2 [1]	Lindisfarne Walk	43 C1	Lohunda Park	21 C2	Lower Road (Shankill)	64 E1
Leopardstown Drive	58 F2	Lindsay Road	25 A4	Lohunda Park View	22 D2	Lower Road (Strawberry Beds)	35 B1
Leopardstown Gardens	58 F2	Linenhall Parade	38 D2 [4]	Lohunda Road	22 D2	Luby Road	37 A3
Leopardstown Grove	58 F2	*Linenhall Street	38 D2	Lombard Court	38 E2 [33]	Lucan	34 D2
Leopardstown Heights	58 E3	(off King Street North)		Lombard Street East	38 E2	Lucan Bypass	34 D2
Leopardstown Lawn	58 F2 [2]	Linenhall Terrace	38 D2 [1]	Lombard Street West	38 D4	Lucan Heights	34 E1
Leopardstown Oaks	58 F2	Link Road	60 E1	Lomond Avenue	25 C4	Lucan Newlands Road	34 D2
Leopardstown Park	58 F2	Link Road	49 C4	Londonbridge Drive	39 A3 [20]	Lucan Road (Chapelizod)	36 D2
Leopardstown Rise	58 E3	(Off Monkstown Crescent)		Londonbridge Road	39 A3	Lucan Road (Lucan)	34 D1
Leopardstown Road	58 D3	Linnbhlá	12 D4 [3]	Long Lane	38 D3	Lucan Road (near Qaurryvale)	35 A1
Leopardstown Road	58 F2	Linnetfields	21 A1	*Long Lane Close	38 D3	Lucan Road (Palmerston)	35 C1
Leopardstown Valley	58 F4	Linnetfields Avenue	8 E4	(off Long Lane)		Lucan-Newlands Road	34 F3
Leslie Avenue	60 F1	Linnetfields Close	8 E4	Long Mile Road	45 B1	Ludford Drive	57 B1
Leslie's Buildings	37 C1 [7]	Linnetfields Court	21 A1	Longdale Terrace	25 A1	Ludford Park	57 B1
Leukos Road	39 A3 [11]	Linnetfields Drive	8 E4	Longdale Way	25 A1	Ludford Road	57 B2
Liberty House	38 E1 [64]	Linnetfields Park	21 A1	Longford Lane	38 D3 [45]	Lugg	52 F4
Liberty Lane	38 D3 [20]	Linnetfields Rise	8 E4	Longford Place	49 C4	Lugmore	54 D3
Library Road (Dún Laoghaire)	50 D4	Linnetfields Square	8 E4	Longford Street Great	38 D3 [8]	Lugmore Lane	53 C3
Library Road (Shankill)	64 E2	Linnetfields View	8 D4	Longford Street Little	38 D3 [9]	Lugnaquilla Avenue	45 B3
Library Square	52 F2	Linnetfields Walk	21 A1	Longford Terrace	49 C4	Luke Street	38 E2 [25]
Library View Villas	38 D1 [61]	Lios na Sidhe	54 F2	Longlands	2 D2	Lurgan Street	38 D2 [3]
Liffey Ave	34 F2	Lioscian	1 B1	Longmeadow	59 C3	Lutterell Hall	7 A2
Liffey Close	34 F2	Lisalea	49 A3 [22]	Longmeadow Grove	59 C3	Luttrell Park	22 D3
Liffey Court	34 F2	Lisburn Street	38 D2 [2]	Long's Place	37 C3 [5]	Luttrell Park Close	22 D3
Liffey Crescent	34 F2	Liscannor Road	24 E4	Longwood Avenue	38 D4	Luttrell Park Court	22 D3
Liffey Dale	34 F2	Liscanor	60 F1 [9]	Longwood Park	46 F4	Luttrell Park Crescent	22 E3
Liffey Downs	34 F2	Liscarne Court	35 A3	Lorcan Avenue	25 C1	Luttrell Park Drive	22 E3
Liffey Drive	34 F2	Liscarne Dale	35 A3 [2]	Lorcan Crescent	25 C1	Luttrell Park Green	22 E3
Liffey Gardens	34 F2	Liscarne Gardens	35 A3	Lorcan Drive	25 B1	Luttrell Park Grove	22 D3
Liffey Glen	34 F2	Lisle Road	46 D1	Lorcan Green	25 C1	Luttrell Park Heath	22 E3 [2]
Liffey Green	34 F2	Lismeen Grove	26 E1 [1]	Lorcan Grove	25 C1	Luttrell Park Lawn	22 D3
Liffey Hall	34 F2 [1]	Lismore	18 E4	Lorcan O'Toole Court	46 D2 [2]	Luttrell Park View	22 D3
Liffey Junction	24 E4	Lismore Road	46 E1	Lorcan O'Toole Park	46 D2	Luttrellstown Avenue	22 E4
Liffey Lawn	34 F2	Lissadel Avenue	37 A4	Lorcan Park	25 C1	Luttrellstown Chase	22 D4
Liffey Park	34 F2	Lissadel Court	37 A4	Lorcan Road	25 B1	Luttrellstown Close	22 E4
Liffey Place	34 F2	Lissadel Crescent	2 F2	Lorcan Villas	25 C1	Luttrellstown Court	22 D4
Liffey Rise	34 F2	Lissadel Drive	37 A4	Lord Edward Street	38 D3	Luttrellstown Dale	22 D4
Liffey Road	34 F2	Lissadel Green	37 A4 [2]	Lordello Road	64 D3	Luttrellstown Drive	22 D4
Liffey Row	34 F2	Lissadel Grove	2 F2	Lords Walk	37 A1	Luttrellstown Glade	22 D4
Liffey Street Lower	38 D2	Lissadel Park	2 F2	Loreto Abbey	47 A4	Luttrellstown Green	22 D4
Liffey Street South	36 F3	Lissadel Road	37 A4	Loreto Avenue (Dalkey)	60 F1	Luttrellstown Grove	22 D4
Liffey Street Upper	38 D2	Lissadel Wood	2 F2	Loreto Avenue	47 A4	Luttrellstown Heath	22 D4
Liffey Street West	37 C2 [19]	Lissen Hall	2 E1	(Nutgrove Avenue)		Luttrellstown Heights	22 D4
Liffey Terrace	36 E2 [7]	Lissen Hall Drive	2 E1	Loreto Court	47 A4	Luttrellstown Lawn	22 D4
Liffey Vale	34 F2	Lissenfield	38 D4 [53]	Loreto Crescent	47 A4	Luttrellstown Oaks	22 D4
Liffey Valley Park	34 F2	Lissenhall Avenue	2 D1	Loreto Grange	67 C3	Luttrellstown Park	22 D4
Liffey View	34 F2	Lissenhall Court	2 D1	Loreto Park	47 A4	Luttrellstown Place	22 D4
Liffey View Apts.	33 A1 [2]	Lissenhall Drive	2 D1	Loreto Road	37 C3	Luttrellstown Rise	22 D3
Liffey Villas	34 F2	Lissenhall Park	2 D1	Loreto Row	47 A4	Luttrellstown Thicket	22 D4
Liffey Walk	34 F2	Little Britain Street	38 D2	Loreto Terrace	46 F4	Luttrellstown View	22 E4
Liffey Way	34 F2	Little Fitzwilliam Place	38 E3 [29]	Loretto Avenue	67 C2 [34]	Luttrellstown Walk	22 D4
Liffey Wood	34 F2	Little Meadow	59 C3 [1]	Loretto Terrace	67 C2 [35]	Luttrellstown Way	22 D4
Lilys Way	21 A1	Littlepace Close	8 E4	Loretto Villas	67 C2 [54]	Luttrellstown Wood	22 E4
Lime Street	38 F2	Littlepace Court	8 E4	*Lorne Terrace	37 B3	Lyllymore Terrace	37 C4 [6]
Limekiln Avenue	45 B3	Littlepace Crescent	8 E4	(off Almeida Avenue)		Lymewood Mews	12 E4
Limekiln Close	45 C3	Littlepace Drive	8 E4	*Losset Hall (Belgard Square)	54 F1	Lynches Lane	34 E4
Limekiln Drive	45 C3	Littlepace Gallops	8 E4	Lotts	38 D2	Lynch's Lane	36 E3 [2]
Limekiln Green	45 B3	Littlepace Meadow	8 E4	Lough Conn Avenue	36 D2	Lynch's Place	38 D1 [2]
Limekiln Grove	45 C2	Littlepace Park	8 E4	Lough Conn Drive	36 D2	Lyndon Gate	24 D4 [4]
Limekiln Lane (Harold's Cross)	37 C4 [16]	Littlepace Road	8 E4	Lough Conn Road	36 D2	Lynton Court	39 A4 [12]
Limekiln Lane (Kimmage)	45 C2	Littlepace View	8 E4	Lough Conn Terrace	36 D2	Lynwood	57 C1
Limekiln Park	45 C3	Littlepace Walk	8 E4	Lough Derg Road	27 A2	Lyons	41 A4
Limekiln Road	45 C3	Littlepace Way	8 E4	Lough na Mona	19 C4	Lyons Road	41 B4
Limelawn Green	22 D2	Littlepace Woods	8 E4	Loughlinstown	64 D1	Lyreen Court	17 C3
Limelawn Park	22 D2	Littlewood	58 D4	Loughlinstown Drive	64 D1	*Lyreen Manor	17 C3
Limes Road	58 D2	Litton Lane	38 D2 [18]	Loughlinstown Park	64 D1	Lyreen Park	18 D2
Limetree Avenue	4 D4	Llewellyn Close	57 A1	Loughlinstown Wood	64 D1		
Limetree Avenue	3 C4	Llewellyn Court	57 A1	Loughmorne House	46 F2 [27]		

STREET NAME	PAGE/GRID REFERENCE	
M		
Ma Tuire Apts.	48	D4
Mabbot Lane	38	E2 [17]
Mabel Street	25	B4
Macken Street	38	F3
Macken Villa	38	F3 [31]
Mackies Place	38	E3 [33]
Mackintosh Park	59	C2
Macroom Avenue	13	B4
Macroom Road	13	B4
Madden Road	37	C3 [31]
*Madden's Court	37	C3
(off Thomas Street)		
Madden's Lane	60	E4
Madison House	47	A2
Madison Road	37	B3 [10]
*Magdalen Terrace	39	A3
(off Oliver Plunket Ave)		
Magennis Place	38	E2 [3]
Magennis Square	38	E2 [29]
Magenta Crescent	25	B1
Magenta Hall	25	B1
Magenta Place	60	D1 [8]
Magna Drive	53	C2
*Maher's Terrace	47	C4
(on Main Street Dundrum)		
Maidens Row	36	E2 [2]
Main Street (Baldoyle)	15	A4
Main Street (Blackrock)	49	A3
Main Street (Blanchardstown)	22	E2
Main Street (Bray)	67	C2
Main Street (Celbridge)	32	D3
Main Street (Clondalkin)	44	E1
Main Street (Clongriffin)	14	E4
Main Street (Dunboyne)	7	B2
Main Street (Dundrum)	47	C4
Main Street (Finglas)	24	E2
Main Street (Howth)	30	D2
Main Street (Leixlip)	33	A1
Main Street (Lucan)	34	D1
Main Street (Malahide)	3	B2
Main Street (Maynooth)	17	C3
Main Street (Newcastle)	42	D4
Main Street (Raheny)	27	A2
Main Street (Rathcoole)	52	F2
Main Street (Rathfarnham)	46	F4
Main Street (Swords)	2	D2
Main Street (Tallaght)	55	A1
Maitland Street	67	B2
Malachi Place	38	F1 [18]
Malachi Road	37	C2 [45]
Malahide	3	B2
Malahide Road (Artane)	26	E2
Malahide Road (Balgriffin)	14	D3
Malahide Road (Coolock)	26	F1
Malahide Road (Marino)	26	D4
Malahide Road (Swords)	2	E2
Malborough Court	60	E2 [8]
Malin House	22	F1
Mallin Avenue	37	B3 [17]
Malone Gardens	38	F3 [12]
Malpas Court	38	D3 [50]
*Malpas Place (off Malpas Street)	38	D3
*Malpas Street (off New Street)	38	D3
Malpas Terrace	38	D3 [46]
Mander's Terrace	38	E4 [10]
Mangerton Road	36	F4
Mannix Road	25	A4
Manor Avenue	46	E3
Manor Close	57	A2
Manor Court (Clonsilla)	22	D2
Manor Court (Maynooth)	17	C3
Manor Crescent	21	B1
Manor Drive	14	D4
Manor Green	57	A2
Manor Grove	46	D2
Manor Heath	57	A1
*Manor Mews	37	C2
(off Norseman Place)		
Manor Mills	17	C3
Manor Park (Ballinteer)	57	A2
Manor Park (Palmerston)	35	C2
Manor Place (Clonsilla)	21	A1

STREET NAME	PAGE/GRID REFERENCE	
Manor Place (Stoneybatter)	37	C2
Manor Rise	57	A2
Manor Road	35	C2
Manor Square	21	A1
Manor Street	37	C2
Manor Villas	46	F1 [4]
Manorfields	21	B1
Mantua Park	2	D1
Maolbuille Road	25	A2
Mapas Avenue	60	E2
Mapas Road	60	E2
Maple Avenue (Carpenterstown)	22	E3
*Maple Avenue	58	D2
(off Blackthorn Drive)		
Maple Close	22	E3
Maple Drive (Carpenterstown)	22	E3
Maple Drive (Dunboyne)	7	B2
Maple Drive (Harold's Cross)	46	F2 [6]
Maple Glen	22	E3
Maple Green	22	E3
Maple Grove (Bray)	67	B2
Maple Grove (Carpenterstown)	22	E3
Maple Grove (Rathcoole)	52	F2
Maple Lawn	22	E3
Maple Lodge	23	A4
Maple Manor	59	C3
Maple Road	47	C2
Maples Road	58	D2
Maplewood Avenue	54	E1
Maplewood Close	54	E1
Maplewood Court	54	E1
Maplewood Drive	54	E1
Maplewood Green	54	E1
Maplewood Lawn	54	E1
Maplewood Park	54	E1
Maplewood Road	54	E1
Maplewood Way	54	E1
Maretimo Gardens East	49	A3
Maretimo Gardens West	49	A3 [4]
Maretimo Place	49	A3 [17]
Maretimo Road	49	A3 [2]
Maretimo Terrace	49	A3 [16]
Maretimo Villas	49	A3 [18]
Marewood Crescent	24	F1
Marewood Drive	11	C4
Marewood Grove	24	F1
Margaret Place	38	F3 [11]
Marguerite Road	25	A4
Marian Crescent	46	E4
Marian Drive	46	E4
Marian Grove	46	E4
Marian Park (Baldoyle)	27	C1
Marian Park (Blackrock)	59	A1
Marian Park (Templeogue)	46	E4
Marian Road	46	E4
Mariavilla	17	C2
Marie Villas	67	C2 [55]
Marigold Avenue	13	C4
Marigold Court	13	C4
Marigold Crescent	13	C4
Marigold Drive	13	C4
Marigold Grove	13	C4
Marigold Park	13	C4
Marina House Apts	49	C4 [32]
Marina Village	3	B2
Marine Avenue	60	E1
Marine Court (Dalkey)	60	E1
Marine Court (Dún Laoghaire)	50	D4 [17]
Marine Cove	28	D1 [4]
Marine Drive	39	A4
Marine Parade	60	E1
Marine Road	50	D4
Marine Terrace (Bray)	68	D2 [17]
Marine Terrace (Dún Laoghaire)	50	D4 [9]
Marine View	48	F3
Marine Villas	30	D1 [7]
Mariners Court	27	C1
Mariners Cove	30	E2
Mariner's Port	38	F2 [16]
Marino	25	C4
Marino Avenue	26	D4
Marino Avenue East	60	E4
Marino Avenue West	60	E4
Marino Court	25	C4 [13]
Marino Crescent	25	C4

STREET NAME	PAGE/GRID REFERENCE	
Marino Green	25	C4
Marino Mart	25	C4 [9]
Marino Park	25	C4
Marino Park Avenue	25	C4
Marion Villas	37	C3 [59]
Mark Street	38	E2 [26]
Market House	67	C2
Market Square	67	C2 [49]
Market Street South	37	C3 [4]
Mark's Alley West	37	C3 [22]
Mark's Lane	38	E2 [4]
Marlay View	57	B2
Marlborough Court	38	E2 [35]
Marlborough Lane	47	B1 [25]
Marlborough Mews	37	B1
Marlborough Park	60	D1 [9]
Marlborough Place	38	E2 [7]
Marlborough Road	47	B1
(Donnybrook)		
Marlborough Road (Glenageary)	60	E1
Marlborough Road	37	B1
(Nth Circular Rd)		
Marlborough Street	38	D2
Marlborough Terrace	68	D2 [16]
Marley Avenue	57	A1
Marley Close	57	A1
Marley Court North	57	A1
Marley Court South	57	A1
Marley Drive	57	A1
Marley Grange	57	A1
Marley Grove	57	A1
Marley Lawn	57	A1
Marley Rise	57	A1
Marley Villas	57	A1 [1]
Marley Walk	57	A1
Marlfield	59	C3
Marlfield Close	54	F3
Marlfield Court	54	F3
Marlfield Crescent	54	F3
Marlfield Green	54	F3
Marlfield Grove	54	F3
Marlfield Lawn	54	F3
Marlfield Mall	54	F3
Marlfield Place	54	F3
*Marmion Court	37	C2
(on Blackhall Street)		
Marne Villas	37	C1 [13]
Marrowbone Lane	37	C3 [66]
Marrowbone Lane	37	C3
*Marrowbone Lane Close	37	C3
(off Marrowbone Lane)		
Marshal Court Apts.	37	C3 [1]
Marshal Lane	37	C3 [68]
*Marshalsea Lane	37	C2
Marsham Court	58	E1
Mart Lane	59	B3
Martello Avenue	50	D4 [14]
Martello Court	4	D4
Martello Mews	48	E1
Martello Terrace (Booterstown)	48	F3 [1]
Martello Terrace (Bray)	67	C1 [2]
Martello Terrace	50	E4 [2]
(Dun Laoghaire)		
Martello Terrace (Sutton)	29	B3 [2]
Martello View	39	B4 [3]
Martello Wood	39	B4 [6]
Martin Grove	24	D4
Martin Savage Park	23	C3
Martin Street	38	D4 [34]
Martin White Chalets	39	A4 [9]
Martin's Row	36	E2
*Martin's Terrace	38	E2
(off Hanover Street East)		
Mary Street	38	D2
Mary Street Little	38	D2 [32]
Maryfield Avenue	26	E2 [1]
Maryfield Crescent	26	E2
Maryfield Drive	26	D2
Maryland	64	E2 [5]
Mary's Abbey	38	D2
Mary's Lane	38	D2
Maryville Road	26	F3
Mask Avenue	26	E2
Mask Crescent	26	E2
Mask Drive	26	E2

STREET NAME	PAGE/GRID REFERENCE	
Mask Green	26	E2
Mask Road	26	E2
Mather Road North	48	E3
Mather Road South	48	D3
Matt Talbot Court	38	E1 [28]
Maunsell Place	38	D1 [52]
Maxwell Court	47	A1 [18]
Maxwell Lane	47	A2
Maxwell Road	47	A1
Maxwell Street	37	C3 [10]
May Lane	37	C2
May Park	26	D3
*May Street (off Fitzroy Ave)	25	B4
Mayberry Park	45	A4
Mayberry Road	44	F4
Mayeston Boulevard	11	B3
Mayeston Close	11	B3
Mayeston Court	11	B4
Mayeston Crescent	11	B3
Mayeston Downs	11	B3
Mayeston Drive	11	B3
Mayeston Lawn	11	B3
Mayeston Rise	11	B4
Mayeston Square	11	B4
Mayeston Walk	11	C4
Mayfair	3	C2
Mayfield	47	A2
Mayfield Park	35	B4
Mayfield Road (Kilmainham)	37	B3 [11]
Mayfield Road (Terenure)	46	F2
Mayfield Terrace (Ballinteer)	57	C2
Mayfield Terrace (Bray)	67	C3 [17]
Maynooth	18	D2
Maynooth Park	18	D4
Maynooth Road (Celbridge)	31	C1
Maynooth Road (Dunboyne)	7	A3
Mayola Court	47	B4
Mayor Street Lower	38	E2
Mayor Street Upper	38	F2
Mayville Terrace	60	F1 [11]
Maywood Avenue	27	B2
Maywood Close	27	B2
Maywood Crescent	27	B3
Maywood Drive	27	B2
Maywood Grove	27	B2
Maywood Lawn	27	B3
Maywood Park	27	B2
Maywood Road	27	B2
McAuley Avenue	26	F2
McAuley Drive	26	F2
McAuley Park	26	F2
McAuley Road	26	F2
McCabe Villas	48	E3
McCarthy Terrace	37	B3 [25]
McCreadies Lane	3	A3
McDowell Avenue	37	B3 [8]
McGrane Court	57	C1 [5]
McKee Avenue	24	E1
McKee Park	37	B1
McKee Road	24	E1
McKelvey Avenue	11	A4
McKelvey Road	11	A4
McMahon Street	38	D4 [27]
McMorrough Road	46	F2 [14]
Meade's Terrace	38	E3 [6]
Meadow Avenue	57	B1 [1]
Meadow Close (Dundrum)	57	A1
Meadow Close	59	A1
(Newtown Park Ave)		
Meadow Copse	21	C1
Meadow Court	60	D4 [2]
Meadow Dale	21	C1 [1]
Meadow Downs	21	C1
Meadow Drive	21	C1
Meadow Green	21	C1
Meadow Grove	57	B1
Meadow Mount	57	A1
Meadow Park	57	A1
Meadow Park Avenue	47	A4
Meadow Vale	59	B2
Meadow View (Dunboyne)	7	B2
Meadow View	57	A1
(Nutgrove Avenue)		
Meadow Villas	57	A1 [2]
Meadow Way	21	C1

STREET NAME	PAGE/GRID REFERENCE	STREET NAME	PAGE/GRID REFERENCE	STREET NAME	PAGE/GRID REFERENCE	STREET NAME	PAGE/GRID REFERENCE
Meadowbank	46 F3	*Merchants Arch	38 D2	Millers Wood	67 B3	Monastery Gate Lawn	44 F1
Meadowbrook	17 C4	(off Temple Bar)		Millfarm	7 C2	Monastery Gate Villas	44 F1
Meadowbrook Avenue	17 C4	Merchant's Quay	37 C2	Millfield (Enniskerry)	66 E3	Monastery Grove	66 E2
(Maynooth)		Merchant's Road	39 A1	Millfield (Portmarnock)	14 F2	Monastery Heath	44 E1
Meadowbrook Avenue (Sutton)	28 D1	Merchant's Square	38 F2 [15]	Millgate Drive	45 C3	Monastery Heath Avenue	44 E1
Meadowbrook Close	17 C4	Meretimo Villas	68 D3 [2]	Millmount Avenue	25 A4	Monastery Heath Court	44 E1
Meadowbrook Court	17 C4	Merlyn Drive	48 D1	Millmount Grove	47 B3	Monastery Heath Green	44 E1
Meadowbrook Crescent	17 C4	Merlyn Park	48 D1	Millmount Place	25 B4	Monastery Heath Square	44 E1
Meadowbrook Drive	17 C4	Merlyn Road	48 D1	*Millmount Terrace	25 B4	Monastery Heights	44 E1 [2]
Meadowbrook Lawn	28 D1	Merrion	48 E1	(Drumcondra)		Monastery Park	44 E1
Meadowbrook Lawns	17 C4	Merrion Close	38 E3 [26]	Millmount Villas	25 A4 [1]	Monastery Rise	44 E1
Meadowbrook Park	28 D1	Merrion Court	48 E1 [1]	Millrace Road	23 B3	Monastery Road	44 E1
Meadowbrook Road	17 C4	Merrion Crescent	48 E2 [3]	Millrose Estate	36 E4 [2]	Monastery Walk	44 E1
Meadowfield	58 E4	Merrion Gates	48 E1 [2]	Millstead	22 F2	Monck Place	37 C1
Meadowlands	59 C1	Merrion Grove	48 E3	Millstream	14 F2	Monks Hill	66 E2
Meadowview Grove	33 C2	Merrion Hall	48 E4	Millstream Road	33 C2	Monks Meadow	4 D4
Meakstown Cottages	11 B3	Merrion Park	48 E3	Milltown (Clonskeagh)	47 C2	Monksfield	44 F1
Meath Market	37 C3 [16]	Merrion Place	38 E3 [8]	Milltown (Peamount)	42 F2	Monksfield Court	44 F1
Meath Place (Bray)	67 C2	Merrion Road	39 A4	Milltown Bridge Road	47 C2	Monksfield Downs	44 F1
Meath Place (Meath Street)	37 C3	Merrion Row	38 E3	*Milltown Collonade	47 B2	Monksfield Grove	44 F1
Meath Road	68 D2	Merrion Square East	38 E3	(on Milltown Road)		Monksfield Heights	44 F1
Meath Square	37 C3 [42]	Merrion Square North	38 E3	Milltown Drive	47 A3	Monksfield Lawn	44 F1
Meath Street	37 C3	Merrion Square South	38 E3	Milltown Grove (Churchtown)	47 A3	Monksfield Meadows	44 F1
*Meath Terrace (on Meath Place)	37 C3	Merrion Square West	38 E3	Milltown Grove (Clonskeagh)	47 B2 [6]	Monksfield Walk	44 F1
*Meathville Terrace	38 D3	Merrion Strand	48 E1	Milltown Hill	47 B2 [7]	Monkstown	49 B4
(on Long Lane)		Merrion Street Lower	38 E3 [27]	Milltown Park	47 B1	Monkstown Avenue	59 B1
Meenan Square	48 D3 [5]	Merrion Street Upper	38 E3	Milltown Path	47 B2	Monkstown Crescent	49 C4
Meetinghouse Lane	38 D2 [33]	Merrion View Avenue	48 D1 [1]	Milltown Road	47 B2	Monkstown Farm	59 C1
Méile an Rí Crescent	34 F3	Merrion Village	48 E1	Milltown Terrace (Dundrum)	47 B3 [4]	Monkstown Gate	49 C4 [29]
Méile an Rí Drive	34 F3	Merton Avenue	37 C4 [25]	Millview	44 E1 [7]	Monkstown Grove	59 C1
Méile an Rí Green	34 F3	Merton Drive	47 B1	Millview Close	3 A3	Monkstown Road	49 B4
Méile an Rí Park	34 F3	Merton Park	37 C4 [27]	Millview Cottages	37 A3 [28]	Monkstown Square	59 B1 [12]
Méile an Rí Road	34 F3	Merton Road	47 B2	Millview Court	3 A2	Monkstown Valley	49 B4
Méile an Rí View	34 F3	Merville Avenue (Fairview)	25 C4	Millview Lawns	3 A3	Montague Court	38 D3 [25]
Mellifont Avenue	50 D4	Merville Avenue (Stillorgan)	58 F1	Millview Road	3 A3	Montague Lane	38 D3 [13]
Mellowes Avenue	24 D1	Merville Road	58 F1	Millwood Court	27 A1	Montague Place	38 D3 [26]
Mellowes Court	24 D2 [3]	Mespil Estate	38 E4	Millwood Park	27 A1	Montague Street	38 D3
Mellowes Crescent	24 D2 [4]	Mespil Road	38 E4	Millwood Villas	27 A1	Monte Vella	60 F2 [9]
Mellowes Park	24 D1	Michael Collins Park	44 D1	Milton Hall	1 C2	Montebello Terrace	68 D2 [2]
Mellowes Road	24 D1	Middle Third	26 E3	Milton Terrace	2 D2	Montpelier Court	37 B2
Melrose Avenue (Clondalkin)	43 C1	Milesian Avenue	2 E2	Milton Terrace	67 C2 [13]	Montpelier Drive	37 B2
Melrose Avenue (Fairview)	25 C4	Milesian Court	2 E2	Milward Terrace	68 D2 [13]	Montpelier Gardens	37 B2 [5]
Melrose Court	25 C4 [16]	Milesian Grove	2 E2	Mine Hill Lane	63 B3	Montpelier Gardens	37 B2
Melrose Crescent	43 C1	Milesian Lawn	2 E2	Minnow Brook	46 F2 [26]	Montpelier Hill	37 B2
Melrose Green	43 C1	Milestown	19 C1	*Minstrel Court	58 F2	Montpelier Manor	49 B4 [2]
Melrose Grove	43 C1	Milestown	6 F4	(Charles Sheil's Houses)		Montpelier Parade	49 B4
Melrose Lawn	34 F4	Milford	3 A2	Misery Hill	38 F2	Montpelier Park	37 B2
Melrose Park (Clondalkin)	43 C1	Military Road (Killiney)	60 E4	Moat Lane	1 A2	Montpelier Place	49 B4 [1]
Melrose Park (Swords)	2 E3	Military Road (Kilmainham)	37 B3	Moatfield Avenue	26 F1	Montpelier View	54 D2
Melrose Park The Avenue	2 E3	Military Road (Phoenix Park)	36 F2	Moatfield Park	26 F1	Montrose Avenue	26 D2
Melrose Park The Close	2 E3	Military Road (Rathmines)	38 D4	Moatfield Road	26 F1	Montrose Close	26 D2
Melrose Park The Crescent	2 E3	Mill Bank	34 D1 [15]	Moatview Avenue	13 B4	Montrose Court	26 D2
Melrose Park The Drive	2 E3	Mill Brook Apts.	35 C1	Moatview Court	13 B4	Montrose Crescent	26 D1
Melrose Park The Green	2 E3	Mill Court Avenue	43 C1	Moatview Drive	13 B4	Montrose Drive	26 D1
Melrose Park The Grove	2 E3	Mill Court Drive	43 C1	Moatview Gardens	13 B4	Montrose Grove	26 D2
Melrose Park The Heights	2 E3	Mill House	62 F3	Mobhi Court	25 A3 [16]	Montrose Park	26 D2
Melrose Park The Lawn	2 E3	Mill Lane (Ashtown)	23 B3 [1]	Mobhi Road	25 A3	Moore Lane	38 D2 [15]
Melrose Park The Park	2 E3	Mill Lane (Leixlip)	33 A1	Moeran Road	45 C1	Moore Street	38 D2
Melrose Park The Rise	2 E3	Mill Lane (Loughlinstown)	64 E2	*Moira Road	37 B1	Moorefield	60 E4
Melrose Park The Villa	2 E3	Mill Lane (Newmarket)	37 C3 [26]	(off Oxmanstown Road)		Moore's Cottages	59 A1 [3]
Melrose Park The Walk	2 E3	Mill Lane (Palmerston)	35 C1	Moland Place	38 E2 [21]	Mooretown	1 B1
Melrose Road	34 F4	Mill Park	44 D1	Molesworth Close	1 A2	Mooretown Avenue	1 C1
Melville Close	11 B4	Mill Race Avenue	53 A2	Molesworth Place	38 E3 [24]	Mooretown Grove	1 C1
Melville Court	11 B4	Mill Race Court	53 A2	Molesworth Street	38 E3	Mooretown Park	1 C1
Melville Cove	11 B4	Mill Race Crescent	53 A2	Mollison Avenue	14 D4	Moorfield	35 A4
Melville Crescent	11 B4	Mill Race Drive	53 A2	Molyneux Yard	37 C3 [19]	Moorfield Avenue	35 A4
Melville Drive	11 B4	Mill Race Gardens	53 A2	Monalea Grove	55 C1	Moorfield Close	35 A4 [2]
Melville Green	11 B4	Mill Race Green	53 A2	Monalea Park	55 C1	Moorfield Drive	35 A4
Melville Grove	11 B4	Mill Race Park	53 A2	Monalea Wood	55 C1	Moorfield Green	35 A4
Melville Lawn	11 B4	Mill Race View	53 A2	Monaloe Avenue	59 C3	Moorfield Grove	35 A4
Melville Park	11 B4	Mill Race Walk	53 A2	Monaloe Court	59 B3 [6]	Moorfield Lawns	35 A4
Melville Rise	11 B4	Mill Road (Blanchardstown)	22 F2	Monaloe Crescent	59 B3 [4]	Moorfield Parade	35 A4
Melville Square	11 B4	Mill Road (Saggart)	53 A2	Monaloe Drive	59 C3	Moorfield Walk	35 A4
Melville Terrace	11 B4	Mill Street (Dun Laoghaire)	50 D4 [19]	Monaloe Park	59 C3	Moracrete Cottages	37 B4 [4]
Melville View	11 B4	Mill Street (The Coombe)	37 C3	Monaloe Park Road	59 C3	Moran's Cottages	47 B1 [12]
Melville Way	11 B4	Millbank	14 F2	Monaloe Way	59 C3	Moreen Avenue	58 D2
Melvin Road	46 F2	Millbourne Avenue	25 A4	Monasterboice Road	46 D1	Moreen Close	58 D2
Memorial Court	37 A2	Millbrook Avenue	27 A1	Monastery	66 E3	Moreen Lawn	58 D2 [2]
Memorial Road	38 E2	Millbrook Court	37 B3 [35]	Monastery Crescent	44 E1	Moreen Park	58 D2
(Custom House Quay)		Millbrook Drive	27 A1	Monastery Drive	44 E1	Moreen Road	58 D2
Memorial Road	37 A3 [9]	Millbrook Grove	27 A1	Monastery Gate	44 F1	Moreen Walk	58 D2
(Inchicore Road)		Millbrook Lawns	55 A1	Monastery Gate Avenue	44 F1	Morehampton Lane	38 F4
Mercer Street Lower	38 D3	Millbrook Road	27 A1	Monastery Gate Close	44 F1	Morehampton Mews	38 F4 [12]
Mercer Street Upper	38 D3	Millbrook Terrace	37 A3 [24]	Monastery Gate Copse	44 F1	Morehampton Road	38 F4
Merchamp	26 F4	Millbrook Village	47 C1 [17]	Monastery Gate Green	44 F1	Morehampton Square	38 F4 [11]

STREET NAME	PAGE/GRID REFERENCE	STREET NAME	PAGE/GRID REFERENCE	STREET NAME	PAGE/GRID REFERENCE	STREET NAME	PAGE/GRID REFERENCE
Morehampton Terrace	47 C1	Mount Norris Villas	68 D2 [19]	Moy Glas Avenue	34 E3	Nangor Place	43 C1 [2]
Morgan Place	37 C2 [14]	Mount Olive Grove	27 B1	Moy Glas Chase	34 E3	Nangor Road (Clondalkin)	44 D1
Morgans Place	23 A3	Mount Olive Park	27 B1	Moy Glas Close	34 E3	Nangor Road (Fox & Geese)	44 F1
Moritz House	55 B2	Mount Olive Road	27 B1	Moy Glas Court	34 E3	Nangor Road (Grange Castle)	43 A2
Morning Star Avenue	37 C2 [24]	Mount Prospect Avenue	27 A4	Moy Glas Dale	34 E3	Nanikin Avenue	27 A3
Morning Star Road	37 B3 [19]	Mount Prospect Drive	26 F4	Moy Glas Dene	34 E3	Nash Street	36 F3
Mornington Avenue	50 E4 [1]	Mount Prospect Grove	26 F4	Moy Glas Drive	34 E3	Nashville Park	30 E2
Mornington Grove	26 E2	Mount Prospect Lawn	26 F4	Moy Glas Glen	34 E3	Nashville Road	30 D2
Mornington Park	26 E2	Mount Prospect Park	26 F4	Moy Glas Green	34 E3	Nassau Street	38 E3
Mornington Road	47 B1	Mount Salus Road	60 F2	Moy Glas Grove	34 E3	Naul Road	1 A3
Morrogh Terrace	25 C3 [2]	Mount Sandford	47 C1 [14]	Moy Glas Lawn	34 E3	(Brackenstown Road)	
Moss Street	38 E2	Mount St. Annes	47 B2	Moy Glas Park	34 E3	Naul Road (Cloghran)	1 C4
Mount Albany	59 A1	Mount Street Crescent	38 F3 [32]	Moy Glas Road	34 E3	Navan Road (Blanchardstown)	22 E1
Mount Albion	57 B1 [3]	Mount Street Lower	38 E3	Moy Glas Vale	34 E3	Navan Road (Cabra)	24 D4
Mount Albion Road	57 B1	Mount Street Upper	38 E3	Moy Glas View	34 E3	Navan Road (Clonee)	8 E3
Mount Alton	55 C1	Mount Symon Avenue	21 C2	Moy Glas Way	34 E3	Navan Road (Dunboyne)	7 B2
Mount Alton Court	56 D1	Mount Symon Close	21 C2	Moy Glas Wood	34 E3	Navan Road (Mulhuddart)	8 F4
Mount Andrew	34 F2	Mount Symon Crescent	21 B2	Moyclare Avenue	28 D1	Neagh Road	46 E2
Mount Andrew Avenue	34 F2	Mount Symon Dale	21 B2	Moyclare Close	28 D1	Neilstown Avenue	35 A3
Mount Andrew Close	34 F1	Mount Symon Drive	21 C2	Moyclare Drive	28 D1	Neilstown Cottages	35 A4 [3]
Mount Andrew Court	34 F1	Mount Symon Estate	21 B2	Moyclare Gardens	28 D1 [6]	Neilstown Crescent	35 A3
Mount Andrew Dale	34 F2	Mount Symon Green	21 B2	Moyclare Park	28 D1	Neilstown Drive	35 A3
Mount Andrew Grove	34 F1	Mount Symon Lawn	21 C2	Moyclare Road	28 D1	Neilstown Gardens	35 A3
Mount Andrew Rise	34 F1	Mount Symon Park	21 C2	Moycullen Road	35 C3	Neilstown Park	35 A3
Mount Annville Road	48 D4	Mount Symon Rise	21 B2	Moygaddy	18 D1	Neilstown Road	35 A3
Mount Annville Wood	48 D4	Mount Tallant Avenue	46 F2	Moyglare	17 A1	Neilstown Village Court	35 A3 [1]
Mount Anville Lawn	48 D4	Mount Temple Road	37 C2	Moyglare Abbey	17 B2	Nelson Street	38 D1
Mount Anville Park	48 D4	Mount Venus Road	56 D4	Moyglare Meadows	17 C2	Nephin Road	24 D4
Mount Argus Avenue	46 F1	Mount View Road	22 D2	Moyglare Road	17 C2	Neptune Terrace	60 E1 [17]
Mount Argus Close	46 F1	Mount Wood	59 C1	Moyglare Village	17 C2	Nerano Road	60 G2
Mount Argus Court	46 F1	Mountain Park	55 A1	Moyle Crescent	44 E1	Nerney's Court	38 D1 [44]
Mount Argus Crescent	46 F1	Mountain Talbot	44 F1	Moyle Road	24 E3	Nethercross Court	2 D1
Mount Argus Green	46 F1	Mountain View	54 D2	Moyne Court	47 B1 [22]	Neville Road	47 A2
Mount Argus Grove	46 F1	Mountain View Apts.	67 C3 [11]	Moyne Park	14 F3	Nevinstown Lane	1 C3
Mount Argus Park	46 F1	Mountain View Avenue	46 F1 [3]	Moyne Road (Balgriffin)	14 E3	New Bancroft Hall	55 A1 [11]
Mount Argus Road	46 F1	Mountain View Cottages	22 D4	Moyne Road (Ranelagh)	47 B1	New Bancroft Place	55 A1 [9]
Mount Argus Square	46 F1 [15]	(Castleknock)		Moynihan Court	55 B1 [6]	New Bancroft Square	55 A1 [12]
Mount Argus Terrace	46 F1	Mountain View Cottages	47 B1 [13]	Moyville	56 E2	New Bawn Drive	55 A2
Mount Argus View	46 F1	(Ranelagh)		Moyville Lawns	56 E1	New Bawn Park	55 A2
Mount Argus Way	46 F1	Mountain View Court	46 F1 [16]	Muckross Avenue	46 D2	New Brighton Terrace	67 C2 [47]
Mount Auburn	60 E3 [2]	(Harold's Cross)		Muckross Crescent	46 D2	New Grange Road	59 A1
Mount Bellew Crescent	34 F2	*Mountain View Court	38 E1	Muckross Drive	46 D2 [1]	New Grove Estate	14 E4
Mount Bellew Green	34 F2	(off Summerhill Place)		Muckross Green	46 D2	New Ireland Road	37 B3
Mount Bellew Rise	34 E2	Mountain View Drive	57 A1	Muckross Grove	46 D2	New Lucan Road	35 B1
Mount Bellew Way	34 E2	Mountain View Park	47 A4	Muckross Parade	38 D1 [32]	New Nangor Road	43 C1
Mount Brown	37 B3	Mountain View Road	60 E4 [5]	Muckross Park	46 D2	New Park Lodge	59 A2 [3]
Mount Carmel Avenue	47 C4	(Ballybrack)		Muirfield Drive	36 F4 [1]	New Park Road	59 A1
Mount Carmel Park	55 C1	Mountain View Road	47 B1	Mulally's Lane	52 F2	New Rathmore Terrace	67 B2 [23]
Mount Carmel Road	47 C4	(Ranelagh)		Mulberry Crescent	22 F4	New Ravenswell Row	67 B2 [20]
Mount Dillon Court	26 E2	Mountain Villa	60 E4 [3]	Mulberry Drive	22 E4	New River Road	23 A2
Mount Drinan Avenue	2 E3	Mountainview Drive	67 C4	Mulberry Park	22 E4	New Road (Clondalkin)	44 E2
Mount Drinan Crescent	2 E3	Mountbrook	48 E3 [2]	Muldowney Court	3 C3	New Road (Howth)	30 E1
Mount Drinan Grove	2 E3	Mountdown Avenue	45 C3	Mulgrave Street	50 D4	New Road (Inchicore)	36 F3
Mount Drinan Lawn	2 E3	Mountdown Drive	45 C3	Mulgrave Terrace	50 D4	New Road (Swords)	2 D2 [5]
Mount Drinan Park	2 E3	Mountdown Park	45 C3	Mulhuddart	9 A4	New Row	36 E2 [12]
Mount Drinan Walk	2 E3	Mountdown Road	45 C3	Mulhuddart Wood	9 A4	New Row South	37 C3
Mount Drummond Avenue	37 C4	Mountfield	3 B3	Mullauns	42 D1	New Row Square	37 C3 [32]
Mount Drummond Court	37 C4 [30]	Mountgorry Wood Apts.	2 E2	Mullinastill Road	64 D2	New Street	3 B2
Mount Drummond Square	38 D4	Mountjoy Parade	38 E1 [36]	Mullingar Terrace	36 E2 [10]	*New Street Garden's	38 D3
Mount Eagle Court	58 E3	Mountjoy Place	38 E1 [22]	Mulroy Road	24 E4	(off New Street)	
Mount Eagle Drive	58 E3	Mountjoy Square	38 E1	Mulvey Park	47 C3	*New Street North	37 C2
Mount Eagle Green	58 E3	Mountjoy Square Apts	38 E1 [65]	Munster Street	24 F4	(off Church Street)	
Mount Eagle Grove	58 E3	Mountjoy Square East	38 E1	Munster Terrace	60 E1 [16]	New Street South	38 D3
Mount Eagle Lawn	58 E3	Mountjoy Square North	38 E1	Murphy's Lane	63 B4	New Vale	64 E3
Mount Eagle Park	58 E3	Mountjoy Square South	38 E1	Murphy's Lane	66 E1	New Vale Cottages	64 D3
Mount Eagle Rise	58 D3	Mountjoy Square West	38 D1	Murphystown Road	58 E3	New Vale Crescent	64 E3
Mount Eagle View	58 E3	Mountjoy Street	38 D1	Murray's Cottages	36 F3 [4]	New Wapping Street	38 F2
Mount Eagle Way	58 E3	Mountjoy Street Middle	38 D1 [9]	Murtagh Road	37 C2 [30]	Newbridge Avenue	39 A3
Mount Eden Road	47 C1	Mountpleasant Avenue Lower	38 D4	Muskerry Road	36 E3	Newbridge Drive	39 A3
Mount Eustace	9 B2	Mountpleasant Avenue Upper	38 D4	Mutton Lane	56 E4	Newbrook Avenue	27 B1
Mount Eustace Avenue	9 B2	Mountpleasant Parade	38 D4 [39]	Myra Cottages	37 A3 [21]	Newbrook Road	27 B1
Mount Eustace Close	9 A2	Mountpleasant Place	38 E4 [22]	Myra Manor	3 A4	Newbury Avenue	13 A4
Mount Eustace Drive	9 B2	Mountpleasant Square	38 D4	Myrtle Avenue	60 D1 [3]	Newbury Drive	13 A4
Mount Eustace Green	9 B2	Mountpleasant Terrace	38 D4 [40]	Myrtle Grove (Bray)	67 B1 [3]	Newbury Grove	13 A4
Mount Eustace Grove	9 A2	*Mountpleasant Terrace	38 E4	Myrtle Grove (Stillorgan)	58 F1	Newbury Lawns	13 B4
Mount Eustace Park	9 B2	Upper (off Mountpleasant Place)		Myrtle Park	60 D1	Newbury Park	13 A4
Mount Eustace Rise	9 B2	Mountpleasant Villas	67 B2 [13]	Myrtle Street	38 D1 [23]	Newbury Terrace	13 A4 [1]
Mount Eustace Walk	9 B2	Mountsandel	59 B4			Newcastle	41 C4
Mount Gandon	34 D1 [9]	Mountshannon Road	37 B3	**N**		Newcastle Demesne	41 B4
Mount Harold Terrace	46 F1 [1]	Mounttown Cottages	49 C4 [26]			Newcastle Farm	41 B4
Mount Hybla Court	23 A4	Mounttown Park	59 C1 [3]	Naas Road (Rathcoole)	52 F1	Newcastle Manor	42 D4
Mount Hybla House	23 A4	Mounttown Road Lower	59 C1	Naas Road (Saggart)	53 B1	Newcastle Road (Lucan)	34 D2
Mount Merrion	48 E4	Mounttown Road Upper	49 C4	Naas Road (Walkinstown)	45 A1	Newcastle Road (Rathcoole)	52 E1
Mount Merrion Avenue	48 F3	Mourne Road	37 A4	Nagle Court	18 D2	Newcomen Avenue	38 E1
		Moy Elta Road	38 F1	Nangor Crescent	44 D1 [5]	Newcomen Court	38 E1 [29]

STREET NAME	PAGE/GRID REFERENCE
Newcourt (Bray)	68 D4
Newcourt (Swords)	2 D1
Newcourt Avenue	68 D3
Newcourt Mews	2 D1
Newcourt Road	68 D3
Newcourt Villas	67 C3 [8]
Newgrange Road	24 F4
Newgrove Avenue	39 B4
Newhall Court	54 D2
Newington Terrace	47 A1 [27]
Newlands Avenue	44 E2
Newlands Drive	44 E2
Newlands Manor	44 D3
Newlands Manor Court	44 D3
Newlands Manor Drive	44 D3
Newlands Manor Fairway	44 D3
Newlands Manor Green	44 D3
Newlands Manor Park	44 D3
Newlands Park	44 E2
Newlands Road (Clondalkin)	44 E2
Newlands Road (Ronanstown)	34 F3
Newman Place	18 D3
Newmarket	37 C3
Newmarket Street	37 C3 [25]
Newpark	59 A2
Newport Street	37 C3
Newtown (Dunboyne)	7 A3
Newtown (Glencullen)	62 E3
Newtown (Rathfarnham)	56 E3
Newtown (Tinnehinch)	66 E4
Newtown Avenue (Blackrock)	49 A3
Newtown Avenue (Coolock)	26 F1
Newtown Close	13 C4
Newtown Cottages (Coolock)	26 F1
Newtown Cottages (St. Margaret's)	11 A1
Newtown Court (Coolock)	13 C4
Newtown Court (Maynooth)	17 B4
Newtown Court (Rathgar)	47 A3 [5]
Newtown Drive	26 F1
Newtown Glendale	20 D4
Newtown Grove	17 C3
Newtown House	47 A3 [12]
Newtown Lower	52 D4
Newtown Lower	51 C4
Newtown Park (Blackrock)	59 A1
Newtown Park (Coolock)	26 F1
Newtown Park (Leixlip)	20 D4
Newtown Park (Tallaght)	55 B1
Newtown Park Court	59 A1 [8]
Newtown Road (Celbridge)	32 D4
Newtown Road (Coolock)	13 C4
Newtown Road (Maynooth)	17 B4
Newtown Road (Maynooth)	17 C3
Newtown Upper	52 D4
Newtown Villas (Blackrock)	49 A3 [1]
Newtown Villas (Braemor Road)	47 A3 [4]
Newtown Way	13 C4
Newtownpark Avenue	49 A4
Newtownpark House	59 A1 [11]
Newtownsmith	50 E4
Niall Street	37 B2 [11]
Nicholas Avenue	37 C2 [7]
Nicholas Street	38 D3
Ninth Lock Road	44 D1
No2 Nth. Road Extension	39 B1
Noel Purcell Park	38 D3 [56]
Nore Road	24 E3
Norfolk Road	24 F4
*Norseman Court (off Noresman Place)	37 C2
Norseman Place	37 C2
North Avenue	48 E3
North Bull Island	27 B4
North Circular Road (Phibsborough)	38 E1
North Circular Road (Phoenix Park)	37 B2
North Clarence St Flats	38 E1 [66]
North Great George's St	38 D1
North Quay Extension	39 A2
North Road (Finglas)	24 D1
North Road (Phoenix Park)	37 A1
North Strand Road	38 F1
North Street	2 D1
North Wall	38 F2
North Wall Quay	38 F2
Northbrook Avenue (Ranelagh)	38 E4
Northbrook Avenue Lower	38 F1
Northbrook Avenue Upper	38 F1
Northbrook Lane	38 E4 [20]
Northbrook Road	38 E4
Northbrook Terrace	38 F1 [1]
*Northbrook Villas (on Northbrook Road Ranelagh)	38 E4
Northcote Avenue	49 C4
Northcote Place	49 C4 [23]
Northcote Terrace	49 C4 [20]
Northern Close	13 B3
Northern Cross Route	23 A2
Northland Drive	24 F3 [2]
Northland Grove	24 F3 [1]
Northumberland Avenue	50 D4
Northumberland Park	50 D4 [11]
Northumberland Place (Dún Laoghaire)	50 D4 [10]
Northumberland Place (Grand Canal St. Upr.)	38 F3 [42]
Northumberland Road	38 F3
Northumberland Square	38 E2 [8]
Northway Estate	11 A4
Northwood	12 E4
Norton's Avenue	37 C1 [11]
Norwood	64 E1
Norwood Park	47 C1 [7]
Nottingham Street	38 F1
Novara Avenue	67 C2
Novara Mews	67 C2 [57]
Novara Park	67 C2 [7]
Novara Terrace	67 C2 [27]
Nugent Road	47 A4
Nunciature Road	23 C4
Nun's Lane	26 E3
Nurney Lawn	14 D4
Nutgrove Avenue	47 A4
Nutgrove Avenue	47 B4 [14]
Nutgrove Court	47 A4 [2]
Nutgrove Crescent	57 A1
Nutgrove Park (Clonskeagh)	47 C2
Nutgrove Way	57 A1
Nutley Avenue	48 D1
Nutley Lane	48 D2
Nutley Park	48 D2
Nutley Road	48 D1
Nutley Square	48 D2 [1]

O

STREET NAME	PAGE/GRID REFERENCE
O'Neill's Park	18 D3
Oak Apple Green	47 A2
Oak Avenue	12 F4
Oak Close	44 F1
Oak Court	12 F4
Oak Crescent	12 F4
Oak Dene	60 E3
Oak Downs	44 D2
Oak Drive (Fox & Geese)	44 F1
Oak Drive (Santry)	12 F4
Oak Glen Park	67 C4
Oak Glen View	67 C4
Oak Green	12 F4
Oak Grove	12 F4
Oak Hall	3 B3
Oak Lawn (Castleknock)	22 F3
Oak Lawn (Santry)	12 F4
Oak Lodge	23 A4
Oak Rise (Clondalkin)	44 D2
Oak Rise (Santry)	12 F4
Oak Road (Donnycarney)	26 D3
Oak Road (Fox & Geese)	44 F1
Oak View	12 E4
Oak Way	44 D2
Oakcourt Avenue	35 C2
Oakcourt Close	35 C2
Oakcourt Drive	35 C2
Oakcourt Grove	35 C2
Oakcourt Lawn	35 C2
Oakcourt Park	35 C2
Oakdale Close	55 B3
Oakdale Crescent	55 B3
Oakdale Drive (Firhouse)	55 B3
Oakdale Drive (Sallynoggin)	59 C2
Oakdale Grove	55 B3
Oakdale Park	55 B3
Oakdale Road	55 B3
Oakdown Road	47 A4
Oakfield Place	38 D4 [50]
Oaklands Avenue	2 D2
Oaklands Crescent	47 A2
Oaklands Drive (Rathgar)	47 A2
Oaklands Drive (Sandymount)	39 A4
Oaklands Park (Sandymount)	39 A4
Oaklands Park (Swords)	2 D2
Oaklands Terrace	46 F2
Oaklawn	19 C4
Oaklawn Close	19 C4
Oaklawn West	19 C4
Oaklee	32 D2
Oakleigh	31 C4
Oakley Court	47 B1 [10]
Oakley Grove	49 A4
Oakley Park (Blackrock)	49 A4
Oakley Park (Clontarf)	26 F4
Oakley Park (Ranelagh)	47 B1 [23]
Oakley Road	47 B1
Oakley Square	47 B1 [20]
Oakpark Avenue	25 C1
Oakpark Close	25 C1
Oakpark Drive	25 C1
Oakpark Grove	25 C1
Oakton Court	60 E4 [1]
Oakton Drive	60 D4
Oakton Green	60 D4 [3]
Oakton Park	64 D1
Oakton Park	60 D4
Oaktree Avenue	22 E3
Oaktree Drive	22 E3
Oaktree Green	22 E3
Oaktree Grove	22 E3
Oaktree Lawn	22 E3
Oaktree Road	58 F1
Oakview Avenue	21 C1
Oakview Close	21 C1
Oakview Court	21 C1
Oakview Drive	21 C1
Oakview Grove	21 C1 [2]
Oakview Lawn	21 C1
Oakview Park	21 C1
Oakview Rise	21 C1
Oakview Walk	21 C1
Oakview Way	21 C1
Oakwood	49 C4 [7]
Oakwood Avenue (Glasnevin)	24 E1
Oakwood Avenue (Swords)	1 C2
Oakwood Close	24 E1
Oakwood Grove Estate	35 A4
Oakwood Park	24 E1
Oakwood Road	24 E1
Oatfield Avenue	35 B3
Oatfield Close	35 B3
Oatfield Crescent (off Oatfield Drive)	35 B2
Oatfield Drive	35 B3
Oatfield Grove	35 B3
Oatfield Lawn	35 B3
Oatfield Park	35 B3
Obelisk Avenue	59 A1 [12]
Obelisk Court (Stillorgan)	59 A1
Obelisk Grove	59 A1
Obelisk Lane	18 E4
Obelisk Rise	59 A1
Obelisk Walk	59 A1
Oblate Drive	36 F3 [14]
O'Brien Road	45 C1
O'Brien's Place North	25 A3 [13]
O'Brien's Terrace	25 A4 [15]
O'Carolan Road	37 C3 [29]
O'Casey Avenue	35 C4
O'Connell Avenue	38 D1 [6]
O'Connell Gardens	39 A3
O'Connell Street	38 D2
*O'Curry Avenue (off O'Curry Road)	37 C3
O'Curry Road	37 C3
O'Daly Road	25 A3
Odd Lamp Road	36 F1
O'Devaney Gardens	37 B2
O'Donnell Gardens	60 D1 [1]
O'Donoghue Street	36 F3
O'Donovan Road	37 C4
O'Dwyer Road	45 C1 [4]
Offaly Road	24 F4
Offington Avenue	29 B2
Offington Court	29 B2
Offington Drive	29 B2
Offington Lawn	29 B2
Offington Manor Apts	29 B1 [4]
Offington Park	29 B1
O'Hanlon's Lane	3 B2
O'Hara Avenue	38 D4 [56]
O'Hogan Road	36 E3 [1]
O'Hogan Road	36 E3
Olaf Hall	58 D2 [8]
Olaf Road	37 C2 [33]
Olcovar	64 E4
Old Bawn Avenue	55 A2
Old Bawn Close	55 A2
Old Bawn Court	55 A1 [5]
Old Bawn Drive	55 A2
Old Bawn Park	55 A2
Old Bawn Road	55 A1
Old Bawn Terrace	55 A2
Old Bawn Way	55 A2
Old Belgard Road	44 F4
Old Blessington Road	55 A1
Old Brazil Way	1 A2
Old Bridge Road	46 D4
Old Brighton Terrace	67 C2 [46]
Old Cabra Road	37 B1
Old Camac Bridge	37 A3
Old Carrickbrack Road	30 D4
Old Connaught	67 A1
Old Connaught Avenue	67 B1
Old Connaught Grove	67 B2
Old Connaught View	67 B2
Old Corduff Road	22 E1
Old Cornmill Road	33 C2
Old County Glen	37 B4
Old County Road	37 B4
Old County Road	37 A4
Old Dublin Road (Stillorgan)	48 E4
Old Dunleary	49 C4
Old Fairgreen	7 B2
Old Fort Road	1 A2
Old Greenfield	17 C3
Old Greenfield	17 C4
Old Hill	20 D4
Old Kilmainham	37 B3
Old Kilmainham Village	37 B3 [2]
Old Mill Court	37 C3 [52]
Old Mountpleasant	38 E4 [9]
Old Naas Road (Bluebell)	36 E4
Old Naas Road (Brownsbarn)	43 C4
Old Naas Road Cottages	36 E4 [1]
Old Quarry (Dalkey)	60 F2
Old Quarry (Kilshane)	10 D2
Old Quay	29 B2
Old Quay Mews	29 B2
Old Quay Terrace	29 B2
Old Rathmichael	64 D3
Old Rathmore Terrace	67 B2 [22]
Old Ravenswell Row	67 B2 [11]
Old Rectory	34 D1 [11]
Old Rectory Park	47 C4
Old Road	14 E2
Old Street	3 B2
Old Yellow Walls Road	2 F2
Oldbawn	55 A2
Oldbridge	34 E3
Oldbridge Close	34 E3
Oldbridge Court	34 E3
Oldbridge Glen	34 E3
Oldbridge Green	34 E3
Oldbridge Grove	34 E3
Oldbridge Park	34 E3
Oldbridge View	34 E3
Oldbridge Walk	34 E3
Oldbridge Way	34 E3

STREET NAME	PAGE	GRID
Oldcarton	18	F1
Oldcastle Avenue	29	B2
Oldcastle Drive	43	B1
Oldcastlepark	43	B1
Oldcastlepark Close	43	B1
Oldcastlepark Green	43	B1
Oldcastlepark Grove	43	B1
Oldcastlepark Lawn	43	B1
Oldcastlepark View	43	B1
Oldchurch Avenue	43	C1
Oldchurch Close	43	C1
Oldchurch Court	43	C1
Oldchurch Crescent	43	C1
Oldchurch Drive	43	C1
Oldchurch Grove	43	C1
Oldchurch Lawn	43	C1
Oldchurch Park	43	C1
Oldchurch Way	43	C1
Oldcourt	67	B3
Oldcourt Avenue (Boghall Road)	67	B3
Oldcourt Avenue (Bohernabreena)	55	B2
Oldcourt Close	55	B2
Oldcourt Cottages	55	B3
Oldcourt Drive	67	B3
Oldcourt Farm	55	B2
Oldcourt Grove	67	B4
Oldcourt Lawn	55	B2 [1]
Oldcourt Lodge	55	B2
Oldcourt Manor	55	B3
Oldcourt Park	67	B3
Oldcourt Road	55	B3
Oldcourt Terrace	67	C3 [15]
Oldcourt View	55	B2
Oldfarm	22	F3
Oldtower Crescent	35	A2
Oldtown Avenue	25	A1
Oldtown Cottages	31	C3
Oldtown Mill	31	C3
Oldtown Mill Road	31	C3
Oldtown Park	25	A1 [3]
Oldtown Road	25	A1
O'Leary Road	37	A3
Olivemount Grove	47	C3 [2]
Olivemount Road	47	C3
Olivemount Terrace	47	C3 [6]
Oliver Bond Street	37	C2
Oliver Plunkett Avenue (Dun Laoghaire)	59	C1
Oliver Plunkett Avenue (Ringsend)	39	A3
Oliver Plunkett Road	59	C1
Oliver Plunkett Square	59	C1 [1]
Oliver Plunkett Terrace	59	C1 [5]
Oliver Plunkett Villas	59	B1 [3]
Olney Crescent	46	F2
Olney Grove	46	F2 [17]
Omni Park	25	B1
O'Moore Road	36	E3
O'Neachtain Road	25	A3 [14]
O'Neill's Buildings	38	D3 [14]
Ongar Chase Estate	21	A1
Ongar Park Estate	21	B1
Ongar Road	21	B2
Ongar Village	21	A1
Ontario Terrace	38	D4 [11]
Onward Close	3	C4
Onward Walk	3	C4
Ophaly Court	47	C4
O'Quinns Avenue	37	B3 [40]
O'Rahilly House Flats	39	A3 [28]
O'Rahilly Parade	38	D2 [26]
Oranmore Road	35	C3
Oratory Mews Court	50	D4 [24]
Orby Avenue	58	E3
Orby Close	58	F3
Orby Court	58	F3
Orby Lawn	58	E3
Orby Park	58	F3
Orby View	58	E3
Orby Village	58	E3
Orby Way	58	E3
Orchard Avenue (Citywest)	53	B1
Orchard Avenue (Clonsilla)	21	C2
Orchard Close	22	D2
Orchard Cottages	59	A1 [1]
Orchard Court	22	E2
Orchard Green	22	D2
Orchard Grove (Blanchardstown)	22	E2
Orchard Grove (Newcastle)	42	D4
Orchard Lane (Blackrock)	59	A1
Orchard Lane (Clondalkin)	44	E1
Orchard Lane (Ranelagh)	38	E4 [24]
Orchard Lawns	35	C3
Orchard Lodge	44	E1
Orchard Road (Ballybough)	25	B4
Orchard Road (Raheny)	27	B2
Orchard Road South	47	B2
Orchard Square	47	C3
Orchard Terrace (Bray)	67	C3 [19]
*Orchard Terrace (Grangegorman Upper)	37	C1
*Orchard View	37	C1
Orchardstown Avenue	46	E4
Orchardstown Drive	46	E4
Orchardstown Park	46	E4
Orchardstown Villas	56	E1
Orchardton	56	E1 [1]
Ordnance Survey Road	36	E1
O'Reilly Avenue	37	B3 [9]
Oriel Street Lower	38	F1
Oriel Street Upper	38	E2
Orlagh Avenue	56	D2
Orlagh Close	56	D2
Orlagh Court	56	D2
Orlagh Crescent	56	D2
Orlagh Downs	56	D2
Orlagh Grange	56	D2
Orlagh Green	56	D2
Orlagh Grove	56	D2
Orlagh Lawn	56	D2
Orlagh Lodge	56	D2
Orlagh Meadows	56	D2
Orlagh Park	56	D2
Orlagh Pines	56	D2
Orlagh Rise	56	D2
Orlagh View	56	D2
Orlagh Way	56	D2
Orlagh Wood	56	D2
Ormeau Drive	60	F1 [2]
Ormeau Street	38	F3 [7]
Ormond Avenue	1	B1
Ormond Close	1	B1
Ormond Crescent	1	B1
Ormond Drive	1	B1
Ormond Grove	1	B1
Ormond Lawn	1	B1
*Ormond Market (off Ormond Quay Upper)	38	D2
*Ormond Place (off Ormond Quay Upper)	38	D2
Ormond Quay Lower	38	D2
Ormond Quay Upper	38	D2
Ormond Road	25	B4
Ormond Road South	47	B1
Ormond Square	38	D2 [37]
Ormond Street	37	C3
*Ormond Terrace (off Sorrento Road)	60	F2
Ormond View	1	B1
Ormond Way	1	B1
O'Rourke Park	59	C2
Orpen	58	F1
Orpen Close	48	F4
Orpen Dale	48	F4 [2]
Orpen Green	48	F4 [6]
Orpen Green	58	F1
Orpen Hill	58	F1
Orpen Rise	58	F1
Orwell Bank	47	A3 [7]
Orwell Court	47	A3 [3]
Orwell Gardens	47	A3
Orwell Mews	47	A2 [8]
Orwell Park (Rathgar)	47	A3
Orwell Park (Templeogue)	45	C4
Orwell Park Avenue	46	D3
Orwell Park Close	46	D3
Orwell Park Crescent	46	D3
Orwell Park Dale	45	C4
Orwell Park Drive	46	D3
Orwell Park Glade	45	C3
Orwell Park Glen	46	D3
Orwell Park Green	46	D3
Orwell Park Grove	45	C3
Orwell Park Heights	45	C4
Orwell Park Lawns	45	C3
Orwell Park Rise	45	C4
Orwell Park View	45	C4
Orwell Park Way	46	D3
Orwell Road	47	A2
Orwell Walk	47	A3
Orwell Woods	47	A2
*Osborne Terrace (Northbrook Road)	38	E4
Oscar Square	37	C3 [23]
Oscar Traynor Road	26	E1
O'Shea's Cottages	59	C3 [4]
Osprey Avenue	45	C3
Osprey Court	64	E3 [3]
Osprey Drive	45	C3
Osprey Lawn	45	C3
Osprey Park	45	C3
Osprey Road	45	C3
Ossory Road	38	F1
Ostman Place	37	C2 [1]
O'Sullivan Avenue	38	E1 [1]
Oswald Road	39	A3
Otranto Place	60	E1
Otterbrook	46	F4 [16]
Oulart	1	C3
Oulton Road	26	E4
*Our Lady's Close (off Our Lady's Road)	37	C3
Our Lady's Road	37	C3
Outer Ring Road	43	B2
Outfarm Lane	22	E3
Outlands	1	B1
Overend Way	57	C1
Ovoca Road	38	D4
Owendoher Lodge	56	E1
Owendore Avenue	46	F4
Owendore Crescent	46	F4
Owen's Avenue	37	B3 [39]
Owensilla	24	F1
Owenstown Park	48	D3
Oxford Lane	38	E4
Oxford Road	38	E4
*Oxford Terrace (on Hawthorn Terrace)	38	F1
*Oxford Terrace (off Church Road)	38	F1
Oxmantown Lane	37	C2 [21]
Oxmantown Road	37	B1

P

STREET NAME	PAGE	GRID
Pace Avenue	8	E4
Pace Crescent	8	E4
Pace Road	8	E4
Pace View	8	E4
Pacelli Avenue	27	C1
Pairc Gleann Trasna	55	A3
Pairc Mhuire	53	A2
Pairc Mhuire	53	A2
Pakenham	49	C4 [28]
Pakenham Road	49	C4
*Palace Street (off Dame Street)	38	D2
Palmer Park	56	E2
Palmer Park	56	F2
Palmers Avenue	35	B2
Palmers Close	35	B2
Palmers Copse	35	B2
Palmers Court	35	B2
Palmers Crescent	35	B2
Palmers Drive	35	B2
Palmers Glade	35	B2
Palmers Grove	35	B2
Palmers Lawn	35	B2
Palmers Park	35	B2
Palmers Road	35	B2
Palmers Walk	35	B2
Palmerston	35	C1
Palmerston Close	47	B1 [21]
*Palmerston Close (rere of Palmerston Road)	47	B1
Palmerston Court	47	A1
Palmerston Gardens	47	B2
Palmerston Grove	47	C2 [5]
Palmerston Lane	47	B2
Palmerston Park (Kennelsfort Road)	35	B2
Palmerston Park (Rathgar)	47	B2
Palmerston Place	38	D1 [8]
Palmerston Road	47	B1
Palmerston Villas	47	A2
Palmerstown Avenue	35	C2
Palmerstown Close	35	B2
Palmerstown Court	35	C2
Palmerstown Drive	35	C2
*Palmerstown Green	35	B2
Palmerstown Heights	35	B2
Palmerstown Lawn	35	B2
Palmerstown Manor	35	B2
Palmerstown Woods	35	B4
Paradise Place	38	D1
Park Avenue (Brackenstown Road)	1	B2
Park Avenue (Castleknock)	22	F3
Park Avenue (Deans Grange)	59	A1
Park Avenue (Sandymount)	39	B4
Park Avenue (Willbrook)	56	F1
Park Avenue West	37	B2 [13]
Park Boulevard	9	B2
Park Close (Sallynoggin)	60	D2
Park Court (Sandymount)	39	A4 [16]
Park Court Apts	23	A3 [4]
Park Crescent (Blackhorse Avenue)	37	A1
Park Crescent (Kimmage)	46	D2
Park Crescent House	24	D4 [6]
Park Drive (Cabinteely)	59	B3
Park Drive (Ranelagh)	47	B1
Park Drive Avenue	22	F3
Park Drive Close	22	F3
Park Drive Court	22	F3
Park Drive Crescent	22	F3
Park Drive Green	22	F3
Park Drive Grove	22	F3
Park Drive Lawn	22	F3
Park Lane (Chapelizod)	36	E2 [1]
Park Lane (Dún Laoghaire)	50	D4 [21]
Park Lane (Sandymount)	39	A4
Park Lawn	27	A4
Park Lodge	22	F3
Park Manor	22	E3
Park Place	37	A2 [4]
Park Road (Dun Laoghaire)	50	D4
Park Road (off Navan Road)	23	C3
Park Road (Sallynoggin)	60	D2
Park Spring's	24	D4 [5]
Park Street	36	F3 [1]
*Park Street (off Hanover St West)	37	C3
Park Terrace (Coombe)	37	C3 [6]
Park View (Cabra)	37	B1
Park View (Castleknock)	23	B4
Lohunda Park View	22	D2
Park View (Enniskerry Road)	58	D4
Park View (Mount Prospect Lawns)	26	F4 [4]
Park View (Portmarnock)	15	A1
Park View (Rathgar)	47	A3 [10]
Park View House	9	B2
Park View Lawns	44	D2
Park View Manor	9	B2
Park Villas (Castleknock)	23	A3
Park Villas (Stillorgan)	48	F4 [3]
Park West Avenue	35	C4
Park West Road	35	C4
Park West Road	36	D4
Parker Hill	47	A1 [12]
Parkgate Street	37	B2
Parkhill Avenue	44	F3
Parkhill Close	45	A3
Parkhill Court	44	F3
Parkhill Drive	44	F3
Parkhill Green	44	F3
Parkhill Heights	45	A3 [1]

STREET NAME	PAGE/GRID REFERENCE
Parkhill Lawn	44 F3
Parkhill Rise	44 F3
Parkhill Road	44 F3
Parkhill Way	45 A3
Parkhill West	44 F4
Parklands (Castleknock)	22 F3
Parklands (Maynooth)	18 D3
Parklands (Santry)	12 E4
Parklands Avenue	55 B2
Parklands Close	18 D3
Parklands Court (Maynooth)	18 D3
Parklands Court (Scholarstown Link Road)	55 B2
Parklands Crescent	18 D3
Parklands Drive	55 B2
Parklands Grove	18 D3
Parklands Lawns	18 D3
Parklands Rise	18 D3
Parklands Road	55 B2
Parklands Square	18 D3
Parklands View	55 B2
Parklands Way	18 D3
Parkmore	23 A3
Parkmore Drive	46 E2
Parknasilla Avenue	64 D2
Parknasilla Close	64 D2
Parknasilla Lane	64 D2
Parknasilla Rise	64 D2
Parknasillog	65 C2
Parkvale (Dundrum)	57 C1
Parkvale (Sutton)	28 D1
Parkview (Kilnamanagh)	45 A3 [2]
Parkview (Swords)	1 B2
Parkview Avenue (Harold's Cross)	46 F1
Parkview Court (Blackhorse Avenue)	37 A1 [1]
Parkview Court (Harold's Cross)	46 F1 [8]
Parkview Place	39 A3 [14]
Parkview Terrace	67 B2 [16]
Parkwood Avenue	55 A2
Parkwood Grove	55 A2
Parkwood Lawn	55 A2
Parkwood Road	55 A2
Parliament Street	38 D2
Parnell Avenue	37 C4
Parnell Cottages	3 B3
Parnell Court	37 C4 [13]
Parnell Hall	37 C4
Parnell Place	38 D1 [16]
Parnell Road (Bray)	67 C2
Parnell Road (Harold's Cross)	37 C4
Parnell Square East	38 D1
Parnell Square North	38 D1
Parnell Square West	38 D1
Parnell Street (O'Connell Street)	38 D1
Parnell Street (Sallynoggin)	60 D1
Parochial Avenue	15 A4 [2]
Parslickstown Avenue	9 A4
Parslickstown Close	9 A4
Parslickstown Court	9 A4
Parslickstown Drive	9 A4
Parslickstown Gardens	9 A3
Parslickstown Green	9 A4
Parson Court	17 C3
Parson Lodge	17 C3
Parson Street	17 C3
Parsons Hall	17 B3
Partridge Terrace	36 F3 [5]
Patrician Park	59 C1 [2]
Patrician Villas	48 F4
Patrick Doyle Road	47 B2
Patrick Street (Dun Laoghaire)	50 D4
Patrick Street (Kevin Street Upr.)	38 D3
Patrick's Row	49 A3 [14]
Patrickswell Court	24 D2 [8]
Patrickswell Place	24 D2
Paul Street	37 C2 [36]
Pavillion Gate	59 A4
Pea Field	48 F3
Peamount	42 D2
Peamount Road	42 D3
Peamount Road	42 E2
Pear Tree Field	58 F1 [5]
Pearse Avenue	60 D2
Pearse Brothers Park	56 F1
Pearse Close	60 D2 [3]
Pearse Drive	60 D2
Pearse Gardens	59 C2
Pearse Green	60 D2
Pearse Grove	38 F3 [38]
Pearse House	38 E2 [1]
Pearse Park	60 D2
Pearse Road (Bray)	67 B2 [12]
Pearse Road (Sallynoggin)	60 D2
Pearse Square (Bray)	67 B2
Pearse Square (Pearse Street)	38 F3
Pearse Street (Sallynoggin)	60 D2
Pearse Street (Westland Row)	38 E2
Pearse Villas	60 D2
Pebble Hill	18 D2
Pebble Hill Lodge	18 D2
Peck's Lane	23 A3
Pelletstown Avenue	23 C3
Pemberton	67 A3
Pembroke Cottages (Booterstown)	48 F3 [2]
Pembroke Cottages (Donnybrook)	47 C1 [2]
Pembroke Cottages (Dundrum)	47 C4 [5]
Pembroke Cottages (Ringsend)	39 A2
Pembroke Gardens	38 F4
Pembroke Lane (Lr Baggot Street)	38 E3
Pembroke Lane (Pembroke Road)	38 F4
Pembroke Park	38 F4
Pembroke Place (Ballsbridge)	38 F4 [15]
Pembroke Place (Pembroke St Upr)	38 E4 [32]
Pembroke Road	38 F4
Pembroke Row	38 E3
Pembroke Street	39 A3
Pembroke Street Lower	38 E3
Pembroke Street Upper	38 E3
Pembroke Terrace	47 C4 [6]
Penrose Street	38 F3 [6]
Percy French Road	45 C1 [3]
Percy Lane	38 F3
Percy Place	38 F3
Peter Place	38 D4 [19]
Peter Row	38 D3
Peter Street	38 D3
Peter's Court	38 D1 [38]
Peterson's Court	38 E2 [16]
Petrie Road	37 C4
Pheasant Run	8 F4
Pheasant Run The Drive	8 F4
Pheasant Run The Green	8 F4
Pheasant Run The Grove	8 F4
Pheasant Run The Park	8 F4
Phelan Avenue	24 D3
Phibblestown Avenue	21 A1
Phibblestown House	21 B1
Phibsborough	38 D1
Phibsborough	37 C1
Phibsborough Avenue	37 C1 [6]
Phibsborough Place	38 D1 [1]
Phibsborough Road	38 D1
Philipsburgh Avenue	25 C4
Philipsburgh Terrace	25 C4
*Philomena Terrace (off Oliver Plunket Ave)	39 A3
Phoenix Avenue	23 A3
Phoenix Court (Arbour Hill)	37 B2 [17]
Phoenix Court (Castleknock)	23 A3
Phoenix Court (North Circular Road)	37 B1 [15]
Phoenix Drive	23 A3
Phoenix Gardens	23 A3
Phoenix Manor	37 B1 [19]
Phoenix Park Way	23 B3
Phoenix Place	23 A3
Phoenix Street	36 F3 [2]
Phoenix Street West	37 C2 [15]
Phoenix Terrace	48 F3
Phoenix View	37 B3 [43]
Phrompstown	66 E1
Pickford's Terrace	38 F2 [13]
Pig Lane	38 E1
Pigeon House Road (Ringsend)	39 B3
Pigeon House Road (Ringsend)	39 A2
*Pile's Terrace (Sandwith St Upper)	38 E3
Pilot View	60 F1 [14]
Pim Street	37 C3
Pimlico	37 C3
Pimlico Cottages	37 C3 [12]
Pine Avenue	59 A2
Pine Copse Road	57 B1
Pine Court (Deans Grange)	59 A1
Pine Court (Portmarnock)	15 A1
Pine Grove	56 D1 [2]
Pine Grove Park	1 C1
Pine Grove Road	1 C1
Pine Haven	48 F3
Pine Hurst	24 E4
Pine Lawn (Deans Grange)	59 A1
Pine Lawn (Tallaght)	55 A2
Pine Road	39 A3
Pine Valley Avenue	57 B2
Pine Valley Drive	57 B3
Pine Valley Grove	57 B3
Pine Valley Park	57 B3
Pine Valley Way	57 B3
Pinebrook Avenue	26 D2
Pinebrook Close	21 C1
Pinebrook Crescent	26 D2
Pinebrook Downs	21 C1
Pinebrook Drive	26 D2
Pinebrook Glen	21 C1
Pinebrook Grove	26 E2
Pinebrook Heights	21 C1
Pinebrook Lawn	21 C1
Pinebrook Rise	26 D2
Pinebrook Road	26 D2
Pinebrook Vale	21 C1
Pinebrook View	21 C1
Pinebrook Way	21 C1
Pinecroft	62 F1
Pinetree Crescent	44 F4 [1]
Pinetree Grove	44 F3 [1]
Pineview Avenue	55 A2
Pineview Drive	55 A2
Pineview Grove	55 A2
Pineview Lawn	55 A2
Pineview Park	55 A2
Pineview Rise	55 A2
Pineview Road	55 A2
Pinewood	60 D4
Pinewood Avenue	24 F1
Pinewood Close	67 C4
Pinewood Court	8 F4
Pinewood Crescent	24 F1
Pinewood Drive	24 F1
Pinewood Green	24 F1
Pinewood Grove	25 A1 [1]
Pinewood Park	56 E1
Pinewood Villas	24 F1
Pinewoods	44 D2
Pinnock Roundabout	1 C3
Pipe Hill	1 C2
Pleasants Lane	38 D3 [15]
Pleasants Place	38 D3 [21]
Pleasants Street	38 D3
Pluckstown	51 A2
Plums Road	58 D1
Plunket Hall	2 E2
Plunkett Avenue (Finglas)	24 D1
Plunkett Avenue (Foxrock)	59 A3
Plunkett Crescent	11 A4
Plunkett Drive	24 D1
Plunkett Green	24 D1
Plunkett Grove	24 D1
Plunkett Hall	7 A2
Plunkett Road	24 D1
Poddle Close	46 E1
Poddle Green	46 E1 [6]
Poddle Park	46 E2
Polo Road	37 A1
Poolbeg Quay	39 A3
Poolbeg Street	38 E2
Poole Street	37 C3 [38]
Poplar Row	38 F1
Poppintree	11 C4
Poppintree Lane	11 C4
Poppintree Parade	11 C4
Poppintree Park Lane West	11 C4
Poppintree Terrace	11 C4
Port Tunnel (East Wall)	38 F1
Port Tunnel (Santry)	25 C4
Port View House	39 A2
Porters Avenue	22 D2
Porters Gate	21 B2
Porters Gate Avenue	21 C2
Porters Gate Close	21 B2
Porters Gate Court	21 B2
Porters Gate Crescent	21 B2
Porters Gate Drive	21 B2
Porters Gate Green	21 B2
Porters Gate Grove	21 B2
Porters Gate Heights	21 C2
Porters Gate Rise	21 C2
Porters Gate View	21 B2
Porters Gate Way	21 B2
Porters Road	22 D2
Portersfield Apts.	22 D2
Porterstown	5 A3
Porterstown Road	22 D2
Portland Close	38 E1 [50]
*Portland Court (off Portland Place)	38 D1
Portland Lock	38 D1
Portland Place	38 D1
Portland Row	38 E1
Portland Square	38 E1 [70]
Portland Street North	38 E1
Portland Street West	37 C3
Portmahon Drive	37 B3
Portmarnock	15 A1
Portmarnock Avenue	4 D4
Portmarnock Crescent	15 A1
Portmarnock Crescent	4 D4
Portmarnock Drive	4 D4
Portmarnock Grove	4 D4
Portmarnock Park	4 D4
Portmarnock Rise	15 A1
Portmarnock Walk	4 D4
Portobello Harbour	38 D4 [6]
Portobello Harbour Apts	38 D4 [58]
Portobello Place	38 D4 [36]
Portobello Road	38 D4
Portside Court	38 F1 [22]
Pottery Road	59 C2
Pound Hill	17 C1
Pound Lane	17 C3
Pound Park	17 C3
Pound Street	33 A1
Power's Court	38 F3
*Power's Square (off John Dillon Street)	38 D3
Prebend Street	37 C2
Premier Square	24 E2
Preston Street	38 E1 [14]
*Price's Lane (Aston Quay)	38 D2
Price's Place (Ranelagh)	38 D4
Priestfield Cottages	37 C4 [4]
Priestfield Drive	37 C4 [28]
Primrose Avenue	38 D1
Primrose Grove	13 C4
Primrose Hill (Celbridge)	32 D4
Primrose Hill (Dún Laoghaire)	49 C4 [25]
Primrose Lane	34 D1
*Primrose Street (off Wellington Street Upper)	38 D1
Prince Arthur Terrace	47 A1 [3]
Prince Edward Terrace Lower	49 A4 [2]
Prince Edward Terrace Upper	49 A4 [3]
Prince of Wales Terrace (Bray)	67 C2 [26]
Prince of Wales Terrace (Sandymount)	39 A4 [7]
Prince's Street North	38 D2 [20]
Prince's Street South	38 E2 [12]
Princeton	48 D3
Prior Hall	37 B3 [36]
Priorswood Road	13 C4
Priory Avenue	48 F4
Priory Chase	31 C4
Priory Close	31 C4

STREET NAME	PAGE/GRID REFERENCE	STREET NAME	PAGE/GRID REFERENCE	STREET NAME	PAGE/GRID REFERENCE	STREET NAME	PAGE/GRID REFERENCE
Priory Court (Celbridge)	31 C4	Raheen Close	54 E1	Rathmichael Dales	64 D3	Reginald Square	37 C3 [43]
Priory Court (Grange Road)	57 A2 [1]	Raheen Court	54 E1	Rathmichael Haven	64 D3	Reginald Street	37 C3
Priory Crescent	31 C4	Raheen Crescent	54 E1	Rathmichael Hill	63 C2	Rehoboth Avenue	37 C4 [3]
Priory Drive (Celbridge)	31 C4	Raheen Drive (Ballyfermot)	36 D3	Rathmichael Lane	63 C2	Rehoboth Place	37 B4
Priory Drive (Stillorgan)	48 F4	Raheen Drive (Tallaght)	54 E1	Rathmichael Manor	64 D2	Reilly's Avenue	37 B4 [6]
Priory East	24 D4	Raheen Green	54 E1	Rathmichael Park	64 E2	Reuben Avenue	37 B3
Priory Green	31 C4	Raheen Park (Ballyfermot)	36 D3	Rathmichael Road	63 C2	Reuben Street	37 B3
Priory Grove (Celbridge)	31 C4	Raheen Park (Bray)	68 D3	Rathmichael Woods	64 E2	*Rhodaville	38 D4
Priory Grove (Stillorgan)	48 F4	Raheen Park (Tallaght)	54 E1	Rathmines	47 A1	(off Mountpleasant Ave)	
Priory Hall (Kimmage)	46 D2	Raheen Road	54 E1	Rathmines Avenue	47 A1	Rialto Buildings	37 B3 [14]
Priory Hall (Stillorgan)	48 F4	Raheny	27 A2	Rathmines Avenue Court	47 A1 [25]	Rialto Cottages	37 B3
Priory Lodge	31 C4	Raheny Park	27 A3	Rathmines Close	47 A1	Rialto Drive	37 B4 [3]
Priory North	24 D3	Raheny Road	27 A1	Rathmines Park	47 A1 [1]	*Rialto Park(off Rialto Street)	37 B3
Priory Road	46 F1	Railpark	18 E3	Rathmines Road Lower	47 A1	Rialto Street	37 B3
Priory Square	31 C4	Railway Avenue (Baldoyle)	28 D1	Rathmines Road Upper	47 A1	Ribh Avenue	26 F2
Priory View	31 C3	Railway Avenue (Inchicore)	36 F3	Rathmintan Close	54 D2	Ribh Road	26 F2
Priory Walk (Celbridge)	31 C4	Railway Avenue (Malahide)	3 B2	Rathmintan Court	54 D2	Richelieu Park	48 E1
Priory Walk (Kimmage)	46 D2	Railway Close	14 F4	Rathmintan Crescent	54 D2	Richmond	59 A1
Priory Way (Celbridge)	31 C3	Railway Cottages	39 A4 [8]	Rathmintan Drive	54 D2	Richmond Avenue (Fairview)	25 B4
Priory Way (Kimmage)	46 D2	Railway Court	3 B2 [3]	Rathmore	14 F2	Richmond Avenue (Monkstown)	49 C4
Priory West	24 D4	Railway Mews	14 F4	Rathmore Avenue	58 D1	Richmond Avenue South	47 B2
Proby Garden	49 A4	Railway Road	60 F2 [2]	Rathmore Crescent	9 B2	Richmond Cottages	38 E1 [9]
Proby Hall	60 E2	Railway Road (Clongriffin)	14 F4	Rathmore Park	27 A2	(Summerhill)	
Proby Park	60 E2	Railway Street	38 E1	Rathmore Villas	46 F2	Richmond Cottages North	38 E1 [37]
Proby Square	49 A4	*Railway Terrace (off Macken St)	38 F3	Rathsallagh Avenue	64 E2	Richmond Court (Marino)	25 C4
Proby's Lane	38 D2 [28]	Rainsford Avenue	37 C3 [3]	Rathsallagh Drive	64 E2	Richmond Court (Milltown)	47 B2
Promenade Road	39 A1	Rainsford Lane	60 E4 [6]	Rathsallagh Grove	64 E2	Richmond Crescent	38 E1 [8]
Prospect Avenue (Finglas Road)	25 A4	Rainsford Street	37 C3	Rathsallagh Park	64 E2	Richmond Estate	25 C4
Prospect Avenue	56 E2	Ralahine	60 D4	Rathvale Avenue	26 F1	Richmond Green	49 C4 [12]
(Stocking Lane)		Raleigh Square	46 D1	Rathvale Drive	26 F1	Richmond Grove	49 C4
Prospect Court	56 E3	Ralph Square	33 A1 [1]	Rathvale Grove	26 F1	Richmond Hill (Monkstown)	49 C4
Prospect Drive	56 E2	Ramillies Road	36 E3	Rathvale Park	26 F1	Richmond Hill (Rathmines)	38 D4
Prospect Glen	56 E2	Ramleh Close	47 C2	Rathvilly Drive	24 D2	Richmond Lane	38 E1 [20]
Prospect Grove	56 E2	Ramleh Park	47 C2	Rathvilly Park	24 D2	Richmond Lodge	25 B4
Prospect Heath	56 E2	Ramor Park	22 E2	Ratoath Avenue	24 D2	*Richmond Manor	38 D2
Prospect Heights	56 E2	Ranelagh	38 E4	Ratoath Drive	23 C1	Richmond Mews	38 D4 [43]
Prospect Lane	47 C2 [1]	Ranelagh Avenue	38 E4	Ratoath Estate	24 D3	Richmond Parade	38 E1 [10]
Prospect Lawn	59 B3	Ranelagh Road	38 E4	Ratoath Road (Cabra)	24 E4	Richmond Park (Herbert Road)	67 A4
Prospect Meadows	56 E2	Raphoe Road	46 D1	Ratoath Road (Hollystown)	9 B1	Richmond Park (Monkstown)	49 B4
Prospect Road	25 A4	Rath Geal	43 C1	Ratra Park	23 C4	Richmond Place (Rathmines)	38 D4 [10]
Prospect Square	25 A4 [5]	Rathbeale Court	1 C1 [2]	Ratra Road	23 C4	Richmond Place South	38 D4 [44]
Prospect Terrace (Kilmainham)	37 A3 [1]	Rathbeale Crescent	1 C1	Ravens Court	24 D2 [5]	(Sth Richmond St)	
Prospect Terrace (Sandymount)	39 B3 [1]	Rathbeale Rise	1 C2	Ravens Rock Road	58 E2	Richmond Road	25 B4
Prospect View	56 E2	Rathbeale Road	1 C1	Ravensdale Drive	46 E2	Richmond Row	38 D4 [7]
Prospect Way	25 A4	Rathborne Avenue	23 C3	(off Ravensdale Park)		Richmond Street North	38 E1
Protestant Row	38 D3 [12]	Rathborne Close	23 C3	Ravensdale Park	46 E2	Richmond Street South	38 D4
Proud's Lane	38 D3 [24]	Rathborne Drive	23 C3	Ravensdale Road	38 F1	Richmond Terrace	68 D2 [12]
Provost Row	37 C2 [46]	Rathborne Place	23 C3	Ravenswell Road	67 C2	Richmond Villas	38 D4 [22]
Prussia Street	37 C1	Rathborne Way	23 C3	Ravenwood Avenue	21 B1	Richview	47 C2
Pucks Castle Lane	63 C3	Rathclaren	67 B3 [2]	Ravenwood Crescent	21 B1	Richview Park	47 B2
Purcell Lane	67 C2 [60]	Rathcoole Park	52 F2	Ravenwood Drive	21 B1	Richview Villas	47 C2 [11]
(off Main Street Bray)		Rathcreedan	52 E1	Ravenwood Estate	21 B1	Riddlesford	67 C4
Purley Park	3 C4	Rathdown Avenue	46 F3	Ravenwood Green	21 B1	Ridge Hall	64 E1
Purser Gardens	47 A1 [10]	*Rathdown Court	46 F2 [10]	Ravenwood Lawn	21 B1	Ridge Hill	64 E1
Putland Road	67 C3	(off Templeogue Road)		Ravenwood Rise	21 B1	Ridgewood Avenue	1 B3
Putland Villas	67 C3 [14]	Rathdown Crescent	46 F3	Ravenwood Road	21 B1	Ridgewood Close	1 B3
Pyro Villas	37 C3 [60]	Rathdown Drive	46 E3	Ravenwood View	21 B1	Ridgewood Court	1 B3
		Rathdown Grove	58 D2 [9]	Raverty Villas	67 B1 [1]	Ridgewood Green	1 B3
Q		Rathdown Park	46 F3	Raymond Street	37 C4	Ridgewood Grove	1 B3
		Rathdown Road	37 C1	Rectory Slopes	67 B3	Ridgewood Park	1 B3
Quarry Cottages	26 E3 [3]	Rathdown Square	37 C1 [20]	Rectory Way	67 A3	Ridgewood Place	1 B3
Quarry Drive	45 C2	Rathdown Terrace	58 D2 [5]	Red Brick Terrace	59 A1 [2]	Ridgewood Square	1 B3
Quarry Road (Cabra)	24 E4	Rathdown Villas	46 F3	Red Cow Cottages	35 C1 [4]	Rinawade Avenue	32 E1
Quarry Road (Ferndale Road)	64 D4	Rathdrum Road	37 B4	Red Cow Lane	37 C2	Rinawade Close	32 E1
Quarryfield Court	44 F2	Rathfarnham	46 F3	Redberry	34 D3	Rinawade Crescent	32 E1
Quartiere Bloom	38 D2	Rathfarnham Mill	46 F4 [12]	Redesdale Court	48 E4	Rinawade Downs	32 E1
Queen's Park	49 B4	Rathfarnham Park	46 F3	Redesdale Crescent	48 D4	Rinawade Glade	32 E1
Queen's Road	50 D4	Rathfarnham Road	46 F3	Redesdale Road	48 D4	Rinawade Grove	32 E1
Queen's Street	37 C2	Rathfarnham Wood	46 F4	Redfern Avenue	3 C4	Rinawade Lawns	32 E1
Quinn's Lane	38 E3	Rathgar	47 A2	Redgap	52 E3	Rinawade Park	32 F1
Quinn's Road	64 E3	Rathgar Avenue	46 F2	Redmond's Court	27 B1 [3]	Rinawade Rise	32 E1
Quinsborough	51 A4	Rathgar Court	47 A1 [28]	Redmond's Hill	38 D3 [11]	Rinawade View	32 E1
Quinsborough Road	67 C2	Rathgar Park	46 F2 [16]	Redwood	9 C1	Ring Street	36 F3 [12]
		Rathgar Park	47 A2 [7]	Redwood Avenue	45 A4	Ring Terrace	36 F3
R		Rathgar Place	47 A1	Redwood Close	45 A4	Ringsend	39 A3
		Rathgar Road	47 A1	Redwood Court (Churchtown)	47 A3	Ringsend Park	39 A2
Radcliffe	29 A1 [3]	Rathgar Villas	46 F2 [11]	Redwood Court (Tallaght)	44 F4	Ringsend Road	38 F3
Radlett Grove	4 D4	Rathingle Road	1 B3	Redwood Drive	44 F4	Rinn na Mara	27 A4 [3]
Rafter's Avenue	37 A4	Rathland Drive	46 E2 [4]	Redwood Grove	48 F3	Ripley Court	67 B3
(off Rafter's Road)		Rathlawns	52 E2	Redwood Heights	45 A4	Ripley Hills	67 B3
Rafter's Lane	37 A4	Rathlin House	22 F1	Redwood Lawn	44 F4	River Close	64 E1 [23]
Rafter's Road	37 A4	Rathlin Road	25 A3	Redwood Park	45 A4	River Drive	24 D3
Raglan Hall Apts.	38 F4 [20]	Rathlyon Grove	55 C2	Redwood Rise	45 A4	River Forest	20 D4
Raglan Lane	38 F4	Rathlyon Park	55 C2	Redwood View	45 A4	River Forest View (Leixlip)	19 C3
Raglan Road	38 F4	Rathmichael	63 C3	Redwood Walk	44 F4	River Forest View (Leixlip)	20 D3
Raheen Avenue	54 E1						

STREET NAME	PAGE	GRID
River Gardens	25	A3 [15]
River Lane (Bray)	67	B2
River Lane (Loughlinstown)	64	E2 [1]
River Lawns	31	C4
River Mall	2	D2
River Road (Ashtown)	23	C3
River Road (Blanchardstown)	22	F2
River Road Cottages	23	A2
River Valley Avenue	1	C2
River Valley Close	1	B2
River Valley Court	1	B2
River Valley Drive	1	C2
River Valley Grove	1	C3
River Valley Heights	1	C2
River Valley Lawn	1	C2
River Valley Park	1	C2
River Valley Rise	1	C3
River Valley Road	1	C2
River Valley View	1	B2
River Valley Way	1	B2
River View	31	C4
Riverbank (Braemor Road)	47	A3 [6]
Riverbank (Dundrum)	57	C1 [11]
Riverbank Hall	24	F3
Riverdale	20	D4
Riverpark View	9	A4 [3]
Riversdale (Dundrum)	57	C1 [10]
*Riversdale (Herbert Hill)	57	C1
*Riversdale (Palmerstown)	35	C1
Riversdale Avenue (Clondalkin)	44	E1
Riversdale Avenue (Palmerston)	35	C1
Riversdale Avenue (Terenure)	46	F3
Riversdale Court	35	C1
Riversdale Crescent	44	E1
Riversdale Drive	44	E1
Riversdale Green	35	B4
Riversdale Grove (Kimmage)	46	E2 [1]
Riversdale Grove (Palmerstown)	35	B1
Riversdale Park (Clondalkin)	44	E1
Riversdale Park (Palmerstown)	35	C1
Riversdale Road	44	E1
Riverside (Clondalkin)	44	E1 [6]
Riverside (Kimmage)	46	E2 [9]
Riverside (Mulhuddart)	9	A4 [4]
Riverside Avenue	13	A4
Riverside Cottages	46	E4
Riverside Crescent	13	A4
Riverside Drive (Coolock)	13	B4
Riverside Drive (Palmerston)	35	C1
Riverside Drive (Rathfarnham)	47	A3
Riverside Grove	13	A4
Riverside Park	13	A4
Riverside Road	13	A4
Riverside Walk	47	C1 [21]
Riverston Abbey	24	D4
Rivervale	23	C3
Rivervale Apts.	67	B2 [27]
Riverview (Grand Canal Docks)	38	F3
Riverview (Oldbawn)	55	A2
Riverview (Palmerstown)	35	C1
Riverview Apts	32	D4
Riverview Court	36	E2 [11]
Riverwood Chase	22	D3
Riverwood Close	22	D3
Riverwood Copse	22	D3
Riverwood Court	22	D3
Riverwood Crescent	22	D3
Riverwood Dale	22	D3
Riverwood Dene	22	D3
Riverwood Drive	22	D3
Riverwood Gardens	22	D3
Riverwood Glebe	22	D3
Riverwood Glen	22	D3
Riverwood Green	22	D3
Riverwood Grove	22	D3
Riverwood Hall	22	D3
Riverwood Heath	22	D3
Riverwood Lawn	22	D3
Riverwood Park	22	D3
Riverwood Place	22	D3
Riverwood Road	22	D3
Riverwood Terrace	22	D3
Riverwood Vale	22	D3
Riverwood View	22	D3
Riverwood Way	22	D3

STREET NAME	PAGE	GRID
Robert Emmett Close	37	C2 [48]
Robert Place	25	B4 [7]
Robert Street (James's Street)	37	C3
Robert Street (Jones's Road)	25	B4 [6]
Robin Villas	35	C1
Robinhood Park	45	B1
Robinhood Road	45	A1
Robswall	3	C3
Robswall Path	4	D3
Robswall Walk	4	D3
Rochestown Avenue	59	C2
Rochestown House Apts.	59	C2 [6]
Rochestown Park	60	D2
Rochfort Avenue	34	F2
Rochfort Close	34	F2
Rochfort Crescent	34	F3
Rochfort Downs	34	F2
Rochfort Green	34	F2
Rochfort Park	34	F2
Rochfort Way	34	F3
Rock Hall	49	A3
Rock Hill	49	A3
*Rock Lane (Baggot St Lower)	38	E3
Rock Lodge	60	E3
Rock Road	49	A3
Rock Road Mansion	42	F1
Rockbrook	56	E4
Rockfield (Dundrum)	57	C1
Rockfield (Lucan)	34	D3
Rockfield (Maynooth)	18	D4
Rockfield Avenue (Kimmage)	46	D2
Rockfield Avenue (Maynooth)	18	D4
Rockfield Close	22	D3
Rockfield Drive (Clondalkin)	44	D2
Rockfield Drive (Coolmine)	22	D3
Rockfield Drive (Kimmage)	46	D2
Rockfield Gardens	18	D3
Rockfield Green	18	D3
Rockfield Lodge	18	D4
Rockfield Manor	18	D4
Rockfield Park (Coolmine)	22	D2
Rockfield Park (Maynooth)	18	D4
Rockfield Rise	18	D3
Rockfield Square	18	D3
Rockfield Walk	18	D3
Rockford Manor	59	B1
Rockford Park	59	B1
Rockford Terrace	49	B4 [14]
Rockfort Avenue	60	F2
Rockingham Avenue	19	C4
Rockingham Green	19	C4
Rockingham Grove	19	C4
Rockingham Park	19	C4
Rockingham Terrace	2	D2
Rocklands	60	F1 [6]
Rockmeadon Court	46	D1 [5]
Rockstown	30	E2
Rockview	57	C3
Rockville	62	F2
Rockville Crescent	49	B4
Rockville Drive	63	A1
Rockville Drive	49	B4
Rockville Estate	49	A4 [9]
Rockville Park	49	B4
Rockville Road	49	A4
Rockwell Cove Apts.	49	A3 [9]
Rockwood	34	D3
Rocwood	58	F2
Roe Lane	37	C2
Roebuck Avenue	48	E3
Roebuck Castle	48	D3
Roebuck Crescent	47	C3 [10]
Roebuck Downs	47	C3
Roebuck Drive	46	D2
Roebuck Hill	48	D3
Roebuck Lawn	47	C3 [9]
Roebuck Road	47	C4
Roebuck Road	48	D3
Roger Casement Park	67	B2
Roger's Lane	38	E3 [15]
Roland Court	47	A1 [20]
Rollins Court	60	D1 [12]
Rollins Villas	60	D1
Ronanstown	35	A4
Roncalli Road	27	C1

STREET NAME	PAGE	GRID
Rookwood Lodge	56	E2
Rookwood View	56	E2
Roosevelt Cottages	24	D4 [1]
Rooske Road	7	B3
Ropewalk Place	39	A3 [30]
Rory O'Connor Park	59	B1
Ros Mór View	56	D2
Rosary Gardens East	50	D4 [2]
Rosary Gardens West	49	C4 [1]
Rosary Road	37	B3
Rosary Terrace (Ringsend)	39	A3
*Rosary Terrace (off Library Road)	50	D4
Rosbeg Court	27	C2
Rosberry	34	E3
Rosberry Avenue	34	E3
Rosberry Court	34	E3
Rosberry Lane	34	E3
Rosberry Park	34	E3
Rosberry Place	34	E3
Rose Park	59	C1
Rose View	35	C1
Roseacre	58	E3
Rosebank	55	A2
Rosebank Court	35	B4 [2]
Rosebank Hall	35	A4 [5]
Rosebank Place	35	A4 [4]
Rosebank View	35	B4 [1]
Rosedale (Clonsilla)	21	B1
Rosedale (Dunboyne)	7	B2
Rosedale Close	21	B1
Rosedale Crescent	21	B1
*Rosedale Terrace (Lower Clanbrassil St)	37	C4
Roseglen Avenue	27	B2
Roseglen Road	27	B2
Rosehaven	22	E3 [1]
Rosehill	59	A1 [5]
Roselawn (Lucan)	34	E1
Roselawn Avenue	22	E2
Roselawn Close	22	F2
Roselawn Court	22	F2
Roselawn Crescent	22	E2
Roselawn Drive (Blanchardstown)	22	E2
Roselawn Drive (Oldcourt)	67	C3
Roselawn Glade	22	E2
Roselawn Grove	22	E2
Roselawn Park	67	C3 [2]
Roselawn Road	22	E2
Roselawn Road	22	F2
Roselawn View	22	E2
Roselawn Walk	22	E2
Roselawn Way	22	F2
Rosemount (Churchtown)	47	C4
Rosemount (Donnycarney)	26	D3
Rosemount Avenue	26	E2
Rosemount Court (Booterstown)	48	E3
Rosemount Court (Dundrum)	47	C4
Rosemount Court (Inchicore Rd)	37	A3 [19]
Rosemount Crescent (Roebuck Road)	47	C3
Rosemount Glade	47	C4
Rosemount Hall	47	C4
Rosemount Park	47	C4
Rosemount Park Drive	10	D4
Rosemount Park Road	10	D4
Rosemount Road	37	C1 [4]
Rosemount Terrace (Arbour Hill)	37	C2 [29]
Rosemount Terrace (Booterstown)	48	E3
Rosemount Terrace (Dundrum)	47	B4 [11]
Rosevale Court	26	F3
Rosevale Mansions	26	F3
Roseville Court	67	B1 [7]
Roseville Terrace	47	C4 [4]
Rosewood Grove	34	F3
Rosmeen Gardens	50	D4
Rosmeen Park	60	D1
Ross Road	38	D3
Ross Street	37	B3
Rossaveal Court	36	D2 [1]
Rossecourt Avenue	34	F3
Rossecourt Green	34	F3

STREET NAME	PAGE	GRID
Rossecourt Grove	34	F3
Rossecourt Heights	34	F3
Rossecourt Lane	34	F3
Rossecourt Rise	34	F3
Rossecourt Square	34	F3
Rossecourt Terrace	34	F3
Rossecourt Way	34	F3
Rossfield Avenue	54	D1
Rossfield Crescent	54	D1
Rossfield Drive	54	D1
Rossfield Gardens	54	D1
Rossfield Green	54	D1
Rossfield Grove	54	D1
Rossfield Park	54	D1
Rossfield Way	54	D1
Rosslyn	67	C2 [37]
Rosslyn Court	67	C2
Rosslyn Grove	67	C2 [4]
Rossmore Avenue (Ballyfermot)	36	D3
Rossmore Avenue (Templeogue)	45	C4
Rossmore Close	46	D4
Rossmore Crescent	46	D4
Rossmore Drive (Ballyfermot)	36	D2
Rossmore Drive (Templeogue)	45	C4
Rossmore Grove	45	C4
Rossmore Lawns	46	D4
Rossmore Park	46	D4
Rossmore Road (Ballyfermot)	36	D2
Rossmore Road (Templeogue)	46	D4
Rostrevor Road	47	A3
Rostrevor Terrace (Lr Grand Canal St)	38	F3 [25]
Rostrevor Terrace (Orwell Road)	47	A2
Rothe Abbey	37	A3
Rowan Avenue	58	D2
Rowan Close	32	D3
Rowan Grove	67	B2
Rowan Hall	47	C1 [15]
Rowan Park	49	B4
Rowan Park Avenue	49	B4
Rowanbyrn	49	B4
Rowanbyrn	59	B1
Rowans Road	58	D2
Rowlagh Avenue	35	A3
Rowlagh Crescent	35	A3
Rowlagh Gardens	35	A3
Rowlagh Green	35	A3
Rowlagh Park	35	A3
Rowserstown Lane	37	A3 [20]
Royal Canal Avenue	23	C3
Royal Canal Bank	25	A4
Royal Canal Bank	38	D1
Royal Canal Terrace	37	C1 [12]
Royal Hibernian Way	38	E3 [10]
Royal Marine Terrace	67	C2 [12]
Royal Oak	12	F4
Royal Terrace East	60	D1
Royal Terrace Lane	60	D1 [10]
Royal Terrace North	60	D1 [2]
Royal Terrace West	60	D1
Royse Road	25	A4
Royston	46	D2
Royston Village	46	D2
Ruby Hall	59	C2
Rugby Road	47	B1
Rugby Villas	47	B1 [6]
*Rus in Urbe Terrace (on Glengeary Road Lr)	60	D1
Rushbrook	22	E2
Rushbrook Avenue	45	C3
Rushbrook Court	45	C4
Rushbrook Crescent	45	C3
Rushbrook Drive	45	C3
Rushbrook Grove	45	C3
Rushbrook Park	45	C3
Rushbrook Road	45	C3
Rushbrook View	45	C3
Rushbrook Way	45	C4
Rusheeney	21	B1
Rusheeney Avenue	21	B1
Rusheeney Close	21	B1
Rusheeney Court	21	B1
Rusheeney Crescent	8	F4
Rusheeney Green	21	C1

STREET NAME	PAGE/GRID REFERENCE
Rusheeney Grove	21 B1
Rusheeney Manor	21 B1
Rusheeney Park	21 B1
Rusheeney View	21 C1
Rusheeney Way	21 B1
Rus-in-Urbe Terrace	60 D1 [19]
Russell Avenue (Fortunestown Way)	54 D1
Russell Avenue (Jones's Road)	38 E1
Russell Avenue East	38 F1 [14]
Russell Close	54 D2
Russell Court	54 D2
Russell Crescent	54 D1
Russell Downs	54 D1
Russell Drive	54 D2
Russell Green	54 D2
Russell Grove	54 D2
Russell House	2 E2
Russell Lane	54 D1
Russell Lawns	54 D2
Russell Meadows	54 D1
Russell Place	54 D1
Russell Rise	54 D1
Russell Street	38 E1
Russell View	54 D2
Russell Walk	54 D1
Russell's Mews	2 E3
Russell's Place	2 E3
Russell's Terrace	2 E4
Rutland Avenue (Clogher Road)	46 E1
Rutland Avenue (Crumlin Road)	37 B4
Rutland Cottages	38 E1 [55]
*Rutland Court	38 E1
Rutland Grove	46 F1
Rutland Place North	38 E1 [48]
Rutland Place West	38 D1
Rutland Street Lower	38 E1
Rutledge Terrace	37 C4 [26]
Ryan's Cottages (Harold's Cross)	46 F1 [7]
Ryder's Row	38 D2 [9]
Rye River Avenue	20 D4
Rye River Close	20 D4
Rye River Court	20 D4
Rye River Crescent	20 D4
Rye River Gardens	20 D4
Rye River Grove	20 D4
Rye River Mall	20 D4
Rye River Park	20 D4
Ryecroft	67 C3
Ryemont Abbey	20 D4
Ryevale Lawns	20 D4
Rynville Manor	67 B4

S

STREET NAME	PAGE/GRID REFERENCE
Sackville Avenue	38 E1
Sackville Gardens	38 E1 [2]
Sackville Place	38 D2 [24]
Saddlers Avenue	9 A4
Saddlers Close	9 A4
Saddlers Court	38 D4 [55]
Saddlers Crescent	9 A4
Saddlers Drive	9 A4
Saddlers Glade	9 A4
Saddlers Grove	9 A4
Saddlers Lawn	9 A4
Sadleir Hall	7 A2
Saggart	53 B2
Saggart Abbey	53 C2
Saggart Lakes	53 B1
Saintsbury Avenue	60 E4
Salamanca	48 D4
Salem Court	47 A1 [17]
Salestown	6 D4
Sallowood View	12 E4
Sallowood Walk	12 E4
Sally Park	55 C1
Sally Park Close	55 C1
Sallyglen Road	60 D2
Sallymount Avenue	47 B1
Sallymount Gardens	47 B1 [1]
Sallymount Terrace	47 B1 [14]
Sallynoggin	60 D2
Sallynoggin Park	59 C2
Sallynoggin Road	59 C2
Salmon Pool Apts	37 A2 [5]
Salthill	49 C4
*Salthill Place (off Crofton Road)	50 D4
Saltzburg	48 D4
Sampson's Lane	38 D2 [14]
San Souci Wood (Bray)	67 C3
Sanderling Apts.	48 E3
Sandford Avenue (Donnybrook)	47 C1
Sandford Avenue (Donore Avenue)	37 C4
Sandford Close	47 B1
Sandford Gardens (Donnybrook)	47 C1 [10]
*Sandford Gardens (off Donore Avenue)	37 C4
Sandford Gardens (Sandford Avenue)	37 C4 [33]
Sandford Lodge	47 B1
*Sandford Park (off O'Donovan Road)	37 C4
Sandford Park (Sandford Avenue)	37 C4 [32]
Sandford Road	47 B1
Sandford Row	47 B1
Sandford Terrace	47 B1
Sandford Wood	1 C1
Sandon Cove	26 E4
Sandwith Street Lower	38 E2
Sandwith Street Upper	38 E3
Sandycove Avenue East	60 E1
Sandycove Avenue North	50 E4
Sandycove Avenue West	60 E1
Sandycove Lane East	60 E1
Sandycove Point	50 E4
Sandycove Road	60 E1
Sandyford	58 D2
Sandyford Downs	58 D3
Sandyford Hall	58 E3
Sandyford Hall Avenue	58 E3
Sandyford Hall Close	58 E4
Sandyford Hall Court	58 E3
Sandyford Hall Crescent	58 E3
Sandyford Hall Drive	58 E4
Sandyford Hall Green	58 E3
Sandyford Hall Grove	58 E4
Sandyford Hall Lawn	58 E3
Sandyford Hall Place	58 E3
Sandyford Hall Rise	58 E3
Sandyford Hall View	58 E3
Sandyford Hall Walk	58 E3
Sandyford Park	58 D2
Sandyford Road	57 C1
Sandyford View	57 C3
Sandyford Village	58 D3
Sandyhill Avenue	24 F1
Sandyhill Court	11 C4
Sandyhill Gardens	24 F1
Sandyhill Terrace	11 C4
Sandyhill Way	11 C4
Sandymount	39 A4
Sandymount Avenue	39 A4
Sandymount Castle	39 A4 [5]
Sandymount Castle Drive	39 A4 [3]
Sandymount Castle Park	39 B4 [2]
Sandymount Castle Road	39 A4 [2]
Sandymount Court	39 A3 [26]
Sandymount Green	39 A4 [1]
Sandymount Road	39 A3
Sans Souci Park	48 F3
Santa Sabina Manor	29 B2
Santry	25 B1
Santry Avenue	12 E4
Santry Close	12 F4
Santry Court	12 F4
Santry Cross	12 D4
Santry Villas	12 E4
Sarah Curran Avenue	56 F1
Sarah Curran Road	56 F1 [1]
Sarah Place	37 A2 [3]
Sarney	6 E2
Sarsfield Court (Inchicore)	36 F3
Sarsfield Court (Lucan)	34 D1 [4]
Sarsfield Park	34 D1
Sarsfield Quay	37 C2 [8]
Sarsfield Road	36 F3
Sarsfield Street (Phibsborough)	38 D1 [5]
Sarsfield Street (Sallynoggin)	60 D1
Sarsfield Terrace	34 D1 [1]
Sarto Lawn	27 C1
Sarto Park	27 C1
Sarto Rise	27 C1
Sarto Road	27 C2
Saul Road	46 E1
Saval Grove	60 E2
Saval Park Crescent	60 E2
Saval Park Gardens	60 E2
Saval Park Road	60 E2
Scariff House	22 F1
Scholarstown Park	56 D2
Scholarstown Road	56 D2
School Avenue	26 E2
School Street	37 C3
School Walk	52 E2
Schoolhouse Court	25 B1
Schoolhouse Lane (Kildare Street)	38 E3 [12]
Schoolhouse Lane (Santry)	25 B1
*Schoolhouse Lane West (off High Street)	38 D3
Schools Road	67 B4
Scott Park	67 C3
Scribblestown	23 C3
Scribblestown Road	23 B3
Sea Road	3 A2
Seabank Court (Dalkey)	60 E1 [21]
Seabank Court (Malahide)	3 C2 [1]
Seabrook Manor Apts.	14 E2
Seabury	48 E1
Seabury Avenue	2 F2
Seabury Close	2 F2
Seabury Court	2 F2
Seabury Crescent	2 F2
Seabury Dale	2 F2
Seabury Downs	2 F2
Seabury Drive	3 A2
Seabury Gardens	2 F2
Seabury Glen	2 F2
Seabury Green	2 F2
Seabury Grove	2 F2
Seabury Heights	2 F2
Seabury Lane	2 F2
Seabury Lawns	2 F2
Seabury Meadows	2 F2
Seabury Orchard	2 F2
Seabury Parade	2 F2
Seabury Park	2 F2
Seabury Place	2 F2
Seabury Road	2 F2
Seabury Vale	2 F2
Seabury View	2 F2
Seabury Walk	2 F2
Seabury Wood	2 F2
Seacliff Avenue	27 C1
Seacliff Drive	27 C1
Seacliff Road	27 C1
Seacourt	26 F4
Seacrest	67 C3
Seafield (Shankill)	64 F2
Seafield (Sutton)	28 D1 [2]
Seafield Avenue (Clontarf)	26 F4
Seafield Avenue (Monkstown)	49 B4
Seafield Close	48 E3
Seafield Court (Loughlinstown)	64 E1
Seafield Court (Malahide)	3 B2
Seafield Crescent	48 E3
*Seafield Downs (off Kincora Road Clontarf)	26 F4
Seafield Drive	48 E2
Seafield Grove	27 A4 [1]
Seafield Park	48 E2 [1]
Seafield Road (Ballybrack)	64 E1
Seafield Road (Booterstown)	48 E2
Seafield Road (Killiney)	60 E4
Seafield Road East	26 F4
Seafield Road West	26 E4
Seafort Avenue	39 A4
Seafort Cottages	39 A4 [18]
Seafort Gardens	39 A3 [10]
Seafort Parade	48 F3
Seafort Terrace	39 A4 [19]
Seafort Villas	39 A4 [20]
Seagrange Avenue	14 F4
Seagrange Drive	27 C1
Seagrange Road	27 C1
Seagrave	14 F2
Seagrave Close	11 B4
Seagrave Court	11 B4
Seagrave Drive	11 B4
Seagrave Rise	11 B4
Seagrave Terrace	11 B4
Seagrave Way	11 B4
Seamount	48 E3
Seamount Drive	3 C3
Seamount Grove	3 C3
Seamount Heights	3 C3
Seamount Park	3 C3
Seamount Road	3 C3
Seamount View	2 E2
Seamus Ennis Road	24 E1
Sean MacDermott Street Lower	38 E1
Sean MacDermott Street Upper	38 D2
Sean Moore Road	39 A3
Sean O'Casey Avenue	38 E1 [47]
Sean Tracey House	38 E1 [12]
Sean Walsh Memorial Park	54 F1
Seapark (Dollymount)	26 F4
Seapark (Malahide)	3 C3
Seapark Drive	26 F4
Seapark Hill	3 C3
Seapark Road	26 F4
Seapoint Avenue (Baldoyle)	15 A4 [1]
Seapoint Avenue (Blackrock)	49 B3
Seapoint Court (Baldoyle)	15 A4 [7]
Seapoint Court (Bray)	67 C1
Seapoint Road	67 C2
Seapoint Terrace (Blackrock)	49 B3 [4]
Seapoint Terrace (Bray)	67 C2 [24]
Seapoint Terrace (Ringsend)	39 A3 [4]
Seapoint Villas	67 C2 [20]
Seatown Park	2 D1
Seatown Park The Avenue	2 D1
Seatown Park The Court	2 D1
Seatown Park The Crescent	2 D1
Seatown Park The Drive	2 D1
Seatown Park The Green	2 D1
Seatown Park The Grove	2 D1
Seatown Road	2 D1
Seatown Terrace	2 D2
Seatown Villas	2 D1
Seatown Walk	2 D2
Seatown West	2 D1
Seaview Avenue East	38 F1
Seaview Avenue North	26 D4
Seaview Cottages	63 C4
Seaview Lawn	64 E2
Seaview Park	64 E2
Seaview Terrace (Donnybrook)	48 D1
Seaview Terrace (Dun Laoghaire)	49 C4 [15]
Seaview Terrace (Howth)	30 D2 [2]
Seaview Wood	64 E2
Second Avenue (Seville Place)	38 F2 [6]
Second Avenue (Tallaght)	44 F4
Sefton	59 C2
Sefton Green	59 C2
Sefton Hall	59 A2 [12]
Selskar Terrace	38 E4 [21]
Serpentine Avenue	39 A4
Serpentine Park	39 A4
Serpentine Road	39 A4
Serpentine Terrace	39 A4
Seskin View Avenue	55 A2
Seskin View Drive	55 A2
Seskin View Park	55 A2
Seskin View Road	55 A2
Setanta Place	38 E3 [11]
Seven Houses	60 D1 [13]
Seven Oaks (Inchicore)	36 F3
Seven Oaks (Whitehall)	25 B3
Seventh Lock Cottages	36 D4
Seventh Lock Place	36 D4
Seville Place	38 E1
Seville Terrace	38 E1 [59]
Seymour Road	67 C2

STREET NAME	PAGE/GRID REFERENCE
Shaldon Grange	62 F2
Shamrock Cottages	38 E1 [31]
Shamrock Hill Mews	47 C1 [23]
Shamrock Place	38 E1 [15]
Shamrock Street	38 D1 [69]
Shamrock Terrace	38 E1 [16]
Shamrock Villas	46 F1
Shanagarry	47 B2 [9]
Shanard Avenue	25 A1
Shanard Road	25 A1
Shanboley Road	25 C1
Shancastle Avenue	35 A2
Shancastle Close	35 A2
Shancastle Crescent	35 A2
Shancastle Drive	35 A2
Shancastle Lawns	35 A2
Shancastle Park	35 A2
Shandon Crescent	24 F4
Shandon Drive	24 F4
Shandon Gardens	24 F4
Shandon Green	24 F4 [8]
Shandon Mill	24 F4 [9]
Shandon Park (Monkstown)	49 B4
Shandon Park (Phibsborough)	24 F4
Shandon Road	24 F4
Shangan Avenue	25 B1
Shangan Court	25 A1
Shangan Crescent	25 A1
Shangan Drive	25 B1
Shangan Gardens	25 B1
Shangan Green	25 B1
Shangan Park	25 B1
Shangan Road	25 A1
Shanganagh Cliffs	64 E2
Shanganagh Grove	64 E3
Shanganagh Road	64 E1
Shanganagh Terrace	60 E4
Shanganagh Vale	60 D4
Shanganagh Wood	64 E2 [8]
Shanglas Road	25 C1
Shanid Road	46 F2
Shankill	64 E3
Shankill View	67 C2 [38]
Shanliss Avenue	25 B1
Shanliss Drive	25 B1
Shanliss Gardens	25 A1 [2]
Shanliss Grove	25 B1
Shanliss Park	25 B1
Shanliss Road	25 A1
Shanliss Walk	25 B1
Shanliss Way	25 B1
Shannon Terrace	37 B3 [4]
Shanowen Avenue	25 A1
Shanowen Crescent	25 B1
Shanowen Drive	25 B1
Shanowen Grove	25 A1
Shanowen Park	25 A1
Shanowen Road	25 B1
Shanowen Square	25 B1
Shanrath Road	25 B1
Shantalla Avenue	25 C1
Shantalla Drive	25 C2
Shantalla Park	25 C2
Shantalla Road	25 C1
Shanvarna Road	25 B1
Sharavogue	60 E2
Shaw Street	38 E2 [10]
Shaw's Lane	38 F3 [13]
Shea's Court	37 C1 [23]
Sheelin Avenue	64 E1
Sheelin Drive	64 E1
Sheelin Grove	64 E1 [7]
Sheelin Hill	64 E1 [13]
Sheelin Walk	64 E1 [14]
Sheephill Avenue	9 C4
Sheephill Green	9 C4
Sheephill Park	9 C4
Sheepmoor Avenue	22 D1
Sheepmoor Close	22 D1
Sheepmoor Crescent	22 D1
Sheepmoor Gardens	22 D1
Sheepmoor Green	22 D1
Sheepmoor Grove	22 D1
Sheepmoor Lawn	22 D1
Sheepmoor Way	22 D1

STREET NAME	PAGE/GRID REFERENCE
Shelbourne Avenue	38 F4 [5]
Shelbourne Lane	38 F4 [3]
Shelbourne Park Mews	38 F3 [50]
Shelbourne Road	38 F3
Shelbourne Village	38 F3 [51]
Shelerin Road	21 C2
Shellys Banks Road	39 B3
Shelmalier Road	38 F1
Shelmartin Avenue	25 C4
Shelmartin Terrace	25 C4 [2]
Shelton Drive	46 D2
Shelton Gardens	46 D2
Shelton Grove	46 D2
Shelton Park	46 D2
Sherborne	47 A2
Sheriff Street Lower	38 E2
Sheriff Street Upper	38 F2
Sherkin Court	25 B3
Sherkin Gardens	25 B3
Sherrard Avenue	38 D1 [28]
*Sherrard Court	38 D1
(off Portland Place)	
Sherrard Street Lower	38 D1
Sherrard Street Upper	38 D1
Sherrards Court	38 D1 [65]
Shielmartin Drive	29 B3
Shielmartin Park	29 B3 [1]
Shielmartin Road	29 B3
Ship Street Great	38 D3
Ship Street Little	38 D3
Shrewsbury	39 A4
Shrewsbury Hall	64 E3
Shrewsbury House	59 C4
Shrewsbury Lawn	59 C4
Shrewsbury Lodge	59 C3
Shrewsbury Park	48 D1
Shrewsbury Road	48 D1
(Ailesbury Road)	
Shrewsbury Road (Shankill)	64 E3
Shrewsbury Woods	59 C4
Sibthorpe Lane	38 E4 [28]
Sidbury Court	68 D2 [5]
Sidmonton Avenue	67 C2
Sidmonton Court	68 D3 [5]
Sidmonton Gardens	67 C2 [36]
Sidmonton Gardens	67 C2
Sidmonton Park	68 D2
Sidmonton Place	67 C2 [6]
Sidmonton Road	67 C2
Sidmonton Square	67 C2 [1]
Sigurd Road	37 C2 [31]
Silchester Court	60 D1
Silchester Crescent	60 D1
Silchester Park	60 D1
Silchester Road	60 D1
Silchester Wood	60 D1 [16]
Silken Vale	17 C3
Silleachain Lane	20 D4
Silloge Avenue	25 A1
Silloge Crescent	25 A1
Silloge Gardens	25 A1
Silloge Road	25 A1
Silver Birches (Dunboyne)	7 B2
Silver Birches (Dundrum)	47 C4
Silver Birches Close	7 B2
Silver Birches Crescent	7 B2
Silver Pines	58 F2 [3]
Silverberry	34 D3
Silverdale	34 D3
Silverpine	67 B3
Silverwood	34 D3
Silverwood Drive	46 E4
Silverwood Road	46 E4
Simmon's Court	48 D1 [3]
*Simmon's Place	38 E1
(off Thompson's Cottages)	
Simmonscourt Avenue	48 D1 [2]
Simmonscourt Castle	48 D1
Simmonscourt Road	39 A4
Simmonscourt Terrace	47 C1 [18]
Simmonstown	41 A1
Simmonstown Mannor	32 D4
Simmonstown Park	32 D4
Simons Ridge	57 C3
Simpsons Lane	39 A3 [32]

STREET NAME	PAGE/GRID REFERENCE
Sion Hill	48 F3
Sion Hill Avenue	46 F1
Sion Hill Court	25 C3 [5]
Sion Hill Road	25 C3
Sion Road	60 D2
Sir Ivor Mall	58 F2 [7]
Sir John Rogerson's Quay	38 F2
*Sitric Place (off Sitric Road)	37 C2
Sitric Road	37 C2
Skeagh	41 A3
Skelligs Court	24 D4
Skelly's Lane	26 D2
Skreen Road	24 D4
Slade	53 A3
Slade Castle	53 A2
Slade Castle Avenue	53 A2
Slade Castle Close	53 A2
Slade Castle Court	53 A2
Slade Castle Heights	53 A2
Slade Castle Lane	53 A2
Slade Castle View	53 A2
Slade Castle Walk	53 A2
Slade Castle Wood	53 A2
Slade Road	53 A2
Slade Row	37 C2 [35]
Slademore Avenue	26 F1
Slademore Close	26 F1
Slademore Court	13 C4
Slademore Drive	26 F1
Slane Road	37 B4
Slaney Close	24 E3
Slaney Road	24 E3
Slate Cabin Lane	57 C3
Slemish Road	37 A1
Slí an Chanáil	19 C4
Slieve Rua Drive	58 D1
Slievebloom Park	45 C1
Slievebloom Road	45 C1
Slievemore Road	37 A4
Slievenamon Road	37 A4
Sloan Terrace	68 D2 [8]
*Sloan Terrace (on Meath Road)	67 C2
Sloperton	49 C4
Smithfield	37 C2
Smithfield Terrace	37 C2 [37]
Smith's Cottages (Donnybrook)	47 B1 [18]
Smith's Lane	46 F1 [13]
Smith's Villas	49 C4 [3]
Smyth Gardens	49 C4 [34]
Snowdrop Walk	13 C4
Snugborough Road	22 F1
Snugborough Road (Extention)	22 D2
Somerset Street	38 F3 [8]
Somerton	59 C2
Somerton Lane	22 E4
*Somerton Mews	59 C2
Somerville Avenue	45 C1
Somerville Drive	46 D1
Somerville Park	45 C1 [7]
Sommerville	47 C4
Sonesta	3 A2
Sophie Baret Residence	48 D4 [2]
Sorbonne	48 D4
Sorrel Dale	22 D2
Sorrel Drive	21 C2
Sorrel Heath	21 C2
Sorrel Park	21 C2
Sorrento Close	60 F2 [25]
Sorrento Court	60 F2 [29]
Sorrento Drive	60 F2 [12]
Sorrento Heights	60 F2 [30]
Sorrento Lawn	60 F2 [13]
Sorrento Mews	60 F2 [28]
*Sorrento Park (on Sorrento Rd)	60 F2
Sorrento Road	60 F2
Sorrento Terrace	60 G2
South Avenue	48 E4
South Bank (Swords)	1 C1
South Bank Road	39 B3
South Circular Road	37 B3
(Dolphin's Barn)	
South Circular Road	37 A2
(Islandbridge)	
South Circular Road	37 B3
(Kilmainham)	

STREET NAME	PAGE/GRID REFERENCE
South Circular Road	37 C4
(Portobello)	
*South City Market	38 D3
(on South Great Georges St)	
South Dock Place	38 F3 [35]
South Dock Road	38 F3 [24]
South Dock Street	38 F3
South Esplanade	68 D2
South Great George's Street	38 D3
South Hill (Howth)	29 C3
South Hill (Milltown)	47 B2
South Hill Avenue	48 F3
South Hill Park	48 E3
South Lotts Road	38 F3
South Park (Cornelscourt)	59 B2
South Park Drive	59 B2
South Winds	60 F1 [4]
South Wood Park	48 F3
Southdene	49 B4 [18]
Southern Cross Avenue	37 A3
Southern Cross Route	57 B3
Southmede	57 C1
Southview Terrace	37 B3 [38]
Spa Road (Inchicore)	36 F3
Spa Road (Phoenix Park)	37 A1
Spafield Terrace	39 A4 [13]
Spawell Cottages	45 C4 [1]
Spencer Dock (North Wall)	38 F2 [12]
Spencer Dock (Guild Street)	38 F2
*Spencer Place	38 F1
(off Spencer Street N)	
Spencer Row	38 E2 [22]
Spencer Street North	38 F1
Spencer Street South	38 D4 [48]
*Spencer Terrace	37 B3
(off Cork Street)	
Spencer Villas	60 E1
Sperrin Road	37 A4
Spiddal Park	35 C3
Spiddal Road	35 C3
Spire View	24 D4
Spire View	37 C1 [22]
Spire View Lane	47 A1
Spitalfields	37 C3 [46]
Spring Garden Lane	38 E2 [14]
Spring Garden Street	38 E1
Springbank Cottages	53 A2
Springdale Court Apts.	26 F2
Springdale Road	26 F2
Springfield (Cabra)	37 A1
Springfield (Tallaght)	54 F1
Springfield Avenue	46 E4
Springfield Close	31 C4
Springfield Crescent	46 E4
Springfield Drive	46 E4
Springfield Lane	63 A1
Springfield Park (Deans Grange)	59 A2
Springfield Park (Templeogue)	46 E4
Springfield Road	46 E3
Springhill Avenue	59 A1
Springhill Cottages	59 B1 [5]
Springhill Park (Dalkey)	60 E2
Springhill Park (Deans Grange)	59 B1
Springlawn	22 E2
Springlawn Close	22 E2
Springlawn Court	22 E2
Springlawn Drive	22 E2
Springlawn Heights	22 E2
Springlawn Park	22 E2
Springlawn Road	22 E2
Springmount Apts.	24 D2
Springvale	56 E2
Spruce Avenue	58 D2
*St Agatha Court	38 E1
(off William St N)	
St Agnes Park	46 D1
St Agnes Road	46 D1
*St Agnes Terrace	46 D1
(on St Agnes Rd)	
St Agnes Terrace (Rathfarnham)	46 F3 [2]
St Aidan's Drive	48 D4
St Aidan's Halting Site	54 D1
St Aidan's Park	25 C4 [6]
St Aidan's Park Avenue	25 C4
St Aidan's Park Road	25 C4

STREET NAME	PAGE/GRID REFERENCE		
St Aidan's Terrace	67	C2	23
St Alban's Park	48	E1	
St Alban's Road	37	C4	
St Alphonsus Avenue	25	A4	11
St Alphonsus Rd	25	A4	
St Andrew Street	38	D3	
St Andrews	34	F2	
St Andrews Drive	34	F2	
St Andrews Fairway	34	F2	
St Andrews Green	34	F2	
St Andrew's Grove	3	B3	
*St Andrew's Lane	38	D3	
(off Exchequer Street)			
St Andrews Park	1	C1	
St Andrews Wood	34	F2	
St Anne's Court	27	A3	2
St Anne's (Kimmage)	46	E2	
St Anne's (Ranelagh)	38	E4	
St Anne's Avenue	27	A3	
St Anne's Drive	27	A3	
St Anne's Park	64	E3	
St Anne's Road North	25	A4	
St Anne's Road South	37	C4	5
St Anne's Square (Blackrock)	49	A3	7
St Anne's Square (Portmarnock)	14	F2	6
St Anne's Terrace (Raheny)	27	A3	
St Anne's Terrace (Ranelagh)	38	E4	
St Anne's Terrace (Rathcoole)	52	E2	
St Ann's Square Lower	14	F2	5
St Anthony's Avenue	44	E2	
St Anthony's Crescent	45	C2	
*St Anthony's Place	38	D1	
(off Temple Street North)			
St Anthony's Road	37	B3	
St Aongus Court	45	B4	
St Aongus Crescent	45	B4	
St Aongus Green	45	B4	
St Aongus Grove	45	B4	
St Aongus Lawn	45	B4	
St Aongus Park	45	B4	
St Aongus Road	45	B4	
St Assam's Avenue	27	A2	
St Assam's Drive	27	A2	
St Assam's Park	27	A2	
St Assam's Road East	27	B2	
St Assam's Road West	27	A2	
St Attracta Road	24	F4	
St Aubyn's Court	64	E1	5
*St Audoen's Terrace	38	D3	
(off High Street)			
St Augustine Street	37	C2	
St Augustine's Park	59	A1	
St Barnabas Gardens	38	F1	12
St Begnet's Villas	60	E1	
St Benedicts Gardens	38	D1	35
St Brendan's Avenue	26	E2	
St Brendan's Cottages	39	A3	6
St Brendan's Crescent	45	B2	
St Brendan's Drive	26	E2	
St Brendan's Park	26	F2	
St Brendan's Road	25	A4	12
St Brendan's Terrace (Coolock)	26	E1	
St Brendan's Terrace	49	C4	19
(Dun Laoghaire)			
St Brendan's Terrace	56	E4	
(Rockbrook)			
St Bricin's Park	37	B2	
St Bridget's Avenue	38	F1	
(North Strand)			
St Bridget's Drive	45	B2	
St Bridget's Flats	47	C2	8
St Brigid's Green	26	E2	
St Brigid's Grove	26	E2	
St Brigid's Avenue	14	F2	4
St Brigid's Church Road	58	F1	
St Brigid's Cottages	22	F2	
(Blanchardstown)			
St Brigid's Cottages (Clondalkin)	44	F2	
St Brigid's Cottages	38	F1	24
(North Strand)			
St Brigid's Court	26	E3	2
St Brigid's Crescent	26	E2	
St Brigid's Drive (Clondalkin)	44	E2	
St Brigid's Drive (Killester)	26	E3	1
St Brigid's Lawn	26	E2	

STREET NAME	PAGE/GRID REFERENCE		
St Brigid's Park	22	F2	
(Blanchardstown)			
St Brigid's Park (Clondalkin)	44	E2	1
St Brigid's Park (Cornelscourt)	59	B3	
St Brigid's Road (Artane)	26	E2	
St Brigid's Road (Clondalkin)	44	E2	
St Brigid's Road Lower	25	A4	
St Brigid's Road Upper	25	A4	
St Brigid's Terrace	67	C2	33
St Broc's Cottages	47	C1	1
St Canice's Court	23	C1	
St Canice's Park	24	F2	
St Canice's Road	25	A2	
St Canice's Square	24	E2	
St Catherine's Avenue	37	C4	
St Catherines Grove	43	C1	3
St Catherine's Lane West	37	C3	14
St Catherine's Park	60	E1	
St Catherine's Road	60	E1	
St Catherine's Terrace	29	A1	2
St Catherine's View	20	E4	
St Clair's Lawn	67	B3	
St Clair's Terrace	67	B3	3
St Clare's Avenue	37	C4	20
St Clement's Road	25	A4	13
St Colmcille's Way	55	C2	
St Columbanus Avenue	47	B3	
St Columbanus Place	47	B3	1
St Columbanus Road	47	B3	
St Columbas Heights	1	C2	
St Columbas Rise	1	C2	
St Columba's Road	45	B2	
St Columba's Road Lower	25	A4	
St Columba's Road Upper	25	A4	
St Columcille's Crescent	2	D2	1
St Columcille's Drive	2	D2	
St Columcille's Terrace	67	C2	18
St Columcills Park	2	D2	
St Conleth's Road	45	C2	
St Cronan's Avenue	1	B1	
St Cronan's Close	1	B2	
St Cronan's Cottages	1	C2	
St Cronan's Court	1	B1	
St Cronan's Grove	1	C1	
St Cronan's Lawn	1	B1	
St Cronan's Road	67	C2	8
St Cronan's View	1	B2	
St Cronan's Way	1	C2	
St David's	26	D2	
St David's Court	26	E4	5
St David's Park	26	D2	
St David's Terrace	37	B1	7
(Blackhorse Avenue)			
St David's Terrace (Glasnevin)	25	A3	3
St Davids Wood	26	D2	
St Declan's Road	25	C4	
St Declan's Terrace	25	C4	5
St Domhnach's Well Street	28	D1	3
St Dominic's Avenue	55	A1	
St Dominic's Court	55	A1	4
St Dominic's Road	55	A1	
St Dominic's Terrace	55	A1	
St Donagh's Crescent	27	B1	
St Donagh's Park	27	B1	
St Donagh's Road	27	B1	
St Eithne Road	24	F4	
St Elizabeth's Court	37	C1	14
St Enda's Drive	56	F1	
St Enda's Park	56	F1	
St Enda's Road	46	F2	
St Finbarr's Court	24	E4	2
St Finbarr's Close	45	B3	
St Finbarr's Road	24	E4	
St Finian's Grove	34	D2	
St Finian's Avenue	34	D2	
St Finian's Close	34	D2	
St Finian's Crescent	34	D2	
St Fintan Road	24	F4	
St Fintan Terrace	24	F4	
St Fintan's Crescent	29	B3	
St Fintan's Grove	29	B3	
St Fintan's Park	59	B1	
(Dean's Grange)			
St Fintan's Park (Sutton)	29	B2	
St Fintan's Road	29	B3	

STREET NAME	PAGE/GRID REFERENCE		
St Fintan's Terrace	35	C1	5
St Fintan's Villas	59	B1	
St Francis Square	38	D3	48
St Gabriel's	59	C3	
St Gabriel's Court	27	A4	2
St Gabriel's Road	26	F4	
St Gall Gardens North	47	B3	2
St Gall Gardens South	47	B3	3
St Gatien Road	56	F1	2
St George's Avenue	25	B4	
(Clonliffe Road)			
St George's Avenue (Killiney)	60	E3	
St George's Villas (Inchicore)	36	F3	18
St Gerard's Road	45	C2	
St Helena's Court	24	E2	3
St Helena's Drive	24	E2	
St Helena's Road	24	E2	
St Helen's	60	E1	22
St Helen's Road	48	E2	
St Helen's Terrace	37	A3	27
St Helen's Villas	48	F2	1
St Helen's Wood	48	E3	
St Helier's Copse	48	F4	1
St Ignatius Avenue	38	D1	17
St Ignatius Road	25	A4	
St Ita's Road	25	A3	6
St Ives	3	B2	
St James Avenue	38	E1	
(Clonliffe Road)			
*St James Place	39	A3	
(Sandymount Road)			
St James Terrace (Sandymount)	39	A3	23
St Jame's Wood	37	A3	25
St James's Avenue	37	B3	21
(James's Street)			
St James's Place (Inchicore)	36	F3	17
St James's Road	45	B2	
St James's Terrace	37	B4	2
(Dolphin's Barn)			
St Jarlath Road	24	F4	
St John Street	37	C3	58
St John's Court (Donnycarney)	26	D3	
St John's	48	E1	
St John's Avenue (Clondalkin)	44	D2	
St John's Avenue (The Coombe)	37	C3	39
St John's Close	44	D2	
St John's Cottages	37	B3	28
St John's Court (Beaumont)	26	D1	
St John's Court (Clondalkin)	44	D2	
St John's Crescent	44	D2	
St John's Drive	44	D2	
St John's Gate	44	D2	
St John's Green	44	D2	
St John's Grove	44	D2	
*St John's Lane(off Strand Road)	48	E1	
St John's Lawn	44	D2	
St John's Park (Dun Laoghaire)	49	C4	
St John's Park East	44	D2	
St Johns Park West	44	D2	
St John's Road	44	D2	
St John's Road East	48	E1	
St John's Road West	44	D2	
(Clondalkin)			
St John's Road West	37	B2	
(Islandbridge)			
St John's Terrace	37	B3	33
(Mount Brown)			
St John's Wood (Clondalkin)	44	D2	
St John's Wood (Clontarf)	26	E4	2
St John's Wood West	44	D2	
St Joseph Street	38	D1	27
St Joseph's	23	C2	
St Joseph's Avenue (Ballybough)	25	B4	2
St Joseph's Avenue	25	A4	
(Drumcondra)			
St Joseph's Cottages	23	C4	3
St Joseph's Court	37	C1	16
St Joseph's Grove	47	C4	9
St Joseph's Mansions	38	E1	60
St Joseph's Parade	38	D1	
St Joseph's Place	38	D1	59
(Dorset Street Lower)			
St Joseph's Place (Prussia Street)	37	C1	15
St Joseph's Road	37	C1	
(Aughrim Street)			

STREET NAME	PAGE/GRID REFERENCE		
St Joseph's Road (Walkinstown)	45	C2	
St Joseph's Square	39	C1	2
*St Joseph's Street	38	D1	
(off Leo Street)			
St Joseph's Terrace (Fairview)	25	C4	4
St Joseph's Terrace	38	E1	35
(North Circular Road)			
St Joseph's Terrace	37	B4	
(off Dolphin's Barn)			
*St Joseph's Terrace	39	A3	
(off Pembroke Street)			
*St Joseph's Terrace	50	D4	
(on Tivoli Road)			
St Joseph's Villas (Summerhill)	38	E1	38
St Judes Apts.	31	C3	3
*St Kevin's Avenue	37	C3	
(off Blackpitts)			
St Kevin's Cottages	38	D4	29
St Kevin's Court	47	A2	
St Kevin's Gardens	47	A2	
St Kevin's Parade	38	D4	52
St Kevin's Park (Rathgar)	47	A2	
St Kevin's Park (Stillorgan)	58	D1	
St Kevin's Road	38	D4	3
St Kevin's Square	67	C2	
St Kevin's Terrace (Bray)	67	C2	14
*St Kevin's Terrace	38	D3	
(New Bride St)			
St Kevin's Villas	60	D1	
St Killian's Avenue	45	B2	
St Killians Crescent	67	B4	
St Killian's Park	44	E1	1
St Laurence Grove	36	E2	4
St Laurence Park	48	F4	
*St Laurence Place	38	D1	
(Fontenoy Street)			
*St Laurence Place	38	F2	
(Lr Sheriff Street)			
St Laurence Place	38	D1	66
(Western Way)			
St Laurence Road	36	E2	
St Laurence Terrace	36	E2	9
(Chapelizod)			
St Laurence's Terrace (Bray)	67	C2	17
St Lawrence Glen	36	E3	3
St Lawrence O'Toole Avenue	14	F2	1
St Lawrence Quay	30	D1	8
St Lawrence Road (Clontarf)	26	D4	
St Lawrence Road (Howth)	30	D1	
St Lawrence's Court	26	D4	
St Lawrence's Terrace (Howth)	30	D2	1
St Loman's Road	34	F2	
St Luke's Avenue	37	C3	
St Luke's Court	26	D1	3
St Luke's Crescent	47	B2	3
St Luke's Gate	37	C3	
St Maelruans Park	55	A1	1
St Maignenn's Terrace	37	B3	4
St Malachy's Drive	45	C2	
St Malachy's Road	25	A3	7
St Margaret's Close	60	E1	30
St Margaret's (Booterstown)	48	F3	
St Margaret's (North Road)	11	B1	
St Margaret's Avenue	27	C2	
(Kilbarrack)			
St Margaret's Avenue	3	B3	
(Malahide)			
*St Margaret's Avenue	37	C3	
(off Pimlico)			
St Margaret's Avenue North	38	E1	34
St Margaret's Court	11	A4	1
St Margaret's Halting Site	11	C4	
St Margaret's Park	3	B3	
St Margaret's Road (Ballymun)	12	D4	
St Margaret's Road (Finglas)	11	A4	
St Margaret's Road (Malahide)	3	B3	
St Margaret's Terrace	37	C3	7
St Mark's Avenue	35	A2	
St Mark's Crescent	35	A3	
St Mark's Drive	35	A3	
St Mark's Gardens	35	A3	
St Mark's Green	35	A3	
St Mark's Grove	35	A3	
St Marnock's Avenue	14	F2	
St Martin's Drive	46	E2	
St Martin's Park	46	E1	

STREET NAME	PAGE/GRID REFERENCE
St Mary's Ave North (Mountjoy Street)	38 D1 [7]
St Mary's Avenue (Rathfarnham)	46 F4
St Mary's Avenue West	36 F3
St Mary's Crescent	45 C1
St Mary's Drive	45 C1
St Mary's Lane	38 F3 [17]
St Mary's Mansions	38 E1 [62]
St Mary's Park (Crumlin)	45 C1
St Mary's Park (Finglas)	23 C2
St Mary's Park (Leixlip)	20 D4
St Mary's Place (Howth)	30 D2 [4]
St Mary's Place North	38 D1 [48]
St Mary's Road (Crumlin)	46 D1
St Mary's Road (Howth)	30 D2 [3]
St Mary's Road North (East Wall)	38 F1
St Mary's Road South (Ballsbridge)	38 F4
St Mary's Street	49 C4 [5]
St Mary's Terrace (Arbour Hill)	37 C2 [34]
*St Mary's Terrace (Bath Street)	39 A3
St Mary's Terrace (Boghall Road)	67 C4 [6]
St Marys Terrace (Bray)	68 D2 [20]
St Mary's Terrace (Chapelizod)	36 E2 [5]
St Mary's Terrace (Dunboyne)	7 B2 [1]
St Mary's Terrace (Mountjoy Street)	38 D1 [10]
St Mary's Terrace (Rathfarnham)	46 F4 [5]
St Mathias Wood	60 D4
St Mel's Avenue	45 B3
*St Michael's Close (off High Street)	38 D3
St Michael's Estate	37 A3 [8]
*St Michael's Hill (off High Street)	38 D3
St Michael's House	47 C4
St Michael's Place	38 D1 [51]
St Michael's Road	25 A3 [8]
St Michael's Terrace (Blackpitts)	37 C3 [57]
St Michael's Terrace (Dun Laoghaire)	49 C4 [18]
*St Michan's Place (off Chancery Street)	38 D2
St Michan's Street	38 D2 [44]
*St Mobhi Avenue (on St. Mobhi Road)	25 A3
St Mobhi Boithirin	25 A3
St Mobhi Drive	25 A3
St Mobhi Grove	25 A3 [10]
St Mobhi Road	25 A3
St Mochtas Avenue	22 D3
St Mochtas Chase	22 D2
St Mochtas Drive	22 D3
St Mochtas Green	22 D3
St Mochtas Grove	22 D3
St Mochtas Lawn	22 D2
St Mochtas Road	22 D3
St Mochtas Vale	22 D3
St Mura's Terrace	38 F1 [17]
St Nathy's House	47 B4 [5]
St Nathy's Villas	47 B4 [17]
St Nessan's Apts	30 E2 [3]
St Nessan's Close	30 D2 [9]
St Nessans Court	30 D2 [12]
St Nessan's Terrace	30 D2 [5]
St Nicholas Place	38 D3 [2]
St Oliver's Park	35 B3
St Pappin's Green	24 F2
St Pappin's Road	25 A2
St Pappin's Street	12 D4 [1]
St Patrick's Avenue (Clondalkin)	44 D1 [1]
St Patrick's Avenue (Dalkey)	60 F2 [1]
St Patrick's Avenue (Fairview)	38 F1 [16]
St Patrick's Avenue (Portmarnock)	14 F2
St Patrick's Close (Kevin Street Upper)	38 D3
St Patrick's Close (Kill O'The Grange)	59 C1 [9]
St Patrick's Cottages	46 F4
St Patrick's Crescent (Kill O'The Grange)	59 C1
St Patrick's Crescent (Rathcoole)	52 E2
St Patrick's Parade	25 A4
St Patrick's Park (Blanchardstown)	22 E2
St Patricks Park (Celbridge)	31 C3
St Patricks Park (Celbridge)	32 D3
St Patricks Park (Clondalkin)	44 D1
St Patricks Park (Dunboyne)	7 B2
St Patricks Park (Stepaside)	58 E4
*St Patrick's Place (off Royal Canal Bank)	25 A4
St Patrick's Road (Clondalkin)	35 A4
St Patrick's Road (Dalkey)	60 F2 [8]
St Patrick's Road (Drumcondra)	25 A4
St Patrick's Road (Walkinstown)	45 C2
St Patrick's Square (Bray)	67 C1 [1]
St Patrick's Square (Dalkey)	60 F2 [4]
St Patrick's Terrace (Inchicore)	36 F3 [9]
St Patrick's Terrace (Kill O' the Grange)	59 C1 [7]
*St Patrick's Terrace (Nth Brunswick St)	37 C2
*St Patrick's Terrace (off Fitzroy Avenue)	25 B4
St Patrick's Terrace (Russell Street)	38 E1
St Patrick's Villas	39 A3 [3]
St Paul's Terrace	60 E1 [5]
St Peter's Avenue	37 C1
St Peter's Close	38 D1 [62]
St Peter's Crescent	45 C2
St Peter's Drive	45 C2
St Peter's Park	7 B2
St Peter's Road (Bray)	67 B1
St Peter's Road (Phibsborough)	24 F4
St Peter's Road (Walkinstown)	45 C2
St Peter's Square	38 D1 [37]
St Peter's Terrace (Bray)	67 B1 [2]
St Peter's Terrace (Dun Laoghaire)	60 E1 [6]
St Peter's Terrace (Howth)	30 D2
St Peter's Terrace (Walkinstown)	45 C2 [1]
St Philomenas	9 C4
St Philomena's Court	9 C4
St Philomena's Park	9 C3
St Philomena's Road	24 F4 [1]
St Raphaels Avenue	31 C4
St Ronan's Avenue	35 A3
St Ronan's Close	35 A3
St Ronan's Crescent	35 A3
St Ronan's Drive	35 A3
St Ronan's Gardens	35 A3
St Ronan's Green	35 A3
St Ronan's Grove	35 A3
St Ronan's Park	35 A3
St Ronan's Way	35 A3
St Stephen's Green East	38 E3
St Stephen's Green North	38 E3
St Stephen's Green South	38 D3
St Stephen's Green West	38 D3
St Sylvester Villas	3 B3
St Teresa's Gardens	37 C3
St Teresa's Place	25 A4 [9]
St Teresa's Road (Crumlin)	46 D2
St Teresa's Road (Glasnevin)	25 A4 [8]
St Thomas Mead	48 E3
St Thomas Road (Ardee Street)	37 C3
St Thomas's Road (Mount Merrion)	48 E3
St Ultan's Flats	38 D4 [21]
St Vincent Street North	38 D1 [4]
St Vincent Street South	38 D4
St Vincent Street West	37 A3
St Vincent's Cottages	23 C4 [2]
St Vincent's Court	25 C3 [7]
St Vincent's Park	49 A4
St Werburghs	2 E2
St Wolston's Abbey	32 D4
St. Agnes Terrace	46 D1 [4]
St. Candice's Court	23 C1
St. Cronan's Cottages	1 C2
St. James's	26 D4
St. John's Well Way	37 B3
St. Laurence Court	36 E3
*St. Samson Court	14 D3
St. Samson Square	14 D3
St. Vincent's Court	26 D3
Stable Lane (Harcourt Street)	38 D3 [19]
Stable Lane (Leeson St Lr)	38 E3 [37]
Stable Lane (Smithfield)	37 C2 [16]
Stackstown	61 B1
Staffordstown	5 C2
Staffordstown Little	5 C1
Stamer Street	38 D4
Stanford Green	45 C1
Stanhope Street	37 C2 [2]
Stanley Street	37 C2 [39]
Stannaway Avenue	46 D1
Stannaway Court	46 D2 [3]
Stannaway Drive	46 E1
Stannaway Road	46 E1
Stapolin Lawns	14 F4
Station Close	35 A4
Station Road (Dunboyne)	7 B3
Station Road (Glenageary)	60 E1
Station Road (Killiney)	60 E1
Station Road (Leixlip)	19 C4
Station Road (off Clover Hill Road)	35 A4
Station Road (Portmarnock)	14 E2
Station Road (Raheny)	27 A2
Station Road (Shankill)	64 E2 [6]
Station Road (Sutton)	29 A1
Station View Apts.	22 E3 [3]
Station Way	14 F4
Stationcourt	22 D3
Stationcourt Hall	22 D3
Stationcourt Park	22 D3
Stationcourt View	22 D3
Stationcourt Way	22 D3
Steelstown	51 C3
Steeven's Lane	37 B2
Stella Avenue	25 A3
Stella Gardens	39 A3
Stepaside	58 E4
Stepaside	62 E1
Stepaside Lane	62 E1
Stepaside Park	62 E1
Stepaside Park	58 E4
Stepaside Village	58 D3
Stephen Street Lower	38 D3
Stephen Street Upper	38 D3
Stephen's Lane	38 E3
Stephen's Place	38 E3 [36]
Stephen's Road	37 A3
Sterling Square Apts.	8 D3
Stillorgan	58 F1
Stillorgan Court	58 E1 [2]
Stillorgan Grove	48 F4
Stillorgan Heath	58 E1 [3]
Stillorgan Heath	58 E1
Stillorgan Park	48 F4
Stillorgan Park Avenue	58 F1
Stillorgan Road (Donnybrook)	48 D1
Stillorgan Road (Foxrock)	59 A2
Stillorgan Road (Mount Merrion)	48 E3
Stillorgan Road (Stillorgan)	58 F1
Stillorgan Wood	58 E1
Stirling Park	47 A3 [2]
*Stirrup Lane (off Church Street)	37 C2
Stockhole Lane	12 F1
Stocking Lane	56 D3
Stockton Court	23 A3
Stockton Drive	23 A3
Stockton Green	23 A3
Stockton Grove	23 A3
Stockton Lawn	23 A3
Stockton Park	23 A3
Stokes Place	38 D3 [27]
*Stone Masons Green	57 A2
*Stone Masons Way	57 A2
Stone Mews	47 A1 [8]
Stonebridge	21 B2
Stonebridge Avenue	21 B2
Stonebridge Close	64 E3 [2]
Stonebridge Drive	21 B2
Stonebridge Lane	64 D2 [1]
Stonebridge Road (Clonsilla)	21 B2
Stonebridge Road (Shankill)	64 D2
Stonepark Abbey	46 F4
Stonepark Court	46 F4
Stonepark Orchard	46 F4 [17]
Stoneview Place	50 D4 [13]
Stoney Park	52 F2
Stoney Road (Dundrum)	47 C4
Stoney Road (East Wall)	38 F1 [2]
Stoneybatter	37 C2
Stoneylea Terrace	67 C3 [10]
Store Street	38 E2
Stormanstown Road	25 A2
Stradbrook Close	59 B1
Stradbrook Gardens	49 B4 [8]
Stradbrook Grove	49 B4
Stradbrook Hall	49 B4 [20]
Stradbrook Hill	59 B1 [4]
Stradbrook Lawn	49 B4
Stradbrook Park	49 B4
Stradbrook Road	49 B4
Straffan Road	17 C4
Straffan Way	17 C4
Straleek	41 B1
Stralem Court	21 B1
Stralem Crescent	21 B1
Stralem Grove	21 B1
Stralem Mews	21 B1
Stralem Terrace	21 B1
Strand Lane	48 E1 [3]
Strand Road (Baldoyle)	15 A4
Strand Road (Ballybrack)	64 E1
Strand Road (Bray)	67 C2
Strand Road (Merrion)	48 E1
Strand Road (Portmarnock)	4 D4
Strand Road (Portmarnock)	15 A1
Strand Road (Portmarnock)	14 F2
Strand Road (Sandymount)	39 B4
Strand Road (Sutton)	29 B2
Strand Street (Malahide)	3 B2
Strand Street (Ringsend)	39 A3
Strand Street Great	38 D2
Strand Street Little	38 D2 [36]
Strand Terrace	47 B2 [2]
Strandmill Avenue	14 F2
Strandmill Park	15 A2
Strandmill Road	15 A2
Strandville Avenue (North Strand)	38 F1 [4]
Strandville Avenue East (Clontarf)	26 D4
Strandville House	26 D4 [4]
Strandville Place	38 F1 [19]
Strangford Drive	42 D4
Strangford Gardens	38 F1
Strangford Road	38 F1
Strasburg Terrace	39 A3 [21]
Stratford	47 A2 [9]
Strathmore Road	60 E4
Streamstown Lane	2 F4
Streamville Court	64 E1 [10]
Streamville Road	27 A1
Strong's Court	38 D1 [67]
Suffolk Street	38 D3
Sugarloaf Crescent	67 C3
Sugarloaf Terrace	67 C3 [21]
Suir Road	37 A3
Sullivan Street	37 B2 [1]
*Summer Arch (off Summer Street North)	38 E1
Summer Place	38 E1 [46]
*Summer Row (off Summer Street North)	38 E1
Summer Street North	38 E1
Summer Street South	37 C3
Summerfield (Blanchardstown)	22 E2
Summerfield (Ringsend)	39 A3 [33]
Summerfield (Tallaght)	55 A2 [1]
Summerfield Avenue	22 E2
Summerfield Close	22 E2
Summerfield Close	60 F2 [10]
Summerfield Green	22 E2
Summerfield Lawns	22 E2
Summerfield Meadows	22 E2
Summerfield Rise	22 E2
Summerhill	38 E1
Summerhill Court	50 E4 [3]

STREET NAME	PAGE/GRID REFERENCE
Summerhill Parade (Dun Laoghaire)	50 D4 [6]
Summerhill Parade (Summerhill)	38 E1
Summerhill Place	38 E1 [26]
Summerhill Road (Dún Laoghaire)	50 D4
Summerhill Road (Dunboyne)	7 A2
Summerseat Court	8 D4
Summerville	39 B1
Summerville Park	47 A1
*Summerville Terrace (on Dalkey Ave)	60 F2
Sunbury Court	47 A2
Sunbury Gardens	47 A2
Suncroft Avenue	14 F2 [3]
Suncroft Drive	54 D2
Suncroft Park	54 D2
Sundale Avenue	54 D2
Sundale Close	54 D2
Sundale Crescent	54 D1
Sundale Green	54 D1
Sundale Grove	54 D2
Sundale Heights	54 D1
Sundale Lawn	54 D1
Sundale Meadows	54 D1
Sundale Parade	54 D1
Sundale Park	54 D2
Sundale Road	54 D2
Sundale Villas	54 D1
Sundale Walk	54 D1
Sundrive Park	46 E1
Sundrive Road	46 E1
Sunnybank Court	47 C4 [1]
Sunnyside	62 F3
Sunville Green	46 D1 [1]
Susan Terrace	37 C3
Susanville Road	25 B4
Sussex Road	38 E4
Sussex Street	50 D4 [16]
Sussex Terrace	38 E4 [11]
Sutton	29 A1
Sutton Castle Apts.	29 B3
Sutton Court	28 D1 [1]
Sutton Downs	28 D1
Sutton Grove	28 D1
Sutton Lane	63 A3
Sutton Lawns	28 D1
Sutton Park	28 D1
Sutton Road	67 B2 [9]
Sutton Villas	67 B2 [17]
Swallowbrook	8 F4
Swallowbrook Crescent	8 F4
Swallowbrook Park	8 F4
Swallowbrook View	8 F4
Swan Alley	37 C3 [51]
Swan Grove	38 E4 [23]
*Swan Hall	54 F1
Swan Place	38 E4 [31]
*Swan Yard (off Harry Street)	38 D3
Swanbrook	67 C4
Swan's Nest Apts.	27 B1 [6]
Swan's Nest Avenue	27 B1
Swan's Nest Court	27 B1 [2]
Swan's Nest Road	27 B1
Swanville Place	47 A1 [4]
Swanward Court	37 C4 [39]
Sweeney's Terrace	37 C3 [36]
Sweetbriar Lane	58 D1
Sweetman's Avenue	49 A3 [21]
Sweetman's Avenue	49 A3
Sweetmount Avenue	47 B4
Sweetmount Drive	57 B1
Sweetmount House	47 B4 [18]
Sweetmount Park	47 B4
Sweetmount Park	57 B1
Swift Hall	59 B4
Swiftbrook (Saggart)	53 A2
Swiftbrook (Tallaght)	54 D1
Swiftbrook Avenue	54 D1
Swiftbrook Close	54 D1
Swiftbrook Drive	54 D1
Swiftbrook Park	54 D1
Swift's Alley	37 C3
Swift's Grove	13 A3
*Swift's Row (off Ormond Quay)	38 D2

STREET NAME	PAGE/GRID REFERENCE
Swiftwood	53 B1
Swilly Road	24 E4
Swords	2 E2
Swords Manor Avenue	1 B2
Swords Manor Court	1 B1
Swords Manor Crescent	1 B1
Swords Manor Drive	1 B1
Swords Manor Grove	1 B2
Swords Manor View	1 B1
Swords Manor Way	1 B1
Swords Road (Collinstown)	12 F2
Swords Road (Malahide)	3 A3
Swords Road (Santry)	25 B1
Swords Street	37 B2 [8]
Sybil Hill Avenue	26 F3
Sybil Hill Road	26 F3
Sycamore Avenue (Cabinteely)	59 B3
Sycamore Avenue (Castleknock)	22 E3
Sycamore Avenue (Tallaght)	45 A3
Sycamore Close (Cornelscourt)	59 B3
Sycamore Close (Kilnamanagh)	44 F3
Sycamore Court	59 C2 [3]
Sycamore Crescent (Cabinteely)	59 B3
Sycamore Crescent (Mount Merrion)	48 E4
Sycamore Drive (Cabinteely)	59 B3
Sycamore Drive (Castleknock)	22 E3
Sycamore Drive (Dundrum)	57 B1 [4]
Sycamore Drive (Tallaght)	45 A3
Sycamore Green (Cabinteely)	59 B3
Sycamore Grove (Cabinteely)	59 B4
Sycamore Grove (Foxrock)	59 A2 [7]
Sycamore House (Shankill)	64 E2 [11]
Sycamore House (Sutton)	28 D1
Sycamore Lawn (Cabinteely)	59 B3
Sycamore Lawn (Castleknock)	22 E3
Sycamore Park (Castleknock)	22 E3
Sycamore Park (Finglas)	24 E1
Sycamore Park (Tallaght)	45 A3
Sycamore Road (Dundrum)	57 B1
Sycamore Road (Finglas)	24 E1
Sycamore Road (Fox & Geese)	45 A1
Sycamore Road (Mount Merrion)	48 E4
Sycamore Street	38 D2 [21]
Sycamore View	22 E3
Sycamore Walk	59 B4
Sydenham	50 D4 [23]
Sydenham Mews	68 D3
*Sydenham Place (on Kilmacud Rd Upr)	47 C4
Sydenham Road (Ballsbridge)	39 A4 [4]
Sydenham Road (Dundrum)	47 C4
Sydenham Villas (Bray)	68 D3 [6]
Sydenham Villas (Dundrum)	57 C1
Sydney Avenue	49 A3
Sydney Parade Avenue	48 E1
Sydney Terrace	49 A3
Sylvan Avenue	45 A3
Sylvan Close	44 F3
Sylvan Drive	44 F3
Sylvester Villas	3 B3
Synge House	47 A3
Synge Lane	38 D4 [25]
Synge Place	38 D4 [24]
Synge Street	38 D4
Synge Way	35 C4
Synnott Place	38 D1
Synnott Row	38 D1 [26]
Synnott Terrace	49 C4 [16]

T

Taaffe's Place	38 F1 [15]
Talbot	2 F3
Talbot Avenue	2 F3
Talbot Court (Blanchardstown)	22 F2
Talbot Court (Malahide)	3 A2
Talbot Downs	22 F2
Talbot Lane (Killiney)	60 E3 [4]
Talbot Lane (Talbot Street)	38 E2 [6]
Talbot Lodge	48 F4
Talbot Park	2 F3
Talbot Place	38 E2
Talbot Road (Killiney)	60 E3 [3]
Talbot Road (Swords)	2 F3

STREET NAME	PAGE/GRID REFERENCE
Talbot Street	38 E2
Tallaght	55 A1
Tallaght Bypass	54 F1
Tallaght Road	45 C4
Tallaght Road	55 B1
*Tallow Hall (Belgard Square)	54 F1
Tamarisk Avenue	45 A3
Tamarisk Close	45 A3
Tamarisk Court	45 A3
Tamarisk Dale	45 A3
Tamarisk Drive	45 A3
Tamarisk Grove	45 A3
Tamarisk Heights	45 A3
Tamarisk Lawn	45 A3
Tamarisk Park	45 A3
Tamarisk View	45 A3
Tamarisk Walk	45 A3
Tamarisk Way	45 A3
Tandys Lane	33 C3
Tandys Lane	34 D3
Taney Avenue	47 C4
Taney Court	47 C4
Taney Crescent	47 C4
Taney Drive	47 C4
Taney Grove	47 C4
Taney Lawn	47 C4
Taney Manor	47 C4
Taney Park	47 C4
Taney Rise	47 C4
Taney Road	47 C4
*Tangier Lane (off Grafton Street)	38 D3
Tara Crescent	55 B2 [3]
Tara Hill Crescent	46 F4
Tara Hill Grove	46 F4 [2]
Tara Hill Road	46 F4
Tara Lawn	27 A1
Tara Street	38 E2
Tassagard Greens	53 B2
Tassagart Drive	53 A2
Tay Lane	52 E2
Taylor's Hill	57 A3
Taylor's Lane (Ballyboden)	56 E1
Taylor's Lane (Pimlico)	37 C3 [13]
Temple Bar	38 D2
Temple Buildings	38 D1 [60]
Temple Cottages	38 D1
Temple Court (Arbour Hill)	37 B2 [16]
Temple Court (Blackrock)	49 A3 [25]
*Temple Court (Off Hogan Place)	38 F3 [46]
Temple Court Apts.	12 E4
Temple Crescent	49 B4
Temple Gardens (Milltown)	47 B2
Temple Gardens (Santry)	12 E4
Temple Grove	32 D3
Temple Hill	49 B4
Temple Hill (on Terenure Road West)	46 E2
Temple Lane North	38 D1 [41]
Temple Lane South	38 D2 [46]
Temple Lawns (Primrose Hill)	32 D4
Temple Manor (Celbridge)	31 C4
Temple Manor (Dunboyne)	7 B2
Temple Manor (Greenhills)	45 C3
Temple Manor Avenue	45 C3
Temple Manor Close	45 C3
Temple Manor Court	45 C3
Temple Manor Drive	45 C3
Temple Manor Grove	45 C3
Temple Manor Way	45 C3
Temple Park	47 B2
Temple Park Apts.	12 E4
Temple Park Avenue	49 B4
Temple Place	38 E4 [26]
Temple Road (Blackrock)	49 A3
Temple Road (Rathgar)	47 B2
Temple Square	47 B2 [5]
Temple Street North	38 D1
Temple Street West	37 B2 [7]
Temple Terrace	60 F2 [16]
*Temple Villas (Arbour Hill)	37 C2
*Temple Villas (on Palmerston Road)	47 B1
Templemore Avenue	47 A2
Templeogue	46 D4

STREET NAME	PAGE/GRID REFERENCE
Templeogue Lodge	46 D4
Templeogue Road	46 E3
Templeogue Wood	46 D4
Templeroan	56 D1
Templeroan Avenue	56 D1
Templeroan Close	56 E1
Templeroan Court	56 D1
Templeroan Crescent	56 D1
Templeroan Downs	56 E1
Templeroan Drive	56 D1
Templeroan Green	56 D2
Templeroan Grove	56 D1
Templeroan Lodge	56 D2
Templeroan Meadows	56 E1
Templeroan Mews	56 D1
Templeroan Park	56 D1
Templeroan Road	56 D1
Templeroan View	56 D1
Templeroan Way	56 D1
Templeview Avenue	14 D4
Templeview Close	14 D4
Templeview Copse	14 D4
Templeview Court	14 D4
Templeview Crescent	14 D4
Templeview Downs	14 D4
Templeview Drive	14 D4
Templeview Green	14 D4
Templeview Grove	14 D4
Templeview Lawn	14 D4
Templeview Park	14 D4
Templeview Place	14 D4
Templeview Rise	14 D4
Templeview Row	14 D4
Templeview Square	14 D4
Templeview Vale	14 D4 [1]
Templeview Walk	14 D4
Templeview Way	14 D4
Templeville Avenue	46 D3
Templeville Drive	46 D3
Templeville Park	46 E3 [1]
Templeville Road	46 D3
Terenure	46 F2
Terenure Park	46 F2
Terenure Place	46 F2 [3]
Terenure Road East	46 F2
Terenure Road North	46 F2
Terenure Road West	46 E2
Terminal Road North	39 C2
Terminal Road South	39 C2
Termon Court	11 C4 [1]
*Terrace Place (off Bella St)	38 E1
Tetrarch Grove	7 C1
Texas Lane	3 A2
The Alders	49 B4 [6]
The Anchorage	49 C4 [33]
The Appian Way	38 E4
The Arches	17 C3
The Avenue (Ballinteer)	57 C2
The Avenue (Ballyboden)	56 E2
The Avenue (Carrickmines)	63 A1
The Avenue (Celbridge)	32 D3
The Avenue (Dunboyne Castle)	7 B3
The Avenue (Grange Manor)	34 D3
The Avenue (Louisa Valley)	19 C4
The Avenue (Lutterell Hall)	7 B2
The Avenue (Manorfields)	21 B1
The Avenue (Mulhuddart)	9 A4
The Avenue (Plunkett Hall)	7 A2
The Avenue (St Wolston's Abbey)	32 D4
The Avenue (Tallaght)	44 F3
The Avenue (Templeogue)	46 D3
The Bawn	3 B3
The Bawn Grove	3 B3
The Beeches (Abberley)	64 E1 [22]
The Beeches (Donaghmede)	27 A1
The Beeches (Kilmacud)	58 D1
The Beeches (Monkstown)	49 B4 [21]
The Beeches (Willbrook)	56 F1 [8]
The Belfry (Citywest Road)	53 C2
The Belfry (Inchicore)	37 A3 [17]
The Belfry (Kilbarrack)	27 B1
The Birch	57 C1 [12]
The Birches	59 A3
The Black Avenue	33 B1

STREET NAME	PAGE/GRID REFERENCE		STREET NAME	PAGE/GRID REFERENCE		STREET NAME	PAGE/GRID REFERENCE		STREET NAME	PAGE/GRID REFERENCE	
The Blackthorn	57	C1 [14]	The Crescent	32	D4	The Green (Dunboyne Castle)	7	B3	The Maples (Monkstown)	49	B4 [4]
The Boulevard	9	A2	(St Wolston's Abbey)			The Green (Larch Hill)	12	F4	The Mayne	8	E2
The Bramblings	26	E3	The Crescent (Swords)	2	D2 [4]	The Green (Lutterell Hall)	7	B2	The Meadow	57	B2
The Briars	35	C1	The Crescent (Tallaght)	44	E4	The Green (Malahide)	3	B2	The Meadows (Dunboyne)	7	B2
The Bridge	64	E3	The Crescent (Tallaght)	44	F3	The Green (Manorfields)	21	B1	The Meadows (Killester)	26	F3
The Burgage	60	F2	The Crescent (Tallaght)	55	A1	The Green (Moyglare Abbey)	17	B2	The Meadows	59	A1
The Castlelands	46	F4 [11]	The Crescent (Temple Manor)	31	C4	The Green (Mulhuddart)	9	A4	(Newtownpark Ave)		
The Cedars (Abberley)	64	E1 [21]	The Crescent (Templelogue)	46	E3	The Green (Oldtown Mill)	31	C3	The Meadows (Oldtown Mill)	31	C3
The Cedars (Monkstown)	49	B4 [5]	The Crescent (Whitehall)	25	B3	The Green (Tallaght)	44	F3	The Meadows East	44	F4
The Charter	12	D4 [4]	The Croft	32	D2	The Green (Templeogue)	46	D3	The Meadows West	44	E4
The Chase	58	F2	The Dale	7	B2	The Green (Woodbrook Glen)	67	C1	The Mews (Clontarf)	26	E4
The Cherries	57	A2 [2]	The Dale (Ballinteer)	57	B2 [4]	The Green Road	60	G2	The Mews (Killester)	26	E3
The Claremont Apts.	12	D4 [4]	The Dale (Belgard)	44	F4	The Greenlands	46	F4	The Mews (Rathmines)	47	A1 [19]
The Cloisters (Grace Park Road)	25	B3 [5]	The Dale (Bray)	67	B2	The Grove (Abbeyfarm)	31	C4	The Mews (Templeogue)	46	E3
The Cloisters	46	F2	The Dale (Carrickmines)	63	A1	The Grove (Ballinteer)	57	B2	The Mill Pond Apts.	44	D1 [4]
(Mount Tallant Avenue)			The Dale (Celbridge)	31	C3	The Grove (Celbridge)	32	D4	The Mills	22	F2
The Close (Ballinteer)	57	C2	The Dale (Kilnamanagh)	44	F3	The Grove (Dunboyne Castle)	7	A3	The Moorings (Chapelizod)	36	E2
The Close (Ballyboden)	56	E2	The Dale (Manorfields)	21	B1	The Grove (Dundrum)	57	A1	The Moorings (Malahide)	3	C3
The Close (Beaumont)	25	C1	The Deanery	31	C3 [1]	The Grove (Grange Manor)	34	D3	The New Road	23	B1
The Close (Celbridge)	31	C3	The Dell	57	A2	The Grove (Louisa Valley)	19	C4	The Nurseries (Ballybrack)	60	E4 [4]
The Close (Dunboyne Castle)	7	B3	The Dingle	35	B2	The Grove (Lutterell Hall)	7	B2	The Nurseries (Mulhuddart)	9	A4
The Close (Grange Manor)	34	D3	The Downs (Dunboyne Castle)	7	A3	The Grove (Plunkett Hall)	7	A2	The Nurseries (Oldcourt)	67	B3
The Close (Lutterell Hall)	7	B2	The Downs	32	D4	The Grove (Raheny)	27	B3 [1]	The Nurseries (Swords)	1	C3
The Close (Manorfields)	21	B1	(St Wolston's Abbey)			The Grove (Sadleir Hall)	7	A2	The Oaks (Abberley)	64	E1 [17]
The Close (Mount Merrion)	48	E3	The Drive (Abbeyfarm)	31	C4	The Grove (Tallaght)	44	E4	The Oaks (Ballinteer)	57	B2
The Close (Oldtown Mill)	31	C3 [2]	The Drive (Ballinteer)	57	B2	The Grove (Tallaght)	44	F3	The Oaks (Belgard)	44	E4
The Close (Plunkett Hall)	7	A2	The Drive (Ballyboden)	56	E1	The Grove (Tallaght)	55	A1	The Oaks (Celbridge)	32	D3
The Close (Tallaght)	44	F3	The Drive (Dunboyne Castle)	7	B3	The Grove (Whitehall)	25	B3	The Oaks (Churchtown)	47	B4
The Close (Tallaght)	55	A2 [2]	The Drive (Grange Manor)	34	D3	The Grove (Woodbrook Glen)	67	C1	The Oaks (Dollymount)	27	A4
The Close (Temple Manor)	31	C4	The Drive (Kilnamanagh)	44	F3	The Haggard (Howth)	30	D2 [6]	The Oaks (Hollystown)	9	C1
The Close (Templeogue)	46	D3	The Drive (Lutterell Hall)	7	B2	The Hall	46	F2	The Oaks (Loughlinstown)	64	D1 [1]
The Coombe	37	C3	The Drive (Manorfields)	21	B1	The Hampton	12	D4 [2]	The Oaks (Rockfield)	57	C1
The Coppice (Palmerstown)	35	C1	The Drive (Mulhuddart)	9	A4	The Haven (Glasnevin)	25	A3 [17]	The Oaks (Swords)	1	B3
The Coppins (Celbridge)	32	D3	The Drive (Oldtown Mill)	31	C3	The Haven (Malahide)	3	B2	The Old Forge	34	D3
The Coppins (Foxrock)	59	A3	The Drive (Sadleir Hall)	7	A2	The Hawthorns (Abberley)	64	E1 [20]	The Old Golf Links	3	C3
The Copse (Ballinteer)	57	B2 [3]	The Drive (Tallaght)	55	A1	The Heath (Tallaght)	44	F4	The Old Hill	34	D1
The Copse (Drumcondra)	25	B3	The Drive (Temple Manor)	31	C4	The Heath (Templeogue)	46	D3	The Orchard (Carpenterstown)	22	D3 [1]
The Court (Ballinteer)	57	B2	The Drive (Woodbrook Glen)	67	C1	The Heath (The Heath)	57	B2	The Orchard (Deans Grange)	59	A1
The Court (Ballybrack)	60	E4	The Drive Apts.	56	E1 [2]	The Hedgerows	59	A3	The Orchard (Killester)	26	E3
The Court (Carrickmines)	59	B4	The Dunes	15	A1	The Heights (Ballinteer)	57	B2	The Orchard (Kimmage)	46	E2
The Court (Celbridge)	31	C3	The Elm (Rockfield)	57	C1	The Heights (Dunboyne Castle)	7	B3	The Orchard (Lucan)	34	D1 [14]
The Court (Clontarf)	26	D4	The Elms (Celbridge)	32	D2	The Hill (Ballinteer)	57	C2	The Orchard (Oldtown Mill)	31	C3
The Court (Donnybrook)	47	C2	The Elms (Dunboyne)	7	B2	The Hill (Malahide)	3	B3	*The Orchard (Palmerston)	35	C1
The Court (Dunboyne Castle)	7	B3	The Elms (Elm Park)	48	E2	The Hill (Monkstown)	49	C4	The Orchard Apts.	35	B3
The Court (Glenamuck Road)	63	A1	The Elms (Loughlinstown)	64	E1 [4]	The Hill (Mulhuddart)	9	A4	The Oval	35	C2
The Court (Larch Hill)	12	F4	The Fairways (Portmarnock)	14	E2	The Hill (Stillorgan)	58	F1	The Paddock (Ashtown)	23	C4
The Court (Lutterell Hall)	7	B2	The Fairways	67	C1	The Hole in the Wall Rd	14	E4	The Paddock (Moyglare Abbey)	17	B2
The Court (Mulhuddart)	9	A4	(Woodbrook Glen)			The Holly (Rockfield)	57	C1	The Paddock (Oldtown Mill)	31	C2
The Court (Oldtown Mill)	31	C3	The Fairways Apts.	8	D3	The Island	36	E2	The Paddock's (Clontarf)	26	E4 [6]
The Court (Plunkett Hall)	7	A2	The Falls	46	F3 [5]	The Killigeen	52	D4	The Paddocks (Dalkey)	60	F1 [3]
The Court (Raheny)	27	B3 [2]	The Forum	58	E2	The Kilmore Apts	12	D4 [7]	The Paddocks (Dunboyne)	7	B2
The Court (Sadleir Hall)	7	A2	The Fosters	48	E3	The Kilns	14	F2	The Paddocks (Kilmainham)	37	A3
The Court (Shankill)	64	E3	The Gables (Dundrum)	57	B1	The Lakelands	46	F4 [8]	The Paddocks (Swords)	2	D2
The Court (Tallaght)	44	F3	The Gables (Foxrock)	59	A3 [5]	The Larches (Abberley)	64	E1 [16]	The Palms	48	D3
The Court (Tallaght)	44	F4	The Gables (Grange View Road)	43	B1	The Laurels (Bluebell)	36	E4 [3]	The Park (Abbeyfarm)	31	C4
The Court (Temple Manor)	31	C4	The Gables (Nutgrove)	57	A1	The Laurels (Dundrum)	47	B4	The Park (Beaumont)	25	C1
The Court (Templeogue)	46	D3	The Gables (Rathgar)	47	A2	The Laurels (Rathfarnham)	46	F4 [13]	The Park (Celbridge)	31	C3
The Court (Whitehall)	25	C2	The Gallops	58	E3	The Laurels (Tallaght)	55	A1 [10]	The Park (Dunboyne Castle)	7	B3
The Courtyard (Bray)	67	B2	The Gardens	63	A1	The Laurels (Terenure)	46	F2	The Park (Grange Manor)	34	D3
The Courtyard (Celbridge)	31	C4	The Garth (Cookstown)	44	E4	The Lawn (Ballinteer)	57	B2	The Park (Larch Hill)	12	F4
The Courtyard (Clonsilla)	22	D3	The Garth (Kingswood Heights)	44	F3	The Lawn (Ballyboden)	56	E2	The Park (Louisa Valley)	19	C4
The Courtyard (Leopardstown)	58	E2	The Gate	44	D1	The Lawn (Finglas)	24	E2	The Park (Oldtown Mill)	31	C3
The Courtyard (Rathfarnham)	46	F4	The Gate Lodge	30	E3	The Lawn (Kinsaley)	2	E3	The Park (Plunkett Hall)	7	A2
The Courtyard (Templeogue)	46	E3	The Glade (Ballinteer)	57	B2	The Lawn (Moyglare Abbey)	17	B2	The Park (Tallaght)	44	F3
The Coutryard (Foxrock)	59	A2 [10]	The Glade (Kingswood Heights)	44	F3	The Lawn (Oldtown Mill)	31	C3	The Park (Tallaght)	55	A2
The Cove	3	A2	The Glade (Oldtown Mill)	31	C3	The Lawn (Plunkett Hall)	7	A2	The Park (Templeogue)	46	D3
The Covert	35	C1 [1]	The Glade (Palmerston)	35	B2	The Lawn (Tallaght)	44	E4	The Park Lands	46	F4 [7]
The Crescent (Abbeyfarm)	31	C4	The Glade (St Wolston's Abbey)	32	D4	The Lawn(Woodbrook Glen)	67	C1	The Pines (Ballinteer)	57	B2
The Crescent (Ballinteer)	57	B2 [1]	The Glebe	34	E2	The Lawns (Abbeyfarm)	31	C4	The Pines (Castleknock)	23	A3
The Crescent (Ballyboden)	56	E2	The Glen (Ballinteer)	57	B2	The Lawns (Temple Manor)	31	C4	The Pines (Killester)	26	E3
The Crescent (Carrickmines)	63	A1	The Glen (Ballyboden)	56	E1	The Lighthouse	4	D3	The Pines (Kilmacud)	58	D1 [3]
The Crescent (Castleknock)	22	F3 [1]	The Glen (Glenageary Road)	60	D1 [14]	The Linden	57	C1 [13]	The Pines (Oldcourt)	67	B3
The Crescent (Donnybrook)	47	C1 [4]	The Glen (Louisa Valley)	19	C4	The Links	14	F2	The Place (Carrickmines)	63	A1
The Crescent (Dunboyne Castle)	7	B3	The Glen (Raheny)	27	B3	The Little Grove	32	D4	The Place (Dunboyne Castle)	7	B3
The Crescent (Grange Manor)	34	D3	The Glens	63	A1	The Lodge (Balgriffen)	14	E2	The Plaza Apts.	9	B2
The Crescent (Larch Hill)	12	F4	The Goulding Apts	12	D4 [8]	The Lodge (Clontarf)	26	D4	The Poplars	49	B4 [1]
The Crescent (Lucan)	33	C2	The Granary	37	C3	The Lodge (Glenageary)	60	D1	The Priory (Cabra)	24	D4
The Crescent (Lutterell Hall)	7	A2	The Grange (Deans Grange)	59	B1	The Maieston	12	D4 [6]	The Priory (Grange Road)	56	F1
The Crescent (Malahide)	4	D3	The Grange (Malahide)	3	B4	The Mall (Baldoyle)	15	A4 [4]	The Priory (Malahide)	3	B2 [4]
The Crescent (Mulhuddart)	9	A4	The Grange (Terenure)	46	F2	The Mall (Leixlip)	33	A1	The Rectory	58	D4
The Crescent (off Beaumont Rd)	25	C2 [8]	The Green (Ballinteer)	57	B2	The Mall (Lucan)	34	D1	The Rise (Ballinteer)	57	B2
The Crescent (Oldtown Mill)	31	C3	The Green (Ballyboden)	56	E1	The Mall (Malahide)	3	B2	The Rise (Ballyboden)	56	E2
The Crescent (Plunkett Hall)	7	A2	The Green (Beaumont)	25	C1	The Maltings	67	C2	The Rise (Carrickmines)	63	A1
The Crescent (Ranelagh)	47	B1	The Green (Carrickmines)	63	A1	The Manor (Templeogue)	46	D4	The Rise (Dalkey)	60	E2
			The Green (Celbridge)	31	C3	The Maples (Bird Avenue)	47	C3	The Rise (Glasnevin)	25	A2

STREET NAME	PAGE/GRID REFERENCE	STREET NAME	PAGE/GRID REFERENCE	STREET NAME	PAGE/GRID REFERENCE	STREET NAME	PAGE/GRID REFERENCE
The Rise (Malahide)	3 B3	Thomastown Crescent	60 D2 [2]	Tor an Rí Parade	34 F3	Turrets Flats	47 A1 [9]
The Rise (Manorfields)	21 B1	Thomastown Road	60 D3	Tor an Rí Terrace	34 F3	Turvey Avenue	37 A3 [2]
The Rise (Mount Merrion)	48 E4	Thomond	64 E2 [9]	Tor an Rí Walk	34 F3	Tuscany Downs	27 A2
The Rise (Newcastle)	42 D4	Thomond Road	36 E3	Torca Road	60 F2	Tuscany Park	28 D1
The Rise (Tallaght)	44 E4	Thompson's Cottages	38 E1 [49]	Torca View	60 F2 [33]	Twin Cottages	49 A4 [5]
The Rise (Tallaght)	44 F3	Thor Place	37 B2 [1]	Torcaill	3 C4	Tymon Close	55 A2
The Road (Manorfields)	21 B1	Thormanby Grove	30 D2 [10]	Torlogh Gardens	25 C4 [8]	Tymon Crescent	54 F2
The Rookery	56 D2	Thormanby Lawns	30 D2	Torlogh Parade	25 C3 [1]	Tymon Grove	55 A2
The Rose	9 B2	Thormanby Lodge	30 E2	Torquay Road	58 F2	Tymon Heights	55 B2
The Rowan (Rockfield)	57 C1	Thormanby Road	30 E2	Torquay Wood	58 F2	Tymon Lane	45 B4
The Rowans (Abberley)	64 E1 [18]	Thormanby Woods	30 E2	Tory Square	22 F1	Tymon Lane	45 B3
The Sand Holes	22 F4 [1]	Thorn Wood	48 E3	Tourmakeady Road	25 B2 [1]	Tymon Lawn	55 A2
The Scalp	63 A4	Thornberry Apts.	8 F4	Tourville Lodge	46 F3 [6]	Tymon Lodge Apts.	45 B3
The Slopes	49 C4	Thorncastle Court Apts.	39 A2 [3]	Tower Avenue	46 F2	Tymon North	45 B4
The Spruce	9 B2	Thorncastle Street	39 A2	Tower Road (Castleknock)	22 F4	Tymon North Avenue	45 B4
The Square (Irishtown)	39 A3 [5]	Thorncliff	47 B2 [8]	Tower Road (Clondalkin)	44 D1	Tymon North Court	45 B4 [1]
The Square (Larch Hill)	12 F4	Thorncliffe Park	47 B3	*Tower Terrace	37 B3	Tymon North Gardens	45 B4
The Square (Lucan)	34 D1 [5]	Thorndale Avenue	26 D2	(off Kilmainham Lane)		Tymon North Green	45 B4
The Square (Tallaght)	54 F1	Thorndale Court	25 C2 [4]	Tower View Cottages	24 F4 [2]	Tymon North Grove	45 B4
The Stables	48 E3 [1]	Thorndale Crescent	26 D2	Townsend Street	38 E2	Tymon North Lawn	45 B4
The Steeple (Moyglare Abbey)	17 B2	Thorndale Drive	26 D3	Townyard Lane	3 B2	Tymon North Park	45 B4
The Steeples	36 E3	Thorndale Grove	26 D3	Traders Wharf	49 C3	Tymon North Place	45 B4 [2]
The Stiles Road	26 E4	Thorndale Lawns	26 D2	Trafalgar Lane	49 B4	Tymon North Road	45 B4
The Summit (Howth)	30 E3	Thorndale Park	26 D2	Trafalgar Terrace (Blackrock)	49 B3	Tymonville Avenue	45 B4
The Sweepstakes	39 A4 [22]	Thornfield Square	44 E1	Trafalgar Terrace (Bray)	67 C2 [31]	Tymonville Court	45 A4
The Sycamores	64 E1 [3]	Thornhill Gardens	31 C2	Tramway Court (Sutton)	29 A1	Tymonville Crescent	45 A4
The Sycamores (Rockfield)	57 C1	Thornhill Heights	31 C2	Tramway Court (Tallaght)	55 A1 [8]	Tymonville Drive	45 A3
The Terrace	63 A1	Thornhill Lane	27 A4	Tranquility Grove	26 D1	Tymonville Grove	45 B3
The Thatch Road	25 C2	Thornhill Meadows	31 C2	Traverslea Close	60 D1	Tymonville Lawn	45 B4
The Thicket	59 A3	Thornhill Road (Bray)	67 A2	*Traverslea Woods	60 D1	Tymonville Park	45 B4
The Turnpike	12 D4 [5]	Thornhill Road (Kilmacud)	48 E4	Traynor Place	37 B3 [41]	Tymonville Road	45 A4
The Vale	35 C1	Thornhill View	67 B1 [5]	Treepark Avenue	45 A3	Tynan Hall	44 F3
The View (Ballinteer)	57 B2	Thornville Avenue	27 B1	Treepark Close	45 A3	Tynan Hall Avenue	44 F3
The View (Carrickmines)	63 A1 [1]	Thornville Drive	27 B2	Treepark Drive	45 A3	Tynan Hall Grove	44 F3
The View (Celbridge)	31 C3	Thornville Park	27 C1	Treepark Road	45 A3	Tynan Hall Park	44 F3
The View (Dunboyne Castle)	7 A3	Thornville Road	27 B1	Trees Avenue	48 E4	Tyrconnell Park	36 F3
The View (Larch Hill)	12 F4	Thornville Terrace	27 B2 [1]	Trees Road Lower	48 E4	Tyrconnell Road	36 F3
The View (Manorfields)	21 B1	Three Rock Close	45 B3 [1]	Trees Road Upper	48 E4	Tyrconnell Street	36 F3 [6]
The View (Oldtown Mill)	31 C3	Three Rock Grove	57 B3	Treesdale	48 F4	Tyrconnell Villas	36 F3 [7]
The View (St Wolston's Abbey)	32 D4	Three Rock Road	58 E2	Tresilian	59 A3	Tyrellstown Boulevard	9 B2
The View (Tallaght)	44 F3	Thundercut Alley	37 C2 [20]	Trim Road	26 D1	Tyrellstown Way	9 B2
The View (Tallaght)	55 B1	Tibradden Close	45 B2 [1]	Trimelston Apts.	47 C3	Tyrone Place	37 A3 [12]
The Village (Clonsilla)	21 C3	Tibradden Drive	45 B2	Trimleston Avenue	48 E2	Tyrrell Place	38 E1 [45]
The Village (Drumcondra)	25 B3 [2]	Tibradden Grove	45 B3	Trimleston Drive	48 E2	*Tyrrel's Lane	39 A3
The Village (Raheny)	27 B3	Tibradden Lane	56 F4	Trimleston Gardens	48 E2	(off Fitzwilliam St Ringsend)	
The Village Centre	34 D1 [12]	Tibradden Road	56 F3	Trimleston Park	48 E2		
The Village Court	34 D1 [13]	Ticknick	63 B2	Trimleston Road	48 E2		
The Village Gate	60 F2	Ticknock Dale	57 C3	Trinity Street	38 D2		
The Walk (Ballinteer)	57 B2	Ticknock Grove	57 C3	Trinity Terrace	38 E1 [44]	**U**	
The Walk (Carrickmines)	63 A1	Ticknock Hill	57 C3	Tristan House Apts.	36 E2 [15]		
The Walk (Dunboyne Castle)	7 B3	Ticknock Road	57 B4	Tritonville Avenue	39 A3 [8]	UCD Village Belgrove	48 D3
The Walk (Louisa Valley)	19 C4	Tiknock	61 B1	Tritonville Close	39 A3 [22]	Ullardmor	60 F2 [27]
The Walk (Manorfields)	21 B1	Timard	17 A1	Tritonville Court	39 A4	Ulster Street	24 F4
The Walk (Oldtown Mill)	31 C3	Timber Mills Apts.	26 E2	Tritonville Crescent	39 A3 [9]	Ulster Terrace (North Strand)	38 E1 [58]
The Walk (Tallaght)	55 A1	Tinkers Hill	21 A4	Tritonville Road	39 A3	Ulster Terrace	58 F1 [4]
The Walk (Templeogue)	46 D3	Tinkler's Path	36 E1	Trosyrafon Terrace	68 D2 [1]	(Stillorgan Grove)	
The Walled Gardens	32 D2	Tinnehinch	66 E4	Tuansgate Apts.	54 F1 [1]	Ulverton Close	60 F1 [5]
The Walled Orchard	33 B1	Tivoli Avenue	46 F1	Tubber Lane Road	33 B2	Ulverton Court	60 F1 [13]
The Warren	2 F3	Tivoli Close	59 C1	Tubbermore Avenue	60 F2	Ulverton Road	60 F1
The Water Rill	2 E2	Tivoli Road	49 C4	Tubbermore Road	60 F2	Upper Cliff Road	30 E2 [2]
The Way (Dunboyne Castle)	7 A3	Tivoli Terrace East	50 D4	Tuckett's Lane	30 D2	Upper Dargle Road	67 A2
The Weir	36 E2	Tivoli Terrace North	49 C4	Tudor Court	2 F2	Upper Glen Road	36 E1
The Wicklow Way	61 C4	Tivoli Terrace South	49 C4	Tudor Lawns	58 F2	Uppercross	34 F1
The Willow	9 B2	Tobernea Terrace	49 B3 [2]	Tudor Road	47 B1	Uppercross Court	55 A1 [7]
The Willow (Rockfield)	57 C1	Tolka Cottages	24 F3	Tulip Court	13 C4	Uppercross Road	37 B3
The Willows (Abberley)	64 E1 [19]	Tolka Estate	24 F2	Tullyhall	34 D4	Urney Grove	60 E2 [7]
The Willows (Celbridge)	32 D3	Tolka Estate Road	24 F3	Tullyhall Avenue	34 D4	Usher Lane	1 A2
The Willows (Glasnevin)	24 F3	Tolka Quay	39 A2	Tullyhall Close	34 D4	Usher Street	37 C2
The Willows (Monkstown)	49 B4 [3]	Tolka Quay Road	39 A2	Tullyhall Court	34 D4	Usher's Island	37 C2
The Willows (Orwell Road)	47 A3 [1]	Tolka Road	25 B4	Tullyhall Crescent	34 E4	Usher's Quay	37 C2
The Wood (Carrickmines)	63 A1	Tolka Vale	24 E3	Tullyhall Drive	34 D4		
The Wood (Tallaght)	55 A2	Tolka Valley Road	24 D3	Tullyhall Green	34 D4		
The Woodlands (Celbridge)	32 D3	Tolka Valley View	24 D3	Tullyhall Park	34 D4	**V**	
The Woodlands (Rathfarnham)	46 F4 [9]	Tom Clarke House	25 B4 [1]	Tullyhall Rise	34 E4		
Theresa House	46 F4 [20]	Tom Kelly Road	38 D4 [16]	Tullyhall Way	34 D4	*Vale Terrace	67 B2
Third Avenue (Seville Place)	38 F2 [7]	Tonduff Close	45 B3	Tullyvale	63 C1	(on lower Dargle Road)	
Third Avenue (Tallaght)	44 F4	Tonguefield Road	46 E1 [1]	Turnapin Cottages	12 F3	Vale View	67 B2 [21]
Thirlestane Terrace	37 C3 [67]	Tonlegee Avenue	26 F1	Turnapin Green	12 F3	Vale View Avenue	59 B3
Thomas Court	37 C3	Tonlegee Drive	26 F1	Turnapin Grove	12 F3	Vale View Close	59 B3
Thomas Davis Street (South)	37 C3 [49]	Tonlegee Road	27 A1	Turnapin Lane	12 F3	Vale View Grove	59 B3
Thomas Davis Street (West)	36 F3	Tootenhill	52 D2	Turnberry	28 D1	Vale View Lawn	59 B3
Thomas Lane	38 D2 [17]	Tootenhill	52 E2	Turnberry Square	28 D1	Valentia Parade	38 D1 [34]
Thomas Moore Road	45 C1	Tor an Rí Close	34 F3	Turnpike Road	45 A2	Valentia Road	25 B3
Thomas Street	37 C3	Tor an Rí Court	34 F3	Turnstone Apts.	48 E3	Valeview Crescent	24 D2 [6]
Thomas Street West	37 C3 [65]	Tor an Rí Lane	34 F3	Turret Road	35 C2	Valeview Drive	24 D2
						Valeview Gardens	24 D2 [2]
						Valley Avenue	64 D1
						Valley Close (Loughlinstown)	64 D1
						Valley Park Avenue	24 D2 [1]

STREET NAME	PAGE/GRID REFERENCE
Valley Park Drive	23 C2
Valley Park Road	23 C2
Valley View	1 B1
Valley View	64 D1
Valley Walk	64 D1
Vally Drive (Loughlinstown)	63 C1
Vanessa Close	31 C3
Vanessa Lawns	31 C3
Vauxhall Avenue	37 B3 [30]
Vavasour Square	38 F3
Venetian Hall	26 E3
Ventry Drive	24 D4
Ventry Park	24 E4
Ventry Road	24 E4
Verbena Avenue (Foxrock)	59 A3
Verbena Avenue (Kilbarrack)	27 C1
Verbena Grove	27 C1
Verbena Lawn	27 C1
Verbena Park	27 C1
Verdemont	22 D2
Vergemount	47 C1 [12]
Vergemount Hall	47 C1 [9]
Vergemount Park	47 C1 [6]
Verney House	62 F3
Vernon Avenue	26 F4
Vernon Court (Clontarf)	39 C1 [3]
Vernon Court (Vernon Avenue)	26 F4
Vernon Drive	26 F3
Vernon Gardens	26 F4
Vernon Grove (Clontarf)	26 F4
Vernon Grove (Rathgar)	47 A2
Vernon Heath	26 F4
Vernon Park	26 F4
Vernon Rise	26 F3
Vernon Street	38 D3
Vernon Wood	39 C1 [4]
*Veronica Terrace (off Oliver Plunket Ave)	39 A3
Verschoyle Avenue	53 C2
Verschoyle Close	53 C2
Verschoyle Crescent	53 C2
Verschoyle Drive	53 C2
Verschoyle Glen	53 C2
Verschoyle Green	53 C2
Verschoyle Heights	53 C2
Verschoyle Park	53 C2
Verschoyle Place (off Lr Mount St)	38 E3
Verschoyle Rise	53 C2
Verschoyle Vale	53 C2
Verville Court	26 E4
Vesey Mews	49 C4
Vesey Park	34 D2
Vesey Place	49 C4
Vesey Terrace	34 D1 [2]
*Vevay Arcade (on Vevay Road)	67 C3
Vevay Crescent	67 C2 [58]
Vevay Road	67 C3
Vevay Villas	67 C3 [18]
Vicar Street	37 C3 [20]
Vico Road	60 F3
*Vico Terrace (0ff Vico Road)	60 F3
Victoria Avenue (Bray)	68 D2
Victoria Avenue (Donnybrook)	47 C1
*Victoria Cottages (off Irishtown Rd)	39 A3
Victoria Lane	25 B4 [9]
*Victoria Lane (off South Zion Road)	47 A2
Victoria Quay	37 C2
Victoria Road (Clontarf)	26 E4
Victoria Road (Dalkey)	60 F2
Victoria Road (Killiney)	60 E3
Victoria Road (Terenure)	46 F2
Victoria Street	38 D4
Victoria Terrace (Dalkey)	60 F2 [11]
Victoria Terrace (Dun Laoghaire)	50 D4 [8]
Victoria Terrace (Dundrum)	47 C4
Victoria Village (Rathgar)	46 F2 [7]
Victoria Village (Rathgar)	47 A2
Victoria Villas (Clontarf)	26 D4
Victoria Villas (Rathgar)	46 F2 [5]
Viking Place	37 C2 [47]
Viking Road	37 C2 [32]

STREET NAME	PAGE/GRID REFERENCE
*Villa Bank (Royal Canal Bank)	38 D1
Villa Blanchard	22 F2
Villa Building Apts.	30 D1 [15]
Villa Nova	48 F4
Villa Park Avenue	24 D4
Villa Park Drive	24 D4
Villa Park Gardens	24 D4
Villa Park Road	24 D4
Village Court Apts.	46 F4 [6]
Village Gate Arcade (on Main Street Bray)	67 C2
Village Green (Rathfarnham)	46 F3 [4]
Village Green (Tallaght)	55 A1
Village Heights	9 A4
Village Square (Tallaght)	55 A1
Village Weir	34 D1 [7]
Villarea Park	60 E1
Villiers Road	47 A2
Violet Hill Drive	24 F3
Violet Hill Park	24 F3
Violet Hill Road	24 F3
Virginia Drive	24 D2
*Virginia Hall (Belgard Square)	54 F1
Virginia Heights	54 F1
Virginia Park	24 D2
Viscount Avenue	12 F4

W

STREET NAME	PAGE/GRID REFERENCE
Wadelai Green	25 A2
Wadelai Road	25 A2
Wade's Avenue	27 A3
Wainsfort Avenue	46 D3
Wainsfort Crescent	46 D3
Wainsfort Drive	46 D2
Wainsfort Gardens	46 D3
Wainsfort Grove	46 E3
Wainsfort Manor	46 D3
Wainsfort Manor Crescent	46 D3
Wainsfort Manor Drive	46 D3
Wainsfort Manor Green	46 D3
Wainsfort Manor Grove	46 D3
Wainsfort Park	46 E3
Wainsfort Road	46 D3
Waldemar Terrace	47 B4 [12]
Walker's Cottages	38 D4 [37]
Walker's Court	38 D4 [38]
Walkinstown	45 B1
Walkinstown Avenue	45 B1
Walkinstown Close	45 B1
Walkinstown Crescent	45 B1
Walkinstown Cross	45 C2
Walkinstown Drive	45 B1
Walkinstown Green	45 B1
Walkinstown Parade	45 B1
Walkinstown Park	45 B1
Walkinstown Road	45 C1
Wallace Road	45 C1 [2]
Walnut Avenue (Clondalkin)	44 F3
Walnut Avenue (Whitehall)	25 B3
Walnut Close	44 F3
Walnut Court	25 B2
Walnut Drive	44 F3
Walnut Lawn	25 B3
Walnut Park	25 B3
Walnut Rise	25 B3
Walnut View	56 E2 [5]
Walsh Road	25 A3
Waltersland Road	58 F1
Waltham Terrace	48 F3
Walworth Road	38 D4 [33]
Warburton Terrace	68 D2 [7]
Ward's Hill	37 C3
Warner's Lane	38 E4 [18]
Warren Avenue	22 E3
Warren Close	22 E3
Warren Court	28 D1 [5]
Warren Crescent	22 E4
Warren Green (Carpenterstown)	22 E3
Warren Green (Sutton)	28 D1
Warren Park	22 E3
Warren Street	38 D4 [35]
Warrenhouse Road	28 D1
Warrenmount	37 C3 [27]
Warrenmount Place	37 C3 [28]

STREET NAME	PAGE/GRID REFERENCE
Warrenpoint	26 E4 [1]
Warrenstown	9 B4
Warrenstown Close	9 B4
Warrenstown Court	9 B4
Warrenstown Drive	9 B4
Warrenstown Garth	9 B4
Warrenstown Green	9 B4
Warrenstown Grove	9 B4
Warrenstown Lawn	9 B4
Warrenstown Park	9 B4
Warrenstown Place	9 B4
Warrenstown Rise	9 B4
Warrenstown Row	9 B4
Warrenstown Vale	9 B4
Warrenstown View	9 B4
Warrenstown Walk	9 B4
Warrenstown Way	9 B4
Warrington Lane	38 F3 [45]
Warrington Place	38 F3
Warwick Terrace	38 E4 [27]
Wasdale Grove	46 F2
Wasdale House	46 F3 [8]
Wasdale Park	46 F2
Washington Lane	46 E4
Washington Park	46 E4
Washington Street	37 C4
Waterfall Avenue	25 B4
Waterfall Road	26 F3
Watergate Estate	55 A1
Waterloo Avenue	38 F1
Waterloo Lane	38 E4
Waterloo Road	38 E4
Watermeadow Drive	54 F2
Watermeadow Park	55 A2
Watermill Avenue	27 A3
Watermill Close	55 A2
Watermill Drive	27 A3
Watermill Grove	55 A2
Watermill Lawn (Raheny)	27 A3 [1]
Watermill Lawn (Tallaght)	55 A2
Watermill Park	27 A3
Watermill Road	27 A3
Watermint Court	24 D3 [3]
Waterside Apts.	38 F3 [49]
Waterside Avenue	2 E2
Waterside Close	2 E3
Waterside Court	2 E2
Waterside Crescent (Portmarnock)	3 C4
Waterside Crescent (Swords)	2 E2
Waterside Drive	2 E2
Waterside Green	2 E3
Waterside Grove	2 E2
Waterside King's Hall	2 E2
Waterside Lawn	2 E2
Waterside Park	2 E2
Waterside Place	2 E3
Waterside Rise	2 E2
Waterside Road	2 E2
Waterside Walk	2 E2
Waterside Way	2 E2
Waterstown Avenue	35 C1
Waterville Road	22 F1
Waterville Row	22 E1
Waterville Terrace	22 F1
Watery Lane (Clondalkin)	44 E1
Watery Lane (Swords)	1 C1
Watkins Buildings	37 C3 [64]
Watling Street	37 C2
Watson Avenue	60 D4
Watson Drive	60 D4
Watson Park	60 D4
Watson Road	60 D3
Watson's Estate	60 D3
Waverley Avenue	25 C4
Waverley Terrace (Bray)	67 C2 [28]
Waverley Terrace (Harolds Cross Road)	46 F1 [12]
Waynestown	5 C1
Wayside Cottages	62 F2
Weaver Lane	38 D1 [39]
Weaver's Close	37 C3 [33]
Weaver's Row (Clonsilla)	21 C2
Weavers Row (The Coombe)	37 C3
Weaver's Square	37 C3 [37]

STREET NAME	PAGE/GRID REFERENCE
Weaver's Street	37 C3
Weavers Walk	21 C2
Webster's Cottages	49 A4 [8]
Wedgewood Estate	58 D2
Weirview	34 D1
Weirview Drive	58 F1
Weldon's Lane	15 A4
Well Road	2 D2 [2]
Wellesley Place	38 E1 [32]
Wellington Cottages	45 C3 [2]
Wellington Court (Bray)	67 C2 [56]
Wellington Court (Whitehall Road West)	46 D2 [5]
*Wellington Gardens (off Oakley Road)	47 B1
Wellington House	38 F4 [18]
Wellington Lane (Tallaght Road)	45 C3
Wellington Lane (Wellington Road)	38 F4
Wellington Park	46 D3
Wellington Place (Leeson Street)	38 F4
Wellington Place North	38 D1 [50]
Wellington Quay	38 D2
Wellington Road (Ballsbridge)	38 F4
Wellington Road (Phoenix Park)	37 A2
Wellington Road (Templeogue)	46 D3 [1]
Wellington Street (Dun Laoghaire)	50 D4 [1]
Wellington Street Lower	38 D1
Wellington Street Upper	38 D1
Wellmount Avenue	24 D2
Wellmount Court	24 D2
Wellmount Crescent	24 D2
Wellmount Drive	24 D2
Wellmount Green	24 D2
Wellmount Parade	24 D2
Wellmount Park	24 D2
Wellmount Road	24 D2
Wellpark Avenue	25 B3
Wellview Avenue	9 A3
Wellview Crescent	9 A3
Wellview Green	9 A3
Wellview Grove	9 A3
Wellview Park	9 A3
Wendell Avenue	4 D4
Werburgh Street	38 D3
Wesbury	58 E1
Wesley Heights	57 C2
Wesley House	38 E4 [38]
Wesley Lawns	57 C2
Wesley Place	37 C4 [7]
Wesley Road	47 A2
West Park Drive	24 F2
West Pier (Dun Laoghaire)	49 C3
West Pier (Howth)	30 D1
West Road	38 F1
West Terrace	36 F3
Westbourne Avenue	43 C1
Westbourne Close	43 C1
Westbourne Court	46 F3
Westbourne Drive	43 C1
Westbourne Grove	43 C1
Westbourne Lodge	56 D1
Westbourne Rise	43 C1
Westbourne Road	46 F3
Westbourne Terrace	67 C2 [52]
Westbourne View	43 C1
Westbrook	46 D2
Westbrook Lawns	53 C2
Westbrook Park	33 C2
Westbrook Road	47 B3
Westbury	34 D3
Westbury Avenue	34 D3
Westbury Close	34 D3
Westbury Drive	34 D2
Westbury Grove	33 C3 [1]
Westbury Park	34 D3
Westend Village	22 E2
Western Park Way	45 B3
Western Parkway Motorway	22 E4
Western Road	37 C4 [29]
Western Way	38 D1
Westerton Rise	57 C1 [1]
Westfield Avenue	33 B1
Westfield Park	68 D3

STREET NAME	PAGE/GRID REFERENCE
Westfield Road	46 F1
Westfield Terrace	49 A3 [10]
Westhampton Place	46 F2 [2]
Westhaven	8 F4
Westland Row	38 E3
Westmanstown	42 D3
Westminster Court	59 A3 [6]
Westminster Lawns	58 F2
Westminster Park	59 A2
Westminster Road	59 A3
Westmoreland Park	47 B1 [4]
Westmoreland Street	38 D2
Weston Avenue	47 B4
Weston Close (Churchtown)	47 B4
Weston Close (Leixlip)	33 B1
Weston Court	33 B2
Weston Crescent	33 B1
Weston Drive	33 B1
Weston Green	33 B1
Weston Grove	47 B4
Weston Heights	33 B2
Weston Lawn	33 B1
Weston Meadow	33 B2
Weston Park (Churchtown)	47 B4
Weston Park (Leixlip)	33 B1
Weston Road	47 B4
Weston Terrace	47 B4 [9]
Weston Way	33 B2
Westpark (Coolock)	26 F2
Westpark (Rathcoole)	52 F2
Westpark (Tallaght)	55 A1
Westview Terrace	67 C2 [29]
Westway Close	9 C4
Westway Grove	9 C4
Westway Lawns	22 F1
Westway Park	9 C4
Westway Rise	9 C4
Westway View	9 C4
Westwood Avenue	23 C2
Westwood Road	23 C2
Wexford Street	38 D3
Whately Place	58 E1
Wheatfield	67 C3
Wheatfield Grove	4 D4
Wheatfield Road (Palmerstown)	35 C2
Wheatfield Road (Portmarnock)	4 D4
Wheatfields Avenue	35 B3
Wheatfields Close	35 B3
Wheatfields Court	35 B3
Wheatfields Crescent	35 B3
Wheatfields Drive	35 B3
Wheatfields Grove	35 B3
Wheatfields Park	35 B3
Wheaton Court	36 F3 [20]
Whelan House Flats	39 A3 [29]
Whelan's Terrace	49 A3 [19]
Whitaker Hall	38 D1
Whitchurch Drive	56 F2
Whitchurch Road	56 F2
White Hall (Ballymount Road)	44 F3
White Oak	47 C3
White Oaks	67 B4
Whiteacre Close	25 B1
Whiteacre Court	25 B1
Whiteacre Crescent	25 B1
Whiteacre Place	25 B1
Whitebank Road	39 B3
Whitebarn Road	47 A4
Whitebeam Avenue	47 C2
Whitebeam Road	47 C2
Whitebeams Road	58 D2
Whitebrook Park	54 E1
Whitechapel Avenue	22 D2
Whitechapel Court	22 D2
Whitechapel Crescent	22 D2
Whitechapel Green	22 D2
Whitechapel Grove	22 D2
Whitechapel Lawn	22 D2
Whitechapel Park	22 D2
Whitechapel Road	22 D2
Whitechurch Abbey	56 F1 [4]
Whitechurch Avenue	56 F2
Whitechurch Close	56 F2
Whitechurch Court	56 F2
Whitechurch Crescent	56 F2
Whitechurch Drive	56 F2
Whitechurch Green	56 F2
Whitechurch Grove	56 F2
Whitechurch Hill	56 F2
Whitechurch Lawn	56 F2
Whitechurch Park	56 F2
Whitechurch Pines	56 F1
Whitechurch Place	56 F2
Whitechurch Road	56 F2
Whitechurch Stream	56 F1
Whitechurch View	56 F2
Whitechurch Walk	56 F2
Whitechurch Way	56 F2
Whitecliff	56 F1
*Whitefriar Gardens (off Whitefriar St)	38 D3
Whitefriar Place	38 D3 [42]
Whitefriar Street	38 D3 [41]
Whitehall	25 B2
Whitehall Close	46 D3
Whitehall Gardens	46 D3
Whitehall Mews	59 A2
Whitehall Park	46 D3
Whitehall Road (Churchtown)	47 A4
Whitehall Road (Kimmage)	46 D2
Whitehall Road West	46 D2
Whitehall Square	45 C2
White's Lane North	38 D1 [3]
White's Road	23 A4
White's Villas	60 F1 [10]
Whitestown	22 D1
Whitestown Avenue	22 D1
Whitestown Crescent	22 D1
Whitestown Drive (Blanchardstown)	22 D1
Whitestown Drive (Tallaght)	54 E2
Whitestown Gardens	22 D1
Whitestown Green	22 D1
Whitestown Grove	22 D1
Whitestown Park	22 D1
Whitestown Road	54 F2
Whitestown Walk	22 D1
Whitestown Way	54 F2
Whitethorn	35 B3
Whitethorn Avenue	26 D2
Whitethorn Close	26 D2
Whitethorn Crescent (Artane)	26 D2
Whitethorn Crescent (Coldcut Road)	35 B3
Whitethorn Drive	35 B3
Whitethorn Gardens	35 B3
Whitethorn Grove (Artane)	26 D2
Whitethorn Grove (Celbridge)	32 D3
Whitethorn Park (Artane)	26 D2
Whitethorn Park (Coldcut Road)	35 B3
Whitethorn Rise	26 D2
Whitethorn Road (Artane)	26 D2
Whitethorn Road (Milltown)	47 C2
Whitethorn Walk (Foxrock)	59 A2 [8]
Whitethorn Walk (Kill O'The Grange)	59 C2 [2]
Whitethorn Way	35 B3
Whitton Road	46 F2
Whitworth Avenue	38 E1 [40]
*Whitworth Parade (off Saint Patrick's Road)	25 A4
Whitworth Place	25 A4 [16]
Whitworth Road	25 A4
*Whitworth Terrace (off Russell Ave)	38 E1
*Wicklow Lane (off Wicklow Street)	38 D3
Wicklow Street	38 D3
Wicklow Way	65 A4
Wigan Road	25 A4
Wilderwood Grove	45 C4
Wilfield	39 A4 [15]
Wilfield Park	39 A4
Wilfield Road	39 A4
Wilford Court	67 B1
Wilfrid Road	46 F1
Wilfrid Terrace	46 F1 [5]
Willans Avenue	21 A1
Willans Drive	21 A1
Willans Green	21 A1
Willans Rise	21 A1
Willans Row	21 A1
Willans Way	21 A1
Willbrook	46 F4
Willbrook Downs	56 F1
Willbrook Estate	56 F1
Willbrook Grove	46 F4 [1]
Willbrook House	38 E4 [36]
Willbrook Lawn	46 F4
Willbrook Park	46 F4
Willbrook Road	46 F4
Willbrook Street	46 F4
William Pallister House	46 F4 [22]
William Street North	38 E1
William Street South	38 D3
William's Lane	38 D2 [27]
William's Park	47 A1
*William's Place Lower (off Portland Place)	38 D1
William's Place South	38 D3 [6]
William's Place Upper	38 D1 [29]
Willie Bermingham Place	37 B3 [31]
Willie Nolan Road	15 A4
Willington Avenue	45 C3
Willington Court	45 C3
Willington Crescent	45 C3
Willington Drive	45 C3
Willington Green	45 C3
Willington Grove	45 C3
Willington Lawn	45 C3 [1]
Willington Park	45 C3
Willow Avenue (Clondalkin)	44 D2
Willow Avenue (Loughlinstown)	64 D1
Willow Bank	49 C4
Willow Bank Drive	56 E1
Willow Bank Park	56 E1
Willow Court (Clondalkin)	44 D2
Willow Court (Loughlinstown)	64 D1
Willow Crescent	64 D1
Willow Drive	44 D2
Willow Gate	57 B1
Willow Grove (Clondalkin)	44 D2
Willow Grove (Cornelscourt)	59 B3
Willow Grove (Kill O'The Grange)	59 C1 [13]
Willow Lodge	23 A4
Willow Mews	48 E1
Willow Park (Dunboyne)	7 B2
Willow Park (Foxrock)	59 A2 [6]
Willow Park (Loughlinstown)	64 D1
Willow Park Avenue	24 F1
Willow Park Close	24 F1
Willow Park Crescent	24 F1
Willow Park Drive	25 A1
Willow Park Grove	24 F1
Willow Park Lawn	24 F1
Willow Park Road	24 F1
Willow Place (Booterstown)	48 F3
Willow Place (Loughlinstown)	64 D1
Willow Road (Dundrum)	57 B1
Willow Road (Fox & Geese)	45 A1
Willow Terrace	48 F2
Willow Vale	60 D4
Willow Wood Close	21 C2
Willow Wood Downs	21 C2 [1]
Willow Wood Green	21 C2
Willow Wood Grove	21 C2
Willow Wood Lawn	21 C2
Willow Wood Park	21 C2
Willow Wood Rise	21 C2
Willow Wood View	21 C2
Willow Wood Walk	21 C1
Willowbank	57 C1
Willowbrook Grove	31 C3
Willowbrook Lawns	31 C3
Willowbrook Lodge	31 C3
Willowbrook Park	31 C3
Willowfield	39 B4
Willowfield Avenue	47 C4
Willowfield Park	47 C4
Willowmount	48 F3 [3]
Willows Court	21 C2
Willows Drive	21 C2
Willows Green	21 C2
Willows Road	21 C2
Willsbrook Avenue	34 E2
Willsbrook Crescent	34 F1
Willsbrook Drive	34 E1
Willsbrook Gardens	34 E1
Willsbrook Green	34 E2
Willsbrook Grove	34 E1
Willsbrook Park	34 E1
Willsbrook Place	34 E1
Willsbrook Road	34 E2
Willsbrook View	34 E2
Willsbrook Way	34 E1
Wilmont Avenue	60 E1 [1]
Wilson Crescent	48 D4
Wilson Road	48 E4
Wilson Terrace	37 C3 [44]
Wilson's Place	38 E3 [35]
Wilton Place	38 E4
Wilton Terrace	38 E4
Windele Road	25 A3 [12]
Windermere	21 B2
Windgate Rise	30 D3
Windgate Road	30 D3
Windmill Avenue (Crumlin)	46 D1
Windmill Avenue (Swords)	1 C2
Windmill Crescent (Crumlin)	46 D1 [2]
Windmill Crescent (swords)	1 A2
Windmill Lands	1 C2
Windmill Lane	38 E2
Windmill Park	46 D1
Windmill Rise	1 C2
Windmill Road	46 D1
Windmillhill	51 C3
Windrush	64 E2 [7]
Windsor Avenue	25 C4
Windsor Court	59 B1 [1]
Windsor Drive	59 B1
Windsor Mews	3 B2 [5]
Windsor Park	59 B1
Windsor Place	38 E3 [32]
Windsor Road	47 B1
Windsor Terrace (Dun Laoghaire)	50 D4
Windsor Terrace (Malahide)	3 B3
Windsor Terrace (Ranelagh)	38 D4
Windsor Villas	25 C4 [3]
Windy Arbour	47 C3
Winetavern Street	38 D2
Wingfield	62 E1
Winton Avenue	47 A2
Winton Grove	46 F2 [19]
Winton Road	38 E4
Wogans Field	33 A1
Wolfe Tone Avenue	50 D4 [4]
Wolfe Tone Quay	37 B2
Wolfe Tone Square East	67 C3
Wolfe Tone Square Middle	67 C3
Wolfe Tone Square North	67 C3
Wolfe Tone Square South	67 C3
Wolfe Tone Square West	67 C3
Wolfe Tone Street	38 D2 [12]
Wolseley Street	37 C4 [24]
Wolstan Haven Avenue	31 C3
Wolstan Haven Road	31 C3
Wolverton Glen	60 E2
Wood Avens	35 A3
Wood Dale Close	55 B2
Wood Dale Crescent	55 B2
Wood Dale Drive	55 B2
Wood Dale Green	55 B2
Wood Dale Green	55 C2
Wood Dale Grove	55 C2
Wood Dale Oak	55 C2 [1]
Wood Dale View	55 C2
Wood Lane	37 C2 [40]
Wood Quay	38 D2
Wood Street	38 D3
Woodbank Avenue	23 C2
Woodbank Drive	23 C2
Woodberry (Carpenterstown)	22 E3
Woodberry (Lucan)	34 D3
Woodbine Avenue	48 E2
Woodbine Close	27 A1
Woodbine Drive	27 A1
Woodbine House	48 E2 [4]
Woodbine Park (Booterstown)	48 E2

STREET NAME	PAGE/GRID REFERENCE
Woodbine Park (Raheny)	27 A1
Woodbine Road (Booterstown)	48 E2
Woodbine Road (Raheny)	27 A1
Woodbine Terrace (Dundrum)	47 C4 [2]
Woodbrook Court	22 D3
Woodbrook Crescent	22 D3
Woodbrook Downs	64 E4
Woodbrook Glen	67 C1
Woodbrook Hall	22 D3
Woodbrook Lawn	67 C3
Woodbrook Park (Carpenterstown)	22 D3
Woodbrook Park (Templelogue)	46 D4
Woodbrook Square	22 D3
Woodcliff Heights	30 E2
Woodfarm Avenue	35 C2
Woodfarm Cottages	35 C1 [6]
Woodfarm Drive	35 C2
Woodfield	56 D2
Woodfield Cottages	36 F3 [8]
Woodfield Place	36 F3 [15]
Woodford	58 E2
Woodford Avenue	44 F1
Woodford Close	44 F1
Woodford Court (Harold's Cross)	46 F1 [10]
Woodford Court (Monksfield)	44 F1
Woodford Crescent	44 E1
Woodford Downs	44 F1
Woodford Drive	44 E1
Woodford Garth	44 E1
Woodford Green	44 F1
Woodford Grove	44 F1
Woodford Heights	44 F1
Woodford Hill	44 F1
Woodford Lawn	44 F1
Woodford Meadows	44 E1
Woodford Parade	44 E1
Woodford Park	44 F1
Woodford Park Road	44 E1
Woodford Rise	44 F1
Woodford Road	44 E1
Woodford Terrace	44 F1
Woodford View	44 F1
Woodford Villas	44 E1
Woodford Walk	44 F1
Woodford Way	44 F1
Woodhaven	47 C2 [10]
Woodhazel Close	25 A1
Woodhazel Terrace	25 A1
Woodlands (Blakestown Road)	22 D1 [2]
Woodlands (Malahide)	14 F1
Woodlands (Maynooth)	17 B3
Woodlands (Rathgar)	47 A2 [1]
Woodlands Avenue (Cornelscourt)	59 C3
Woodlands Avenue (Stillorgan)	48 E4
Woodlands Court	15 A1
Woodlands Drive (Johnstown Road)	59 C3
Woodlands Drive (Stillorgan)	48 E4
Woodlands Park (Johnstown Road)	59 C3
Woodlands Park (Mount Merrion)	48 F4
Woodlands Road	59 C3
Woodlawn	12 F4
Woodlawn Avenue	12 F4
Woodlawn Close	12 F4
Woodlawn Court	12 F4
Woodlawn Crescent (Churchtown)	47 B4
Woodlawn Crescent (Coolock Lane)	12 F4
Woodlawn Drive	12 F4
Woodlawn Green	12 F4
Woodlawn Grove (Churchtown)	47 B4 [7]
Woodlawn Grove (Coolock Lane)	12 F4
Woodlawn Park (Churchtown)	47 B4
Woodlawn Park (Coolock Lane)	12 F4
Woodlawn Park (Dun Laoghaire)	59 C1 [4]
Woodlawn Park (Tallaght)	55 C2
Woodlawn Park Avenue	55 B1
Woodlawn Park Drive(Firhouse)	55 B1
Woodlawn Park Grove	55 C2
Woodlawn Rise	12 F4
Woodlawn Terrace	47 B4 [2]
Woodlawn View	12 F4
Woodlawn Villas	59 C1 [16]
Woodlawn Walk	12 F4
Woodlawn Way	12 F4
Woodleigh	47 A2 [2]
Woodley Court	58 D1 [4]
Woodley Park	58 D1
Woodley Road	60 D3
Woodpark (Ballinteer)	57 B2
Woodpark (Blanchardstown)	22 F2
Woods End	22 F2
Woodscape	34 D3
Woodside (Clontarf)	26 F4
Woodside (Howth)	30 D2
Woodside (Leixlip)	19 C4
Woodside (Rathfarnham)	47 A3
Woodside Drive	47 A3
Woodside Grove	47 A3
Woodside Road	57 C3
Woodstock Court	47 B1 [2]
Woodstock Gardens	47 B1 [24]
Woodstock Park	56 D1
Woodstown	55 C2
Woodstown Abbey	56 D2
Woodstown Abbey	55 D2
Woodstown Avenue	55 C2
Woodstown Close	55 C2
Woodstown Court	55 C2 [2]
Woodstown Crescent	55 C2
Woodstown Dale	55 C2
Woodstown Drive	55 C2
Woodstown Gardens	55 C2
Woodstown Green	55 C2
Woodstown Heath	55 C2
Woodstown Height	55 C2
Woodstown Hill	55 C2
Woodstown House	46 F4 [21]
Woodstown Lane	56 D2
Woodstown Lawn	55 C2
Woodstown Meadow	55 C2
Woodstown Parade	55 C2
Woodstown Park	55 C2
Woodstown Place	55 C2
Woodstown Rise	55 C2
Woodstown Road	55 C2
Woodstown Vale	55 C2
Woodstown Walk	55 C2
Woodstown Way	55 C3
Woodthorpe	58 E1 [5]
Woodtown Way	56 D3
Woodvale Avenue	21 C1
Woodvale Crescent	21 C1
Woodvale Drive	21 C1
Woodvale Garth	21 C1
Woodvale Green	21 C1
Woodvale Grove	21 C1
Woodvale Park	21 C1
Woodvale Way	21 C1
Woodview (Celbridge)	32 D2
Woodview (Lucan)	33 C2
Woodview Close	27 A1
Woodview Cottages	46 F3 [1]
Woodview Court (Dunboyne)	7 B3
Woodview Court (Stillorgan)	58 F1 [1]
Woodview Court Apts.	33 C2
Woodview Drive	67 C3 [4]
Woodview Grove	22 E2
Woodview Heights (Dunboyne)	7 B3
Woodview Heights (Lucan)	33 C2
Woodview Park (Ardara Avenue)	27 A1
Woodview Park (Castleknock)	23 A3
Woodville Avenue	34 E1
Woodville Close	34 E1
Woodville Court	26 E1
Woodville Green	34 E1
Woodville Grove	34 E1
Woodville House	26 D1 [4]
Woodville Lawn	34 E1
Woodville Road	25 A4 [7]
Woodville Walk	34 E1
*Wormwood Gate (off Bridge Street Lower)	37 C2
Wyattville	64 D1
Wyattville Close	64 D1
Wyattville Hill	64 D1
Wyattville Park	64 D1
Wyattville Road	64 D1
Wyckham Grove	57 C1
Wyckham Park Road	57 B1
Wyckham Place	57 C1
Wyckham Way	57 C1
Wynberg Park	49 B4
Wyndham Park	67 C2
Wynnefield House	47 A1
Wynnefield Park	47 A1 [21]
Wynnefield Road	47 A1
Wynnsward Drive	47 C2
Wynnsward Park	47 C2
Wyteleaf Grove	14 D4
Wyvern Estate	60 E3

X

STREET NAME	PAGE/GRID REFERENCE
Xavier Avenue	38 F1 [3]

Y

STREET NAME	PAGE/GRID REFERENCE
Yale	48 D3
Yankee Terrace	49 A4
Yarnhall Street	38 D2 [45]
Yeates Hall	59 B4
Yeates Way	35 C4
Yellow Meadows Ave	44 F1
Yellow Meadows Drive	44 E1
Yellow Meadows Estate	44 F1
Yellow Meadows Grove	44 E1
Yellow Meadows Lawn	44 E1
Yellow Meadows Park	44 E1
Yellow Meadows Vale	44 E1
Yellow Road	25 C2
Yellow Walls	3 A2
Yellow Walls Road	3 A2
Yellownook Avenue	59 C3
Yewlands Terrace	46 F2
York Avenue	47 A1
York Road (Dun Laoghaire)	49 C4
York Road (Rathmines)	47 A1
York Road (Ringsend)	39 A2
York Street	38 D3
York Terrace	49 C4 [4]

Z

STREET NAME	PAGE/GRID REFERENCE
Zion Road	47 A2
Zoo Road	37 A2
*Zuma Terrace (on Mount Drummond Ave)	37 C4

LIST OF STREETS NOT NAMED ON MAP BUT SHOWN AS SMALL NUMBERS

PAGE/GRID REF		STREET NAME
1	A2	1 Grove Court (Brackenstown Road)
1	C1	1 Elmwood Court
		2 Rathbeale Court
2	D2	1 St Columcille's Crescent
		2 Well Road
		3 Colmcille Court
		4 The Crescent (Swords)
		5 New Road (Swords)
3	A2	1 Hillcrest (Malahide)
3	B2	1 Fair Haven
		2 Haven View
		3 Railway Court
		4 The Priory (Malahide)
		5 Windsor Mews
3	C2	1 Seabank Court (Malahide)
4	D4	1 Alder Court
7	B2	1 St Mary's Terrace (Dunboyne)
		2 Avondale Square
7	B3	1 Congress Park
		3 Hamilton Court (Dunboyne)
9	A4	1 Ashmount
		2 Ashfield Park (Huntstown Way)
		3 Riverpark View
		4 Riverside (Mulhuddart)
11	A4	1 St Margaret's Court
11	C4	1 Termon Court
12	D4	1 St Pappin's Street
		2 The Hampton
		3 Linnbhla
		4 The Charter
		5 The Turnpike
		6 The Maieston
		7 The Kilmore Apts
		8 The Goulding Apts
		9 The Claremont Apts.
13	A4	1 Newbury Terrace
13	B4	1 Greenlawns
		2 Clonshaugh Rise
		3 Ferrycarrig Green
		4 Clonshaugh Court
14	D4	1 Templeview Vale
		2 Elmfield Close
		3 Clonmellon Grove
		4 Beechbrook Grove
14	F2	1 St Lawrence O'Toole Avenue
		2 Church Avenue (Portmarnock)
		3 Suncroft Avenue
		4 St Brigid's Avenue
		5 St Ann's Square Lower
		6 St Anne's Square (Portmarnock)
		7 Hazel Court
15	A4	1 Seapoint Avenue (Baldoyle)
		2 Parochial Avenue
		3 Back Lane (Baldoyle)
		4 The Mall (Baldoyle)
		5 Breffni Gardens
		6 Brookstone Lane
		7 Seapoint Court (Baldoyle)
		8 College Street (Baldoyle)
		9 Admiral Court
17	C3	1 Kelly's Lane (Maynooth)
		2 Fagan's Lane
		3 Coates Lane
		4 Geraldine Court
		5 Court House Square
		6 Leinster Cottages
		7 Charter House

PAGE/GRID REF		STREET NAME
18	D3	1 Leinster Lodge Apts.
		2 Leinster Court
20	D4	1 Cypress Springs
21	A1	1 Hayworth Close
21	C1	1 Meadow Dale
		2 Oakview Grove
21	C2	1 Willow Wood Downs
		2 Cedar Grove
22	D1	1 Briarwood Park
		2 Woodlands (Blakestown Road)
		3 Briarwood Road
		4 Ashcroft Grove
22	D2	1 Coolmine Mews
		2 Kirkfield
22	D3	1 The Orchard (Carpenterstown)
22	E3	1 Rosehaven
		2 Luttrell Park Heath
		3 Station View Apts.
22	F2	1 Herbert Crescent
22	F3	1 The Crescent (Castleknock)
		2 Castleknock Court
22	F4	1 The Sand Holes
23	A3	1 Beech Park Crescent
		2 Hadleigh Green
		3 Beechpark Close
		4 Park Court Apts
		5 Castleknock Manor
23	B3	1 Mill Lane (Ashtown)
23	B4	1 Castleknock Gate
23	C2	1 Eastwood
23	C4	1 Baggot Terrace
		2 St Vincent's Cottages
		3 St Joseph's Cottages
		4 Ashtown Lodge
24	D1	1 Cardiffsbridge Grove
		2 Casement Close (off Barry Road)
24	D2	1 Valley Park Avenue
		2 Valeview Gardens
		3 Mellowes Court
		4 Mellowes Crescent
		5 Ravens Court
		6 Valeview Crescent
		7 Church View (Finglas)
		8 Patrickswell Court
24	D3	1 Clearwater Court
		2 Cassian Court
		3 Watermint Court
24	D4	1 Roosevelt Cottages
		2 Convent View Cottages (Cabra)
		3 Convent View Crescent
		4 Lyndon Gate
		5 Park Spring's
		6 Park Crescent House
24	E1	1 Georges Road
		2 Gofton Hall
		3 Heath Square
24	E2	1 Ballygall Place
		2 Glenhill Villas
		3 St Helena's Court
		4 Johnstown Gardens
		5 Collins Row
		6 Glebe View (Finglas)
24	E4	1 Kilkieran Court
		2 St Finbarrrts Court
24	F2	1 Drapier Green
		2 Glasnamana Place
		3 Johnstown House
24	F3	1 Northland Grove
		2 Northland Drive

PAGE/GRID REF		STREET NAME
		3 Glasnevin Oaks
		4 Bellevue Cottages
		5 Cremore Villas
24	F4	1 St Philomena's Road
		2 Tower View Cottages
		3 Delvin Road
		4 Bengal Terrace
		5 Fertullagh Road
		6 Connaught Parade
		7 Clareville Court
		8 Shandon Green
		9 Shandon Mill
25	A1	1 Pinewood Grove
		2 Shanliss Gardens
		3 Oldtown Park
25	A3	1 Claremont Avenue
		2 Church Avenue (Glasnevin)
		3 St David's Terrace (Glasnevin)
		4 Barron Place
		5 Comyn Place
		6 St Ita's Road
		7 St Malachy's Road
		8 St Michael's Road
		9 Addison Place
		10 St Mobhi Grove
		11 Clonmore Court
		12 Windele Road
		13 O'Brien's Place North
		14 O'Neachtain Road
		15 River Gardens
		16 Mobhi Court
		17 The Haven (Glasnevin)
25	A4	1 Millmount Villas
		2 De Courcy Square
		3 Enniskerry Road (Phibsborough)
		4 Devery's Lane
		5 Prospect Square
		6 Glendalough Road
		7 Woodville Road
		8 St Teresa's Road (Glasnevin)
		9 St Teresa's Place
		10 Botanic Villas
		11 St Alphonsus Avenue
		12 St Brendan's Road
		13 St Clement's Road
		14 Botanic Park
		15 O'Brien's Terrace
		16 Whitworth Place
25	B1	1 Ailesbury
25	B2	1 Tourmakeady Road
25	B3	1 Clonturk Avenue
		2 The Village (Drumcondra)
		3 Clare Park Villas
		4 Beaucourt
		5 The Cloisters (Grace Park Road)
		6 Clonturk Court
		7 All Hallows Lane
25	B4	1 Tom Clarke House
		2 St Joseph's Avenue (Ballybough)
		3 Clonturk Gardens
		4 Kingston Lodge
		5 Holycross Avenue
		6 Robert Street (Jones's Road)
		7 Robert Place
		8 College Manor
		9 Victoria Lane
		10 Edgewood (Richmond Road)
		11 College Mews
25	C1	1 Ivy Court
		2 Beaumont Court

PAGE/GRID REF		STREET NAME
		3 Beaumont Wood
25	C2	1 Chestnut Court
		2 Dromnanane Road
		3 Dromnanane Park
		4 Thorndale Court
		5 Laragh Flats
		6 Collindale
		7 Beaumont Hall
		8 The Crescent (off Beaumont Rd)
25	C3	1 Torlogh Parade
		2 Morrogh Terrace
		3 Calderwood Grove
		4 Croydon Terrace
		5 Sion Hill Court
		6 Collins Court (Collins Avenue)
		7 St Vincent's Court
		8 Collins Close
25	C4	1 Annadale Avenue
		2 Shelmartin Terrace
		3 Windsor Villas
		4 St Joseph's Terrace (Fairview)
		5 St Declan's Terrace
		6 St Aidan's Park
		7 Fairview Green
		8 Torlogh Gardens
		9 Marino Mart
		10 Fairview Passage
		11 Fairview Terrace
		12 Caragh Court
		13 Marino Court
		14 Fairview Court
		15 Bushfield Square
		16 Melrose Court
		17 Elton Court (Marino)
		18 Belmount Court
26	D1	1 Kilbarron Court
		2 Cromcastle Close
		3 St Luke's Court
		4 Woodville House
		5 Kilmore Court
		6 Cromcastle Court
26	D3	1 Cherrymount Crescent
		2 Cherrymount Grove
26	D4	1 Brighton Avenue (Clontarf)
		2 Hollybrook Court Drive
		3 Hollybrook Court
		4 Strandville House
		5 Haddon Park
		6 Crescent House
		7 Kilronan Court
		8 Glenbrian Hall
		9 Hollybrook Wood
		10 Hollybrook Manor
26	E1	1 Lismeen Grove
		2 Brookville Crescent
		3 Coolock Village Close
26	E2	1 Maryfield Avenue
		2 Artane Cottages Lower
		3 Artane Cottages Upper
26	E3	1 St Brigid's Drive (Killester)
		2 St Brigid's Court
		3 Quarry Cottages
		4 Killester Court
		5 Killester Park
26	E4	1 Warrenpoint
		2 St John's Wood (Clontarf)
		3 Lambourne Village
		4 Knights Bridge
		5 St David's Court
		6 The Paddock's (Clontarf)
26	F1	1 Elton Court (Coolock)
		2 Ayrefield Park
26	F2	1 Gorsefield Court

PAGE/ GRID REF   **STREET NAME**

26   F4   1 Park View (Mount Prospect Lawns)

27   A1   1 Elton Walk
2 Glentworth Park
3 Invermore Grove
4 Curracloe Drive
5 Laracor Gardens
6 Gables

27   A3   1 Watermill Lawn (Raheny)
2 St Annғs Court

27   A4   1 Seafield Grove
2 St Gabriel's Court
3 Rinn na Mara

27   B1   1 Howth Junction Cottages
2 Swan's Nest Court
3 Redmond's Court
4 Briarsfield Walk
5 Briarfield Villas
6 Swan's Nest Apts.

27   B2   1 Thornville Terrace
2 Greendale Court

27   B3   1 The Grove (Raheny)
2 The Court (Raheny)

27   C1   1 Bayside Crescent

27   C2   1 Mariners Court
2 Del Val Court

28   D1   1 Sutton Court
2 Seafield (Sutton)
3 St Domhnach's Well Street
4 Marine Cove
5 Warren Court
6 Moyclare Gardens

29   A1   1 James McCormack Gardens
2 St Catherine's Terrace
3 Radcliffe

29   B1   1 Corrbridge Terrace (off Claremont Road)
2 Avalon Apts.
3 Corr Castle Apts
4 Offington Manor Apts

29   B3   1 Shielmartin Park
2 Martello Terrace (Sutton)

30   D1   1 Dunbo Terrace
2 Evora Terrace
3 Findlater Building Apts.
4 Dunbo Hill
5 Howth Terrace
6 Harbour View (Howth)
7 Marine Villas
8 St Lawrence Quay
9 Island View Apts.
10 Howth House Apts
11 Abbey Terrace
12 Evora Crescent
13 Cuan na Mara
14 Howth Peninsula Apts.
15 Villa Building Apts.

30   D2   1 St Lawrence's Terrace (Howth)
2 Seaview Terrace (Howth)
3 St Mary's Road (Howth)
4 St Mary's Place (Howth)
5 St Nessan's Terrace
6 The Haggard (Howth)
7 Hillside Terrace
8 Dungriffan Villas
9 St Nessan's Close
10 Thormanby Grove
12 St Nessans Court
13 Crosstrees Court
15 Forge Court
16 Campbell Court

30   E2   1 Cannon Rock View
2 Upper Cliff Road
3 St Nessan's Apts

31   C2   1 Crodaun Court

31   C3   1 The Deanery
2 The Close (Oldtown Mill)
3 St Judes Apts.

32   D4   1 Balfe Gardens

33   A1   1 Ralph Square
2 Liffey View Apts.

33   C3   1 Westbury Grove

34   D1   1 Sarsfield Terrace
2 Vesey Terrace
3 Hanbury Lane (Lucan)
4 Sarsfield Court (Lucan)
5 The Square (Lucan)
6 Dispensary Lane (Lucan)
7 Village Weir
8 Brookvale
9 Mount Gandon
10 Gandon Mews
11 Old Rectory
12 The Village Centre
13 The Village Court
14 The Orchard (Lucan)
15 Mill Bank

34   D2   1 Arthur Griffith Court

34   E1   1 Edmondsbury Court

34   F2   1 Liffey Hall

34   F3   1 Foxborough Hall
2 Foxborough Crescent

35   A3   1 Neilstown Village Court
2 Liscarne Dale
3 Collinstown Crescent

35   A4   1 Ballymanagin Lane
2 Moorfield Close
3 Neilstown Cottages
4 Rosebank Place
5 Rosebank Hall

35   B4   1 Rosebank View
2 Rosebank Court

35   C1   1 The Covert
2 Glenside Villas
3 Clarkeville Terrace
4 Red Cow Cottages
5 St Fintan's Terrace
6 Woodfarm Cottages

35   C2   1 Culmore Park
2 Glenaulin Green

35   C4   1 Cherry Orchard Way

36   D2   1 Rossaveal Court

36   D3   1 Le Fanu Drive

36   E2   1 Park Lane (Chapelizod)
2 Maidens Row
3 Hibernian Terrace
4 St Laurence Grove
5 St Mary's Terrace (Chapelizod)
6 Isolde Gardens
7 Liffey Terrace
8 Clayton Terrace
9 St Laurence Terrace (Chapelizod)
10 Mullingar Terrace
11 Riverview Court
12 New Row
13 Isolde House Apts.
14 Distillery House Apts.
15 Tristan House Apts.

36   E3   1 O'Hogan Road
2 Lynch's Lane
3 St Lawrence Glen
4 Convent Lawns

36   E4   1 Old Naas Road Cottages
2 Millrose Estate
3 The Laurels (Bluebell)
4 Hollybrooke

36   F3   1 Park Street
2 Phoenix Street
3 Inchicore Terrace North
4 Murray's Cottages
5 Partridge Terrace
6 Tyrconnell Street
7 Tyrconnell Villas
8 Woodfield Cottages

    9 St Patrick's Terrace (Inchicore)
10 Abercorn Terrace
11 Granite Terrace
12 Ring Street
13 Inchicore Square
14 Oblate Drive
15 Woodfield Place
16 Hampton Court (Tyreconnell Road)
17 St James's Place (Inchicore)
18 St George's Villas (Inchicore)
19 Abercorn Square
20 Wheaton Court

36   F4   1 Muirfield Drive
2 Bernard Curtis House
3 La Touche Court (Bluebell)
4 Grove Court (Bluebell)
5 Landsdowne Valley Park

37   A1   1 Parkview Court (Blackhorse Avenue)

37   A2   1 Islandbridge Court
2 Hospital Lane
3 Sarah Place
4 Park Place
5 Salmon Pool Apts

37   A3   1 Hybreasal
2 Turvey Avenue
3 Connolly Gardens
4 Goldenbridge Gardens
5 Goldenbridge Terrace
6 Camac Close
7 Kearn's Place
8 St Michael's Estate
9 Memorial Road (Inchicore Road)
10 Camac Court
11 Heuston Square
12 Tyrone Place
13 Lady's Lane
14 Prospect Terrace (Kilmainham)
15 Carrickfoyle Terrace
16 Goldenbridge Walk
17 The Belfry (Inchicore)
18 Beaconsfield Court
19 Rosemount Court (Inchicore Rd)
20 Rowserstown Lane
21 Myra Cottages
22 Harcourt Lodge
23 Ashmount Court
24 Millbrook Terrace
25 St Jame's Wood
26 Bulfin Court
27 St Helen's Terrace
28 Millview Cottages

37   A4   1 Iveagh Gardens
2 Lissadel Green

37   B1   1 Glenmore Road
2 Glencar Road
3 Everton Avenue
4 Ardmore Avenue
5 Glenard Avenue (Cabra)
6 Doon Avenue
7 St David's Terrace (Blackhorse Avenue)
8 Aughrim Place
9 Carnew Street
10 Ashford Street
11 Dunard Road
12 Aughrim Villas
13 Arklow Street
14 Drumalee Court
15 Phoenix Court (North Circular Road)
16 Ashford Place
17 Ashford Cottages
18 Auburn Walk
19 Phoenix Manor

37   B2   1 Thor Place
2 Halliday Square
3 Sullivan Street
4 Kinahan Street
5 Montpelier Gardens
6 Arbour Terrace
7 Temple Street West
8 Swords Street
9 Black Street
10 Findlater Street (Nth Circular Rd)
11 Niall Street
12 Finn Street
13 Park Avenue West
14 De Burgh Road
15 Brodin Row
16 Temple Court (Arbour Hill)
17 Phoenix Court (Arbour Hill)

37   B3   1 Irwin Street
2 Old Kilmainham Village
3 Cromwell's Quarters
4 Shannon Terrace
5 Cameron Square
6 St Maignenn's Terrace
7 Donnellan Avenue
8 McDowell Avenue
9 O'Reilly Avenue
10 Madison Road
11 Mayfield Road (Kilmainham)
12 Ewington Lane
13 Glenmalure Park
14 Rialto Buildings
15 Herberton Park
16 Clarke Terrace
17 Mallin Avenue
18 Ave Maria Road
19 Morning Star Road
20 Emerald Square
21 St James's Avenue (James's Street)
22 Church Avenue South (Dolphin's Barn)
23 Fatima Mansions (off James's Walk)
24 Irwin Court
25 McCarthy Terrace
26 Almeida Avenue
27 Almeida Terrace
28 St John's Cottages
29 Carrick Terrace
30 Vauxhall Avenue
31 Willie Bermingham Place
32 Brandon Terrace
33 St John's Terrace (Mount Brown)
34 Knocknarrow Terrace
35 Millbrook Court
36 Prior Hall
37 Faulkner's Terrace
38 Southview Terrace
39 Owen's Avenue
40 O'Quinns Avenue
41 Traynor Place
42 Burke Place
43 Phoenix View

37   B4   1 Dolphin House
2 St James's Terrace (Dolphin's Barn)
3 Rialto Drive
4 Moracrete Cottages
5 Dolphin Park
6 Reilly's Avenue
7 Dolphin Court

37   C1   1 Aughrim Lane
2 Annamoe Parade
3 Cherrymount Park
4 Rosemount Road
5 Fingal Place
6 Phibsborough Avenue
7 Leslie's Buildings

PAGE/GRID REF — STREET NAME

8 Great Western Square
9 Great Western Villas
10 Kirwan Street Cottages
11 Norton's Avenue
27 A1 12 Royal Canal Terrace
13 Marne Villas
14 St Elizabeth's Court
15 St Joseph's Place (Prussia Street)
16 St Joseph's Court
17 Castle Terrace (Phibsborough Ave)
18 Great Western Avenue
19 King's Court
20 Rathdown Square
21 Aughrim Court
22 Spire View
23 Shea's Court
37 C2 1 Ostman Place
2 Stanhope Street
3 George's Lane
4 Blackhall Parade
5 Brown Street North
6 Friary Avenue
7 Nicholas Avenue
8 Sarsfield Quay
9 Hendrick Place
10 Arran Quay Terrace
11 Church Street New
13 Blackhall Street
14 Morgan Place
15 Phoenix Street West
16 Stable Lane (Smithfield)
17 Arran Street West
18 Burgess Lane
19 Liffey Street West
20 Thundercut Alley
21 Oxmantown Lane
22 Catherine Lane
23 Fitzwilliam Place North (Grangegorman)
24 Morning Star Avenue
25 Church Avenue West (Church Street)
26 Father Mathew Square
27 Ard Right Place
28 Houghton Terrace
29 Rosemount Terrace (Arbour Hill)
30 Murtagh Road
31 Sigurd Road
32 Viking Road
33 Olaf Road
34 St Mary's Terrace (Arbour Hill)
35 Slade Row
36 Paul Street
37 Smithfield Terrace
38 Ellis Street
39 Stanley Street
40 Wood Lane
41 Friary Grove
42 Coke Lane
43 Lincoln Lane
44 Ellis Court
45 Malachi Road
46 Provost Row
47 Viking Place
48 Robert Emmett Close
49 Haymarket House
37 C3 1 Marshal Court Apts.
2 Grand Canal Place
3 Rainsford Avenue
4 Market Street South
5 Long's Place
6 Park Terrace (Coombe)
7 St Margaret's Terrace
8 Huxley Crescent
9 Darley's Terrace
10 Maxwell Street
11 Fingal Street
12 Pimlico Cottages

13 Taylor's Lane (Pimlico)
14 St Catherine's Lane West
15 Allingham Street
16 Meath Market
17 Brabazon Street
18 Brabazon Row
19 Molyneux Yard
20 Vicar Street
21 Garden Lane
22 Mark's Alley West
23 Oscar Square
24 Cow Parlour
25 Newmarket Street
26 Mill Lane (Newmarket)
27 Warrenmount
28 Warrenmount Place
29 O'Carolan Road
30 Geoffrey Keating Road
31 Madden Road
32 New Row Square
33 Weaver's Close
34 Ardee Row
35 Brabazon Place
36 Sweeney's Terrace
37 Weaver's Square
38 Poole Street
39 St John's Avenue (The Coombe)
40 Brabazon Square
41 Gray Square
42 Meath Square
43 Reginald Square
44 Wilson Terrace
45 Catherine Street (Swift's Alley)
46 Spitalfields
47 Hanover Street West
48 Brickfield Lane
49 Thomas Davis Street (South)
50 John's Lane West
51 Swan Alley
52 Old Mill Court
53 Ebenezer Terrace
54 Harman Street
55 Donore Terrace
56 Hammond Street
57 St Michael's Terrace (Blackpitts)
58 St John Street
59 Marion Villas
60 Pyro Villas
61 Ivy Terrace
62 Coombe Court
63 Emerald Terrace
64 Watkins Buildings
65 Thomas Street West
66 Marrowbone Lane
67 Thirlestane Terrace
68 Marshal Lane
37 C4 1 Hamilton Street
2 Ingram Road
3 Rehoboth Avenue
4 Priestfield Cottages
5 St Anne's Road South
6 Lyllymore Terrace
7 Wesley Place
8 Arbutus Avenue
9 Greenmount Avenue
10 Emmet Street (Harold's Cross)
11 Greenville Avenue
12 Gilbert Road
13 Parnell Court
14 Greenmount Square
15 Hatter's Lane
16 Limekiln Lane (Harold's Cross)
17 Clanbrassil Close
18 Harold's Cross Cottages
19 Greenmount Court
20 St Clare's Avenue

21 Donovan Lane
22 Griffith Square
23 Briansboro Terrace
24 Wolseley Street
25 Merton Avenue
26 Rutledge Terrace
27 Merton Park
28 Priestfield Drive
29 Western Road
30 Mount Drummond Court
31 Boyne Court
32 Sandford Park (Sandford Avenue)
33 Sandford Gardens (Sandford Avenue)
34 Leonard's Court
35 Greenville Place
36 Harold Bridge Court
37 Armstrong Street
38 Le Vere Terrace
39 Swanward Court
40 Darley Street
41 Argus House
38 D1 1 Phibsborough Place
2 Lynch's Place
3 White's Lane North
4 St Vincent Street North
5 Sarsfield Street (Phibsborough)
6 O'Connell Avenue
7 St Mary's Ave North (Mountjoy Street)
8 Palmerston Place
9 Mountjoy Street Middle
10 St Mary's Terrace (Mountjoy Street)
11 Belvidere Court
12 Hardwicke Place
13 Graham Court
14 Frederick Lane North
15 Grenville Lane
16 Parnell Place
17 St Ignatius Avenue
18 Glengarriff Crescent
19 De Velara Place
20 Eccles Court
21 Cavendish Row
22 Kelly's Lane (Phibsborough)
23 Myrtle Street
24 Leo Avenue
25 Josephine Avenue
26 Synnott Row
27 St Joseph Street
28 Sherrard Avenue
29 William's Place Upper
30 Killarney Parade
31 Kenmare Parade
32 Muckross Parade
33 Derrynane Parade
34 Valentia Parade
35 St Benedicts Gardens
36 Arranmore Avenue
37 St Peter's Square
38 Peter's Court
39 Weaver Lane
40 Gardiner Row
41 Temple Lane North
42 Bath Lane
43 George's Place (Temple Street)
44 Nerney's Court
45 Hardwicke Lane
46 Frederick Court
47 Britain Place
48 St Mary's Place North
50 Wellington Place North
51 St Michael's Place
52 Maunsell Place
53 Blessington Lane
54 Graham's Row
55 Berkeley Avenue
56 Blessington Court
57 Berkeley Place

58 Bethesda Place
59 St Joseph's Place (Dorset Street Lower)
60 Temple Buildings
61 Library View Villas
62 St Peter's Close
63 Dorset Place
64 Glengariff Parade
65 Sherrards Court
66 St Laurence Place (Western Way)
67 Strong's Court
68 Broadstone Avenue
69 Shamrock Street
38 D2 1 Linenhall Terrace
2 Lisburn Street
3 Lurgan Street
4 Linenhall Parade
5 Anne Street North
6 George's Hill
7 Anglesea Row
8 Green Street Little
9 Ryder's Row
10 Jervis Lane Upper
11 Jervis Lane Lower
12 Wolfe Tone Street
13 Chapel Lane (Parnell Street)
14 Sampson's Lane
15 Moore Lane
16 Henry Place
17 Thomas Lane
18 Litton Lane
19 Earl Place
20 Prince's Street North
21 Sycamore Street
22 Cope Street
23 Ball's Lane
24 Sackville Place
25 Findlater Place
26 O'Rahilly Parade
27 William's Lane
28 Proby's Lane
29 Hotel Yard
30 Bachelors Way
31 Byrne's Lane (Jervis St)
32 Mary Street Little
33 Meetinghouse Lane
34 Campbell's Court
35 Dominick Lane
36 Strand Street Little
37 Ormond Square
38 Foster Place South (College Green)
39 Aston Place
40 Crampton Quay
41 Church Lane (College Green)
42 Dame Lane
43 Abbey Cottages
44 St Michan's Street
45 Yarnhall Street
46 Temple Lane South
47 Fownes Street Upper
48 Cows Lane
49 Copper Alley
49 Curved Street
38 D3 1 Hanover Lane
2 St Nicholas Place
3 Castle Street (Cork Hill)
4 Iveagh Buildings
5 Cathedral Lane
6 William's Place South
7 Dame Lane
8 Longford Street Great
9 Longford Street Little
10 Aungier Place
11 Redmond's Hill
12 Protestant Row
13 Montague Lane
14 O'Neill's Buildings
15 Pleasants Lane
16 Dame Court

PAGE/GRID REF	STREET NAME
17	Harry Street
18	Clonmel Street
19	Stable Lane (Harcourt Street)
20	Liberty Lane
21	Pleasants Place
22	Camden Villas
23	Aungier Lane
24	Proud's Lane
25	Montague Court
26	Montague Place
27	Stokes Place
28	Glovers Alley
29	Balfe Street
30	Johnson's Court
31	Lemon Street
32	Duke Lane Upper
33	Anne's Lane
34	Coppinger Row
35	Chatham Row
36	Johnson Place
37	Bow Lane East
38	Digges Lane
39	Fade Street
40	John Field Road
41	Whitefriar Street
42	Whitefriar Place
43	Cathedral View Court
44	Cathedral View Walk
45	Longford Lane
46	Malpas Terrace
47	Hanover Square
48	St Francis Square
49	Coolevin Road
50	Malpas Court
51	Christchurch Square
52	John's Lane East
53	Church Lane South
54	Camden Buildings
55	Bride Close
56	Noel Purcell Park

38 D4

PAGE/GRID REF	STREET NAME
1	Fitzgerald Street
2	Desmond Street
3	St Kevin's Road
4	Kingsland Park Avenue
5	Kingsland Parade
6	Portobello Harbour
7	Richmond Row
8	Blackberry Lane (Rathmines)
9	Bessborough Parade
10	Richmond Place (Rathmines)
11	Ontario Terrace
12	Atlumney Villas
13	Cheltenham Place
14	Harcourt Lane
15	Albert Place West
16	Tom Kelly Road
17	Florence Street
18	Albert Terrace (Charlemont Street)
19	Peter Place
20	Charlemont Gardens
21	St Ultan's Flats
22	Richmond Villas
23	Gordon Place
24	Synge Place
25	Synge Lane
26	Avenue Road
27	McMahon Street
28	Camden Market
29	St Kevin's Cottages
30	Camden Court
31	Lennox Terrace
32	Charlotte Way
33	Walworth Road
34	Martin Street
35	Warren Street
36	Portobello Place
37	Walker's Cottages
38	Walker's Court
39	Mountpleasant Parade
40	Mountpleasant Terrace

PAGE/GRID REF	STREET NAME
41	Bannaville
42	Garden View
43	Richmond Mews
44	Richmond Place South (Sth Richmond St)
45	Alexandra Terrace (Portobello)
46	Bloomfield Park (Rathmines)
47	Grove Avenue (Harold's Cross)
48	Spencer Street South
49	Bloomfield Cottages
50	Oakfield Place
51	Arbutus Place
52	St Kevin's Parade
53	Lissenfield
54	Harold's Cross Cottages
55	Saddlers Court
56	O'Hara Avenue
57	Adelaide Court
58	Portobello Harbour Apts
59	Hazelwood House

38 E1

PAGE/GRID REF	STREET NAME
1	O'Sullivan Avenue
2	Sackville Gardens
3	Ardilaun Road
4	Ballybough Lane
5	Charlemont Parade
6	Clonmore Terrace
7	Clinch's Court
8	Richmond Crescent
9	Richmond Cottages (Summerhill)
10	Richmond Parade
11	Bailey's Row
12	Sean Tracey House
13	Killarney Avenue
14	Preston Street
15	Shamrock Place
16	Shamrock Terrace
17	Aldborough Parade
18	Drumcondra Park
19	Belvidere Avenue
20	Richmond Lane
21	Fitzgibbon Lane
22	Mountjoy Place
23	Langrishe Place
24	Gloucester Place Upper
25	Gloucester Place
26	Summerhill Place
27	Bella Street
28	Matt Talbot Court
29	Newcomen Court
30	Gilford Place
31	Shamrock Cottages
32	Wellesley Place
33	Brendan Behan Court
34	St Margaret's Avenue North
35	St Joseph's Terrace (North Circular Road)
36	Mountjoy Parade
37	Richmond Cottages North
38	St Joseph's Villas (Summerhill)
39	Clonmore Villas
40	Whitworth Avenue
41	Foster Place North
42	Ballybough Avenue
43	Ballybough Court
44	Trinity Terrace
45	Tyrrell Place
46	Summer Place
47	Sean O'Casey Avenue
48	Rutland Place North
49	Thompson's Cottages
50	Portland Close
51	Beaver Close
52	Gloucester Diamond
53	Gloucester Place Lower
54	Gloucester Place Lower
55	Rutland Cottages

PAGE/GRID REF	STREET NAME
56	Buckingham Village
57	Duke Row
58	Ulster Terrace (North Strand)
59	Seville Terrace
60	St Joseph's Mansions
61	Lourdes House
62	St Mary's Mansions
63	Avondale House
64	Liberty House
65	Mountjoy Square Apts
66	North Clarence St Flats
67	Clarence St Great North
68	Croke Villas
69	Campbell's Row (off Portland Street N)
70	Portland Square
71	Campbell's Lane (off Belvidere Ave)
72	Aldborough House

38 E2

PAGE/GRID REF	STREET NAME
1	Pearse House
2	Erne Place Lower
3	Magennis Place
4	Mark's Lane
5	Deverell Place
6	Talbot Lane (Talbot Street)
7	Marlborough Place
8	Northumberland Square
9	Beresford Lane
10	Shaw Street
11	Leinster Market
12	Prince's Street South
13	Card's Lane (Pearse St)
14	Spring Garden Lane
15	Dowling's Court
16	Peterson's Court
17	Mabbot Lane
18	Harbour Court
19	Abbey Street Old
20	Frenchman's Lane
21	Moland Place
22	Spencer Row
23	Emerald Place
24	Corn Exchange Place
25	Luke Street
26	Mark Street
27	Custom House Harbour
28	Bracken's Lane
29	Magennis Square
30	Brunswick Villas (Pearse Street)
31	Crinan Strand
32	Champions Avenue
33	Lombard Court
34	Harbour Master Place
35	Marlborough Court
36	George's Dock

38 E3

PAGE/GRID REF	STREET NAME
1	Cumberland Street South
2	Boyne Lane
3	Bass Place
4	Erne Place Little
5	Grant's Row
6	Meade's Terrace
7	Holles Row
8	Merrion Place
9	Baggot Court
10	Royal Hibernian Way
11	Setanta Place
12	Schoolhouse Lane (Kildare Street)
13	Leinster Lane
14	Clare Lane
15	Roger's Lane
16	Leeson Lane
17	Duke Lane Lower
18	Dawson Lane
19	College Lane (Trinity College)
20	Erne Terrace Front
21	Erne Terrace Rere
22	Devlin's Place

PAGE/GRID REF	STREET NAME
23	Harmony Row
24	Molesworth Place
25	Kildare Place
26	Merrion Close
27	Merrion Street Lower
28	Baggotrath Place
29	Little Fitzwilliam Place
30	Bell's Lane
31	Ely Place Upper
32	Windsor Place
33	Mackies Place
34	Holles Place
35	Wilson's Place
36	Stephen's Place
37	Stable Lane (Leeson St Lr)
38	Fitzwilliam Court (Fitzwilliam Square)
39	Hagan's Court
40	Convent Close
41	Herbert Lane

38 E4

PAGE/GRID REF	STREET NAME
1	Leeson Close
2	Hatch Lane
3	Leeson Place
4	Dartmouth Place
5	Dartmouth Terrace
6	Dartmouth Lane
7	Cambridge Terrace (Ranelagh)
8	Chelmsford Avenue
9	Old Mountpleasant
10	Mander's Terrace
11	Sussex Terrace
12	Convent Place
13	Hatch Place
18	Warner's Lane
19	Leeson Walk
20	Northbrook Lane
21	Selskar Terrace
22	Mountpleasant Place
23	Swan Grove
24	Orchard Lane (Ranelagh)
25	Berystede
26	Temple Place
27	Warwick Terrace
28	Sibthorpe Lane
29	Dexter Terrace
30	Leeson Village
31	Swan Place
32	Pembroke Place (Pembroke St Upr)
33	Burlington Gardens
34	Burleigh Court
35	Crosbie House
36	Willbrook House
37	Cullen's Wood House
38	Wesley House
39	Flemming House

38 F1

PAGE/GRID REF	STREET NAME
1	Northbrook Terrace
2	Stoney Road (East Wall)
3	Xavier Avenue
4	Strandville Avenue (North Strand)
5	Hibernian Avenue
6	Gaelic Street
7	Hyacinth Street
8	Courtney Place
9	Annesley Avenue
10	Enaville Road
11	Crescent Gardens
12	St Barnabas Gardens
13	Boolavogue Road
14	Russell Avenue East
15	Taaffe's Place
16	St Patrick's Avenue (Fairview)
17	St Mura's Terrace
18	Malachi Place
19	Strandville Place
20	James's Street North
21	Leinster Street East
22	Portside Court
23	Austin's Cottages

PAGE/GRID REF	STREET NAME
	24 St Brigid's Cottages (North Strand)
	25 Caledon Court
38 F2	1 Emerald Street
	2 Bellman's Walk
	3 First Avenue (Seville Place)
	4 Blythe Avenue
	5 Laurence Place East
	6 Second Avenue (Seville Place)
	7 Third Avenue (Seville Place)
	8 Fourth Avenue (Seville Place)
	9 Carbury Terrace
	10 Irvine Cottages
	11 Alexander Terrace (North Wall)
	12 Spencer Dock (North Wall)
	13 Pickford's Terrace
	14 Ferryman's Crossing
	15 Merchant's Square
	16 Mariner's Port
38 F3	1 Clarence Place Great
	2 Eblana Villas (Lr Grand Canal St)
	3 Island Villa
	4 Carlingford Parade
	5 Hastings Street
	6 Penrose Street
	7 Ormeau Street
	8 Somerset Street
	9 Gerald Street
	10 Bath Avenue Place
	11 Margaret Place
	12 Malone Gardens
	13 Shaw's Lane
	14 Albert Place East
	15 Love Lane East
	16 Estate Cottages (Northumberland Rd)
	17 St Mary's Lane
	18 Haddington Place
	19 Cranmer Lane
	20 Lansdowne Lane
	21 Erne Place
	22 Brunswick Place
	23 Conway Court
	24 South Dock Road
	25 Rostrevor Terrace (Lr Grand Canal St)
	26 Greenore Terrace
	27 Hogan Avenue
	28 Grattan Court East
	29 Grattan Place
	30 Albert Court (Grand Canal St. Lower)
	31 Macken Villa
	32 Mount Street Crescent
	33 Leitrim Place
	34 Emerald Cottages
	35 South Dock Place
	36 Berkeley Terrace
	37 Lansdowne Terrace
	38 Pearse Grove
	39 Camden Lock
	40 Clanwilliam Terrace
	41 Clanwilliam Square
	42 Northumberland Place (Grand Canal St. Upr.)
	43 Lansdowne Crescent
	44 Lansdowne Villas
	45 Warrington Lane
	46 Temple Court (Off Hogan Place)
	47 Cannon Mews East
	48 Beggars Bush Court
	49 Waterside Apts.
	50 Shelbourne Park Mews
	51 Shelbourne Village
38 F4	1 Eastmoreland Place
	2 Eastmoreland Lane
	3 Shelbourne Lane
	4 Herbert Cottages
	5 Shelbourne Avenue
	6 Carlton Villas (Ballsbridge)
	7 Lansdowne Gardens
	8 Beatty's Avenue
	9 Dodder View Cottages
	10 Granite Place
	11 Morehampton Square
	12 Morehampton Mews
	13 Estate Cottages (Shelbourne Rd)
	14 Ballsbridge Terrace
	15 Pembroke Place (Ballsbridge)
	16 Crampton Avenue
	17 Iveragh Court
	18 Wellington House
	19 Clyde Court
	20 Raglan Hall Apts.
39 A2	1 Fishermans Wharf
	2 Alexandra Quay
	3 Thorncastle Court Apts.
39 A3	1 Cambridge Street
	2 Fitzwilliam Street (Ringsend)
	3 St Patrick's Villas
	4 Seapoint Terrace (Ringsend)
	5 The Square (Irishtown)
	6 St Brendan's Cottages
	7 Cambridge Avenue
	8 Tritonville Avenue
	9 Tritonville Crescent
	10 Seafort Gardens
	11 Leukos Road
	12 Clonlara Road (Ringsend)
	13 Kyle-Clare Road
	14 Parkview Place
	15 Canon Mooney Gardens
	16 Caroline Row
	17 Havelock Terrace
	18 Dodder Terrace
	19 Ennis Grove
	20 Londonbridge Drive
	21 Strasburg Terrace
	22 Tritonville Close
	23 St James Terrace (Sandymount)
	24 Cambridge Court
	25 Lansdowne Hall
	26 Sandymount Court
	28 O'Rahilly House Flats
	29 Whelan House Flats
	30 Ropewalk Place
	31 Kennedy Court
	32 Simpsons Lane
	33 Summerfield (Ringsend)
39 A4	1 Sandymount Green
	2 Sandymount Castle Road
	3 Sandymount Castle Drive
	4 Sydenham Road (Ballsbridge)
	5 Sandymount Castle
	6 Churchill Terrace
	7 Prince of Wales Terrace (Sandymount)
	8 Railway Cottages
	9 Martin White Chalets
	10 Gilford Court
	11 Homelee
	12 Lynton Court
	13 Spafield Terrace
	14 Adair
	15 Wilfield
	16 Park Court (Sandymount)
	17 Dromard Terrace
	18 Seafort Cottages
	19 Seafort Terrace
	20 Seafort Villas
	21 Claremont Court (Sandymount)
	22 The Sweepstakes
	23 Ballsbridge Park
	24 Lansdowne Square
	25 Ballsbridge Gardens
	26 Ballsbridge Avenue
	27 Ballsbridge Wood
39 B1	1 Alverno
	2 Haddon Court
39 B3	1 Prospect Terrace (Sandymount)
39 B4	1 Gilford Terrace
	2 Sandymount Castle Park
	3 Martello View
	4 Bethany House
	5 Hempenstal Terrace
	6 Martello Wood
39 C1	1 Churchgate Avenue
	2 St Joseph's Square
	3 Vernon Court (Clontarf)
	4 Vernon Wood
43 C1	1 Bawnogue Cottages
	2 Nangor Place
	3 St Catherines Grove
44 D1	1 St Patrick's Avenue (Clondalkin)
	2 Leinster Terrace
	3 Beech Row (Nangor Road)
	4 The Mill Pond Apts.
	5 Nangor Crescent
	6 Cherrywood Villas
44 D2	1 Church View (Clondalkin)
	2 Green Isle Court
44 E1	1 St Killian's Park
	2 Monastery Heights
	3 Bettysford
	4 Castle Crescent
	5 Friar's Walk
	6 Riverside (Clondalkin)
	7 Millview
44 E2	1 St Brigid's Park (Clondalkin)
44 F1	1 Knockmitten Close
	2 Knockmitten Lane North
44 F3	1 Pinetree Grove
	2 Belgard Close
44 F4	1 Pinetree Crescent
45 A3	1 Parkhill Heights
A3	2 Parkview (Kilnamanagh)
45 B2	1 Tibradden Close
45 B3	1 Three Rock Close
	2 Ballymount Cottages
45 B4	1 Tymon North Court
	2 Tymon North Place
45 C1	1 Field Avenue
	2 Wallace Road
	3 Percy French Road
	4 O'Dwyer Road
	5 Esposito Road
	6 Landsdowne Valley
	7 Somerville Park
	8 Harty Court
45 C2	1 St Peter's Terrace (Walkinstown)
45 C3	1 Willington Lawn
	2 Wellington Cottages
45 C4	1 Spawell Cottages
46 D1	1 Sunville Green
	2 Windmill Crescent (Crumlin)
	3 Father Kit Court
	4 St. Agnes Terrace
	5 Rockmeadon Court
	6 Brug Chroimlinn
46 D2	1 Muckross Drive
	2 Lorcan O'Toole Court
	3 Stannaway Court
	4 Beechfield Mews
	5 Wellington Court (Whitehall Road West)
46 D3	1 Wellington Road (Templeogue)
46 D4	1 Hillcrest (Templeogue)
	2 Hillcrest Manor
46 E1	1 Tonguefield Road
	2 Cloyne Road
	3 Faughart Road
	4 Clonmacnoise Grove
	5 Bedford Court
	6 Poddle Green
	7 Larrisa Court
46 E2	1 Riversdale Grove (Kimmage)
	2 Hazel Park
	3 Kimmage Court
	4 Rathland Drive
	5 Brookfield Green
	6 Brookfield Court (Kimmage)
	7 Hazelbrook Apts.
	8 Clonard Court
	9 Riverside (Kimmage)
	10 Baroma
	11 Clonallen
	12 Cranford Court (Kimmage)
46 E3	1 Templeville Park
	2 Fortfield Court
46 E4	1 Butterfield Meadow
	2 Brookmount Court
46 F1	1 Mount Harold Terrace
	2 Le Bas Terrace
	3 Mountain View Avenue
	4 Manor Villas
	5 Wilfrid Terrace
	6 Fitzpatrick's Cottages
	7 Ryan's Cottages (Harold's Cross)
	8 Parkview Court (Harold's Cross)
	9 Gandon Close
	10 Woodford Court (Harold's Cross)
	11 Kenilworth Manor
	12 Waverley Terrace (Harolds Cross Road)
	13 Smith's Lane
	14 Kengar Mews
	15 Mount Argus Square
	16 Mountain View Court (Harold's Cross)
	17 Casimir Court
	18 Kerrygold House
	19 Kenilworth Lodge
46 F2	1 Ashdale Park
	2 Westhampton Place
	3 Terenure Place
	4 Eagle Hill Avenue
	5 Victoria Villas (Rathgar)
	6 Maple Drive (Harold's Cross)
	7 Victoria Village (Rathgar)
	8 Frankfort Court
	9 Frankfort Flats
	10 Rathdown Court (off Templeogue Road)
	11 Rathgar Villas
	12 Greenlea Place
	13 Brighton Green
	14 McMorrough Road
	15 Earls Court (Terenure)
	16 Rathgar Park
	17 Olney Grove
	18 Eaton Hall
	19 Winton Grove
	20 Beechlawn Manor
	21 Beechlawn Mews
	22 Eaton Court (Terenure)
	23 Carlisle Court
	24 Fairfield House
	25 Beaumont House

PAGE/GRID REF	STREET NAME
	26 Minnow Brook
	27 Loughmorne House
46 F3	1 Woodview Cottages
	2 St Agnes Terrace (Rathfarnham)
	3 Dodder Park Drive
	4 Village Green (Rathfarnham)
	5 The Falls
	6 Tourville Lodge
	7 Le Brett Terrace
	8 Wasdale House
	9 Crannagh Castle
	10 Crannagh Court
46 F4	1 Willbrook Grove
	2 Tara Hill Grove
	3 Beaufort Villas
	4 Glenann
	5 St Mary's Terrace (Rathfarnham)
	6 Village Court Apts.
	7 The Park Lands
	8 The Lakelands
	9 The Woodlands (Rathfarnham)
	10 Beaufort Court
	11 The Castlelands
	12 Rathfarnham Mill
	13 The Laurels (Rathfarnham)
	14 Loftus Square
	15 Blackburn Square
	16 Otterbrook
	17 Stonepark Orchard
	18 Castle Court (Rathfarnham)
	19 A.W. Pugin House
	20 Theresa House
	21 Woodstown House
	22 William Pallister House
	23 Frances Ball House
	24 De Bret House
	25 Hogan House
47 A1	1 Rathmines Park
	2 Leinster Square
	3 Prince Arthur Terrace
	4 Swanville Place
	5 Castlewood Terrace
	6 Castlewood Place
	7 Grosvenor Park
	8 Stone Mews
	9 Turrets Flats
	10 Purser Gardens
	11 Esker Villas
	12 Parker Hill
	13 Alma Terrace
	14 Observatory Lane
	15 Belgrave Place (Rathmines)
	16 Cambridge Villas
	17 Salem Court
	18 Maxwell Court
	19 The Mews (Rathmines)
	20 Roland Court
	21 Wynnefield Park
	22 Mount Anthony Estate
	23 Louis Lane
	24 Castlewood Close
	25 Rathmines Avenue Court
	26 Cosy Lodge
	27 Newington Terrace
	28 Rathgar Court
47 A2	1 Woodlands (Rathgar)
	2 Woodleigh
	3 Highfield Court
	4 Cowper Mews
	5 Garville Place
	6 Garville Drive
	7 Rathgar Park
	8 Orwell Mews
	9 Stratford
	10 Garville Court

PAGE/GRID REF	STREET NAME
47 A3	1 The Willows (Orwell Road)
	2 Stirling Park
	3 Orwell Court
	4 Newtown Villas (Braemor Road)
	5 Newtown Court (Rathgar)
	6 Riverbank (Braemor Road)
	7 Orwell Bank
	8 Crannagh Way
	9 Landore
	10 Park View (Rathgar)
	11 Ard Na Gréine
	12 Newtown House
	13 Dodder Vale
47 A4	1 Castle Court (Rathfarnham)
	2 Nutgrove Court
47 B1	1 Sallymount Gardens
	2 Woodstock Court
	3 Collier's Avenue
	4 Westmoreland Park
	5 Field's Terrace
	6 Rugby Villas
	7 Beechwood Park (Rathmines)
	8 Bushfield Avenue
	9 Charleston Court Flats
	10 Oakley Court
	11 Cullenswood Road
	12 Moran's Cottages
	13 Mountain View Cottages (Ranelagh)
	14 Sallymount Terrace
	15 Chelmsford Lane
	16 Belgrave Villas (Rathmines)
	17 Bushfield Place
	18 Smith's Cottages (Donnybrook)
	19 Beechdale Mews
	20 Oakley Square
	21 Palmerston Close
	22 Moyne Court
	23 Oakley Park (Ranelagh)
	24 Woodstock Gardens
	25 Marlborough Lane
47 B2	2 Strand Terrace
	3 St Luke's Crescent
	4 Balnagowan
	5 Temple Square
	6 Milltown Grove (Clonskeagh)
	7 Milltown Hill
	8 Thorncliff
	9 Shanagarry
	10 Dodder Bank
47 B3	1 Dartry Cottages
	1 St Columbanus Place
	2 St Gall Gardens North
	3 St Gall Gardens South
	4 Milltown Terrace (Dundrum)
47 B4	1 Glenbower Park
	2 Woodlawn Terrace
	3 Beaumont Close
	4 Briarly Court
	5 St Nathy's House
	6 Ardtona Avenue
	7 Woodlawn Grove (Churchtown)
	8 Henley Court
	9 Weston Terrace
	10 Frankfort
	11 Rosemount Terrace (Dundrum)
	12 Waldemar Terrace
	13 Airfield Drive
	14 Nutgrove Avenue
	15 Annadale
	16 St Nathy's Villas
	17 Sweetmount House

PAGE/GRID REF	STREET NAME
47 C1	1 St Broc's Cottages
	2 Pembroke Cottages (Donnybrook)
	3 Belmont Park (Donnybrook)
	4 The Crescent (Donnybrook)
	5 Harmony Avenue
	6 Vergemount Park
	7 Norwood Park
	8 Brookvale Road (Donnybrook)
	9 Vergemount Hall
	10 Sandford Gardens (Donnybrook)
	11 Auburn Road (Donnybrook)
	12 Vergemount
	13 Eglinton Square
	14 Mount Sandford
	15 Rowan Hall
	16 Cedar Hall
	17 Millbrook Village
	18 Simmonscourt Terrace
	19 Brookfield (Donnybrook)
	20 Harmony Court
	21 Riverside Walk
	22 Eglinton Wood
	23 Shamrock Hill Mews
	24 Donnybrook Castle
47 C2	1 Prospect Lane
	2 Beech Hill Villas
	3 Beech Hill Crescent
	4 Beech Hill Terrace
	5 Palmerston Grove
	6 Clonskeagh Drive
	7 Clonskeagh Square
	8 St Bridget's Flats
	9 Crannagh
	10 Woodhaven
	11 Richview Villas
47 C3	1 Annaville Grove
	2 Olivemount Grove
	3 Friarsland Avenue
	4 Harlech Villas
	5 Gledswood Drive
	6 Olivemount Terrace
	7 Glenard Hall
	8 Belfield Close
	9 Roebuck Lawn
	10 Roebuck Crescent
47 C4	1 Sunnybank Court
	2 Woodbine Terrace (Dundrum)
	3 Alexandra Villas
	4 Roseville Terrace
	5 Pembroke Cottages (Dundrum)
	6 Pembroke Terrace
	7 Claremont Terrace
	8 Glenville Terrace
	9 St Joseph's Grove
48 D1	1 Merrion View Avenue
	2 Simmonscourt Avenue
	3 Simmon's Court
	4 Ailesbury Close
48 D2	1 Nutley Square
	2 Donnybrook Close
	3 Donnybrook Green
	4 Greenfield Manor
48 D3	1 Hopkins Square
	2 Finglas Square
	3 Hayden Square
	4 Hyde Square (Fosters Avenue)
	5 Meenan Square
48 D4	1 Edenwood (Goatstown)
	2 Sophie Baret Residence
48 E1	1 Merrion Court

PAGE/GRID REF	STREET NAME
	2 Merrion Gates
	3 Strand Lane
48 E2	1 Seafield Park
	2 Bellevue Court
	3 Merrion Crescent
	4 Woodbine House
48 E3	1 The Stables
	2 Mountbrook
48 E4	1 Greygates (Sycamore Crescent)
	2 Beaufield Mews
	3 Ashurst (Mount Merrion)
48 F2	1 St Helen's Villas
48 F3	1 Martello Terrace (Booterstown)
	2 Pembroke Cottages (Booterstown)
	3 Willowmount
	4 Cherbury Mews
48 F4	1 St Helier's Copse
	2 Orpen Dale
	3 Park Villas (Stillorgan)
	4 Cedar Square (Stillorgan)
	5 Grove House Gardens
	6 Orpen Green
49 A3	1 Newtown Villas (Blackrock)
	2 Maretimo Road
	3 Ben Inagh Park
	4 Maretimo Gardens West
	5 Craigmore Gardens
	6 George's Place (Blackrock)
	7 St Anne's Square (Blackrock)
	8 Bath Place
	9 Rockwell Cove Apts.
	10 Westfield Terrace
	11 Idrone Mews
	12 Brusna Cottages
	13 Collins Court (Blackrock)
	14 Patrick's Row
	15 Eagle Hill
	16 Maretimo Terrace
	17 Maretimo Place
	18 Maretimo Villas
	19 Whelan's Terrace
	20 Carbury Place
	21 Sweetman's Avenue
	22 Lisalea
	23 Frascati Court
	24 Frascati Hall
	25 Temple Court (Blackrock)
49 A4	1 Avondale Park (Blackrock)
	2 Prince Edward Terrace Lower
	3 Prince Edward Terrace Upper
	4 Lindenvale
	5 Twin Cottages
	6 Fieldview Cottages
	7 Cullen's Cottages
	8 Webster's Cottages
	9 Rockville Estate
	10 Avoca Hall
	11 Brookfield Grove
	12 Brookfield Court (Blackrock)
49 B3	1 Ardenza Terrace
	2 Tobernea Terrace
	3 Ardenza Park
	4 Seapoint Terrace (Blackrock)
49 B4	1 Montpelier Place
	2 Montpelier Manor
	3 The Willows (Monkstown)
	4 The Maples (Monkstown)
	5 The Cedars (Monkstown)
	6 The Alders
	7 The Poplars
	8 Stradbrook Gardens
	9 Brighton Terrace (Monkstown)

Street Index 136

PAGE/ GRID REF — STREET NAME

10 Belgrave Place (Monkstown)
11 Belgrave Terrace (Monkstown)
12 Brooklawn Avenue
13 Brooklawn Wood
14 Rockford Terrace
15 Beaupark Downs
16 Drayton Close
17 Heathfield
18 Southdene
19 Arundel
20 Stradbrook Hall
21 The Beeches (Monkstown)
22 Brighton Lane
23 Knocknagow

49 C4 1 Rosary Gardens West
2 Barrett Street
3 Smith's Villas
4 York Terrace
5 St Mary's Street
7 Oakwood
8 Harbour Terrace
9 Grosvenor Terrace (Dun Laoghaire)
10 Clifton Lane
11 Clifton Avenue
12 Richmond Green
13 Clifton Terrace
14 Alma Place
15 Seaview Terrace (Dun Laoghaire)
16 Synnott Terrace
17 Bentley Villas
18 St Michael's Terrace (Dun Laoghaire)
19 St Brendan's Terrace (Dun Laoghaire)
20 Northcote Terrace
21 Knapton Court
22 Knapton Lawn
23 Northcote Place
24 Cambridge Terrace (Dun Laoghaire)
25 Primrose Hill (Dún Laoghaire)
26 Mounttown Cottages
27 Knapton Terrace
28 Pakenham
29 Monkstown Gate
30 Alma Park
31 Clearwater Cove
32 Marina House Apts
33 The Anchorage
34 Smyth Gardens

50 D4 1 Wellington Street (Dun Laoghaire)
2 Rosary Gardens East
3 Desmond Avenue
4 Wolfe Tone Avenue
5 Charlemont Avenue
6 Summerhill Parade (Dun Laoghaire)
7 Haddington Terrace
8 Victoria Terrace (Dun Laoghaire)
9 Marine Terrace (Dún Laoghaire)
10 Northumberland Place (Dún Laoghaire)
11 Northumberland Park
12 Dungar Terrace
13 Stoneview Place
14 Martello Avenue
15 Crosthwaite Terrace
16 Sussex Street
17 Marine Court (Dún Laoghaire)
18 Charlemont Terrace
19 Mill Street (Dun Laoghaire)
20 Anglesea Lane
21 Park Lane (Dún Laoghaire)

23 Sydenham
24 Oratory Mews Court
25 Crofton Terrace
26 Connaught Place
27 Albert Terrace (Dún Laoghaire)
28 Crofton Mansions

50 E4 1 Mornington Avenue
2 Martello Terrace (Dun Laoghaire)
3 Summerhill Court

52 F2 1 Eaton House

54 D1 1 Brookfield Court (Tallaght)
2 Jobstown Village Square

54 F1 1 Tuansgate Apts.

55 A1 1 St Maelruans Park
2 High Street (Tallaght)
3 Avonbeg Court
4 St Dominic's Court
5 Old Bawn Court
6 College View (Tallaght)
7 Uppercross Court
8 Tramway Court (Tallaght)
9 New Bancroft Place
10 The Laurels (Tallaght)
11 New Bancroft Hall
12 New Bancroft Square

55 A2 1 Summerfield (Tallaght)
2 The Close (Tallaght)
3 Allenton Crescent

55 B1 1 Bolbrook Drive
2 Bolbrook Avenue
3 Bolbrook Close
5 Avonmore Avenue
6 Moynihan Court

55 B2 1 Oldcourt Lawn
2 Killininny Court Apts
3 Tara Crescent

55 B3 1 Allenton Road
1 Ely Crescent
2 Ely Grove
3 Ely Green
4 Ferncourt Drive
5 Ferncourt Crescent
6 Beechdale Close

55 C1 1 Brookmount Lawns
2 Knocklyon Mews
3 Homeville Court
4 Homeville
5 Balrothery Cottages

55 C2 1 Wood Dale Oak
2 Woodstown Court
3 Knocklyon Gate Apts

55 C3 1 Hunters Hall

56 D1 1 Coolamber Court
2 Pine Grove
3 Ballyroan Court

56 E1 1 Orchardton
2 The Drive Apts.

56 E2 1 Beechview
2 Cypress Avenue
3 Larch Drive
4 Beech Walk
5 Walnut View

56 F1 1 Sarah Curran Road
2 St Gatien Road
3 Fonthill Abbey
4 Whitechurch Abbey
5 Edenbrook Court
6 Forthill Court
8 The Beeches (Willbrook)

57 A1 1 Marley Villas
2 Meadow Villas
3 Barton Court

57 A2 1 Priory Court (Grange Road)
2 The Cherries
3 Elm Way (Grange Wood)
4 Highfield Court (Rathfarnham)

57 B1 1 Meadow Avenue
2 Hawthorn Drive
3 Mount Albion
4 Sycamore Drive (Dundrum)
5 Hillview Glade
6 Hillview Court

57 B2 1 The Crescent (Ballinteer)
2 Ballinteer Court
3 The Copse (Ballinteer)
4 The Dale (Ballinteer)

57 C1 1 Westerton Rise
2 Ashgrove Terrace
3 Eagle Terrace (Dundrum)
4 Castle Court (Dundrum)
5 McGrane Court
6 Ballyolaf Manor
7 Castleview (Dundrum)
8 Ashgrove Court
9 Dundrum Gate Apts
10 Riversdale (Dundrum)
11 Riverbank (Dundrum)
12 The Birch
13 The Linden
14 The Blackthorn

57 C2 1 Clonlea Wood
2 College Park Court
3 College Park Drive

58 D1 1 Drummartin Crescent
2 Carrick Lawn
3 The Pines (Kilmacud)
4 Woodley Court

58 D2 1 Balally Terrace
2 Moreen Lawn
3 Blackthorn Grove
4 Blackthorn Court
5 Rathdown Terrace
6 Blackthorn Green
7 Blackthorn Close (Sandyford)
8 Olaf Hall
9 Rathdown Grove

58 D3 1 Churchland's

58 E1 1 Dale Close
2 Stillorgan Court
3 Stillorgan Heath
4 Convent Court
5 Woodthorpe

58 E3 1 Glencairn Garth

58 F1 1 Woodview Court (Stillorgan)
2 Ard Lorcain Villas
3 Grange Cottages
4 Ulster Terrace (Stillorgan Grove)
5 Pear Tree Field
6 Dunstaffnage Hall Apts

58 F2 1 Leopardstown Court
2 Leopardstown Lawn
3 Silver Pines
4 Ellesmere
5 Ballymoss Parade
6 Arkle Square
7 Sir Ivor Mall
8 Fey Yerra

58 F4 1 Ballyogan Park

59 A1 1 Orchard Cottages
2 Red Brick Terrace
3 Moore's Cottages
4 Hawthorn Manor
5 Rosehill
6 Ardagh Close
8 Newtown Park Court
9 Galloping Green
10 Avila Apts

11 Newtownpark House
12 Obelisk Avenue

59 A2 1 Knocksinna Grove
2 Knocksinna Court
3 New Park Lodge
4 Foxrock Mount
5 Chestnut Park
6 Willow Park (Foxrock)
7 Sycamore Grove (Foxrock)
8 Whitethorn Walk (Foxrock)
9 Birch Dale (Foxrock)
10 The Coutryard (Foxrock)
11 Kelston Hall
12 Sefton Hall

59 A3 1 Brighton Cottages
2 Kilteragh Pines
3 Avalon
4 Brighton Lodge
5 The Gables (Foxrock)
6 Westminster Court

59 B1 1 Windsor Court
2 Grange Grove
3 Oliver Plunkett Villas
4 Stradbrook Hill
5 Springhill Cottages
6 Grange Terrace
7 Abbey Court (Monkstown)
9 Faber Grove
10 Deans Court
11 Devon Close
12 Monkstown Square

59 B3 1 Kerrymount Close
4 Monaloe Crescent
5 Clonkeen Lawn
6 Monaloe Court

59 C1 1 Oliver Plunkett Square
2 Patrician Park
3 Mounttown Park
4 Woodlawn Park (Dun Laoghaire)
5 Oliver Plunkett Terrace
6 Fitzgerald Park
7 St Patrick's Terrace (Kill O' the Grange)
8 Dunedin Drive
9 St Patrick's Close (Kill O'The Grange)
10 Highthorn Woods
11 Aspen Park (Kill O'The Grange)
12 Birch Dale (Kill O'The Grange)
13 Willow Grove (Kill O'The Grange)
14 Carriglea Court (Kill O'The Grange)
16 Woodlawn Villas

59 C2 1 Hillview Cottages
2 Whitethorn Walk (Kill O'The Grange)
3 Sycamore Court
4 Hazel Lawn (Kill O'The Grange)
5 Eaglewood Apts
6 Rochestown House Apts.
7 Eaglewood House
8 Eaglewood Mews

59 C3 1 Little Meadow
2 Cabinteely Court
3 Cabinteely Park
4 O'Shea's Cottages

59 C4 1 Kilbogget Villas
2 Church Villas

60 D1 1 O'Donnell Gardens
2 Royal Terrace North
3 Myrtle Avenue
4 Emmet Street (Sallynoggin)
5 Eden Villas
6 Laurel Hill
7 Granite Hall

PAGE/GRID REF	STREET NAME
	8 Magenta Place
	9 Marlborough Park
	10 Royal Terrace Lane
	11 Beechwood Grove
	12 Rollins Court
	13 Seven Houses
	14 The Glen (Glenageary Road)
	15 Glengara Close
	16 Silchester Wood
	17 Carlisle Terrace (Dún Laoghaire)
	18 Durham Place
	19 Rus-in-Urbe Terrace
60 D2	1 Honey Park
	2 Thomastown Crescent
	3 Pearse Close
60 D3	1 Auburn Road (Cabinteely)
	2 Granville Crescent
60 D4	1 Annabeg
	2 Meadow Court
	3 Oakton Green
60 E1	1 Wilmont Avenue
	2 Congress Gardens
	3 Albert Park
	4 Claremont Villas
	5 St Paul's Terrace
	6 St Peter's Terrace (Dun Laoghaire)
	7 Findlater Street (Dun Laoghaire)
	8 Devitt Villas
	9 Dixon Villas
	10 Glen Terrace
	11 Glasthule Buildings
	12 Hastings Terrace
	13 Brighton Terrace (Dun Laoghaire)
	14 Lawson Terrace
	15 Killiney Terrace
	16 Munster Terrace
	17 Neptune Terrace
	18 Cliff Terrace
	19 Beaufort
	20 Ballygihen Villas
	21 Seabank Court (Dalkey)
	22 St Helen's
	23 Chester Square
	24 Dundela Haven
	25 Arkendale Woods
	26 Arkendale Court
	27 Adelaide Villas (Dun Laoghaire)
	28 Adelaide Terrace (Dun Laoghaire)
	29 Atmospheric Road
	30 St Margaretπs Close
	31 Avondale Court (Dalkey)
60 E2	1 Barnhill Lawn
	2 Killiney Towers
	3 Barnhill Park
	4 Kilcolman Court
	5 Edwin Court
	6 Fairlawns
	7 Urney Grove
	8 Malborough Court
	9 Castlepark Court
60 E3	1 Hill Cottages
	2 Mount Auburn
	3 Talbot Road (Killiney)
	4 Talbot Lane (Killiney)
60 E4	1 Oakton Court
	2 Dale View Park
	3 Mountain Villa
	4 The Nurseries (Ballybrack)
	5 Mountain View Road (Ballybrack)
	6 Rainsford Lane
	7 Firgrove
60 F1	1 Carysfort Drive
	2 Ormeau Drive

PAGE/GRID REF	STREET NAME
	3 The Paddocks (Dalkey)
	4 South Winds
	5 Ulverton Close
	6 Rocklands
	7 Bayswater Terrace
	8 Bullock Steps
	9 Liscanor
	10 White's Villas
	11 Mayville Terrace
	12 Castlelands Grove
	13 Ulverton Court
	14 Pilot View
	15 Bailey View
	16 Castlelands
	17 Churchill Mews
	18 Bartra Rock Apts.
60 F2	1 St Patrick's Avenue (Dalkey)
	2 Railway Road
	3 Anastasia Lane
	4 St Patrick's Square (Dalkey)
	5 Cats Ladder
	6 Dalkey Grove
	7 Barnhill Grove
	8 St Patrick's Road (Dalkey)
	9 Monte Vella
	10 Summerfield Close
	11 Victoria Terrace (Dalkey)
	12 Sorrento Drive
	13 Sorrento Lawn
	14 Coliemore Villas
	15 Seafield Terrace
	16 Temple Terrace
	17 Grosvenor Terrace (Dalkey)
	18 Charlotte Terrace
	19 Heany Avenue
	20 Desmond Cottages
	21 Ardbrugh Villas
	22 Burmah Close
	23 Dalkey Court
	24 Kilbegnet Close
	25 Sorrento Close
	26 Craiglands
	27 Ullardmor
	28 Sorrento Mews
	29 Sorrento Court
	30 Sorrento Heights
	31 Ardbrugh Close
	32 Castle Cove (Dalkey)
	33 Torca View
63 A1	1 The View (Carrickmines)
64 D1	1 The Oaks (Loughlinstown)
	2 Cherry Court (Loughlinstown)
	3 Cois Coillte
	4 Holly Court
64 D2	1 Stonebridge Lane
64 E1	1 Killiney Court
	2 Killiney Oaks
	3 The Sycamores
	4 The Elms (Loughlinstown)
	5 St Aubyn's Court
	6 Ennel Court
	7 Sheelin Grove
	8 Glencarr Court
	9 Domville Grove
	10 Streamville Court
	12 Bayview Glade
	13 Sheelin Hill
	14 Sheelin Walk
	16 The Larches (Abberley)
	17 The Oaks (Abberley)
	18 The Rowans (Abberley)
	19 The Willows (Abberley)
	20 The Hawthorns (Abberley)
	21 The Cedars (Abberley)
	22 The Beeches (Abberley)
	23 River Close

PAGE/GRID REF	STREET NAME
64 E2	1 River Lane (Loughlinstown)
	2 Clonasleigh
	3 Beechfield Haven
	4 Athgoe Drive
	5 Maryland
	6 Station Road (Shankill)
	7 Windrush
	8 Shanganagh Wood
	9 Thomond
	10 Beechwood House
	11 Sycamore House (Shankill)
64 E3	1 Guilford Terrace
	2 Stonebridge Close
	3 Osprey Court
64 E4	1 Kiltuck Park
67 B1	1 Raverty Villas
	2 St Peter's Terrace (Bray)
	3 Myrtle Grove (Bray)
	4 Arbutus Grove
	5 Thornhill View
	6 Fernbrook
	7 Roseville Court
67 B2	1 Auburn Villas (Bray)
	2 Glenburgh Terrace
	4 Ashley Heights
	5 Dargle Crescent
	6 Copper Beech Grove
	9 Sutton Road
	10 Dargan Street
	11 Fairgreen Road
	12 Pearse Road (Bray)
	13 Mountpleasant Villas
	15 Diamond Terrace
	16 Parkview Terrace
	17 Sutton Villas
	18 Esmonde Terrace
	19 Old Ravenswell Row
	20 New Ravenswell Row
	21 Vale View
	22 Old Rathmore Terrace
	23 New Rathmore Terrace
	25 Gertrude Terrace
	26 Herbert View
	27 Rivervale Apts.
	28 Dargle Court
	29 Brookwood
67 B3	1 Ballynoe Court
	2 Rathclaren
	3 St Clair's Terrace
	4 Killarney Court
	5 Kilgrastor Court
67 B4	1 Ballywaltrim Cottages
	2 Ballymorris
67 C1	1 St Patrick's Square (Bray)
	2 Martello Terrace (Bray)
67 C2	1 Sidmonton Square
	3 Eglinton Road
	4 Rosslyn Grove
	5 James Connolly Square
	6 Sidmonton Place
	7 Novara Park
	8 St Cronan's Road
	9 Cill Manntan Park
	10 Kilmantain Place
	11 Father Colohan Terrace
	12 Royal Marine Terrace
	13 Milton Terrace
	14 St Kevin's Terrace (Bray)
	15 Darley Cottages
	16 Brabazon Cottages
	17 St Laurence's Terrace (Bray)
	18 St Columcille's Terrace
	20 Seapoint Villas
	21 Dunbur Terrace
	22 Elmgrove Terrace
	23 St Aidan's Terrace
	24 Seapoint Terrace (Bray)
	25 Goldsmith Terrace
	26 Prince of Wales Terrace (Bray)
	27 Novara Terrace

PAGE/GRID REF	STREET NAME
	28 Waverley Terrace (Bray)
	29 Westview Terrace
	30 Augustine Villas
	31 Trafalgar Terrace (Bray)
	32 Fairgreen Terrace
	33 St Brigid's Terrace
	34 Loretto Avenue
	35 Loretto Terrace
	36 Sidmonton Gardens
	37 Rosslyn
	38 Shankill View
	39 Florence Terrace (Bray)
	40 Florence Villas (Bray)
	41 Carlton Terrace
	42 Carlton Villas (Clontarf)
	43 Alexander Terrace (Bray)
	44 Belton Terrace
	45 Church Terrace (Bray)
	46 Old Brighton Terrace
	47 New Brighton Terrace
	48 Killarney Villas
	49 Market Square
	50 Fairgreen Court
	51 Bayview (Bray)
	52 Westbourne Terrace
	53 King Edward Court
	54 Loretto Villas
	55 Marie Villas
	56 Wellington Court (Bray)
	57 Novara Mews
	58 Vevay Crescent
	59 Bull Lane
	60 Purcell Lane (off Main Street Bray)
67 C3	1 Cherry Tree Drive
	2 Roselawn Park
	4 Woodview Drive
	5 Kennedy Park
	8 Newcourt Villas
	9 O'Byrne Villas
	10 Stoneylea Terrace
	11 Mountain View Apts.
	14 Putland Villas
	15 Oldcourt Terrace
	16 Lauderdale Terrace
	17 Mayfield Terrace (Bray)
	18 Vevay Villas
	19 Orchard Terrace (Bray)
	20 Bray Head Terrace
	21 Sugarloaf Terrace
67 C4	3 Bentley Avenue
	6 St Mary's Terrace (Boghall Road)
68 D2	1 Trosyrafon Terrace
	2 Montebello Terrace
	3 Esplanade Terrace
	4 Brennans Terrace
	5 Sidbury Court
	6 Dargan Court
	7 Warburton Terrace
	8 Sloan Terrace
	9 Belgrave Villas (Bray)
	10 Belgrave Terrace (Bray)
	11 Claremount Terrace
	12 Richmond Terrace
	13 Milward Terrace
	14 Brennans Parade
	15 Claddagh Terrace
	16 Marlborough Terrace
	17 Marine Terrace (Bray)
	18 Jones Terrace
	19 Mount Norris Villas
	20 St Marys Terrace (Bray)
	21 Fitzwilliam Terrace
	23 Convent View (Bray)
68 D3	1 Eaton Court (Bray)
	2 Meretimo Villas
	3 Grosvenor Avenue
	4 Brookfield Avenue (Bray)
	5 Sidmonton Court
	6 Sydenham Villas (Bray)